OXFORD HISTORICAL MONOGRAPHS

Liberal Anglican Politics

Whiggery, Religion, and Reform

1830–1841

RICHARD BRENT

CLARENDON PRESS · OXFORD
1987

Oxford University Press, Walton Street, Oxford OX2 6DP

Oxford New York Toronto Melbourne Auckland
Delhi Bombay Calcutta Madras Karachi
Petaling Jaya Singapore Hong Kong Tokyo
Nairobi Dar es Salaam Cape Town
Associated companies in Beirut Berlin Ibadan Nicosia

OXFORD is a trade mark of Oxford University Press

Published in the United States
by Oxford University Press, New York

British Library Cataloguing in Publication Data
Brent, Richard
Liberal Anglican politics: Whiggery,
religion and reform, 1830–1841.—(Oxford
historical monographs)
1. Liberal Party—History
I. Title
324.24104'09 JN1129.L42
ISBN 0–19–822942–9

Set by Litho Link Limited
Printed in Great Britain
at the University Printing House, Oxford
by David Stanford
Printer to the University

FOR E.J.B. AND J.G.B.

'[C]onsidered merely in its results on the temporal conditions of mankind, neither conquest, legislation, nor philosophy, has at any period affected society so intimately, so extensively, and so permanently, as Christianity'.

S. Hinds, *The History of the Rise and Progress of Christianity* (London, 1828), p. 1.

'. . . though the establishment of toleration in the world may owe much to the man for whom religion was a matter of comparative indifference, the basic argument for religious liberty has always had to find its roots in the nature of religion itself'.

H. Butterfield, *Historical Development of the Principle of Toleration in British Life* (London, 1956), p. 9.

'Much harder to believe in, and more necessary to insist upon, is the Christian dimension of liberalism: it is something which has rather to be inferred and supplied, from scanty and unsuitable testimonies; and one has to guess how far this estimated quantity affected or accredited liberalism'.

J. R. Vincent, *The Formation of the British Liberal Party* (London, 1972), p. 16.

Acknowledgements

I WOULD like to thank the owners of manuscript material cited in the bibliography for permission to use their collections, and the archivists and librarians in the institutions listed there for making them available. I acknowledge the gracious permission of Her Majesty the Queen for use of the Melbourne Papers as reproduced on microfilm. In particular I would like to thank the Earl of Bessborough, with acknowledgements to the West Sussex County Record Office and the County Archivist; Lord Blake; the Keeper of Western Manuscripts, Bodleian Library; the British Library Board; the Broadlands Archive Trustees; the Keeper of the Archives, University of Cambridge; the Keeper of Manuscripts, Cambridge University Library; Castle Howard Archives; the Congregational Memorial Hall Trust; the Governing Body of Christ Church; Durham University Library; Department of Palaeography and Diplomatic, University of Durham; Lady Margaret Fortescue; Mrs P. Goedhuis and the University of Nottingham Library Manuscripts Department; the Directors of the Goodwood Estate Company Ltd., with acknowledgements to the West Sussex County Record Office and the County Archivist; Major Sir Charles Graham; the Keeper of Manuscripts, Guildhall Library, City of London; the Earl of Halifax; the Keeper of Manuscripts, the John Rylands Library; the Librarian, Lambeth Palace Library; Lord Monteagle; the Director, the National Library of Ireland; the Trustees of the National Library of Scotland; the Marquis of Normanby; the Master and Fellows of Oriel College, Oxford; the Keeper of the Archives, University of Oxford; the Protestant Dissenting Deputies of the Three Denominations; Lady Ravensdale and the Hertfordshire County Record Office; the Library Committee of the Religious Society of Friends; the Librarian, Rhodes House Library; Staffordshire County Record Office; the Master and Fellows of Trinity College, Cambridge; University College London Library; Dr Williams's Trust.

This book is a revised version of an Oxford D.Phil. thesis. It is a great pleasure to record my thanks to my supervisor, Angus Macintyre, and my examiners, Boyd Hilton and John Walsh, for their advice and help over the years. It is equally a pleasure to have this opportunity to record my thanks to Derek Beales, Maurice Cowling, Colin Matthew, and Barry Supple, who, in addition to the above, have given me considerable encouragement and support. I am grateful to Michael Brock, who kindly allowed me to consult his own transcriptions from the Ellice, Grey, Knowsley, and Lambton manuscripts. I also owe a particular debt to the following, who read the typescript, in part or in whole, during the various stages of its gestation, and made important suggestions, both as to style and content: David Cannadine, Mark Jones, Peter Mandler, Jon Parry, Stephen Taylor, and Mark Vessey. Finally, I would like to express my gratitude to the Master and Fellows of St John's College, Cambridge, who, by electing me into a Fellowship under Title Λ, enabled me to complete this essay.

St John's College, Cambridge   RICHARD BRENT
11 December 1986

Contents

Figures and Tables

Note on Terminology

Throughout this book reference is made to three groups of Whigs: older Foxites (or Foxites), 'young' Whigs, and 'liberal Anglicans'. These are anachronistic terms. While they are useful descriptions for the purpose of analysis, the reader should also be aware of their limitations. As revealed in the course of this work, the edges of these groups shade into each other: in the 1820s, for example, there was not always much to distinguish 'young' Whigs from liberal Anglicans. Likewise, in the crisis of 1834–5, some liberal Anglicans adopted the political strategy of the older Foxites, although their views on matters of policy differed considerably. Such ambiguities are part and parcel of political activity; the historian imposes order on the past at the risk of being over-schematic, but with the aim of increasing historical understanding.

The word 'liberal', as a political term, was a recent addition to the language of British politics in the 1820s and 1830s.[1] It is used in this book simply to mean 'progressive', in accordance with increasing contemporary usage, and not to indicate the existence of a Liberal party of the mid-Victorian kind. 'Liberal Anglican', a historical coinage, is applied here to a distinctive group of Whig politicians and like-minded theologians in the universities whose policies and doctrines tended to dominate liberal governments in the years following the passing of the Great Reform Act of 1832. For a more extended definition of this term, the reader should consult Chapter 1, Chapter 3, and Chapter 4.

---

[1] For a discussion of the difficulties involved in using 'liberal' as a political term, see J. E. Cookson, *The Friends of Peace: Anti-War Liberalism in England, 1793–1815* (Cambridge, 1982), 2–4.

Introduction:
The Politics of Church Reform

THIS book is an essay in the history of English liberalism. This description summarizes both its limitations and its ambitions. It is an essay because it does not offer a full account of liberal politics in the decade following the first Reform Act. It harbours no wish to rival the work of Elie Halévy in his history of the growth of nineteenth-century English liberalism, or that of Norman Gash in his appraisal of English politics in the years following the passing of the Great Reform Act in 1832.[1] The desire behind this book is simply to affirm one aspect of Whiggery which, in the justified concern of historians to trace the origins of the stability, equipoise, and prosperity of mid-Victorian Britain, has been overlooked or buried. But therein also lies its ambition. If this work has any interest for the more general historical reader, it is in the claim that no history of nineteenth-century English liberalism can be complete if it fails to take account of the role which Anglicanism played in the development of Whiggery in this period. The thesis of this book is that the Whigs were no more immune from the contagion of nineteenth-century Christian renewal than were their Tory opponents, and that this affected their outlook on policy and politics every bit as much as it did that of their Conservative rivals.

This claim, it is hoped, appears neither unduly novel nor startling. It is in accord with what practical historical reasoning would lead one to expect. It is, after all, the exceptional country which can congratulate itself that religion does not form a divisive (or at least formative) issue in the conduct of its national politics. The current examples of Northern Ireland, Iran, Latin America, and the 'moral majority' of North

[1] E. Halévy, *A History of the English People in the Nineteenth Century* (London, 1949–52); N. Gash, *Reaction and Reconstruction in English Politics 1832–1852* (Oxford, 1965).

America easily spring to mind if the proposition is doubted. Superficially, the claim that early nineteenth-century English political liberalism (which in the eyes of such exponents as Leslie Stephen was primarily concerned with sloughing off 'primitive' Christianity) was unsuccessful in accomplishing its own secularization might appear less plausible. Here again a moment's historical reflection will dispel doubt. Dr Hilton has shown the Evangelical basis of the political economy which characterized the liberal Toryism of the 1820s; the work of Professors Morrell, Thackray, Corsi, and Cannon, amongst others, has demonstrated the role religion played in the development of nineteenth-century scientific thought; Doctors Butler, Matthew, and Parry, and Professor Shannon have stressed the importance of the Church of England in Gladstone's understanding of mid and late nineteenth-century liberalism; Professor Turner has shown the degree to which the liberal classical scholarship of Victorian England was permeated by a theological tendentiousness.[2] To suggest, as this book does, that early nineteenth-century liberal politics was, in part and vitally, Anglican in outlook, is only to suggest that it was part and parcel of a more general liberal culture.

The argument contained in this book is that Whig governments had a distinctive religious outlook in the 1830s, that this is best termed 'liberal Anglicanism', and that in politics this was revealed most clearly on questions involving the Church of England. Of course, a distinctively 'liberal Anglican' position is not discernible on all questions of church reform in this decade. The purpose of this introductory chapter is to explain why this was the case, and to do so with reference to the history of the nineteenth-century church reform movement. It should not be unduly surprising that all demands to ensure the survival of an efficient church establishment did not pro-

---

[2] A. J. B. Hilton, *Corn, Cash, Commerce: The Economic Policies of the Tory Governments 1815–1836* (Oxford, 1977); J. Morrell and A. Thackray, *Gentlemen of Science* (Oxford, 1981); S. F. Cannon, *Science in Culture: The Early Victorian Period* (New York, 1979); P. Corsi, 'Baden Powell', D. Phil. thesis (Oxford, 1980); P. Butler, *Gladstone: Church, State, and Tractarianism* (Oxford, 1982); H. C. G. Matthew (ed.),*The Gladstone Diaries* (Oxford, 1978), v. xxiii–lxxii; *idem*, *The Gladstone Diaries* (Oxford, 1982), vii. xxv–cxiii; J. P. Parry, 'Religion and the Collapse of Gladstone's First Government', *Historical Jour.*, xxv (1982), 71–101; R. Shannon, *Gladstone* (London, 1982), i; F. M. Turner, *The Greek Heritage in Victorian Britain* (New Haven, 1981).

voke party political controversy. A political preoccupation with the progress of infidelity, and more particularly, with the church's failure to meet this challenge was not novel to the politics of the 1830s. Richard Watson, the Whig Bishop of Llandaff, for example, informed Pitt in 1800 that he feared Britain and Ireland were in imminent danger due to the 'rapid progress' which infidelity was making 'in the minds of the people'.[3] It was not to be on the issue of rehabilitating and renewing the Church of England that either the Whigs or the Tories in the 'decade of reform' displayed a distinctive outlook. Rather it was to be on issues which involved an adjustment of the relations of church and state undertaken in the light of the repeal of the Test and Corporation Acts in 1828 and the passing of Catholic Emancipation in 1829.

One historian, altogether discounting novelty, has suggested that the church reforms passed by the Whig governments of the 1830s were the product of the 'third church reform movement', which had commenced in the late eighteenth century.[4] Certainly, by the 1830s, the need to reform the church to make it a more efficient propagator of Christian truth was accepted by Anglican politicians of most political persuasions. Many of the reforms proposed by the Ecclesiastical Commission of 1835 were already in general circulation. Watson himself, for example, had drawn up a series of proposals on his appointment to the see of Llandaff in 1782. In his paper of September that year, presented to the Whig Prime Minister, Lord Shelburne, he recommended the equalization of episcopal revenues and the appropriation of a proportion of the revenues of the deans and chapters to augment the incomes of the lower clergy. He hoped that both measures would encourage the church in the better performance of its spiritual duties. Bishops, no longer coveting richer sees, would rest content in their respective dioceses and not politick for translations; the lower clergy, no longer pluralists in order to keep body and soul together, would be resident and active parish priests.[5] These suggestions bear a striking resemblance to the later proposals of the Ecclesiastical Commissioners. Their first report recommended, among

[3] R. Watson, *Anecdotes* (London, 1817), 351.
[4] G. F. A. Best, *Temporal Pillars* (Cambridge, 1964), ch. 5 *passim*.
[5] Watson, *Anecdotes*, 96–7.

other things, the redistribution of episcopal incomes so that no bishop would receive less than £4,500 and not more than £5,500 a year. Their second report advised the abolition of all non-residentiary canonries and the reduction of resident canonries to four per cathedral (the 1840 Act excepted Canterbury, Durham, Ely, and Westminster, which were reduced to six, Winchester and Exeter, and Llandaff and St David's which were reduced to five and two canonries respectively), and the banning of residents from holding estates. The revenue thus released was to be applied to the augmentation of parochial incomes.[6] Just as parliamentary reform in 1832 might be conceived, in part, as the delayed enactment of proposals made by Wyvill and Pitt, so the origins of ecclesiastical reform may be traced to the reform movement of the last quarter of the eighteenth century.

Admittedly Watson, for many years the only reforming cleric on the bench, sprang from the tradition of economical reform which was closely associated with Shelburnite Whiggery. But this did not long remain the sole source of church reform proposals from within the establishment, any more than such proposals retained a partisan character. The desire 'to make the clergy attentive to the duties of the Church'[7] grew in the late eighteenth century with the arrival of two external threats to Anglicanism. The first of these was the French Revolution, which, understood after the fashion of Burke, was an attack on Christendom. Holland noted retrospectively that Burke's antipathy towards the revolutionaries was not so much on account of their cavalier treatment of Louis XVI, as due to the Convention's abolition of ecclesiastical revenues.[8] The upheavals in France pointed to the importance of a strong religious establishment in maintaining order in the country. As Best has put it, the church reform movement should be understood in the context of the perceived 'social crisis' at the end of the century. Significantly Pitt himself, the Prime Minister in a time of foreign war and domestic disaffection, contemplated the introduction of a church reform measure in

---

[6] Best, *Temporal Pillars*, 302–4; Halévy, *History of the English People*, 210
[7] *The Parliamentary History of England*, xxxvi (1802–3), 1515.
[8] H. R. V. Fox (Lord Holland), *Memoirs of the Whig Party During My Time*, (ed. 4th, Lord Holland, London, 1852), 5.

1800.[9] The second impetus for reform was the growth of the Evangelical movement. Its supporters, insisting that the Church of England observe its own discipline, highlighted thereby the inadequate financial basis of the reformed church. It was the series of Evangelical-inspired prosecutions of clergymen for non-residence, brought under the statute of 21 Henry VIII, which prompted the Tory Sir William Scott's non-residence Bill of 1802. By 1800 not only Whig but also Tory politicians saw the necessity for extensive church reform as the prerequisite for a residential parochial clergy. Non-residence, they argued, was the result of the failure of the church at the Reformation to secure adequate means for a married clergy. The financial sins of the sixteenth century were being visited on the sons of the eighteenth-century church. As Scott declared in parliament: 'till the situation of the lower clergy is improved with respect to their incomes, their parsonage houses, and other circumstances, which I trust will soon become the subjects of parliamentary attention, nothing radical, nothing permanent can be projected'.[10] Parliament heeded such warnings. In 1803 Scott himself asked the Commons for leave to bring in a Bill to repair and build parsonage houses, and to provide a sum to augment the stipends of curates. Perceval, the Evangelical Prime Minister, introduced a Bill in 1808 'for the maintenance of stipendiary curates'; the following year, and for the subsequent eleven years, parliament voted an annual sum of £100,000 for endowing and augmenting benefices in populous districts.[11]

To this concern for the performance of the existing parochial clergy, parliament added another interest, namely church extension. Richard Yates, a Tory Anglican clergyman, pointed out in a pamphlet published in 1815 that the real threat to the church came not so much from the rise of dissenting Christian sects, as from the growth of heathen populous districts, for which there was no adequate Christian provision. Tightening church discipline, according to Yates, was a minor, even irrelevant, reform, when the 'Mine of Heathenism' to be found

[9] Best, *Temporal Pillars*, 144; Watson, *Anecdotes*, 350.
[10] *Parl. Hist. of England*, xxxvi, 488.
[11] Ibid., 1514; W. L. Mathieson, *English Church Reform 1815–1840* (London, 1923), 18; Watson, *Anecdotes*, 488.

in the metropolis, 'the very centre and heart of British Prosperity, Liberty and Civilization', was contemplated. He demanded an Act of Parliament which would apportion 'the Population into appropriate Divisions', supply 'the means of Public Worship', and so provide 'for the useful and efficient discharge of the Pastoral Offices in districts not hitherto so provided'.[12] Paying tribute to Yates' pamphlet, Vansittart, the Evangelical Chancellor of the Exchequer in Liverpool's Tory government, proposed and carried in 1818 a grant of £1,000,000 for the building of churches; in 1824 the Commons voted an additional grant of £500,000. The government's aim was to provide enough church accommodation for every third person to attend divine worship.[13] By 1820 not only had the main areas of church reform been established, but the agreement of politicians from different parties on the necessity of reform, if not on specific measures, had been obtained.

What this meant was that, by the 1830s, most proposals for church reform, in a party political sense, were uncontroversial. They were simply legislative attempts at reinvigorating an establishment, the intrinsic worth of which was almost universally recognized by a still overwhelmingly Anglican parliament. Church reform was a political baton which was easily passed from cleric to Whig, to Tory, and back to Whig, in the relay race against infidelity. For example, Archbishop Howley suggested a review of the property of the church which Grey, as Prime Minister, instituted by founding the Ecclesiastical Revenues Commission in 1832. Peel, on becoming Prime Minister in 1834, formed the Ecclesiastical Duties and Revenues Commission of 1835, its task to prepare proposals for the reform of the church. The Whigs made this body permanent in 1836 as the Ecclesiastical Commissioners, and they implemented its proposals regarding the episcopate, pluralism, and deans and chapters in 1836, 1838, and 1840 respectively. These measures were not without controversy, but these controversies were confined to church factions, and in this instance were not associated with party alignments.

Evangelicals such as Fowell Buxton protested that the 'excessive' salaries of the bishops had not been curtailed

[12] R. Yates, *The Church in Danger* (London, 1815), 19, 51–2, 120, 127–8.
[13] Mathieson, *English Church Reform*, 19.

sufficiently to increase the incomes of the lower clergy. High Churchmen such as Phillpotts, the Bishop of Exeter, opposed the reduction of cathedral canonries and chapters because it involved the destruction of supposed centres of ecclesiastical learning, while Inglis, the MP for Oxford University and an Evangelical turning High Churchman, objected to the measure as an unlawful legislative interference in the distribution of private property. Sydney Smith, the Whig Low Churchman, more mindful of the realities of nineteenth-century Anglican life, defended the existence of cathedral stalls as worthy objects of ambition for the lower clergy and as inducements to good clerical behaviour, given that the salaries of the parochial clergy were in themselves too low to inspire diligence. Some, such as Archdeacon Manning, later to defect to the Church of Rome, took the institution of the Ecclesiastical Commissioners as a permanent body to be a sign of an increasingly Erastian church; others, such as the Congregationalist, Edward Baines, saw it as marking the undue dominance of the episcopate within that body.[14] But since these disputes concerning the Whig proposals of church reform were primarily about the internal organization of the Anglican Church, they were not disputes on which governments fell or on which party divisions occurred. Although they delayed the passage of some reform measures, most notably the Deans and Chapters Act, they did not divide Whig from Tory, Peel from Russell. Partisan contests were of a markedly different order.

The religious issues on which party political conflicts took place in the 1830s, and thus in which liberal Anglicanism may be most clearly traced, included whether parliament was justified in appropriating the surplus revenues of the Irish Church to non-ecclesiastical purposes, whether the universities of Oxford and Cambridge should admit non-Anglicans to their degrees, and whether the state should fund schools not under the direction of the Anglican Church or the British and Foreign School Society. The stands taken on these topics became, to a very great extent, the determinants of Whiggery and Toryism

[14] *Hansard*, 3rd ser., xxxv (1836), 44, 344–5; S. Smith, 'Letters to Archdeacon Singleton on the Ecclesiastical Commission', *Collected Works* (London, 1854), pp. 603–44; P. J. Welch, 'Contemporary Views on the Proposals for the Alienation of Capitular Property in England 1832–1840', *Jour. of Eccles. History*, v (1954), 188; O. Brose, *Church and Parliament* (Stanford & London, 1959), 139–40, 144.

in this period. The Whig government of 1835, for example, was formed on the Irish appropriation issue, while the debate concerning Russell's English education proposals of 1839 became a set-piece of party warfare. It is thus with these issues that this book is primarily concerned. A history of church questions in English politics before 1841 is not presented here.[15] The uncontroversial legislative recommendations of the Ecclesiastical Commissioners and the largely uncontested settlement of the English tithe question are not examined in detail in the main body of the work because it is chiefly when party conflict occurred on ecclesiastical topics that liberal Anglicanism can be most clearly seen and described. These issues became politically contentious when they involved a change in the existing balance between church and state, when they were concerned not with the internal well-being of Anglicanism, but with its monopoly of national institutions. Such questions were concerned with the role of Dissent in national life. It was the presence or absence of a Nonconformist interest in church reform which made the subject a matter of party and ideological political dispute. Without this involvement, Anglicans of all persuasions were prepared to collaborate in improving the Church of England, so prevalent was the commitment to reform. Few believed the church to be in a state of near perfection. When, however, the consideration of Nonconformity was foremost, the distinctive attitudes of the political parties on religious topics clearly revealed themselves.

The significance of a Dissenting interest in turning a measure of church reform into a politically important battle may be illustrated clearly with reference to the commutation of English tithes in 1836 and the various attempts of the Whig governments to abolish church-rates.[16] The former measure was at the edge of the divide between the politically controversial and the partisanly neutral. It was the failure of Tory back-benchers

---

[15] The reader interested in such topics should consult the already extensive literature on church reform, including: G. I. T. Machin, *Politics and the Churches in Great Britain 1832 to 1868* (Oxford, 1977); Mathieson, *English Church Reform*; Best, *Temporal Pillars* and Brose, *Church and Parliament* on the Ecclesiastical Commission; E. J. Evans, *The Contentious Tithe* (London, 1976) on English tithe reform.

[16] For a full discussion of church-rates in the 1830s, see R. Brent, 'The Whigs and Protestant Dissent in the Decade of Reform: The Case of Church Rates, 1833–1841' *English Historical Review* (forthcoming).

to turn this Bill into a matter of church and state, which enabled both party front-benchers to vote for its passage through parliament. The reverse was the case with regard to church-rates. Unquestionably seen by Tories as materially affecting the future existence of the Church of England, the Whig proposals were partisanly opposed by the Conservatives. The Whigs, however, initially believed that this was not the case. In this respect the issue of church-rates was at the edge of the divide between reforms which the Whigs were prepared to concede to Dissent, and those they were not. As long as it was possible to view the existence of church-rates as a practical grievance, the Whigs were prepared to legislate on the matter; when abolition, largely as a result of Dissenting propaganda, was taken to be the first step to church disestablishment, Whig enthusiasm waned. A brief examination of these two cases will indicate in what way church reform became a politically contentious topic.

Superficially, at least, English tithe reform was a question which involved the interests of Dissent. The tithe, after all, was a tax on the produce of the land, its proceeds, for the most part, ending up in the pockets of the clergy. It was a compulsory contribution to the upkeep of the Anglican Establishment, a contribution which in Ireland had resulted in a notorious antagonism between the church and the rural Catholic population. In England a comparable compulsory contribution, the church-rate, had resulted in a series of vestry battles between Dissenter and churchman, and in demands for its abolition. The commutation of English tithes might well have been seen as a means of settling the relations between church and Dissent in rural England. Certainly there is some evidence to suggest that the Whig measure was precipitated by rural, and sometimes Dissenting, disturbances. The Quakers had conscientiously refused to pay tithes since the seventeenth century, while from the late eighteenth century onwards demands for the abolition of tithes had increased. In 1790 an assembly of Unitarians at Warrington declared their wish to abolish tithes, and in 1833 and 1834 the Quakers sent petitions to the Commons for that purpose. In 1832 the London Yearly Meeting of the Quakers issued a 'Brief Statement why the Religious Society of Friends object to the Payment of Tithes'.

The post-war agricultural depression exacerbated the severity of the tax, since it fell on gross product and not net profit, and led, in the 'Captain Swing' riots of 1830, to demands for its reduction or abolition in south-east England.[17] The effect of the Whig proposal of 1836, moreover, was to reduce the income of the church.

The important principle of the Act was not so much that commutation was to be compulsory (although on that issue Russell's measure differed from Peel's Bill of 1835), as that important financial restrictions were placed on the rent-charge which was to succeed the tithe. Commutation, the transference of a payment in kind to a payment in cash, was not to be based on the nominal value of the tithe, but was to be calculated in relation to the actual payments received by the clergy. The new rent-charge was neither to exceed nor fall below a certain proportion of the gross value of the average sum paid, or agreed to be paid, over the previous seven years. Under the terms of the 34th clause of the Bill as printed on 13 April 1836, if the value of the produce actually received by the clergyman was less than £60 for every £100 of the estimated value of the tithe, the sum to be taken for calculating a permanent commutation was to be £60 for every £100 whereas, if the sum was £75 or more for every £100, the sum to be taken was to be reduced to £75. It was this clause which Russell believed to be central to the Bill, telling his Cabinet colleague, Hobhouse, that if the government were to lose the vote on it, he would abandon the measure.[18] In the debate on that clause, which occurred on 13 May 1836, Finch, the Conservative MP for Stamford, opposed it as an unwarranted reduction in clerical incomes. He argued that the Bill unjustifiably appropriated part of the church's revenues to the landed proprietors in a manner analogous to the Whigs' proposed appropriation of the surplus revenues of the Irish Church to non-ecclesiastical purposes. Because the Tories opposed the latter, they should

---

[17] Evans, *The Contentious Tithe*, 58, 61; W. R. Ward, *Religion and Society in England* (London, 1972), 22; *idem*, 'The Tithe Question in England in the Early Nineteenth Century', *Jour. of Eccles. History*, xvi (1965), 69; E. J. Hobsbawm and G. Rudé, *Captain Swing* (London, 1969), 158; G. Ditchfield, 'Parliament, the Quakers and the Tithe Question 1750–1835', *Parliamentary History*, 4 (1985), 106 n.

[18] *Parliamentary Papers 1836*, vi. 181; B. L. Addit. MSS 56558 (Hobhouse Diary): 13 May 1836.

also oppose the former: both were measures of church spolia-
tion. In the event the government won the vote, but only by
the narrow majority of 78 to 70.[19]
Nevertheless, Finch's attempt to rally the forces of the
church in opposition to the Bill was unsuccessful. The measure
never caught fire as a church and state issue, and the Tory
leadership refused to be drawn in debate. On the third reading,
perhaps with characteristic disingenuousness, Peel declared
that his object 'was to protect the interests of the Church', an
object he believed he had obtained in agreeing to the third
reading of the Bill.[20] Russell was equally judicious and conciliatory in introducing his measure. By not referring to the Dissenters, he had made it clear that he did not consider the Bill to
be in their interest. On the contrary, the reason for the measure,
according to Russell, was 'the growing discontent of the Members of the agricultural interest and of the tithe-payers at this
mode of payment, and . . . the universal disposition of the
clergy . . . to get rid of this objectionable payment'. In a similar
spirit of disinterested charity, although the Whig Dissenter,
Edward Baines, hailed the act as a 'boon' for the church,
neither he nor the Dissenters in the country opposed it.[21] The
Bill consequently passed through the Commons with scarcely
any party rancour. As Knatchbull, one of the leading Tory
country gentlemen, remarked during the committee stage: 'nothing could be more gratifying . . . than that this important
question should have been brought forward and discussed as
it had been, so wholly free from party or political bias'.[22]
    Although some liberals, such as Warburton, objected to the
Bill for not abolishing tithes altogether, while others, such as
the Radical D. W. Harvey, complained that a portion of the
church's revenues had not been appropriated for the general
welfare of the people, the only opposition of real note came
from the farming interest. They believed that the Bill had been
too favourable to the tithe owners. Lennard, the liberal MP
for Maldon, claimed that the Bill was called 'the Clergyman's
Bill' in the country, and complained in particular that it was

[19] *Hansard*, 3rd ser., xxxiii (1836), 906, 911.
[20] Ibid., xxxiv (1836), 974.
[21] Ibid., xxxi (1836), 187; *ibid.*, xxxiv (1836), 977.
[22] Ibid., xxxii (1836), 631.

too generous in its provisions for the collection of tithe arrears. Parrott, speaking on behalf of the tithe-payers of the West Country, complained that the 34th clause would have the effect of raising actual payments by between a fifth and a third. One Whig Cabinet minister, Lord Holland, reflected that the measure was 'too favourable to the Church, [and] was allowed, and probably for that bad reason, to pass the House of Lords'.[23] Whether rightly or wrongly, the Whig government responded to the farmers' demands. Having secured the passage of the 34th clause in May, in June they amended it so that the upper and lower limits of £60 and £75 were replaced by granting the Commissioners the power to raise or diminish the future rent-charge by up to a fifth of the average amount paid in the last seven years. The point of this change was to introduce a flexible lower limit to the rent-charge, so that farmers would not be in the position of having to meet a substantially increased annual charge after commutation, as some had feared. It was a concession which agriculturists, such as Ayshford Sandford, the Whig MP for West Somersetshire, were pleased to accept.[24]

The truth of the matter was that the English Tithes Commutation Act did not involve the great party issues of church and state, since it was not so much a concession to Dissent as a sop to the agricultural community. It was a Bill designed primarily to eradicate a source of dispute between two Anglican sections of rural England. The reason for the absence of a Nonconformist interest was simply that the existence of payments in kind was not a special grievance of Dissenters. There was, indeed, no correlation between the existence of rural Dissent and the incidence of tithing in kind. As Professor Ward has shown, Nonconformity was strongest where the pressure for enclosure had been greatest (and tithes subsequently commuted), in particular in Lincolnshire and the East Riding of Yorkshire. In the south-east, where the agricultural depression was at its worst, and tithes were blamed for the pauperization of the agricultural labourer, Dissent made little progress. Only the Primitive Methodists of Norfolk were an exception to this rule. Paradoxically, rural Methodism seems to have been a response, in part, to the tithe commutations of the Napoleonic

---

[23] Ibid., xxxi (1836), 696; Evans, *The Contentious Tithe*, 127.
[24] *Parl. Papers 1836*, vi. 243; *Hansard*, 3rd ser., xxxiv (1836), 596.

period, which were the result of the enclosure movement. In consequence, local clergymen, accepting land in lieu of this annual payment, often became pillars of the local gentry, sat on the bench, and socially distanced themselves from their flocks. It was the increasingly secular identification of the clergy with the local landowners, rather than tithes, which provoked the spread of a rural Dissenting interest to rival the Established Church.[25] In any case, rural Dissent was associated primarily with agricultural labourers, rather than with the farmers who actually paid the tithe. Although their wages might suffer, especially in times of agricultural depression, as a result of this impost, labourers did not directly encounter the church on this issue. Consequently it was unsurprising that Dissent (which in any case was politically organized most strongly in the towns) did not have strong views on the Whig measure. Likewise, given that no politically controversial issue of church and state was involved, it was not surprising that Whigs and Tories were able to collaborate on the passage of this Act. The settlement of the English tithes question, however important for the welfare of the church and the agricultural community, was not one which fundamentally affected the nature of the British state.

Ultimately both Whigs and Tories were to believe that the contrary was the case with respect to the abolition of church-rates. Nevertheless, initially, liberal Anglican Whigs such as Russell, Howick, and Morpeth refused to see the abolition of this impost (which fell on all occupants of property within a parish, and funded not only the maintenance of the church fabric, but also the means of public worship) as altering unacceptably the balance between church and state. Admittedly, the Whigs could not prevent the Tories from seeing the issue in this light, and thus from ensuring that all Whig proposals became occasions for party warfare. Where defenders of the Anglican Church failed on the question of English tithes, they were abundantly successful on the issue of church-rates. The Tory front-bench duly denounced Whig schemes as heralding the destruction of the church. Sir William Follett, for example,

[25] Ward, *Religion and Society*, 124; *idem*, 'The Tithe Question' 80–1; E. J. Evans, 'Some Reasons for the Growth of English Rural Anti-Clericalism c. 1750–c. 1830', *Past and Present*, lxvi (1975), 90–91, 100, 104.

the former Conservative Solicitor-General, opposed the government's measure of 1837, arguing that the Dissenters desired 'nothing more or less than the recognition of the voluntary principle'.[26] As political defenders of the Church, the Tories could not condone such aspirations as apparently realized in the Whigs' Bill. The Whigs themselves were no less vociferous in their claims to be defenders of the Anglican establishment, and of the principle that the entire nation should contribute to the upkeep of the church. In 1840 Russell declared that 'The principle on which they alone could maintain the Established Church was, that it was for the common good, and that was a principle which entitled them to ask for that burden to be laid upon all.'[27] But what distinguished the liberal Anglicans on this issue, and made them sympathetic towards Nonconformist grievances, was their belief that the abolition of church-rates would not adversely affect the position of the Anglican Church.

They believed that the existence of church-rates, as far as the Dissenters were concerned, was a genuine and practical grievance which could be alleviated without materially affecting the interests of the church. Their existence was, in the words of the Whig Cabinet minister, Poulett Thomson, a 'grievance of conscience', since Dissenters were required to pay for the upkeep of a church which was contrary to their religious principles.[28] This impost, the liberal argument ran, merely alienated Dissent from Anglicanism, and so hindered the performance of the Church of England in its role as a national church. Abolishing church-rates would render Anglicanism more palatable to Protestant Nonconformity. Whig measures for the abolition of this tax consequently were designed to ensure at the same time that the church was not deprived of funds. Thus Althorp, in 1834, proposed that the abolished rate be replaced by a sum of £250,000, to be an annual charge on the land tax. In 1837 Spring Rice likewise proposed that a new fund, created by the improved management of church lands, be used to repair the fabric of the churches in lieu of church-rates. But by the end of the decade the growing violence

---

[26] *Hansard*, 3rd ser., xxxvii (1837), 401.
[27] Ibid., lii (1840), 97.
[28] P. R. O. 30/22 2A (Russell Papers), fo. 344: memo. by P. Thomson, Mar. 1836.

of Nonconformity in its agitation for disestablishment made the Whig claim that church-rates were merely a practical grievance increasingly implausible. As a result, liberal Anglicans abandoned this measure of church reform.

By the late 1830s the tone of political Dissent had become more militant and insistent, especially in regard to the advocacy of the voluntary church principle in opposition to church establishments. The consequence was that demands for the abolition of church-rates became linked to those for the destruction of the Church of England. In 1839, for example, the Leicester Voluntary Church Association issued an address urging increased parliamentary pressure for the abolition of church-rates. Unable to make a clear separation between demands for the abolition of the tax and those for the destruction of the Anglican establishment, the Whigs ceased to deal with the former as a practical grievance. Once it appeared that conceding on this issue would have the appearance of upsetting the balance of church and state, the Whigs ceased to be compliant. The government thus gave only half-hearted support to Easthope's Bill of 1841 for the abolition of church-rates. Morpeth, for example, a Whig Cabinet minister, offered as a reason for his dislike of the measure his belief that it left too much 'to chance and option whence the funds' for the maintenance of the church should come.[29] Because the Dissenters had fatally linked the issue to the future of the Anglican Church, liberal Whigs became increasingly reluctant to appease them.

It will be thus apparent that the liberal Anglican Whigs had a distinctive attitude towards church reform. It is unfair to view them as either entirely implementing proposals which were common to both political parties, or as being the passive respondents to Dissenting 'pressure from without'. It is one of the aims of this book to explain what it meant to be a liberal Anglican Whig in post-Reform politics. In Chapter 1 the intellectual and political origins of liberal Anglicanism are discussed. It is shown how, in response to the ailing fortunes of the Whig party in the 1820s, a number of Whigs, primarily liberal Anglican in their views, attempted to revitalize the party by extending its appeal to Evangelicals, moderate Nonconformists,

[29] *Hansard*, 3rd ser., lviii (1841), 784.

and trimming Radicals. On the one hand this task involved a series of parliamentary agitations on such issues as anti-slavery, parliamentary reform, and Catholic emancipation. But in addition it involved a re-working of Whig doctrine, nothing less than its transformation from the primarily constitutional concerns of Fox to an interest in the moral and educational welfare of the British nation. This change was largely the work of Lord John Russell, though other Whigs such as Spring Rice, Hobhouse, and Mulgrave also participated, and so it is to an analysis of Russell's political writings that most of this chapter is devoted. Chapter 2 indicates how, on the issue of Irish appropriation, these liberal Anglican Whigs achieved a position of influence within the Whig party. The years 1834–5 saw a struggle between the High Church Whigs such as Stanley and Graham, the older Foxite defenders of a broad aristocratic coalition of defence against Radical insurgency, such as Grey, and the proponents of liberal Anglicanism. In the event, the High Churchmen were forced to leave the party, leaving the older Foxite Whigs and the liberal Anglicans in a not always easy alliance. Nevertheless, this was a coalition dominated by the liberal Anglicans.

The next two chapters deal with the question of whether liberal Anglicanism was a rhetorical device to achieve office, or represented an appreciation of the new-modelled Whiggery. In Chapter 3 it is shown how these liberal Anglican Whigs, in marked contrast with their Foxite elders, possessed a distinctive Anglican faith, and, in particular, were admirers of a group of liberal theologians associated with Trinity College, Cambridge, and Oriel College, Oxford. These dons they patronized, offering preferment to them in the church as well as seeking their advice on political and ecclesiastical questions. Chapter 4 demonstrates the theological basis of these dons' liberal politics, as well as their consonance with the beliefs of liberal Anglican politicians. As a consequence it is suggested that liberal Anglicanism was a sincerely held political doctrine which owed far more to Anglican thinkers than to those secular theorists, such as Grote or Mill, who are more commonly associated with the development of nineteenth-century liberalism.

Chapters 5 and 6 demonstrate the influence of liberal

Anglicanism on the legislative proposals of the Whig governments. In Chapter 5 the movement for university reform is
shown to have been as much the product of an alliance between
liberal Anglican dons and politicians as a consequence of
Nonconformist agitation. The university reform movement
marked the coming of age of liberal Anglicanism, since it
demonstrated the existence of a political alliance between
Westminster, Oxford, and Cambridge in addition to the private relations based on intellectual and personal sympathy.
This chapter also illustrates the practical changes in national
establishments which these liberal Anglican desired, and
which were the consequences of the more abstract speculations
outlined in the previous chapter. In Chapter 6 it is shown that
just as liberal Anglicans attempted to transform the ancient
universities into national institutions open to all Christians,
regardless of sect, so they wished to institute a national system
of elementary education in which Dissenter could sit down
with Anglican, Catholic with Protestant. Russell's proposals
of 1839 marked the high point of liberal Anglicanism. They
enjoyed the support of most Dissenters and Catholics, liberal
Anglicans, and Evangelicals. Only the High Church Tories
were furious in their opposition, doubting the feasibility of
providing a common religious education which would not also
have been a diminution of faith. But thereafter, as the weakness
of the Whig majority constantly revealed itself, the Whig leaders increasingly found themselves under attack from Evangelicals and Nonconformists within the liberal coalition.

The concluding chapter of the book deals with some of the
tensions within the liberal coalition, and so illustrates some
of the limits to liberal Anglican success. Whig relations with
Protestant Dissent, Irish Catholics, and English Evangelicals
are studied in considering Whig attitudes towards the anti-
slavery movement during this decade. The increasing isolation
of Whiggery from these groups is described, as the first two
became increasingly Radical and militant, while the last began
to develop Tory sympathies. Nevertheless the extent of these
changes should not be exaggerated. As a brief analysis of the
1841 general election indicates, the liberal coalition was still
sufficiently strong to unite on a suitable rallying cry (in this
case free trade). Although the Whigs lost the election, it was

by no means as damaging to them as previous by-elections had indicated it would be.

From this epitome, it will be apparent that the argument contained in this book is elaborated stage by stage in the course of the seven chapters. Each chapter is the stone in the span of an arch. Individual chapters contain so much miscellaneous historical information; read together they constitute an extended argument. The early chapters will doubtless raise as many questions as they answer, but it is hoped that these will be dealt with satisfactorily as the book proceeds. The argument relies for its plausibility on the accumulation of evidence. No more than probability is claimed for the conclusions of this book, despite the fashionable pursuit of certainty. But this requires no apology, for, as Bishop Butler insisted in 1736, in a work which profoundly influenced the outlook of many Anglicans in the nineteenth century, 'probability is the very guide of life'.[30]

The achievement of liberal Anglicanism in the decade of reform was considerable. If not all legislative proposals reached the statute book, liberal Anglican politicians were none the less able to transform the language of political liberalism, and so the English political agenda itself. If university and education reform proposals were not successful in the 1830s, they dominated domestic politics for a political generation. Not until 1868 were church-rates abolished, not until 1869 was the Irish Church disestablished, not until 1870 was a national system of elementary education instituted in England, and not until 1871 were Dissenters allowed to graduate at Oxford and Cambridge Universities. Many of the reforms of Gladstone's first government owe their political origins to the earlier ideas and actions of liberal Anglican politicians. Liberal Anglican schemes for forging a united, Christian, and non-sectarian British nation out of the apparently antagonistic elements of Protestant and Catholic, Anglican and Nonconformist, Irish and English, High Churchmen, Broad Churchmen, and Evangelicals, were absorbed into the language and practice of British politics.

[30] J. Butler, *The Analogy of Religion* (London, 1834), 3.

The Political and Intellectual Origins of Liberal Anglicanism: from Foxism to Constitutional Moralism

WHEN the first 'Whig' government for over twenty years was formed in 1830, it owed more to the politics of the order it was pledged to replace than to the order which it heralded. Although the granting of civic rights to Protestant Nonconformists and Roman Catholics had already changed the rules of the political game, which the Whigs were to alter yet further, Grey's administration was an amalgam of parliamentary groups, of the form which had largely dominated English politics since the eighteenth century. Indeed, it was by no means obviously worthy of the epithet 'Whig', any more than Canning's coalition of 1827 had been truly Tory. Far from being propelled into office by a popular enthusiasm for reform, it was primarily the product of political discontents at Westminster.[1] Certainly it was unclear, when the MPs returned to London in the autumn of 1830, following the election, that parliamentary reform was to become the monopoly of Whiggery. In September the Norfolk Whig, Coke, had expressed his belief that Wellington would introduce a Reform Bill, if only to stay in office, a remark highlighted by three national newspapers, including the government's own mouthpiece.[2] It was the Duke's declaration in the House of Lords against reform, on 2 November, which transformed the political situation. Huskissonites could no longer equivocate about their opposition to the government, while ultra-Tories were provided with an opportunity to express theirs. For widely diverse reasons, these two groups were prepared to forget their differences with the Whig party (itself still fragmented after

---

[1] M. G. Brock, *The Great Reform Act* (London, 1973), 103.
[2] Ibid., 113–4.

splits in 1827–8) to bring down the government. Significantly this was achieved on an economy motion proposed by Sir Henry Parnell: it was uncertain that the friable opposition could even agree on parliamentary reform, while there was every reason to suppose it would not. Opinions on the issue within the anti-Wellingtonian alliance ranged widely, from Knatchbull, the MP for Kent, who was prepared to support a moderate concession if it prevented the rick-burning and agricultural distress of the southern counties, to Brougham, who, returned for Yorkshire largely through the influence of Leeds merchants and manufacturers in opposition to the Whig aristocracy, saw reform as a popular Whig cause.[3] Grey's Cabinet of November 1830 reflected this initial disunity.

It was a confused, not to say fractious, coalition. Old Foxites, such as Grey and Holland, rubbed shoulders with one ultra-Tory (the Duke of Richmond), Canningites (Melbourne and Palmerston), Whig members of the coalition of 1827 (Lansdowne and Durham), and their Whig opponents (Althorp and Russell). If these were the most obvious intra-party divisions, in the politics of the 1830s they were not always the most important. Holland and Grey, for example, occupied opposing camps on the question whether or not peers should be created in 1832 in order to ensure a successful reading of the Reform Bill in the House of Lords.[4] Other policy disagreements were more lasting: on Ireland and the use of coercion; on foreign policy and English intervention in Portugal and the Near East; on political economy, especially with regard to agricultural protection in England and public works programmes in Ireland; on the introduction of the ballot and other constitutional innovations. In addition to these topics, the most politically divisive questions involved religious considerations. A broad spectrum of theological opinion found its way into Grey's Cabinet, which ranged from Deism, Unitarianism, and liberal Anglicanism, through Evangelicalism to High Anglicanism. On issues involving the funding of the church and the role of religion in elementary and higher education this mixture proved explosive, and it was on a church rather than a secular reform issue that Grey's Cabinet fell in 1834. At times it seemed that only family connections united the

<hr />

[3] Ibid., 95, 104, 128–9.   [4] Ibid., 278.

government's fissile elements. The Radically inclined Durham might be at odds with the more conservative Grey, but they were at least related by marriage; however suspicious Foxites might be of Canningites following the coalition of 1827, at least the Foxite Duncannon and the Canningite Melbourne were brothers-in-law.

The broad-bottom origins of the ministry superficially make it appear more akin to the Fox–Grenville coalition of 1806–7 or the Liverpool administration of 1812–27 than to Peel's Government of 1841–6 or Russell's of 1846–52. This appearance has coloured modern interpretations of the Whig party in post-reform England. Southgate, for example, in recounting the passing of the Whigs as a political force, has stressed, not altogether unreasonably, the anachronistic nature of their politics. The Whig party, he said, was nothing but the 'specialised subsidiary' of an archaic aristocratic connection, which sustained itself with the fiction that 'it *led* the liberal forces in the community'. In time the Whigs appreciated their own delusions, and realized that far from controlling the pace of progress, they were 'trimmers'—a verdict finally confirmed by the Aberdeen coalition of 1852, which reflected the fact that the Whigs 'were unable to reign alone'.[5] Historians have often noticed the weakness of Whiggery, its outmodishness, its aristocratic nature, and its eighteenth-century view of politics and policies. The Whig government, on such an understanding, represented a belated vindication of Foxite principles. Leslie Mitchell has argued that Foxite articles of faith 'provided the basis for action when the vagaries of politics wafted the Whigs back into office in 1830'; Smith, likewise, has claimed that 'Whig principles and political attitudes survived from the days of Rockingham and Burke to those of Grey and Russell until their translation into practical politics'. Whigs were, in the words of Mitchell, eighteenth–century whales stranded on nineteenth-century beaches.[6]

In such circumstances, it is not surprising that historians such as Gash have argued that the Whigs, however willing to serve the state, however experienced in holding office and

[5] D. Southgate, *The Passing of the Whigs* (London, 1962), 66, 231.
[6] L. Mitchell, *Holland House* (London, 1980), 60, 194; E. A. Smith, *Whig Principles and Party Politics: Earl Fitzwilliam and the Whig Party 1748–1833* (Manchester, 1975), xi.

sociable out of it, were unable to command and discipline the
popular forces which they had encouraged, and for whom
deference had ceased to be the natural state of mind. On this
interpretation, the Whigs in the 1830s lost any distinctive
identity they might once have possessed, and buffeted by waves
of Radicalism, Peelite Conservatism, and unreconstructed
Toryism, took on board whatever ballast was most convenient
to keep them afloat.[7] But, paradoxically, by the end of the
decade of reform, the Whig party had emerged from the confusion of the early 1830s with a distinctive political identity,
which, despite ritual incantations, owed little to Fox and much
to younger Whigs, such as Russell. In foreign policy the Whigs
were aggressive and imperialist, whereas Fox had been pacific
and anti-interventionist; in economic affairs the Whigs adopted
the tenets of political economy and became the advocates of
free trade, while Fox, when not ignorant of such matters, had
been contemptuous of Pitt's steps in that direction; in social
policy the Whigs displayed a concern for popular education
and the conditions of the working classes, whereas Fox, by
and large, had been silent. Above all, the Whigs emerged as
sympathizers with Nonconformist religion, both Catholic and
Protestant, willing to legislate in its interests, to encourage its
adherents to participate in government and to admit them to
a full share of national life. There were of course limits to such
sympathies. The coalition between Whigs and Nonconformists
was not uniformly harmonious, but one liable to fracture at a
number of different points. It was a coalition, in addition,
which not all Whigs supported and some were to regret. None
the less, it was an impressive achievement; it was, moreover,
an important one.

Since the end of the Napoleonic wars Dissenters had been
agitating with increasing strength for the redress of their
grievances. Until the late 1820s, the existence of the Corporation Act of 1661 and the Test Act of 1673 nominally
excluded Protestant Nonconformists from many offices at both
a national and a local level by a requirement that they
should take the sacrament according to Anglican rites. The
Parliamentary Test Act of 1678 excluded Catholics from
parliament by imposing on them a declaration against transub-

[7] See, for example, Gash, *Reaction and Reconstruction*, 186.

stantiation. Both Catholics and most Protestant Nonconformists were compelled by law to pay for the upkeep of the Anglican Church, were excluded from the ancient centres of higher learning on account of their religion, and forced to conform to Anglican rites if they were to be registered by the state at birth, marriage, and death. The Anglican state interfered at every significant point of their lives. In so far as legislation had been passed to meet their grievances, it had been at the expense of political stability. The repeal of the Test and Corporation Acts in 1828 and the passage of Catholic Emancipation in 1829 had resulted in the break-up of the political coalition which had governed England since 1812. Such concessions by the Anglican Tory party had not so much appeased Dissenters as increased their appetite for agitation in order to seek political redress for their outstanding grievances. The passage of the Reform Act in 1832 exacerbated this condition, since it increased the political influence of Dissent. It had, in the words of Gash, given 'greater political strength to the intellectual and sectarian enemies of the Establishment'.[8] The question was whether or not it was possible for either political party to work with this potentially disruptive force. The Whigs in the 1830s proved they were able to do so, whereas the Tories in the 1820s had split on the issue.

In the decade of reform, the Whig appeal to Nonconformity proved remarkably potent. Vincent has shown how, in twenty-eight constituencies between 1830 and 1847, Dissenting ministers cast 362 votes for the liberal candidates as against 21 votes for the conservatives. Close, likewise, has demonstrated that in three borough elections in the 1830s Dissenters cast 1,195 votes for the liberal party as against only 174 for the Tories. In Ireland too, the Whigs successfully garnered dissenting Catholic support. In 1832 those Catholics who wished to repeal the Irish Act of Union passed in 1800 won 39 seats as compared with 36 pro-Unionist Whig supporters; by 1841 the Repealers returned only 18 MPs as against 47 Whig-liberals: it was a triumphant vindication of the Whig governments.[9] This Whig

[8] Ibid., 62.

[9] J. R. Vincent, *Pollbooks: How Victorians Voted* (Cambridge, 1967), 67–8; D. H. Close, 'The General Elections of 1835 and 1837 in England and Wales', D.Phil. thesis (Oxford, 1967), 141; A. D. Macintyre, *The Liberator: Daniel O'Connell and the Irish Party 1830–1847* (London, 1965), 299.

success was not exclusively wrought by their own hands. It would not be altogether untrue to say that Dissenters initially adopted the Whigs, rather than forced the Whigs to adapt to them. This was partly because Dissenting political self-consciousness was a phenomenon which took time to develop. It was not until the late 1830s and the emergence of provincial anti-church-rate campaigns and pro-disestablishment societies that Dissenters fully sundered themselves from the conservative, and primarily Unitarian, leadership of metropolitan London. Once that occurred, as a pressure group like the Anti-Corn Law League showed, it was easier for Nonconformity to take an independent political line. Dissent, with the obvious exception of Wesleyan Methodism, also had historical reasons to expect that it would find sympathetic supporters in the ranks of the Whigs. One Foxite myth concerned the co-operation which had taken place in the late eighteenth century between the Whig opposition and the leaders of Dissent in demanding the abolition of religious penalties, however briefly that co-operation actually had lasted.

But while such remarks might explain why Dissenters were initially sympathetic towards the Whigs, they do not explain why the Whigs were able to respond to their demands. Indeed, as Dissenters were to find out, much to their disappointment, not all Whigs were prepared to respond. It was not until 1834 and after that the Whigs willingly took up Dissenting causes. It was then that the party committed itself to appropriating the surplus revenues of the Irish Church to non-ecclesiastical purposes, and that the Irish administration positively discriminated in favour of Catholics; that, in face of the reluctance of the universities of Oxford and Cambridge to admit Dissenters to degrees, London University was given its charter and provision was made for Dissenters attending Durham University to graduate; that the first attempt was made to establish a non-sectarian national system of elementary education in England; that a non-Anglican registration of marriages was permitted; that Bills were introduced for the abolition of church rates. The profusion of such proposals was the consequence of a struggle within the Whig coalition which occurred in 1834–5. In order to understand how such propositions became politically possible within the party, it is necessary to understand the conflict, which emerged between three sections in particular, and which resulted in the triumph of the pro-Dissenting liberal Anglicans.

To describe these sections in the 1830s in terms of the political groups of the 1820s is misleading. The repeal of the Test and Corporation Acts, the Catholic Relief Act, and the government's commitment to parliamentary reform had rendered such distinctions obsolete, without, at the same time, having produced recognizable alternatives. There were, for example, a number of former followers of the liberal Tory Prime Minister, George Canning, in the government, committed, as he had been, to freer trade and concessions to Dissenting minorities, and these included Grant, Palmerston, and Melbourne. It makes little sense, however, to term these Canningite, when others, of a similar outlook, such as Sandon, Acland, and Wortley, were to be found after 1830 on the Tory benches.[10] The term had ceased to be an indication of how politicians were to act. This was equally true of the Whigs. Both Lansdowne and Durham had supported the alliance with Canning in 1827, but their politics diverged in the 1830s. While Lansdowne remained wedded to a cautious and hesitant outlook on reform, in 1834 Durham spoke out strongly for triennial parliaments, household suffrage, and the secret ballot. In the 1830s, politics were in an obvious state of flux, and it was not with reference to past activity that future performance could be measured. In terms of the struggle for control of the Whig coalition, which occurred in the mid-1830s, it is safer for historians to classify Whig politicians according to their political expectations, rather than their past histories.

The first section of coalitionists consisted of those who feared the consequences of reform. These were the Cassandras of the Whig party, and included such politicians as Graham, Ripon, Richmond, and Stanley. As might be expected, their origins were diverse. Richmond had been an ultra-Tory supporter of the Duke of Wellington, who turned to parliamentary reform as a result of his leader's conversion to Catholic Emancipation, while Stanley was the heir to the earldom of Derby and a member of a traditionally Whig family. Although such

[10] For this list of Huskissonites (the followers of Canning, after his demise), see Os C 67 (Ossington Papers): Sandon to Denison, 22 Jan. 1829.

politicians conceded the necessity for some reforms in church
and state, they believed that the government had little time
to act before the forces of democracy and Dissent overwhelmed
the establishments of the country. Of no one was this more
true than Graham, whose prose was almost hysterical in
expressing his fears for the future, perhaps because he regretted
his earlier enthusiasm for reform and complicity in drafting
the Reform Bill. He believed, indeed, that the first session of
parliament following the passing of the Reform Act was the
last opportunity the government had for carrying moderate
reforms, capable of preventing 'the overthrow of Property and
the destruction of the Kingly Power'.[11] One issue in particular
became the touchstone by which they judged the validity of
their fears, namely the reform of the Church of England.
It was a question which involved both property rights and
religion. They wished to defend the integrity of the church
against those who wished to appropriate its endowments to
non-ecclesiastical purposes. To acquiesce in such demands,
according to these politicians, would be to condone the state's
interference in any form of private property, including that of
the landlord, and to herald the destruction of Anglicanism,
which ever since the Revolution Settlement of 1689, had been
the keystone of Britain's constitution. How the government
acted on that issue was to determine whether or not these
politicians continued to support it. Their defence of the Anglican Church made them the 'High Church' party in the Cabinet.

A second group of politicians existed, who, although sceptical about the benefits of reform, were equally sceptical about
the benefits of not conceding, if only to a limited extent, to
repeated and vociferous demands for change. Such politicians
included Earl Grey, Whig leader since 1807, Viscount Melbourne, a member of the Canning government, and Viscount
Palmerston, who had held office continuously from 1807 to
1828, nineteen of those years as Secretary at War. Given that
the leadership of this group was in the hands of Grey, and
that his closest political allies were Lord Holland and the
Marquis of Lansdowne, it is sensible to refer to them for bre-
vity's sake as the old Foxites. These politicians were less concerned about particular proposals for reform than the means

[11] Bod. Film 108 (Graham Papers): Graham to Brougham, 13 Dec. 1832.

of carrying them out. In short, they believed that the prosperity of the country depended on the maintenance of the reform coalition of 1830, and thus the exclusion of English Radicals and Irish Catholics from positions of political prominence. Grey's discontent with the Whig government of 1835 was based on his belief that too much influence had been conceded to the Irish Catholic leader, O'Connell, and throughout the late 1830s he hoped for a political realignment, which would result in something akin to the coalition he had formed in 1830. Melbourne, conversely, defended the governments over which he presided on the ground that, after the resignations of Stanley, Graham, Ripon, and Richmond in 1834, and the King's dismissal of the government in November of that year, he had none the less managed to recruit an administration, which, in overall composition if not in individuals, was similar to Grey's; he was pleased, in particular, that he had excluded from office Durham, O'Connell, and Brougham. Their overriding concern for the stability of the government meant that these politicians preferred legislative inaction, particularly on issues affecting the relations of church and state: reform proposals precipitated disputes and threatened to break up ministries. Grey spent from 1832 to 1834 ensuring that the question of the Irish Church surplus would not appear on the Cabinet's agenda; Melbourne, according to Archbishop Whately 'the highest conservative I ever knew',[12] opposed the introduction of a national system of education, a leading liberal cause at the end of the decade, just as Irish appropriation had been earlier. This legislative negativism on religiously contentious issues initially appealed to the first section of coalitionists, because it ensured that Radical proposals were stifled, but in the course of the 1830s it appeared increasingly to be a weakness. The reluctance to take a positive stand against further reform seemed an injudicious form of compromise. This was a view, which was confirmed for Graham and Stanley by the willingness of this second group of politicians to accept the reform proposals in religious matters of the third group within the coalition, namely those of the liberal Anglicans.

These politicians saw the governments of the 1830s as welcome opportunities for implementing the reforms, which had

[12] E. J. Whately, *Life and Correspondence of Richard Whately DD* (London, 1875), 466.

been contemplated in the 1820s. They included Lord John Russell, Lord Morpeth, Viscount Howick, Hobhouse, and Poulett Thomson. They saw no incompatibility between admitting Dissenters and Roman Catholics as members of the political nation (reforms which they actively approved rather than accepted as acts of political survival) and maintaining the Anglican Church. This was because they believed that there were Christian truths which were common to members of all Christian sects, and which were independent of dogma: the beliefs these groups shared were more fundamental (and more important) than those on which they differed. In the 1830s such politicians actively promoted the appropriation of the Irish Church surplus to non-ecclesiastical purposes, the admission of Nonconformists to the universities of Oxford and Cambridge, and the institution of a non-sectarian form of elementary education — causes which in the eyes of politicians such as Graham and Stanley eroded the position of the Anglican Church, and which Grey and Melbourne considered as dangerously unsettling to the reform coalitions of the 1830s. These liberal Anglican politicians, aided and abetted by liberal Evangelical Whigs, such as Althorp and Radnor, who were most influential in the 1820s and whom E. A. Wasson has termed 'young Whigs',[13] increasingly dominated the government after 1834, and were responsible for giving it the distinctive tone which was apparent by the end of the decade. How they were able to do so is the subject of this book; their origins in the Whig politics of the 1820s is the subject of this chapter. To understand how they were able to embrace the liberal, religious reforms which so endeared them to Dissenters, which so angered more conservative coalitionist Anglicans, and to which others, such as Grey and Melbourne, were so indifferent, it is necessary to understand the state of the Whig party in the 1820s in the light of the Foxite inheritance.

In retrospect, Charles James Fox acquired a singular and not always deserved reputation for populism. Politicians and historians saw him as keeping alive the spirit of liberty and reform following the disintegration of the Whig party in 1794, and as moulding the rump in his own image. In 1859, as he

[13] E. A. Wasson, 'The Young Whigs: Lords Althorp, Milton, and Tavistock and the Whig Party 1809–1830', Ph.D. thesis (Cambridge, 1976).

entered the twilight of his own career, Lord John Russell reflected that in the 1790s Fox 'placed on a height [his] beacon to save the wandering friends of freedom from destruction'. The son of Newcastle's corrupt Paymaster General, according to Leslie Mitchell, bequeathed to the nineteenth-century Whigs a tradition of acting as 'the guardians of many reform movements'.[14] But Fox's heirs were not immediately clear as to the value of his legacy. They generally accepted that Fox's career could be split into three phases, namely the years of the Fox–North coalition of 1782–3, of opposition to Pitt, especially after 1794, and of the Fox–Grenville coalition of 1806. Whig politicians, however, tended to celebrate or denigrate each of these phases as they corresponded to their current political predilections. Brougham, writing in 1838, excluded from office and taking up Radical causes, disapproved of both the Fox-North coalition and, if to a lesser extent, the Ministry of All The Talents. The Fox he celebrated was the 'leader of the patriot band which, during the almost hopeless struggle from 1793 to 1806, upheld the cause of afflicted freedom'.[15] Holland, on the other hand, somewhat suspicious of Whig–Radical *rapprochements* in 1818, declared that Fox's opposition to Pitt was motivated by his 'ambition of power and distinction'; Holland reserved his praise for the final period of Fox's life when 'his sole, steady, *chastened-down* desire was that of doing good'.[16] Lansdowne, who, with Holland's support, led the Whigs into a coalition with Canning, not surprisingly also praised the Fox–Grenville coalition, while condemning the Fox–North coalition which had defeated his father's administration in 1783. For Lansdowne, the lesson of eighteenth-century politics was that coalitions were not only just but necessary: 'Otherwise the court might bear down everything before it'.[17] Fox's career, as might be expected from a politician who did not find it inconsistent both to uphold and to condemn

[11] J. Russell, *The Life and Times of Charles James Fox*, (London, 1859–66), i. xi; L. Mitchell, *Holland House* 49.

[15] [H. Brougham], 'Remarks on an Article in the *Edinburgh Review*, No. 135, on the Times of George the Third and George the Fourth', *Edinburgh Review*, lxviii (1838), 220.

[16] T. Moore, *Memoirs, Journal, and Correspondence*, ed. Lord John Russell (London, 1853–56), ii. 198.

[17] Ibid., ii. 291.

the exercise of royal prerogatives, proved an exemplary source for Whigs of all political persuasions. The Foxite legacy can be demonstrated best by examining the activities of Fox and his followers.

Certainly it was not clear that Fox had been, any more than rhetorically, the champion of the people, or even regarded it as a desirable role to assume in politics. While in the 1820s it was a useful fiction for Russell and Hobhouse to claim that the Foxites had been the judicious leaders of an extra-parliamentary populace, it was not a claim which Fox's career or the activities of his followers, who were still in charge of the party in the pre-Reform decade, justified. Fox had been at best a reluctant promoter of parliamentary reform and found the aristocratic Society of the Friends of the People, formed in 1792, an embarrassment, since it exacerbated the divisions in a party already divided on its attitude towards the French Revolution. Neither Fox nor his immediate friends, such as Fitzpatrick or Lord Robert Spencer, ever belonged to it.[18] Fox's flirtation with Radicalism evaporated as soon as he perceived that more orthodox parliamentary means were available to achieve power. In 1805 he actively discouraged Wyvill's request to institute a petitioning movement for parliamentary reform.[19] Such a lack of interest was perfectly in keeping with the party of aristocratic Whiggery which Fox led, and which could trace its ancestry via Rockingham to Newcastle and the Whig oligarchs of the 1740s. It was also perfectly in keeping with a politician who had begun his political career as a supporter of Grafton, an opponent of Wilkes and an office-holder under Lord North. It was a party which concerned itself primarily with circumscribing the powers of the crown rather than with relieving the discontents of the people, even if, when in opposition, it was prepared to enlist popular protest if this tactic furthered the aristocratic end of storming the royal closet. Fox was acting in perfect accord with the example of his patron, Rockingham, when he held office in 1783 and 1806 as a consequence of parliamentary manœuvres, and at the expense of public support. It should be no surprise that anti-slavers,

---

[18] Fox, *Memoirs of the Whig Party*, i. 13–5.
[19] R. W. Willis, ' "An Handful of Violent People": The Nature of The Foxite Opposition, 1794–1801', *Albion*, viii (1976), 241.

Dissenters, and parliamentary reformers supported Pitt in 1784 rather than Fox.

The Foxites' traditionally ambiguous support for popular causes also revealed itself in the ministry of 1806–7. The result was a negative legacy of popular distrust of Whiggery which Fox's immediate heirs were reluctant to dispel. When the government increased the property tax by over half at the same time as improving its collection, it did not enhance its standing with the independents, who were opposed to government extravagance and interference.[20] The alliance with the Grenvilles resulted in an embargo on parliamentary reform, an embargo which the Whigs might well have introduced of their own accord in any case.[21] Above all, the failure of the Whigs to stand by their revised Mutiny Bill, which would have allowed Roman Catholics to be members of the general staff, revealed the hollowness of their claim to have the interests of Dissenters at heart. Even Holland was ashamed at the government's action and confessed in his memoirs: 'The surrender of our opinion was, as I then thought and still think, quite wrong.'[22] The consequence, as Whig politicians realized, was the alienation of Radical and Dissenting support from the Foxites. Whitbread, one of the more liberal of their number, acknowledged that Fox's actions had lowered the public's esteem for politicians, adding, in 1808, that 'the last administration completed the job'.[23] Radical leaders such as Henry White, the editor of the *Independent Whig*, Cobbett, and Burdett turned against both Whiggery and the idea of a party connection which was central to its existence. Lord Cochrane, Burdett's colleague as a Radical MP for Westminster, asserted: 'it had become unmistakably manifest that the two great factions into which the politicians were divided had no other object than to share the general plunder.' As Dinwiddy has remarked, there was a strong radical reaction 'against Fox's claim to be entitled the man of the people'.[24]

The Whig heirs of Fox did not learn anything from this state of affairs. If they had any opinions on the issue, they

[20] A. D. Harvey, 'The "Talents" Ministry', *Historical Jour.*, xv (1972), 641.
[21] J. Dinwiddy, 'Charles James Fox and The People', *History*, lv (1970), 346.
[22] Fox, *Memoirs of the Whig Party*, i. 202.
[23] H. Maxwell (ed.), *The Creevey Papers* (London, 1903), i. 92.
[24] Dinwiddy, 'Charles James Fox and The People', 347, 349, 359.

were rather that public opinion was fickle and perfidious. They did not abandon the cautious shuffling which had characterized the government of 1806–7. Far from cultivating Catholic support, Grey did the contrary. He wished to make a royal veto on Irish episcopal appointments an indispensable condition of granting further concessions to Catholics, even though a synod of Irish Catholic bishops in September 1808 had rejected the suggestion.[25] In 1812 he declined to present Catholic petitions to the Lords.[26] Such attitudes encouraged the rise of an independent repeal agitation in Ireland and the emergence of O'Connell as the leader of the movement for Catholic Emancipation: the Whig alliance with the moderate Catholic leader, Lord Fingall, became increasingly irrelevant.[27] A comparable development occurred on the issue of parliamentary reform. By the summer of 1809 it had become clear that Grey would not press ahead with reform motions, and the running was left to such Radicals as Burdett; in June 1810, when Burdett was in the Tower for contempt of parliament, and reform petitions—the first for some years—were being sent to the Commons, Grey declared he stood firm by the principles of the constitution, with the proviso that he supported the reform of obvious abuses.[28] The consequence of fearing too close an association with intemperate Radicalism was that no reform motion was proposed in parliament in the years 1812–17.[29] Far from being the torch-bearers of liberty in the dark years of early nineteenth-century reaction, excluded from office for their pains, Whig leaders did their best to ensure that the torch was passed to other hands.

This was an eminently reasonable position to take. Immediate political history demonstrated that the Whigs achieved office through parliamentary negotiation and not through popular elections. The former 'Friends of the People', such as Grey, Tierney, and Mackintosh, became supporters

---

[25] Lt. Gen. Hon. C. Grey, *Some Account of the Life and Opinions of Charles, Second Earl Grey* (London, 1861), 208, 210; M. Roberts, *The Whig Party 1807–1812* (London, 1939), 45.

[26] H. R. V. Fox (Lord Holland), *Further Memoirs of the Whig Party 1807–1821 with Some Miscellaneous Reminiscences*, ed. Lord Stavordale (London, 1905), 125.

[27] Roberts, *The Whig Party*, 78, 101–2.

[28] Ibid., 246, 271.

[29] Ibid., 295.

of coalitions. The last two even accepted preferment from the anti-Catholic Addington. After 1806, Grey became a devotee of the alliance with the Grenvilles, even acknowledging Lord Grenville as his leader after Fox's death, seeing him as the person 'best qualified to take the chief direction of the party' in which they both acted.[30] Although the Whigs never held office in this period, there was every reason to suppose that, until the 1820s, holding office was an imminent possibility. As the succession of ministries (Portland, Perceval, Liverpool), political negotiations, and deaths indicate, opportunities were not lacking. Moreover, after the defeat of Napoleon in 1815, it was likely that a reconfiguration of politics would occur around those issues which many had thought war rendered inexpedient: the recognition of political rights of minorities, parliamentary reform, and political economy. Thus there were rumours that the Whigs would enter government in September 1809, January 1811, and February and May 1812; it was not improbable that Liverpool's administration might have fallen in 1816, following its defeat on the property tax, and in 1820, when it was forced to withdraw the Bill of Pains and Penalties relating to Queen Caroline. Unfortunately for the Whigs these opportunities came to nothing, a result not entirely unconnected with the fact that the leadership preferred the irresponsibility and purity of opposition to the compromises of government. Holland, for example, believed that Grey's unwillingness to open negotiations with Canning or Lord Wellesley in 1812, as a result of a 'mistaken and misplaced' notion of dignity, was in part responsible for the Whigs' subsequent exclusion from office.[31]

Even those Whigs who urged the leadership, in the name of Fox, to play a more active role in popular politics did not do so because they especially wished to take up the causes of excluded minorities. Whitbread's activities as leader of the inappositely nicknamed 'mountain' harked back to a populism which sought to use public agitation to further attacks on the crown. The campaign in 1809 against the Duke of York for his sale of army commissions was simply an exposure of the corrupt influence of the royal princes; it was followed by such

---

[30] Grey, *Life and Opinions of 2nd Earl Grey*, 358.
[31] Fox, *Further Memoirs*, 134.

proposals as Althorp's, Milton's, and Folkestone's to exclude
princes of the blood from holding offices of state.[32] The 'mountain' had little impact on questions of either political economy
or, to any great extent, of parliamentary reform. On the latter
issue the supporters of Whitbread were divided, and only col-
lectively voted for such measures as Madocks's reform motion
which opposed the Treasury's trading in seats and influencing
votes in the Commons.[33] Until 1812, Whitbread saw the Whigs'
prime route to office being through the reversionary interest
of the crown, and not through popular acclaim. Thus in 1811,
anticipating the Regent's dismissal of Perceval's government,
he drew up lists of potential office-holders, even going so far
as to offer Creevey a seat at the Admiralty Board under Lord
Holland.[34] The main political aim of the 'mountain' was to
separate the Foxites from the Grenvillites by taking up such
divisive, eighteenth-century country party issues as retrenchment and, most controversially in the Napoleonic period,
peace, thereby appealing to traditionally independent members of the Commons. Whitbread conspicuously stayed aloof
from Metropolitan Radicals, for example in not attending the
annual Reform dinner at the Crown and Anchor Tavern in
1809; Creevey, in like-minded fashion, claimed that he thought
'upon the whole unfavourably' of Burdett.[35] Such opinions
were in keeping with politicians who believed that 'the great
agriculturalists', such as the Whig Duke of Bedford, were
'almost without exception, real friends of liberty and Reform'.[36]

The consequence of such a political outlook was that by the
1820s the Whig party was in a moribund state. The alliance
with the Grenvillites had failed to yield any political fruit, and
under the impact of the coercive measures of Liverpool's government, in particular the suspension of Habeas Corpus, it
had broken up. Significantly, Grey's son ended his account of
his father's life and opinions in 1817. A combination of illness,
indifference, and laziness led to Grey's withdrawal from active
politics, to the extent that in 1824, when a change of govern-

[32] Wasson, 'The Young Whigs', Ph.D. thesis, 60.

[33] Ibid., 64–5.

[34] Maxwell, *The Creevey Papers*, i. 143.

[35] A. Hone, *For the Cause of Truth* (Oxford, 1982), 173; Maxwell, *The Creevey Papers*,
i. 107.

[36] Ibid., 94–5.

ment was thought to be imminent, Grey declared: 'it would be quite impossible for me to support the fatigue and anxiety which must attend any leading situation in Government'.[37] In the 1820s Lord Holland began to compose his *Memoirs*, which were 'essentially a valediction'.[38] In 1830, before the fall of Wellington's government, he reflected in his journal that neither his age, position, nor inclination rendered it likely that he would 'take a more active part' in politics than he had done for the past fifteen years.[39] Nor could the followers of Whitbread afford to be sanguine. They failed to capitalize on whatever successes they had in rousing the independent members. Having succeeded in defeating the government on the property tax in 1816, Brougham threw away whatever chance the Whigs had of forming an administration by publicly attacking the Regent; likewise, in 1819, when it appeared that the government might fall, the independents, having flirted with the Whigs, returned to the government's fold.[40] Brougham acknowledged the failure of this form of country party politics when, after his unsuccessful attempt to storm the royal closet on the back of the Queen Caroline affair, he began looking in the mid-1820s to a junction with Canning as his route to office. The Whig party fell into disarray, losing its leadership in the Commons in the spring of 1821 and its ability to muster party votes. From 1822 to 1826 the number of government–opposition clashes fell from 88 to just 20.[41]

In view of divisions in the party and its political impotence, it was not surprising that it was the cult of Fox which kept the party together through its vicissitudes. The myth of a glorious past distracted attention from the humiliations of an undignified present. Provincial Fox clubs were founded, busts or portraits of Fox were prominently displayed, and the practice of holding a public dinner on Fox's birthday spread to all parts of the country. Cockburn commented that the Fox dinners 'animated and instructed, and consolidated the whig

[37] Grey, *Life and Opinions of 2nd Earl Grey*, 425.

[38] W. E. Thomas, 'Lord Holland', *History and Imagination*, eds. H. Lloyd Jones, V. Pearl, B. Worden (London, 1981), 307.

[39] Fox, *Further Memoirs*, 211.

[40] H. K. Olphin, *George Tierney* (London, 1934), 172, 201–5; A. Mitchell, *The Whigs in Opposition 1815–1830* (Oxford, 1967), 123–4.

[41] Ibid., 183.

party'. One such dinner occurred in Norwich in 1820, attended by the Duke of Sussex. The table centre-piece consisted of a 'wonderful erection of sugar, representing the Temple of Liberty'; this was surmounted by Fame holding a flag in Whig colours, inscribed with the initials of Magna Carta; other flags had the legends 'Bill of Rights' and 'Trial by Jury'.[42] But for all such ostentatious display, the cult ceased to have any meaning by the 1820s. This was expressed most symbolically by the failure to reach an agreement on a suitable inscription for Westmacott's statue of Fox, finished by 1819. The committee responsible for the commission, unable to decide between Mackintosh's and Grey's epitaphs, in 1823 finally persuaded Mrs Fox to have just the dates and name inscribed on the monument. Creevey believed this was because Holland House thought that any reminder of 'the two great and brilliant features of Fox's public life' (his resistance to the American war and opposition to the Bourbons) would prevent the Whigs coming into office.[43] By the late 1820s Fox dinners and clubs were ceasing to exist, as indeed were Pitt clubs. Grey's son thought that the passing of the Reform Act in 1832 had rendered the pre-Reform distinctions between Whig and Tory obsolete, a conclusion with which historians of pre-1830 Whiggery have concurred. 'For a Foxite', wrote Leslie Mitchell, 'the issues that had dominated political life since 1789 had disappeared'.[44]

It was in these circumstances of depression and dispersal, that a new generation of Whigs made their political entry. These more youthful politicians, 'young Whigs' and liberal Anglicans, acting in what was in effect a political vacuum, sought to reinvent Whiggery as a form of political action rather than nostalgia. Russell recollected that his political leaders thought the party should 'stand by, profess no principles and hazard no opinions'; thus 'discountenanced by my betters and elders I had to consider the position, the character and prin-

[42] On the cult of Fox, and Cockburn's comment, see L. Mitchell, *Holland House* 42–56; A. M. W. Stirling, *Coke of Norfolk and His Friends* (London, 1908), 224–5.

[43] See N. Penny, 'The Whig Cult of Fox in Early Nineteenth-Century Sculpture', *Past and Present*, lxx (1976), 100–2; Dinwiddy, 'Charles James Fox and The People', 355–6; Maxwell, *The Creevey Memoirs*, i. 299–300.

[44] L. Mitchell, *Holland House*, 159–60; A. Mitchell, *The Whigs in Opposition*, 56; Grey, *Life and Opinions of 2nd Earl Grey*, v.

ciples of the Whig party'. In one of his novels, Lord Mulgrave complained that 'Lord Cholera', a Whig politician modelled on Lord Grey, 'forsook the lead that was virtually his' and obliged younger politicians 'to grasp the independence and to wield the influence he let fall from his hands'.[45] In the absence of any others, these Whigs gradually sought, and obtained, influence in the running of the party. Duncannon, in March 1823, already acting as a party whip, urged the introduction of opposition dinners as a form of union; Russell himself suggested the formation of a committee of seven to ten politicians to act as a form of opposition cabinet. At the end of the decade it was a combination of young Whigs and liberal Anglicans who elected Althorp leader of the party in the Commons, a post unoccupied since Tierney's retirement in 1821.[46] Aware of the failure of their elders, these Whigs looked less to political alignments at Westminster than to an increase in party members through popular election as the route to office. They wished to establish the Whigs as leaders of the 'popular' elements in the country, neglected by their leaders, by associating the party more closely with such causes as parliamentary reform and the removal of Dissenting grievances.

Such aspirations were not altogether unrealistic in the politics of the 1820s. In a letter to Tierney in 1818, Abercromby, a leading Scottish Whig, expressed his belief that 'the diffusion of knowledge and wealth of the middle classes' had resulted in their determination to have a share in the running of the country; it was the Whig opposition's task 'to take the lead in giving a tone to this great body of people'; if they did not, 'they will be in danger of falling into contempt . . . as an incapable and useless body'.[47] The 1818 general election, which resulted in gains for the Whigs, appeared to provide evidence of the strength of a public opinion beyond Westminster. The conservative politician Huskisson reflected on the results: 'I

---

[45] R. Russell (ed.), *Early Correspondence of Lord John Russell* (London, 1913), i. 213; J. Russell, *Selections from the Speeches of Earl Russell 1817–1841 and from Despatches 1859–1865 with Introductions* (London, 1870), i. 31; [C. H. Phipps (Earl of Mulgrave)], *The English at Home* (London, 1830), ii. 97–8.

[46] These initiatives, unfortunately, came to nothing. See A. Mitchell, *The Whigs in Opposition*, 36–7; E. A. Wasson, 'The Coalitions of 1827 and the Crisis of Whig Leadership', *Historical Journal*, xx (1977), 587–606.

[47] Olphin, *George Tierney*, 184.

cannot be indifferent to what the Opposition (not the Whigs but the high popular party) will consider as a triumph in so many populous indications of their strength'.[48] The year 1819 saw a revival of the reform movement in the country when a large meeting at Birmingham elected Sir Charles Worseley as 'the legislatorial representative' for the city; a further meeting was convened at Manchester to choose a representative for that town, a meeting which turned into the Peterloo massacre. The Whig Foxite leadership continued to refuse to exploit this reservoir of popular feeling. Although they condemned the killings at Manchester, Holland acted only half-heartedly in organizing county petitions of protest, while Mackintosh and Grey were against all such exertions. Only after Fitzwilliam took the lead in Yorkshire did the other Whig leaders agree to participate in county meetings. In parliament it was left to Russell to propose a reform measure. Although Tierney as Whig leader in the Commons had declared in favour of reform in November 1819, he delayed taking up the question in a more specific manner, with the result that Russell made his first proposal in that year. Continued Whig inactivity propelled Russell into taking further action in the following years, 'evidently displeased', as his friend, the poet, Tom Moore, noted in his diary, 'with the shilly-shally conduct of his party'.[49]

Such Whigs as Russell, Althorp, and Ebrington became activists, both in the country and at Westminster. They feared that, in the presence of an indifferent Foxite leadership, the Radicals would seize the parliamentary initiative and emerge as the leaders of the reforming elements in the country. In the early 1820s, what was particularly alarming was that the larger, more populous seats returned an increasing number of Radical MPs.[50] The Whig response was fourfold. At Westminster they sponsored various reform measures, of which Russell's campaign for parliamentary reform was but one example. Althorp, for his part, took up the Irish issue: in February 1824 he called for papers relating to the state of the church and the

---

[48] J. E. Cookson, *Lord Liverpool's Administration: The Crucial Years 1815–1822* (Edinburgh & London, 1975), 142–3.

[49] Stirling, *Coke of Norfolk and His Friends* 220; A. Mitchell, *The Whigs in Opposition* 127–8; Olphin, *George Tierney* 215, 223–4; Moore, *Memoirs*, iii. 272.

[50] P. Fraser, 'Party Voting in the House of Commons 1812–1827', *English Historical Review* lxxxi (1983), 769.

numbers of Roman Catholics in the country, and sustained an interest in that question even after the defeat of the 1825 Catholic Relief Bill.[51] 'Young' and Liberal Anglican Whigs, such as Althorp, Spring Rice, and Ebrington, also participated in older parliamentary campaigns, such as those for the abolition of slavery and the reform of the penal system, with the result that the first of these, at least, became an almost exclusively Whig campaign.[52] Secondly, these more activist politicians also sought to concert action with the Radicals at Westminster, and so institute a Whig-led association, if not alliance. At a Whig-Radical club, the Clarendon, Duncannon chaired meetings at which opposition tactics were discussed, while in 1823 Hobhouse, who in that year dined at Holland House for the first time in five years, drew up a 'sort of manifesto respecting the advantages of the opposition acting together in concert'.[53]

In the country these Whigs lent their names and presence to various reform movements. Russell, for example, chaired a parliamentary reform meeting in the parish of St. George's, Bloomsbury, in November 1820, and in 1828 wished both to establish a 'Committee for the Promotion of Religious Liberty' and to organize petitioning movements on the model of the anti-Catholic Brunswick clubs in order to promote Catholic Emancipation. In 1822 Althorp had received the freedom of the City of Nottingham—a Dissenting stronghold—and in 1830 chaired the election campaign of the Radical candidate for Middlesex, Joseph Hume, whose nomination for that county he had secured. Ebrington joined the Catholic Association and contributed to its rent. Milton consulted O'Connell on the Catholic Relief Bill of 1825 and in the 1826 election received the praise of the Nonconformist-owned *Leeds Mercury*.[54] All but the last mentioned Whig politician held office in the

[51] Wasson, 'The Young Whigs' (Ph.D. thesis), 258–9, 262.

[52] P. F. Dixon, 'The Politics of Emancipation: The Movement for the Abolition of Slavery in the British West Indies 1807–1833', D. Phil. thesis (Oxford, 1971), 367–74; H. G. Bennet, one of Wasson's 'Younger Whigs', became a leading Whig advocate for the reform of the penitentiaries. See C. G. Oakes, *Sir Samuel Romilly 1757–1818* (London, 1935), 379.

[53] P. Fraser, 'Party Voting', 776.

[54] Hone, *For the Cause of Truth*, 35; Wasson, 'The Young Whigs' (Ph.D. thesis), 240, 261, 294, 296; G. I. T. Machin, *The Catholic Question in English Politics 1820–1830* (Oxford, 1964), 147.

governments of the 1830s. Admittedly they were aware that
the cultivation of Dissent could, at times, be electorally disastrous, as the Bedfordshire election of 1820 indicated, when the
Whig candidates lost to a 'no Popery' cry.[55] In their parliamentary and extra-parliamentary activities they sought to create
a coalition which would be more broadly-based than mere
Dissent. In 1820 Creevey attacked Russell 'for his buttering
of Wilberforce', when he hoped to secure Evangelical involvement on the Whig side of the Queen Caroline affair. Althorp
stomped the country campaigning for agricultural improvements, addressing meetings in at least nine counties.[56] Such
an attempt at creating a broad reforming coalition of Dissenters
and Evangelicals, progressive agriculturalists and liberal Anglicans, anti-slavers and political reformers, was in keeping with
the brief precedent set by the lawyer, Samuel Romilly, who
achieved the peak of his political career when he was elected
MP for Westminster in 1818, a few months before his suicide.
By taking up such issues as penal and criminal law reform,
anti-slavery, and parliamentary reform, Romilly acquired supporters as diverse as the Evangelical Wilberforce, the Quaker
Mrs Fry, and the Radicals Burdett and Bentham, while
remaining firmly within the Whig fold as the protégé of Lord
Lansdowne. His untimely death, combined with the party
divisions of 1818–20, eclipsed his achievement.[57]

Finally, such Whigs went beyond haphazard political
encounters with assorted reform movements in the country.
They also re-thought Whig party dogma, a re-thinking which,
however inadvertently, enabled these more progressive Whigs
to embrace liberal reforms in the 1830s, which their leaders
tended to accept only as bitter acts of necessity. This is not
to argue that such a formulation of Whig thought was a deliberate and calculated act, anticipating the events of the 1830s.
It is only to suggest that the necessities of the 1820s made
them fortuitously responsive to the demands of the later
decade. This rhetorical re-working was primarily the work of
the liberal Anglican Russell, who, in the 1820s, emerged as a

[55] Ibid., 71.
[56] Maxwell, *The Creevey Papers* i. 309; Cookson, *Lord Liverpool's Administration* 252;
Wasson, 'The Young Whigs' (Ph.D. thesis), 241.
[57] Oakes, *Sir Samuel Romilly*, 58, 89, 299, 311, 314, 343.

leading Whig author, with five works of history and three of fiction to his credit. The most famous of these was his *Essay on the History of the English Government and Constitution*. This had two English editions (in 1821 and 1823) and two French editions in 1821, was re-issued in England in 1865, and published in Germany in 1872. Other works were equally successful. His biography of Lord William Russell had three English editions in 1819 and 1820, and brought him a £300 profit; his essay on *The Establishment of the Turks in Europe* (1828) was published in England and France, while *Essays and Sketches of Life and Character* (1820) appeared in England and America. Something of the public for whom Russell wrote may be inferred from the form which his publications took. Russell did not write for a mass provincial audience or engage in pamphlet warfare. These were works primarily produced for the approbation of the London literary world, although Russell had been known to contribute to *The Times* and the *Edinburgh Review*. Perhaps not surprisingly, they received the quasi-paternal praises of the Hollands, John Whishaw, the lawyer and habitué of Holland House, and the 'Whig Dr Johnson', Samuel Parr. But Russell's readership, as anecdotal evidence as well as sales indicate, extended beyond the immediate family coterie. The Evangelical leader of the anti-slavery movement was an admirer of the biography of William Russell, as were Whishaw's Malmesbury friends, the Smiths.[58]

These works are not notable for their literary or intellectual merit. As Burrow has remarked, Russell's historical account of England's liberties was 'heavily dependent on Hallam' and, it should be added, his life of William Russell owed much to Fox's history of the reign of James II. His description of the four stages of civilization, to be found at the commencement of *An Essay on the History of the English Government and Constitution*, owed more to late seventeenth-and early eighteenth-century 'Machiavellian theories of the civic humanist tradition' than to more modern Scottish conjectural history as pioneered by Millar and Hume.[59] Although Burrow is unfair in his

[58] The Earl of Ilchester, *Chronicles of Holland House 1820–1900* (London, 1937), 38; J. Whishaw, *The Pope of Holland House*, ed. Lady Seymour (London, 1906), 212, 222; Moore, *Memoirs*, v. 114; C. Buxton, *Memoirs of Sir Thomas Fowell Buxton, Bart.* (London, 1866), 94.

[59] J. W. Burrow, *A Liberal Descent* (Cambridge, 1981), 29–30.

suggestion that Russell made no serious attempt to explain how England appeared to be an exception to the general cyclical law of growth followed by decay[60] (the explanation being the predominance of Christian virtue in England, a form of public spirit which continental Europe and the ancient republics lacked), Russell's works are treated here less as the products of intellectual lucubrations than the statements of political faith which contemporaries took them to be. The *Monthly Review* believed that a study of Russell's *An Essay on the History of the English Government and Constitution* would reveal the 'political creed' of one of the country's legislators, while Lord Holland's son, General Charles Fox, praised Russell's 'exposition of Whiggish principles' in the *Life of William Lord Russell*. The *Gentleman's Magazine* in its review of Russell's verse-play, *Don Carlos*, referred to an insinuation that it had been published 'with retrospective views of a political nature'; and the *Quarterly* reviewed Russell's *Causes of the French Revolution* on the assumption that these historical events reflected on the current state of politics: 'We, let it be observed, are but in the second month of a States General: we are approaching the Night of Sacrifices, and by just the same steps which the French took before us', it intoned ominously in 1833.[61]

Russell himself was fully aware of the political implications of his writings. In the preface to his biography of William Russell, he admitted that he had not undertaken the work on the ground of ancestral piety alone, but also had a view to its 'general utility'; likewise his own biographer commented that Russell's *An Essay on the History of the English Government and Constitution* was a 'political confession of faith' made by the man who 'beyond all others was to shape the creed of the Whig party'.[62] This was not unusual. Fox used his history, albeit written in retirement at St Anne's Hill and published posthumously, as a vindication of his Whiggism,[63] and Mackintosh attempted to combine, with no very great success, a literary and a political career. With the aid of other liberal Anglican

[60] Ibid., 30.

[61] *Monthly Review*, xcvii (1822), 161; R. Russell, *Early Corresp. of Lord John Russell*, i. 203; *Gentleman's Magazine*, xciii (1823), i. 246; *Quarterly Review*, xlix (1833), 160.

[62] J. Russell, *Life of William Lord Russell* (London, 1820), i. viii; S. Walpole, *Life of Lord John Russell* (London, 1889), i. 101.

[63] J. Dinwiddy, 'Charles James Fox as Historian', *Historical Journal*, xii (1969), 24.

Whigs, such as Spring Rice, Thomson, Hobhouse, and Morpeth, Russell began to refashion Whiggery and so provide a justification for his dalliance with reformers. This approach to politics had to be defended against both Whig and Radical scepticism. Since the Whigs by no means possessed an honourable tradition of reform, Russell had to refurbish the Whig myth of befriending the people, and demonstrate the practical virtues of an association with an aristocratic party. At the same time, he had to convince his leaders that reform did not imply Radicalism, that it was consonant with sound government, consitutional propriety, and Whig practice. Russell operated from within the very heart of Whiggery and sought to reconcile two positions which many thought incompatible: Whiggery's preservation and its fruitful association with the reform movements of the nineteenth century. In this attempt, Russell, along with his Whig associates, changed the preoccupation of the Whig party from an obsession with the power of the crown to a concern for the moral welfare of the people.

Not surprisingly, for a group of politicians who wished not to overthrow Whiggery but to ensure its continued survival, these Whigs first directed their attention to Whig history. Their version was a populist idealization, in which Whig heroes were to be found on the side of the people as defenders of constitutional liberties. On this understanding they criticized the shortcomings of their current leaders. Russell's disillusionment with Grey began at an early age. In 1809, because the Whig leader had failed to sponsor British intervention in support of the Spanish liberal constitutionalists, Russell accused him of acting inconsistently with 'true Whiggism'; Grey had 'Tory opinions' masked by a Whig 'cloak'. He later contended that Lord Holland, who became the keeper of the Foxite conscience after the Whig leader's death, and vigorously supported British intervention on the Iberian peninsula, was the only true Whig in England.[64] Hobhouse's disaffection with the Whig leadership also commenced when he was of university age. When up at Cambridge, he founded a Whig club in order to sustain what he believed to be the principles of 1688, while all around Whig politicians abandoned the 'good old cause'.

[64] R. Russell, *Early Corresp. of Lord John Russell*, i. 132, 156; BL Addit. MSS 51677 (Holland House Papers), fo. 4: Russell to Holland, 7 Aug. 1810.

In later life Hobhouse continued to contrast the pusillanimous
modern Whig with his forbears. In so doing, he noted 'the
absurdity of the Whigs sheltering their present insignificance
behind the good conduct of the Revolution Whigs and of the
usual complaint that those who object to the modern Whigs
must necessarily be opponents of the Revolution'.[65] Both
Russell's and Hobhouse's early political careers were spent
defending the liberties of Englishmen, while their leaders
appeared neglectful of the example which Fox had set in the
1790s. Russell, for example, opposed the suspension of Habeas
Corpus in 1817, the issue on which the Whig opposition split,
in a speech which the Radical Burdett complimented.
Hobhouse opposed the passing of the Six Acts; the Whig
leadership, on the other hand, agreed to the introduction of
at least one of them, a modified Seditious Meetings Bill.[66]
Hobhouse pointedly urged that the people of England should
continue to talk 'of the Bill of Rights and the glorious Revolution and the birth-right of Britons'.[67]

This outlook was scarcely the orthodox history of the day.
It was by no means obviously the case that Whiggery from
the seventeenth to the nineteenth centuries consisted in a con-
tinous defence of the liberties of the people. Indeed, the Russell
family's own history in the eighteenth century was less than
glorious. The 4th Duke of Bedford was scarcely an orthodox
Whig, being an opponent of Walpole from 1732 to 1741 and
a member of the opposition led by Carteret; he fell out with
Pelham in 1751 and in the early years of George III's reign
attached himself to Bute. No Russell held political office from
the 1770s until the formation of Fox's second administration
in 1806. The somewhat dubious historical lesson had to be
made explicit. Indeed, it was not an uncommon assumption
in post-Napoleonic England that Russell's Whig heroes had
been enemies of the people. For this harmful state of affairs,
Russell blamed 'the Tory prejudices' of Hume's *History of England* and the French Revolution, which Tories had taken 'in
the gross as a receipt in the full for every bad law; for every

[65] R. E. Zegger, *John Cam Hobhouse* (Columbia, 1973), 44; [J. C. Hobhouse], *A Trifling Mistake in Thomas Lord Erskine's Recent Preface* (London, 1819), 24.

[66] *Hansard*, xxxv (1817), 742, 746; Zegger, *John Cam Hobhouse*, 77; A. Mitchell, *The Whigs in Opposition*, 106.

[67] J. C. Hobhouse, *A Supplicatory Letter to Lord Viscount Castlereagh* (London, 1819), 44.

ancient abuse; for maintaining error and applauding incapacity'. Russell therefore revised Hume's account of seventeenth-century politics. For example, he exculpated Shaftesbury from Hume's charge that he had conspired to introduce arbitrary rule under Charles II, and had initiated the Popish Plot of September, 1678. He praised the earl for the part he played in passing the Habeas Corpus Act. His revisionist conclusion was that, far from abusing his talents, 'there never was a statesman against whom more unfounded charges had been brought'. Russell likewise attempted to preserve the reputation of his seventeenth-century ancestor, Lord William Russell, who had gone to the scaffold on a charge of treason. In Chapter VI of his biography, Russell showed that there was no 'treasonable' interest involved in William Russell's conversations with the French minister, Rouvigny, while, in a later chapter, he denied the existence of a Rye House Plot to assassinate the King. Russell penned the exemplary portrait of a politician 'who, heir to wealth and title, was foremost in defending the privileges of the people'; 'few men have deserved better of their country'.[68]

Not content with this vindication of pre-Revolution Whigs, Russell attempted the more difficult historiographical revision of their post-Revolutionary successors. Russell's Walpole was no 'Venetian oligarch', but rather 'one of the wisest statesmen Great Britain ever possessed'; a politician whose temper inclined him to 'mildness and moderation', and who presided over a period of government when there were scarcely any 'violations of personal freedom'. Russell commented: 'It is astonishing to see after twenty-five years of power, how little could be brought against Walpole even when his enemies were in power.'[69] Russell's greatest and most flattering historiographical revision was reserved for Charles James Fox, whose whole life, in this novel understanding, was an instance of the Whig spirit of liberty.[70] He excused Fox from any inconsistency

[68] J. Russell, *William Lord Russell*, i. viii, 57–8, 67–8, 123–4, 125–6, 163–4, ii. 108, 148; *idem, An Essay on the History of the English Government and Constitution* (2nd edn., London, 1823), 435–6. All subsequent citations are from this edition unless otherwise stated.

[69] [J. Russell], *Memoirs of the Affairs of Europe from the Peace of Utrecht* (London, 1824 & 1829), ii. 401; J. Russell, *English Government and Constitution*, 216, 217, 221.

[70] J. Russell, *Speeches and Despatches*, i. 243.

in forming a coalition with his enemy, Lord North, in 1783, on the ground that a change in political circumstances had meant that the alliance was necessary 'to oppose the secret intrigues of the court'. Russell was equally sympathetic about Fox's hesitancy to introduce reform in 1806. Such caution was necessary to avoid 'a precipitate course of action'. Russell concluded his defence in a somewhat bitter tone, since he did not feel that the political achievements of his hero were currently appreciated. According to Russell, Fox's name remained 'as a beacon for all prudent men to avoid his generous devotion, and a monument of the ingratitude of mankind to those who endeavour to spare their lives or promote their welfare'.[71] As a timely act of reminder to the Whig leader, whose enthusiasm for Foxite reform appeared to have waned, Russell dedicated the second edition of his *Essay on the History of the English Government and Constitution* to Grey, 'the constant friend of Mr. Fox', in order to indicate what should have been the identity of Fox's, Russell's, and the Whig leader's understanding of Whiggery.[72]

In explaining the history of the English constitution, Russell highlighted the possibility of reform which was free from any association with Radicalism. He made every effort to dissociate Whiggery from a Radical revolutionary tradition. Thus with regard to the Commonwealth he argued that the Independents and Presbyterians, who sought 'to bring human institutions at once to perfection', in the end only promoted anarchy. The Whig leaders of the Revolution of 1689, on the other hand, knew from experience that the establishment of a republic would result in the 'overthrow' of their work. This good sense, Russell argued, later justified itself at the Hanoverian succession in 1715. The Whig constitution then succeeded in securing 'the liberty of the subject', despite the 'Commonwealth' criticisms of Swift and Bolingbroke, who had argued that radical changes, such as the complete separation of the executive and legislature, were required. In 1689 all the Whig leaders had desired was 'the preservation of the English religion and laws' and 'to preserve the constitution'; 'none of them wished

---

[71] [J. Russell], *Essays and Sketches of Life and Character by a Gentleman who has left his Lodgings*, ed. J. Skillet, (London, 1820), 157, 160–2.

[72] J. Russell, *English Government and Constitution*, v.

for anything more than a regular execution of our ancient constitutional laws'. As interpreted by Russell the Revolution simply consisted in the restoration of the ancient constitution, which he demonstrated had existed under the Tudors, only to be usurped by the Stuarts.[73]

When from 1819 to 1831 he presented his proposals for parliamentary reform to the Commons, Russell dissociated himself from the Radicals by appealing to a Whig notion of the 'ancient constitution'. He argued that altering and enlarging the basis of representation in the Commons was 'the old custom of England'; he suggested that, traditionally, the composition of the Commons had changed repeatedly in order to adapt to new circumstances, so much so that until the Revolution the constitution 'never was, for any fifty consecutive years during a long period of time, settled and stationary'. All Russell demanded was another act of adaptation to remove the 'pollutions' and 'impurities' or 'excrescences' from the 'Gothic' constitution in order to restore to the Commons 'the esteem and reverence of the people', which it had customarily enjoyed since the time of Edward I when 'the House of Commons did represent the people of England'. This was not, said Russell, an innovatory and Radical plan, but 'temperate and rational reform', 'wholesome and salutary change', the work of those who stood between the 'bigotry' of 'ignorant worshippers of antiquity' and the 'fanaticism' of 'wild and visionary' men. By dressing his political attitudes in the historical language of judicious reform, Russell seemed to make such proposals once more respectable. When the Whig Coke of Norfolk commissioned Francis Chantrey to execute a relief in celebration of the passing of the Reform Act, it took the form of King John granting Magna Carta to Coke and his friends dressed as barons.[74]

This attitude towards the Whig past distinguished these Whigs from Macaulay, who, whatever his later reputation, was not the custodian of high Whiggery in this period. While Russell praised the moderation and temperance of the

---

[73] Ibid., 92, 110, 212–5, and esp. Chs. 1–7 for the historical account; *idem, William Lord Russell*, i. 120–1, 186.

[74] J. Russell, *Speeches and Despatches*, i. 184, 187, 228, 231, 270, 282, 303–5, 342, 351–2; Penny, 'The Whig Cult of Fox in Sculpture', 104.

Revolutionary Whigs, Macaulay, in his articles on Milton, Hallam, and Hampden, denigrated their achievements in order to curry support for the Puritan leaders of the Great Rebellion of 1640. According to Macaulay the Revolution was not so much glorious as discreditable to England, since it had required foreign aid; it was 'in a great measure effected by men who cared little about their political principles'. The reign of William III was 'the Nadir of the national character'.[75] Under Macaulay's pen, the heroes Russell celebrated became villains. Shaftesbury was an example of 'the low standard of political morality' into which the country had sunk after the Restoration, while Walpole was marred by 'an insatiable love of power'.[76] Macaulay praised instead the visionaries of the Rebellion, from whom Russell had attempted to dissociate his brand of Whiggery. He defended Milton's support for the Commonwealth, and described the Puritans not as 'vulgar fanatics' but as 'a brave, a wise, an honest and a useful body'. Cromwell himself possessed a 'high, stout, honest English heart', and Macaulay bestowed lavish praise on Hampden, the 'celebrated Puritan leader', after whom were named the pro-reform clubs inspired by the Radical Major Cartwright. If the execution of Charles I in retrospect proved a mistake, it was only because it had made him a 'martyr',[77] and so excited sympathy for royalist causes. Macaulay distinguished himself as a Radical Whig, a defender of the Rebellion and the Commonwealth rather than the Revolution. He supported parliamentary reform not as a return to the ancient constitution, but as a means of defending property and order from a 'fearful peril'. Macaulay did not consider the problems of the 1830s to be identical with those of the Revolution. He believed that the period from the reign of Henry VII to the death of George III formed an 'age' in British history, its theme being the struggle between parliament and crown. This was suc-

---

[75] T. B. Macaulay, *Critical and Historical Essays* (London, 1894), 91–3. Compare this equivocation with the unqualified approval given 20 years later to the Revolution in his *History of England from the Accession of James the Second* (London, 1899), i. 654–5. The account here substantially concurs with that of John Clive who wrote in his *Macaulay* (New York, 1975), p. 94 that in 1825 the historian was 'within the radical line of the Whig tradition'.

[76] Macaulay, *Critical and Historical Essays*, 86, 292.

[77] Ibid., 23, 25, 79–80, 84, 193.

ceeded by another conflict 'between a large portion of the people on the one side and the Crown and Parliament united on the other', a conflict which was the product of 'the progress of society' and 'the development of the human mind'.[78] While Russell argued for the continuity of political concerns, Macaulay contemplated the Whig past 'at dusk', and the pedigree he provided for reform was consequently more radical than Russell wished to allow in the 1820s.

None the less Russell was careful to construct an appeal to Radical sympathizers. These, such as Burdett, attacked the utility of political parties on the ground that when in office they were liable to become corrupt. For such Radicals, this truth was exemplified by the recent history of the Whig party. Russell, alternatively, sought to show the error of this view, and in so doing to point out the advantages which a party (by implication, the Whig party) had in securing the passage of liberal reforms. He argued that those who decried the value of party had paradoxically increased the influence of the crown under Pitt's administration. Their belief in the 'corruption of all public men' had split the opposition to Pittite tyranny, had forced the leaders of reform to adopt increasingly extreme positions in order to compete for support in the country, and had thus precipitated the passage of coercive measures in the Commons. As a result, the people and the constitution were separated. Party, on the other hand, safeguarded political virtue by attaching politicians to 'steady and lasting principles', and so encouraged them to behave consistently. Moreover, by 'embodying the various opinions of the nation', it united people and constitution, and so secured popular interests. Party, according to Russell, was one of the benefits of the Whig Revolution, since it was by means of party that the Whigs had pursued not their own particular interests, but the preservation of 'the constitution in its utmost need'. Radicals who abjured the Whig party aided the re-creation of pre-Revolutionary conditions. Russell urged the union of 'the party of the people within and without the walls of Parliament'.[79] This was a

---

[78] Ibid., 98; T. B. Macaulay, *A Speech delivered in the House of Commons on Lord John Russell's Motion* (London, 1831), 26.

[79] Dinwiddy, 'Charles James Fox and The People', 349; [J. Russell], *Essays and Sketches*, 165–8; J. Russell, *English Government and Constitution*, 187–9, 446–7; idem, *William Lord Russell*, i. 123; idem, *Speeches and Despatches*, i. 244.

double-faceted cry. It was an appeal to the Radicals to end their quarrel with the Whigs and engage in joint reforming endeavours. At the same time it was a warning to the Whig leadership that their future lay not with an association with the Tories, but with the more popular elements of the political nation.

In reaffirming the tradition of Whiggery as primarily a pious concern with the preservation of the country's liberties, those Whigs who followed Russell created an alibi for their activist selves. Proposing reform was neither revolutionary nor dangerous, if in accord with precedent. Party was not the vehicle for corrupt and self-interested men, but the means of joining people to government, a constitutional safeguard, of which the Whig party was the historical exemplar. Above all, proposals of reform were patriotic undertakings. Just as William Russell had been 'a warm friend not to liberty merely, but to English liberty', so his relation Lord John Russell, in seeking the restoration of ancient liberties, was a friend not merely of the people, but of the English people.[80] These Whigs adopted a patriotic posture, which had eluded the party since the ascendancy of Pitt, and Fox's championship of the early stages of the French Revolution. Russell was unashamed in his conviction that the English nation was 'the wisest, the happiest and best', and that the English constitution was 'the most perfect'.[81] This Whiggish chauvinism had its clearest expression in the jingoistic foreign policy of Lord Palmerston at the end of the 1830s, a policy which such liberal Anglican Whigs as Hobhouse, Howick, and Thomson admired, even though Russell, not completely liberated from the influence of Lord Holland, dissented.[82] In particular, these politicians emerged as the defenders of empire, which Hobhouse expanded in India, and Russell in later life campaigned to preserve. In 1870, with regard to British colonies, Russell wrote: 'it would be a spectacle for Gods and men to weep at to see this brilliant luminary cut up into spangles'.[83] In domestic politics Whig nationalism

---

[80] J. Russell, *William Lord Russell*, ii. 108.

[81] [J. Russell], *Essays and Sketches*, 62; J. Russell, *English Government and Constitution*, xii.

[82] Zegger, *John Cam Hobhouse*, 224, 243; Grey Papers, box 24 file 2: Howick to Grey, 2 Feb. 1841; G. Poulett Scrope, *Memoir of the Life of the Rt. Hon. Charles Lord Sydenham GCB* (London, 1843), 326.

[83] Zegger, *John Cam Hobhouse*, 283; J. Russell, *Speeches and Despatches*, i. 153.

took a peculiarly British form. It recognized the equal value of each of the component parts of the United Kingdom, rather than seeing them as the consequence of a series of English conquests. In the 1830s Whigs were strongly unionist, in marked contrast to the opposition which Grey had given to the Irish Act of Union in 1801, not because they believed that Ireland was a subject colony of the English, but because they considered it to be an integral part of a grander United Kingdom. Spring Rice, attacking O'Connell's Repeal movement in a speech which made his reputation as a leading liberal politician, suggested that Ireland be renamed 'West Britain' (and Scotland 'North Britain'). Morpeth, a Chief Secretary for Ireland, referred to the Irish as his 'British fellow-countrymen'; Mulgrave, a Lord Lieutenant of Ireland, stated that his aim had been 'to treat the English and Irish as "one nation" '.[84] Whig nationalism was not a eulogy on the glories of English conquest, but a doctrine which emphasized the unimportance of distinctive local nationalisms within the liberal state. In this sense, it was a liberal and not a conservative notion.

This revived reform doctrine viewed the constitution as a mechanism, the continuance of which depended on its equilibrium or balance. Russell wrote that the 'perfection of civil society' consisted in the 'union of liberty with order'. This he explained more fully as a balance of the legislative, judicial, and executive powers, which he compared 'to what is called in mechanics a combination of forces'.[85] At one level such a doctrine might have been a recipe for conservatism. If reform was merely the restoration of balance (the Revolution Settlement of 1689), it entailed the restoration of a constitution which had excluded Catholics from full citizenship, and had passed over any consideration of the economic and moral welfare of the nation. Indeed, in the circumstances of post-Napoleonic England, it was something of a Tory argument. Graham, for example, left the Whigs for the Tories in the mid-1830s on the ground that thereby he was preserving the

---

[84] J. C. Hobhouse (Lord Broughton), *Recollections of a Long Life*, ed. Lady Dorchester (London, 1909–11), iv. 336; T. Spring Rice, *Speech on the Repeal of the Union* (London, 1834), 29; H. Lonsdale, *The Worthies of Cumberland* (London, 1872), iii. 149; C. H. Phipps (Earl of Mulgrave) *Speech in the House of Lords on the Motion of the Earl of Roden for Certain Papers referring to the State of Ireland* (2nd edn., London, 1837), 49.

[85] J. Russell, *English Government and Constitution*, x, 152.

Revolution Settlement of 1689.[86] To some extent Russell was able to ensure that it was not used in this fashion. He invoked a notion of constitutional progress, which held that certain constitutional provisions were justified by a contingent necessity; when the contingency passed, so might the legal provision. For example, the Whigs did not revoke the Test Acts after the Revolution so that the church would support the new constitution, but since by 1828 'all ground of necessity' was no longer appropriate as an argument for their retention, they might be abolished.[87] He recognized additionally that changes in the social composition of the country might unbalance the constitution, even though there had been no change in formal consitutional arrangements. He suggested as a maxim of political science that 'no government can be stable which does not keep pace with the increasing improvement of the people; and that any government which fails to make such advances must soon come to find ruin'.[88] Neither of these innovations in the constitutional theory of balance was a justification for promoting reform measures designed to improve, rather than simply to reflect, the people's advance. Yet it was precisely this improvement in the condition of the people, which these liberal Anglican Whigs desired.

In his *Essay on the History of the English Government and Constitution* Russell argued for a reform of the criminal law, suggested a reform of the Poor Laws, and lamented the corruption of public opinion. In government he was the leading promoter of elementary education, as well as being a Vice-President of the British and Foreign Schools Society.[89] Hobhouse took up the causes of prison and factory reform, and was involved in such activities as the Royal Humane Society, and with such activists as the Evangelical prison reformer, Thomas Fowell Buxton.[90] Morpeth was a leading sanitary reformer, and Mulgrave as Home Secretary, introduced the Drainage of Buildings Bill in order to prevent one cause of the 'melancholy and

[86] C. S. Parker, *Life and Letters of Sir James Graham* (London, 1907), i. 195–6.
[87] J. Russell, *Speeches and Despatches*, i. 264.
[88] Ibid., i. 210.
[89] J. Russell, *English Government and Constitution*, 242, 262 ff., 436; Walpole, *Russell*, i. 329; J. Alexander, 'Lord John Russell and the Origins of the Committee of Council on Education', *Historical Jour.*, xx (1977), 399.
[90] Zegger, *John Cam Hobhouse*, 158–66, 169.

degenerate condition', which produced a demoralized poor.[91] The causes, which the Whigs took up, reflected not only the problems of urbanization and industrialization, but also their interest in the notion of public virtue as the ground of a country's stability and prosperity. In the first edition of his essay on government, Russell included a chapter entitled 'that the excellence of the English Government does not consist in the laws only but in the spirit and good sense of the nation'; in the second edition he commented that 'The proposition that good laws without virtue in the society where they are established are of little or no avail is one so generally admitted that it seems useless to waste a word respecting it'. Russell might have derived this concern for the moral welfare of the people from Machiavelli, whom he termed 'the most profound of political writers' and 'the Whig commentator on Roman History'.[92] It was a theme he explored more fully in his published writings of 1828–32, which were so removed from the constitutional Whiggery of his earlier days that his biographer, Walpole, noted: 'It is remarkable that his own ideal of writing history apparently was altered in the ten or twelve years which elapsed between the publication of *The Life of Lord Russell* and that of *The Causes of the French Revolution*.'[93] In Russell's writings a constitutional moralism replaced constitutional, and primarily Foxite, mechanics.

In his life of Lord William Russell, Russell gave not only an account of the constitutional struggles of the seventeenth century, but also a description of a 'virtuous citizen', one to whose public spirit 'we owe the permanency and excellence of our ancient constitution'. William Russell exemplified the dutiful aristocrat who was charitable in his concern for others, mindful of his privileges and piously virtuous in both domestic and public surroundings. Along with the mass of the English gentry he was 'rich in honour and virtue'.[94] Russell hinted elsewhere at the characteristics of the virtuous man. In his

[91] Lonsdale, *Worthies of Cumberland*, iii. 158; C. H. Phipps (Marquis of Normanby), *Speech in the House of Lords on moving the Second Reading of the Drainage of Buildings Bill* (London, 1841), 17.

[92] J. Russell, *English Government and Constitution* (1st edn., London, 1821), Ch. 29; idem, *English Government and Constitution*, 383, 482; idem, *Speeches and Despatches*, i. 236.

[93] Walpole, *Russell*, i. 102.

[94] J. Russell, *William Lord Russell*, i. 44, ii. 179.

essay 'The Wandering Jew', he described the quality of benevolence (not indiscriminate giving, but the 'wise and painstaking' exercise of charity). On presenting the Reform Bill in 1831 he suggested three ways in which the virtuous aristocrat might distinguish himself: by 'relieving the poor', 'evincing private wealth', and 'performing important duties'. Russell also stipulated two securities for his good conduct, namely the possession of property, which assured his independence, and 'the fear of shame', that is the desire for the community's approbation. If these continued to exist, then so might the 'good sense' of a nation as a whole. The absence of one of these securities spelled the corruption of a polity. Russell reminded his readers that 'the precipitate fall of a state like that of Rome into an abyss of profligacy and venality' was the consequence of a 'whole people' being delivered 'from a sense of shame'.[95]

The concern for good character was personal to these Whigs and not merely rhetorical. In 1826 Russell contested Huntingdonshire on 'Tavistock's principle', which entailed bans on canvassing, on paying for the transportation of electors to the poll, and on entertaining supporters in the town. This quest for political purity before the Great Reform Act resulted in the loss of the seat.[96] Ebrington in 1817 preferred to resign his seat in parliament rather than vote against the wishes of his patron, the Duke of Buckingham.[97] In 1846 Hobhouse, representing Nottingham, one of the most corrupt boroughs in England, refused to pay for the customary bribery and consequently lost his seat. Hobhouse, indeed, exemplified a concern for his probity which at times verged on the self-indulgent. He noted complacently in his diary that in a fit of candour he had told a large dinner party that his own political conduct 'was prompted by no other desire than that of doing public good in a small way . . . by being an example of political integrity'. He commented that, while he believed this was true, he was perhaps 'a fool for saying so'. In 1833 he resigned not only his office, but also his seat, when Althorp moved an amendment against the repeal of the House and Window

[95] [J. Russell], *Essays and Sketches*, 213; J. Russell, *Speeches and Despatches*, i. 333; idem, *English Government and Constitution*, 234, 320, 332, 460–1.

[96] Wasson, 'Coalitions of 1827 and the Crisis of Whig Leadership', 596.

[97] DCRO MSS 1262M FH 24 (Fortescue Papers): notes on the life of the 2nd Earl Fortescue.

Duties, a measure which was contrary to the wish of his Westminster electors. As a consequence, claimed Hobhouse, he 'never felt more self-satisfied in his life', never more certain that he had acted in a way which 'became' him, and which would be both 'creditable' to himself and 'useful to the public'.[98] If public virtue and political sagacity were contradictory qualities, they each brought their own rewards.

According to Russell, the virtue of politicians in general was guaranteed by public opinion, which he understood as the bar at which action had to be justified. Consequently 'the greatest benefit' derived from publicity was that it corrected and neutralized 'the vices of our institutions': a 'free press' monitored the performance of a country's rulers. Russell, however, was no democrat. Public opinion was primarily a test of grievance and only rarely a prescriber of remedies: MPs might defer to the former, but should retain their responsibility, judgement, and independence in proposing reforms. Moreover Russell did not praise public opinion *per se*, but rather its exertion 'in favour of the wholesome rights and established liberties of the people'. With regard to England, he feared that it might have increased 'in bulk and velocity' more than in 'quality, value and might'. This he attributed to a decline in constitutional learning, the extinction of the Jacobite threat and so of a concern for the safety of the country, the enormous increase in manufacturing towns, and the disposition of an uneducated populace to adopt extreme political positions.[99] Russell was conscious of what he perceived to be England's degenerate condition. The cause of this he explored further by means of historical parallels.

The first of these was his enquiry into the decay of the Turkish empire, which led to its defeats at the hands of Europeans. This was a fashionable theme, a reflection of the liberal preoccupation with philhellenism, an interest uniting Whigs and Radicals in such extra-parliamentary activities as the Greek Committee, established in March 1823. Its membership included, for example, both Russell and Joseph Hume.[100] Russell attributed the Turkish decline to indulgence in luxury, a

---

[98] Zegger, *John Cam Hobhouse* 238; Hobhouse, *Recollections of a Long Life*, iii. 54, iv. 311.
[99] J. Russell, *English Government and Constitution*, 431–2, 436–9, 463–4; idem, *Speeches and Despatches*, i. 307. [100] Zegger, *John Cam Hobhouse* 121.

lack of mechanical and literary genius, a despotic government, and above all barbarism and want of knowledge. These last two were the result of the Turks' religious fanaticism. This, 'the inseparable companion of their ignorance', prevented the acquisition of their opponents' skills. To have done so, to have surmounted 'any of those dangers which Providence' had placed in their way, would have been, for them, 'an impious interference' with the decree of the Almighty. Although religion did not account for the aboriginal ignorance of the Turks, it did provide an explanation of the their continued barbarism. By implication, Christianity contributed to the superiority of nations.[101] Morpeth also examined this theme in his historical verse drama, *The Last of the Greeks*, in this case to explain the fall of Constantinople. According to Morpeth, Constantine was a man of 'Christian virtue' and Constantinople, by tradition, 'the seat of pure religion' and 'the first Christian city'. But it fell because its 'sins deserved it'; its public spirit had deserted it. On the eve of the Turkish invasion Constantinople harboured 'uncharitable priests', 'lust' in its chambers, 'faction' in the streets, in short 'one wide, unawed and withering corruption'.[102] The decline in public virtue coincided with the abandonment of Christian values.

Russell elaborated this notion of a decline in Christian values as the cause of a country's decay in his essay on *The Causes of the French Revolution*. This work, unlike his explanation of the causes of the English Revolution, began not with an account of the imbalance of the constitution, but with a description of the corruption of the French court and administration, and, in particular, with the erosion of its members' ideals of honour and glory, which had once kept licentiousness in check. The result was the predominance of private interests over public, of venality over equity, of barbarism over civility. Eighteenth-century France possessed 'a nobility disfigured by every vice', possessed of 'scarcely any virtue but courage', and privileged 'to insult and maltreat the people whose burden they did not share'. According to Russell, another way of behaving arose in opposition to this state of affairs, and this,

---

[101] [J. Russell], *The Establishment of the Turks in Europe* (London, 1828), 106–16.
[102] G. W. F. Howard (Lord Morpeth), *The Last of the Greeks; Or the Fall of Constantinople: A Tragedy* (London, 1828), 32, 39, 45.

the spirit of the French Revolution, was expressed in the writings of Voltaire, Rousseau, and the other *philosophes*. To this phenomenon, which he called 'The Progress of Public Opinion', Russell devoted more than two-thirds of the work.[103]

These authors, argued Russell, were simply a 'club', 'living in a vicious age, and joining the sins of a corrupt society to the errors and weaknesses and vanities of the literary profession . . . They were swine running down a precipice and thought themselves eagles mounting above the clouds'. The cause of this indictment of the Revolutionary spirit was its religious infidelity: the Revolutionaries, in espousing militant atheism, overthrew the restraint of religion, and so let loose man's unruly passion. For Russell an unnatural self-control was the key to virtue. He therefore criticized Rousseau's notion of rule by the general will on the ground that it was the object of government to restrain, not to encourage, 'the wickedness of man'; likewise Rousseau's religion of nature could not inculcate 'a regular observation of a system of morality', but only excited man's feelings to a vague admiration for purity and benevolence. Russell charged Voltaire with encouraging a 'spurious benevolence that spares the vicious as easily as it relieves the virtuous', and accused Diderot and Helvetius of creating a system which was 'as contrary to taste as to religion and morality'. The consequence was that in the Revolution 'the vices of a corrupt capital set themselves in judgement upon the profligacy of a cankered court'. In criticizing the corruption of the court, the *philosophes* 'tore up the tares and wheat together', and in so doing set in train the machine of destruction which was the Revolution.[104]

In the course of this work, therefore, Russell preached the importance of the Christian religion as the foundation of public spirit, good order, and virtuous government. 'The morality of a nation', he wrote, 'is intimately connected with its religion. Take away religion and in the minds of most men, you take away the obligation to restrain the passions—to speak the truth—to respect the rights and feelings of others'.[105] This was a preoccupation he shared with other liberal Anglican Whigs.

[103] [J. Russell], *The Causes of the French Revolution* (London, 1832), 80.
[104] Ibid., 193, 207, 234, 266, 271, 272.
[105] Ibid., 129.

Morpeth, in his speeches to Mechanics' Institutes in the 1840s, persistently argued that it was 'an indispensable principle' that 'all acquirements should be grounded on a religious basis', and Mulgrave, in his novel *The English at Home*, urged that religion was the cure for immorality.[106] In the *Edinburgh Review* in 1839, Spring Rice limned a portrait of a declining England ('The population of England is not what it was'); he suggested that the populace's concentration in towns, their ignorance, and their privations would produce 'calamities of the most frightful kind'. This precipitate collapse, he thought, could be averted if all parties were equally active in furthering 'the great cause of religion and moral education', and this he termed the 'greatest of all national duties'.[107] This utilitarian interest in Christianity affected not only these Whigs' praise of religion as an inducement to social order, but also their understanding of it as a body of dogmatic knowledge and discipline. They believed that the Christianity, which they advocated, would lead to a socially unifying rather than a divisive way of life, one which would bind a nation together rather than encourage internal strife. This understanding of Christianity Russell began to work out in opposition to the social tyranny of Iberian Catholicism, which he had encountered on his youthful trips to Spain and Portugal, and in the reports of the Spanish ex-Catholic priest and sometime habitué of Holland House, Joseph Blanco White.[108] It was an experience he shared with others. Hobhouse returned from his journey to Portugal in 1809 with evidence of, and prejudice against, 'an ignorant and tyrannical priesthood', which he had encountered there.[109]

Two of Russell's literary works, the novella *The Nun of Arrouca*

---

[106] G. W. F. Howard (Earl of Carlisle), *Lectures and Addresses in Aid of Popular Education* (London, 1852), 70; [C. H. Phipps (Earl of Mulgrave)], *The English in France* (London, 1828), i. 189–90.

[107] [T. Spring Rice], 'Ministerial Plan of Education', *Edinburgh Review*, lxx (1839), 177, 179.

[108] Walpole, *Russell*, i. 36–41; J. H. Thom (ed.), *Life of the Revd Blanco White* (London, 1845), i. 179; see also Lord Seymour's comment (a junior minister in Melbourne's second government): 'I consider any religious opinion to be necessarily false which *militates* against the existence of society . . .' [W. H. Mallock and Lady Gwendolen Ramsden (eds.), *Letters, Remains, and Memoirs of Edward Adolphus Seymour, Twelfth Duke of Somerset KG* (London, 1893), 76].

[109] Hobhouse, *Recollections of a Long Life*, i. 8.

and the play *Don Carlos*, were disguised polemics against the unpleasant social consequences of Catholic dogmatism, which was seen as a corrupting and degenerate influence. In the former, a nun, torn between her faith and her love, was compelled by her uncle to remain true to her religion. In consequence, she wasted away and died prematurely. In effect, it was an anti-Catholic tract on the 'sinfulness' of chastity. *Don Carlos*, set in sixteenth-century Spain, concerned the treachery of the Spanish Inquisition's attack on the unconventional heir to the throne. The latter, disregarding the dogmatic injunctions of the Catholic Church, befriended Protestants, read the Bible, and believed that Christianity consisted in

> . . . words of peace
> Forgiveness ev'n for sin; brotherly love
> And charity that beareth hope to all.

Act III, scene II took place at Don Carlos's trial before the Great Inquisitor, Valdez, whose right to usurp God's judgement of sinners Carlos denied. After many twists and turns in a melodramatic plot, the play ended with the death of Carlos, the repentance of King Philip, who had belatedly recognized the injustice of the Inquisitor, and the arrest of Valdez. Protestant values (if not Protestantism itself) triumphed.[110]

This was a distinctive form of Protestantism, as Russell revealed in the second volume of his *Memoirs of the Affairs of Europe from the Peace of Utrecht*. This work contained a condemnation of evangelical enthusiasm in the form of an attack on Wesleyan Methodism, which Russell described as being akin to 'some very powerful drug' or 'quack medicine'. Russell suggested that its central doctrine, namely enthusiastic conversion, was 'inconsistent with the spirit of Christianity'; that Wesleyans might become intolerant, in the belief that they were especially chosen for salvation; finally, that its doctrines encouraged antinomianism, fraud, and cant. Russell believed that in carrying Methodism to excess, Wesleyans had become 'infected with worse vices than their neighbours whom they despised.' Consequently Methodists were wrong to believe that their religion was a solution to the corruption of the people

---

[110] [J. Russell], *The Nun of Arrouca* (London, 1822); *idem, Don Carlos* (London, 1822), 42, 68.

in eighteenth-century England.[111] Russell searched elsewhere
for a religion which would be both tolerant and elevating.

In the same work Russell praised the rational Protestantism
of the early eighteenth-century latitudinarian divines, Clarke
and Hoadly. The liberalism of these theologians, according to
Russell, emphasized religious toleration and the comprehension of Protestants within the Church of England. This was
possible because these divines distinguished the truths of
Christianity from disputed sectarian dogmas, including the
doctrine of the Trinity. Being controversial, the latter could
not be the universal touchstone of a Christian faith. As Russell
wrote: 'A learned and pious writer has said with equal
ingenuity and truth, "We do not know enough of the mysteri-
ous doctrines of religion to quarrel about them." ' It would
therefore be wrong to bar someone's entry to the Anglican
Church, because he could not agree with all its particular
dogmas. The fact was that it was impossible to know whether
all dogmas were equally Christian truths. Consequently Russell praised Samuel Clarke because he did not want disputed
tenets to be made terms of communion, and because he
approved confining Christian truths to the 'primitive' doctrines
of the New Testament. Russell also praised Bishop Hoadly—
an ornament of human nature—for his rational pursuit of the
foundations of belief. Russell approved Hoadly's contention
that contemporary disputes concerning Christian dogma were
the consequence of erroneous interpretations of Christ's laws:
because Christ's Kingdom was of the next world, argued
Hoadly, it was impossible, in this world, to be absolutely sure
of His commands. Hoadly advocated toleration because
human incapacity, rather than contests between divine truth
and error, was responsible for doctrinal disputes, which in
turn produced the greatest of all sins, schism.[112]

In his later religious writings Russell dwelt on two themes
in particular: man's fallibility in understanding God's laws
and the existence of primitive biblical truths of Christianity.
The first consideration led Russell to question the church's
authority to determine the meaning of Christianity. He praised
the Reformation for releasing Christians from the dictatorship

---

[111] [J. Russell], *Affairs of Europe*, ii. 567, 579–82, 584.
[112] Ibid., ii. 498, 501, 508–15.

of the church, by invoking the doctrine of private judgement. This, said Russell, resulted in a return to a direct consideration of the Scriptures. Indeed, his account of the growth of religion was the story of corruption of scriptural truth by the interposition of various false authorities between reader and biblical text. This produced the Nicene Creed ('not authorized by Scripture'), the Athanasian Creed ('repugnant to the word of Christ'), and the doctrine of transubstantiation, which could not be found in the Scriptures at all. According to Russell, the essence of faith did not lie 'in a belief in the metaphysical articles of belief [*sic*]', or in 'the doctrines of the Church of Rome or the Church of Antioch or the Church of England or the Church of Scotland', but in an adherence to scriptural truth, and 'an inward sense of the want of something higher and holier than human concerns; producing a fervent desire to have the soul saved alive and a confiding trust that through Christ by trusting in his merits and obeying his words that mercy might be vouchsafed by God'.[113] Such a belief might appear naïve and direct, almost childlike. It was certainly a definition which was devoid of an overriding sense of sin and of the disharmonies of this world. It lacked any notion that Christianity, truly understood, could be in conflict with the order of this world. Or, as Russell wrote with an unfounded, if pious, optimism regarding disturbances in Ireland: 'Let us teach these great truths to the people of Ireland and we may hope that they will cease to applaud murder.'[114]

Because he believed that true religious belief was both unproblematic and uncontroversial, Russell did not see any incompatibility between his desire to remove religious divisions from political and social life, and his belief that religious sentiment (and so a religious establishment) was the foundation of a healthy state. Russell's prejudice against involving religious issues in politics was cultivated by a study of nineteenth-century Spain and seventeenth-century England, and promulgated in his life of William Russell. In that work, he expressed his view that 'It is not to the credit of either the

[113] J. Russell, *Essays on the Rise and Progress of the Christian Religion in the West of Europe* (London, 1873), 287, 338; Ogden MSS 84: unpublished treatise on religion by J. Russell.
[114] J. Russell, *Recollections and Suggestions 1813–1873* (Boston, 1875), 141.

piety or the wisdom of the age that political questions
were treated by divines and decided by reference to
Scripture.'[115] Russell's belief that religion was the only secure
basis of a constitution was the consequence of his own investigation into the nature of public virtue. It was responsible for
his advocacy of tolerant, comprehensive religious establishments on Erastian principles. Russell supposed that state
support for religion would act as a check on religious
enthusiasm, since, if religion was left simply to voluntarily–
funded clubs, the way 'to fanaticism and dissension' would be
opened: the minister would have a financial incentive to
appease his congregation rather than to propagate true religion. He was not so indifferent to religious dogma that he agreed
with Paley that the state should always finance the religion of
the majority; there were, said Russell, 'some religions so
degrading and enslaving that no benevolent monarch or just
senate . . . would make them the established religion of their
dominees'. On the other hand, his religious scruples were not
such that he believed the church should be in any way independent of the state. Declaring that Warburton's theory of
an alliance between church and state was 'an arbitrary though
very splendid fiction', Russell insisted on the 'complete and
unbroken' subordination of church to state. For Russell, such
a subordination was not an intolerant intrusion of the profane
in the sacred, as High Churchmen were to complain, because
religion was not incompatible with the secular order. Nor
should the preferment given to one denomination precipitate
conflicts with other, less fortunate, sects, since, according to
Russell, Christianity was a universal, undogmatic, and comprehensive religion. With a pardonable fear, one Methodist
critic of Russell complained that 'the national religion in the
adulterated form which Lord John Russel (*sic*) eulogizes falls
so infinitely short of the standard of genuine Christianity as
to leave thousands of its members in as great moral darkness
and depravity as the unhappy lot of Jew or Heathe'.[116] For
such critics Russell had performed an elaborate sleight of hand.
He had retained, in his own view, the desirability of establish-

---

[115] J. Russell, *William Lord Russell*, ii. 12.
[116] [J. Russell], *Affairs of Europe*, ii. 537–8; H. Sandwith, *A Reply to Lord John Russell's Animadversions on Wesleyan Methodism* (London, 1830), 30.

ments by removing all that was socially objectionable or theologically divisive.

In the years between 1819 and 1834 Russell changed from a Foxite to a constitutional moralist who saw a liberal Anglicanism as ensuring the preservation of the state. In so doing, with the aid of other liberal Anglican Whigs, he altered the concerns of Whiggery from an interest in the mechanics of the constitution to a consideration of its moral foundations. These Whigs attempted to show that the reforms they advocated were virtuous and patriotic endeavours, respectable enterprises for ambitious aristocrats with a sense of social change and public duty. By 1834 they had acquired a doctrine which could accommodate Dissent, and hence reform, by having a highly restricted notion of what constituted the essentials of a sound religious establishment. At the same time they justified the continued existence of such institutions by imposing on them an elevated sense of social duty. Of nothing was this more true than the Church of England, the institution with which the Whigs were preoccupied for much of the 1830s. It was to be preserved because a national religion was a constitutional necessity: if it was morally elevating, it secured the prosperity of the country. It could be made acceptable to Dissent because Nonconformists and Anglicans shared a restricted body of Christian truth, even if, at times, they were reluctant to recognize the fact.

According to one hostile reviewer Russell identified himself with 'the dogmas of modern liberalism'; he praised 'the most alluring examples of a laxity and boldness of thinking on theological subjects' which was gaining ground in England, and which had already 'prostrated in the dust some of the most valuable allies of British Protestantism on the Continent'.[117] It was the fear that the Whig government was acting on such liberal principles which prompted the High Church revival at Oxford. When Keble took the pulpit at St. Mary's on the 44th anniversary of the storming of the Bastille and the beginning of the infidel French Revolution, he did so in order to declaim against the alienation of the nation 'from God and Christ', as symbolized in the Whigs' Irish Church Temporalities Act of 1833.[118] The fears of Evangelicals and

[117] Ibid., 6. [118] J. Keble, *National Apostasy* (Oxford, 1833), iii, 11.

High Churchmen were a little premature; Russell and his sympathizers had yet to fulfil the promise of their political careers. These liberal Anglican Whigs achieved a position of dominance within the party as a result of an internal struggle, which occurred on the issue of the appropriation of the surplus revenues of the Established Church in Ireland to non-ecclesiastical purposes. The political history and importance of this issue are detailed in the following chapter.

2

The Political Emergence of Liberal Anglicanism and the Question of Irish Appropriation

This Church Question approaches the Catholic Question in importance & equals it in urgency & I am afraid we must all regulate our conduct with respect to it upon equally uncompromising principles.

Althorp MSS H (Papers of the 3rd Earl Spencer), box 7: Confidential, Althorp to Grey, 20 October 1832.

THE first politically contentious issue of ecclesiastical reform involved the Irish Church, and in particular the Whig proposal to appropriate its surplus revenues to educational purposes. It was on this issue that the liberal Anglican Whigs achieved a position of dominance within the Whig party, and it was on this issue that their distinctive religious attitude clearly displayed itself. Indeed, being the issue on which Melbourne formed his second government in April 1835, it defined what it meant to be a Whig sympathizer in this period. It is therefore to the politics of this church reform that this chapter is devoted. In order to understand in what way this measure was distinctively Whig, it is necessary to explain the principles which this policy involved. The government's proposal implied a recognition on its part that the property of the church was not akin to that of a private corporation, which it might administer as it chose, but was held in trust, subject to the performance of certain duties. The Whigs claimed on this ground that parliament had a right to interfere in its administration; it had a right to ensure that the terms of the trust were met. The Whigs asserted that the purpose of the church's endowment was 'the moral and religious instruction of all parties'. In his speech to the Commons Russell further specified the aims of the trust as being 'for the benefits of the subjects of the realm, for their religious instruction, for the well-being and harmony of the state'. The Whigs contended that the Irish Church did not fulfil these functions, or, more precisely, that the religious instruction offered by the church was given to only 'a small class of the people', namely the Protestant minority of the country.[1] The Whigs consequently advocated a transfer of funds from the established church to some other non-exclusive body capable of furthering the end of religious instruction. They suggested that this body should be the Irish National Board of Education as established by the government in 1831.

This proposal was politically contentious for two reasons, both of which affected the standing of the church in relation to Dissent. It implied that as far as the fundamental truths of Christianity were concerned there was no difference between the Protestant and Roman Catholic religions: in this regard, there were no grounds for supposing that Anglicanism was superior to Catholicism. Children from various religious sects consequently could receive a common religious education. This was the principle on which the Irish national system of education operated, even if it also recognized the need for additional and separate, denominational religious instruction. The Whig proposal also contained the assertion, if only implicitly, that the choice between Christian sects as far as the question of establishment was concerned, should be made on the basis of their popularity: there was no inherent reason why the state should prefer the Church of England to any other brand of Christianity. This was because first, the church's popularity was the condition of its efficacy as a proselytizing institution; second, it was impossible for the legislature to judge authoritatively the doctrinal truth of any particular sect. The government's policy on the Irish Church encapsulated the liberal position on religion. It recognized the importance of religion for the welfare of the state and of individual citizens, while maintaining that sectarian differences were both negligible and incapable of authoritative resolution. In so doing, it threatened to alter the balance of church and state in relation to Catholic Dissent, by entrusting the latter, via the National Board of Education, with state funds. This policy was opposed by those Tories who argued that it was indeed possible to establish which of all the competing sects was the 'true' church

[1] *Hansard*, 3rd ser., xxvii (1835), 371, 382, 663.

(and this was the Church of England and Ireland as by law established), and by those Radicals who wished for a purely secular state.

Not all politicians in the 1830s regarded the Irish Church measure as embodying liberal Anglican ideals. The critics of the Whig government formed in 1835 denied that it was committed to any religious point of view at all. They held that if it avowed any principle, it was simply that of expediency. With both their political predictions and ambitions thwarted by the formation of Melbourne's Cabinet, the critics suggested that the Whigs sponsored Irish appropriation not on account of a long-standing belief in its benefits, but because of their immediate political needs. They hinted that the Whigs supported appropriation in order to secure the votes of English and Irish Radicals, and so secure a majority in parliament. Irish appropriation, they contended, was not so much a Whig as a Radical policy. Stanley and Ripon, for example, the leaders of the third-force 'Derby Dilly',[2] who had expected to benefit from a fine electoral balance between Whigs and Tories following the 1835 election, claimed that the Whigs had 'sold themselves body and soul to the Radicals', who had them 'completely in their power'. The Tories likewise accused the Whigs of forming a 'close union' with O'Connell, and, in supporting appropriation, of proposing a measure 'calculated to please only one tail'.[3] The fears of conservative Whig politicians such as Grey appeared to corroborate these charges. He believed that the government had been formed at the expense of Whig independence, as the consequence of an agreement with the Radicals. In late August 1835 he wrote to his son, a Cabinet minister, that 'the effect of all' that had been done was 'to promote the views of O'Connell'. Grey believed that the important political battle was yet to be fought with 'the Repealers and the Radicals'. While the Whigs associated with their ultimate antagonists, they prevented the formation of a 'settled Government'. The Whigs, Grey argued,

---

[2] O'Connell coined the derogatory term 'Derby Dilly' to describe followers of Lord Stanley in 1834–5. Stanley was heir to earldom of Derby, while a 'dilly' (an abbrev. of 'diligence') was a common term for a public stagecoach. The implication was Stanley had only enough supporters to fill a coach.

[3] Derby Papers, box 173/1: Stanley to Ripon, 13 Oct. 1835; *Hansard*, 3rd ser., xxvii (1835), 391; *ibid.*, xxviii (1835), 1345.

had lost their political integrity. His evidence was O'Connell's claim, which the government had not contradicted, that Melbourne's administration 'acted upon a different principle' form that of its Whig predecessors.[4]

It is the claim of these doubters which will be assessed in this chapter. The question at issue is whether the Whigs sought this policy in order to achieve power, as the Tories and some subsequent historians have suggested,[5] or whether the events of 1834–5 merely provided the occasion for liberal Anglican Whigs to avow a policy which they had long nurtured. It has already been shown that the liberal attitudes towards religion, which the Irish Church measure embodied, were intrinsic to the doctrine which the liberal Anglican Whigs, led by Russell, had developed prior to 1834. In what follows it will be contended that the conflicts of this period over the Irish Church primarily originated in disputes within the pre-1834 Whig party, and that the policy of 1835 was neither of O'Connell's making nor desire. Given this, it is possible to suggest that the real significance of the formation of the government of 1835 was that it marked the political coming of age of liberal Anglican politics, a coming of age on an issue affecting the relations of church and state with Dissent.

Intimations of internal disarray in Grey's Cabinet on the Irish Church question began to appear just two months after the Great Reform Act received the royal assent. In August 1832 Stanley, the Irish Chief Secretary, following disagreements with his superior Lord Anglesey, the Lord Lieutenant of Ireland, and other members of the Cabinet, sought his own removal to a more agreeable post before an Irish Church measure could be introduced. Grey refused to comply, and by late October, as the draft Irish Church measure reached the Cabinet, Stanley's predicted disputes materialized, along with threats of resignation. These were contained, but when the

---

[4] Grey Papers, box 25 file 2: Grey to Howick, 20 Aug. 1835, 8 Feb. 1836; BL Addit. MSS 51557 (Holland House Papers), fo. 64: Grey to Holland, 13 Sept. 1835.

[5] See e.g., the contention of A. D. Kriegel in 'The Politics of the Whigs in Opposition 1834–5', *Jour. of British Studies*, vii (1968), ii. 85–6 that appropriation was adopted by the Whigs in order 'to maintain their precarious hold on the opposition'. Cf. I. D. C. Newbould's claim in 'Whiggery and the Dilemma of Reform', *Bulletin of the Inst. of Historical Research*, liii (1980), 232 that appropriation was a safe way of 'keeping the radicals at bay'.

Bill was presented to the Commons in the following year, rival factions were clearly discernible within the parliamentary party. It took no great prescience for Ellice, the government's Chief Whip until August 1832, and as such a senior party manager, to predict in 1833 that 'The question which will make or mar the Government is the Irish Church.' Perhaps in retrospect what was remarkable was that the political disruption of 1834 had been delayed for two years. Three distinctive parties emerged on this question. They were the High Church party of Stanley and Graham, who eventually resigned from the government in 1834; that of the old Foxite Grey, who lost his battle for Whig unity; and that of Russell and the liberal Anglican Whigs, who were to triumph in the party in the wake of the government's dismissal by the king in November 1834.[6]

The High Church party in the Cabinet consisted of Stanley and Graham, the First Lord of the Admiralty, aided by the country-gentleman Tory, the Duke of Richmond, and the Earl of Ripon, formerly and briefly Prime Minister. Stanley came from a moderate Whig family, and, when he entered the Commons in 1822, he allied himself with the more conservative Whigs. For example, he spoke and voted against Hume's motion of 1824 for an enquiry into the Irish Church establishment. Likewise in the 1820s he did not participate in Russell's attempts to rejuvenate Whiggery, but remained relatively silent on such 'progressive' issues as parliamentary reform and Catholic emancipation. In 1827 he followed Lansdowne into the coalition with Canning, becoming an Under-Secretary in the Colonial Office, of which he was to become Secretary in 1833.[7] His main ally in the Cabinet was Sir James Graham, who entered the Whig government in 1830 with a reputation for Radicalism. Durham, the Radical Lord Privy Seal, believed him to be 'a kind of pocket vote' for himself. He came from a Tory, Evangelical, and Cumberland land-owning family, but possessed the firm belief that the stability of the country required reforms in the landed aristocracy.[8] At the same time

[6] Grey Papers, box 11 file 8: Stanley to Grey, 4 Aug. 1832; Bod. Film 109 (Graham Papers): Ellice to Graham, nd. [1833].
[7] T. E. Kebbel, *The Life of the Earl of Derby* (London, 1893), 7, 15.
[8] H. Brougham, *Life and Times* (London, 1871), iii. 380; J. T. Ward, *Sir James Graham* (London, 1967), 13, 66–8.

he was afraid of the consequences of change. In particular, he feared that it would give an unwelcome impetus to Radicalism. Morpeth, who became Melbourne's Irish Secretary in the 1835 government, commented that he was in politics 'what the most menacing interpreters are in Scripture prophecy', a fact which Le Marchant, Brougham's private secretary, attributed to excessive timidity. 'He would be afraid of his own shadow', he wrote, 'I never saw equal moral pusillanimity'.[9]

Although Stanley and Graham differed from Tory backbenchers in seeing the necessity for ecclesiastical reform, they understood this as a device to pre-empt the Radicals, and so secure the establishments of the country. It was a reform which they advocated only out of a sense of the imminence of revolution. In October 1832 Graham wrote to Littleton, the MP for South Staffordshire, that the Commissioners of Inquiry into the revenues of the Church of England, instituted in that year, should quicken the pace of their investigations; if they were to delay, their task would be transferred to 'ruder hands' and conducted 'in an adverse spirit'. By December, Graham was encouraging Brougham to bring forward church reform measures, since 'by lagging behind' they could not 'arrest the progress of the mountain'. The following year he warned of the 'extreme' danger involved in allowing questions 'to be wrested from the hands of the Executive'.[10] What limited the extent of Graham's concessions, however, was not so much a calculation concerning the minimum required to save the church from Radical attacks, as a determination to resist on principle any alienation of church property to non-ecclesiastical purposes. These Whig politicians made their position clear in the correspondence surrounding Durham's memorandum dissenting from Stanley's Irish Church Bill, drafted in the autumn of 1832. In his reply Stanley asserted that the principle of his measure was 'non-alienation', and that 'by that principle the Government were determined to stand'. Both he and Graham made it equally clear that if the Cabinet refused to

⁹ Lady Caroline Lascelles (ed.), *Extracts from the Journals kept by George Howard, Earl of Carlisle* (London, 1871), 181; A. Aspinall (ed.), *Three Early Nineteenth-Century Diaries* (London, 1952), 366.

¹⁰ Bod. Film 108 (Graham Papers): Graham to Littleton, 6 Oct. 1832, Graham to Brougham, 13 Dec. 1832; Bod. Film 109 (Graham Papers): Graham to Stanley, 21 Dec. 1833.

abide by this principle, they would break up the government. Althorp, the Chancellor of the Exchequer, commented that Stanley's proposal operated on 'High Church Principles', and added, somewhat ominously, 'I really think that in the present state of Ireland none but a High Church man can go through with him to the end of it'.[11]

The strength of this High Church party in the Cabinet, as they themselves clearly recognized, depended on Grey's tacit support. Graham remarked to Ellice: 'If Lord Grey will consent to remain our Head I have no fears whatever respecting the future; if he abandons the Helm, the Crew will mutiny and the ship will drift in the rocks'.[12] The reason they were so dependent on Grey was because they were in a minority in the Cabinet. They relied therefore on Grey's pursuit of ministerial unity to quell dissent. This was clearly revealed in the events of the autumn and winter of 1832. At the first meeting of the Cabinet to discuss Stanley's Church Bill, dissent was not confined to Durham, but also included Althorp and Russell, the Paymaster General. The following day Russell composed a letter of resignation, while Althorp informed the Prime Minister that he could not agree to the plan 'without some important modifications'. By the following Cabinet, however, Grey's manœuvres had managed to isolate Durham, and to prevent the resignation threats from materializing.[13] It is unclear if Grey greatly sympathized with Stanley, whose demands for a clear Cabinet declaration against appropriation he described as 'rather unreasonable'. It was, however, abundantly obvious that Grey's priority was to prevent a breach in his administration, even at the expense of bringing the ecclesiastical question to a final resolution. Grey's position was that the country, having successfully weathered reform,

[11] Knowsley Papers: copy, Observations on Mr Stanley's Plan of Church Reform for Ireland by Lord Durham with Mr Stanley's replies annexed, 17 Nov. 1832; Althorp MSS H (Papers of the 3rd Earl Spencer), box 7: confidential, Althorp to Grey, 20 Oct. 1832; ibid., box 8: private, Grey to Althorp, 17 Nov. 1832; on Stanley as the 'dog' preventing real church reform, see SCRO MSS D260/M/F/5/26 (Hatherton Papers), ix. 19: E. J. Littleton Jour., 21 [July 1833].

[12] Bod. Film 109 (Graham Papers): Graham to Ellice, 15 Sept. 1833.

[13] Ellice Papers: Durham to Ellice, 18 Oct. 1832; BL Addit. MSS 38080 (Russell Papers), fo. 58: Grey to Russell, 25 Oct. 1832; Walpole, *Russell*, i. 188–92; Althorp MSS H (Papers of the 3rd Earl Spencer), box 7: confidential, Althorp to Grey, 20 Oct. 1832; ibid., box 8: private and confidential, Grey to Althorp, 21 Oct. 1832.

needed to enjoy a period of stability and tranquillity to consolidate its gains. This meant that Radicalism had to be discouraged. As he explained to Ellice, 'having carried the Reform
Bill and having thus provided for the people a real reform and
the means of redressing their grievances in a constitutional
manner; it is the interest of anybody who wished to avoid
confusion to promote and encourage a quiet course of
conduct'.[14] This attitude often assumed the appearance of
statesmanlike haughtiness, since its effect was to suppress the
discussion of what many considered the most important issue
in politics: the church. It was a position which at times frustrated the High Churchmen as well as the liberals. Stanley, for
example, initially reacted to Durham's memorandum by
demanding that the Cabinet come to a formal resolution on
the issue, a position he was reluctant to relinquish. It was also
a position which failed to quell the demand for church reform
outside the formal mechanisms of government. At the end of
December Russell was still insisting that the Cabinet, despite
Stanley's claims to the contrary, had not agreed to the principle
of non-alienation; at the beginning of January 1833 Althorp
was pressing for a measure to 'diminish the pressure of the
Church Rates upon the Dissenters'.[15]

Both Stanley's and Grey's political positions were weakened
further by their comparative isolation from the parliamentary
party. In November 1832 Ellice warned Grey that 'the first
point to be decided at every discussion relative to the measures
of your Cabinet is not whether you can come to some compromise of opinion amongst yourselves and act in concert upon
it, but whether your decision when made and the proceedings
to grow out of it will be satisfactory to a majority of the popular
party in the House of Commons'.[16] Grey was to find himself
isolated not merely from such nominal Radicals as Durham,
but also from a large section of Whigs. This was unsurprising

[14] Grey Papers: Stanley to Grey, 15 Nov. 1832; Althorp MSS H (Papers of the 3rd
Earl Spencer), box 7: Grey to Althorp, 1 Dec. 1832, Althorp to Grey, 2 Dec. 1832;
ibid., box 8: Grey to Althorp, 2 Dec. 1832; Ellice Papers: Grey to Ellice, 11 Jan. 1833.

[15] Grey Papers: Stanley to Grey, 15 Nov. 1832; Graham Papers: Stanley to Grey,
29 Nov. 1832; Knowsley Papers: Grey to Stanley, 2 Dec., 7 Dec. 1832; Lambton
Papers: Russell to Stanley, 30 Dec. 1832; Brougham Papers, MS 13668: copy, Stanley
to Russell, 31 Dec. 1832.

[16] Ellice Papers: Ellice to Grey, 5 Nov. 1832.

given the circumstances surrounding his return to active leadership of the party in the summer of 1830, which was due less to his popular appeal than to the absence of alternatives. Following the death of the inefficient Tierney in January 1830, the anti-coalitionist Whigs in March chose Althorp as their new leader in the Commons. In this move towards an active opposition to Wellington's ministry, Grey had played no part. It was not until the end of June that he declared against the Duke's government and accepted the *fait accompli* wrought by the party in the Commons. These MPs were primarily prepared to accept Grey as leader because he alone of the old Foxite Whig leadership had remained untainted by the failed policy of seeking an alliance with the moderate Tories with the hope that this might bring about Whig reforms. Grey thus found himself at the head of a movement he had not initiated, and it was in this section of the party, which included such Cabinet ministers as Russell and Althorp, that the move to appropriate the surplus revenues of the Irish Church found its most influential supporters.[17] Their strength was increased by the general election of December 1832, which, while resulting in a 'Great Superiority' of Whigs to Radicals, also saw the return of a substantial number of Whigs committed to Althorp's position on the Irish Church Bill. In 1832 Ellice claimed that four-fifths of Whig supporters would vote for a motion to appropriate the surplus revenues of the Irish Church, while Charles Wood, who succeeded him as Chief Whip in that year, claimed in 1833 that if a motion were put down expressing dissatisfaction with the Irish Church Bill of that Session, it would bring out between 200 and 250 liberals against Stanley's measure.[18]

The consequence was considerable back-bench support for Irish appropriation, led by Ebrington, the Evangelical eldest son of Earl Fortescue, and friend and associate of Russell.[19] This support had considerable moral authority since the movement to appropriate the surplus revenues of the Irish Church

[17] On circumstances surrounding Grey's return to active leadership, see G. M. Trevelyan, *Lord Grey of the Reform Bill* (London, 1929), 212–8.

[18] Ellice Papers: Ellice to Grey, 5 Nov. 1832; Knowsley Papers: Wood to Stanley, 5 Jan. 1833.

[19] Grey Papers: Ellice to Grey, 9 Jan. 1833. On Ebrington's lobbying, see NLS MSS 15015 (Ellice Papers), fo. 268: copy, Ebrington to Ellice, 7 Jan. 1833.

had been associated with the Whig party since Hume's motion to inquire into its services and revenues of 6 May 1824. More than 30 of those who had voted for this motion sat in the parliament of 1833, and these included such office-holders as Rice, Russell, Ellice, and Hobhouse. Wood estimated that in total approximately 25 or 26 of the government's 'steadiest friends', and eight more actually in the government, had voted with Hume in 1824.[20] Furthermore, the supporters of this group included such influential Whigs as Duncannon (Melbourne's brother-in-law), Tavistock (Russell's brother), and Abercromby (the Duke of Devonshire's former agent), in short 'every . . . *moderate* man who knows anything of the state of Ireland'.[21] To some, if only to a limited extent, Clause 147 of the Irish Church Temporalities Bill satisfied the aspiration of this section, in so far as it sanctioned parliament's right to appropriate the surplus revenues of the Irish Church which the Perpetuity Purchase fund created. When, however, the government dropped this clause in June 1833 on the ground that this action was necessary in order to secure the passage of the Bill through the Lords, 149 voted for its retention, including such Whigs as Paul Methuen, the Wiltshire land-owner and close friend of Hobhouse, Russell's half-brother, Lord Charles Russell, E. J. Stanley, who became Chief Whip on Wood's resignation in 1835, Abercromby, who entered the Cabinet in 1834, and Sir Henry Parnell, who had been sacked from the Cabinet in 1832 for his vote on the Russo-Dutch loan. The Whigs had feared that they would lose their majority on this vote. Le Marchant, then Brougham's private secretary, recalled that 'we were in serious danger of requiring the support of the Tories and indeed Lord Grey canvassed the Tories at the Queen's Ball'.[22] In the autumn of 1833 back-bench attempts to secure the reform of the Irish Church commenced in earnest. These efforts, when combined with the support of leading Whigs such as Russell, were to render Grey's policy on religious issues—one of maintaining unity by procrastination and suppression—redundant.

[20] *Hansard*, new ser., xi (1824), 588; Knowsley Papers: Wood to Stanley, 5 Jan. 1833.
[21] Ellice Papers: Ellice to Grey, 5 Nov. 1832; BL Addit. MSS 51724 (Holland House Papers), fo. 4343: Duncannon to Holland, 6 Jan. 1833.
[22] *Hansard*, 3rd ser., xviii (1833), 1098–102; Aspinall, *Nineteenth-Century Diaries*, 339.

At the end of October 1833 Ebrington wrote to Grey in an attempt to convince him that no proposal on Irish tithes would be satisfactory which did not deal with the surplus revenues of the Irish Church. He proposed a motion to establish a commission to enquire into the Church's provision of divine services and the numbers attending them. Grey forwarded this letter to Althorp and to Russell. Following a conversation on 27 November in the course of a shooting party at Woburn, Russell persuaded Grey to show the proposed motion to Wellesley, who had replaced Anglesey as the Lord Lieutenant of Ireland. Duncannon meanwhile lobbied Littleton, who had succeeded Stanley as Chief Secretary, writing that '*nothing* will induce the House of Commons to pass a measure in support of the Irish Church but the conviction that it is to be followed up by some satisfactory arrangement of the Surplus Revenues'. Ebrington's proposal did not reach the Irish administration until after the Cabinet had discussed the Irish tithes scheme then being prepared for the forthcoming parliamentary session, and had rejected Wellesley's proposal to finance the Anglican and Roman Catholic Churches out of a common fund on the ground that it was politically impracticable. Littleton was later to make the bitter claim that Grey had postponed Cabinet discussion *sine die* in order to avoid disagreements, and had been so petty as to remove his franking privileges in order to discourage him from pursuing this policy. Not surprisingly, in these circumstances, Ebrington's proposal met with a favourable response from Littleton and Wellesley as a new reforming initiative. Littleton informed Ebrington in late December that 'it would be difficult for any person to feel the imperious urgency of that Question' more deeply than he did, and that he could 'rely on the Lord Lieutenant's intention to recommend in the strongest terms ... the appointment of some such Commission' as had been suggested. In accord with Russell's advice, Ebrington withdrew his motion: it no longer appeared necessary. Althorp wrote encouragingly to Ebrington: 'For myself I shall be very glad if the Government are compelled to take some more decided part'. As Russell had promised, he brought the question before the Cabinet in the New Year, but on 15 February the Cabinet disappointingly resolved once more to postpone indefinitely any discussion on

Wellesley's proposal to inquire into the state of the Irish Church. This decision followed Grey's threats of resignation throughout the parliamentary recess, first out of tiredness, then out of opposition to Palmerston's Portuguese policy. Grey once more had managed to silence temporarily liberal Anglican and 'young' Whigs such as Russell, Duncannon, and Althorp.[23]

Grey's policy of stalling, however, was beginning to collapse on other ecclesiastical issues. In November 1832 Brougham had begun to discuss English church reform with the Whig Bishop of Chichester, Edward Maltby, who acted as a mediator between the Lord Chancellor and the episcopate. By February 1833 Maltby could report that most bishops had shown a willingness to co-operate with the government on this issue. Still the government did nothing, and Brougham acted unilaterally when he presented a Bill on pluralities and non-residence to the Lords on 16 May 1834, rumoured by some to be an attempt to secure his position in the event of Grey's resignation.[24] Likewise, although such members of the government as Littleton appreciated that the abolition of church cess in Ireland would lead to demands for the abolition of church-rates in England, nothing was done until the defeat of the Attorney-General at Dudley at the hands of the Dissenters precipitated the government's introduction of a Bill to abolish this impost in April 1834.[25] When the government brought on its Irish tithe measure at the beginning of May 1834 it was in a state of disarray, with Grey expressing his intention to retire at the end of the session. Russell chose this occasion to press the appropriation issue once more. On the day the debate commenced in the Commons without a pledge to institute a Commission of Inquiry, he sent in his resignation. Grey

[23] DCRO MSS 1262M FC 89 (Fortescue Papers): Ebrington to Grey, 31 Oct. 1833, Russell to Ebrington, 16 Nov. [1833]; BL Addit. MSS 37306 (Wellesley Papers), fos. 162, 193, 201: Duncannon to Littleton, 6 Nov. 1833, Melbourne to Wellesley, 22 Nov. 1833, Melbourne to Littleton, 22 Nov. 1833; Grey Papers C3/1B: Howick Jour., 22 May 1834; DCRO MSS 1262M FC 89 (Fortescue Papers): Russell to Ebrington, 28 Nov. 1833, Littleton to Ebrington, 24 Dec. 1833, Althorp to Ebrington, 26 Dec. 1833; Derby Papers, box 130 bundle 12: Russell to Stanley, 15 July 1834.
[24] Brougham Papers, MSS 44136, 43939: Maltby to Brougham, 27 Nov. 1832, note by Le Marchant, n.d. [Feb. 1833]; Aspinall *Nineteenth-Century Diaries*, 282, 302.
[25] Brougham Papers, MS 44585: Littleton to Brougham, 24 Mar. 1833; *Morning Chronicle*, 1 Mar. 1834; Brougham Papers, MSS 46819, 46822: Campbell to Brougham, n.d. [Feb. 1834], Campbell to Le Marchant, n.d. [Feb. 1834].

succeeded in dissuading him from this rash course of action. But four days later, in his speech on the Bill, Russell 'upset the coach' by once more raising the question of appropriation, and so repeated the crisis of 1832. There was one important difference. This time it was acted out not in private rooms, but before the parliamentary party. After Russell's speech, Stanley and Graham threatened to resign, but, at a Cabinet held on the following day, Stanley agreed to withdraw his threat. For the time being it appeared that the dispute had again been settled in a spirit of mutual, if reluctant, compromise. On Thursday the 8th Howick recorded in his journal: 'I heard everything was patched up again this morning and to go on', and on the 18th Stanley wrote to Richmond, who was out of town during the crisis, that Althorp intended to oppose the appropriation resolution tabled by H. G. Ward, the moderate Radical MP for Sheffield, for the 27th.[26]

But unlike previous Irish Church crises, since parliament was sitting and the Cabinet dissent was public, the initiative could pass to the back-benchers, and they sufficiently prolonged the crisis to provoke the resignations, which occurred three weeks later on 27 May.[27] Two weeks after Russell's speech, Duncannon and Wood were in receipt of the information that friends of the government intended to proceed with a resolution pledging the House of Commons to consider the question of appropriation early next Session, regardless of the Cabinet's wishes. Le Marchant reported to Brougham that such stalwarts as Carter and Ebrington were attending meetings designed to provoke government action on the Irish Church issue. On 25 May Abercromby, who had personally remonstrated with Althorp the day after the dropping of Clause 147, held a meeting to discuss his intention to move a resolution pledging the Commons to take up the appropriation question. It was the Cabinet's apprehension that, even if it could itself agree to move the previous question and so avoid debating Ward's Irish Church resolution, it would not be supported by its troops, which forced the resignations of Stanley, Graham,

[26] Grey Papers C3/1B: Howick Jour., 2, 6, 8 May 1834; Goodwood Papers, MSS 689, fo. 21: Stanley to Richmond, 18 May 1834.
[27] NLS MSS 11806 (Minto Papers), fo. 42: Lansdowne to Minto, n.d. [end of June 1834].

Richmond, and Ripon. Whig back-bench pressure had forced the issue.[28]

The events of May did not as yet demonstrate so much a liberal victory in Whig circles as a temporary set-back for Grey's strategy. The Cabinet still refused to commit itself to Irish appropriation, and instead moved an adjournment to Ward's motion on 27 May. Russell was still contemplating resignation. On 2 June Althorp announced a lay Commission of Inquiry, which, if in January it had been sought as a liberal measure, now appeared to be a delaying device in order to keep open the possibility of reunion with Stanley. When Ward again proposed his resolution, the government dismissed it as being too abstractly formulated, and moved the previous question.[29] Moreover, the reconstruction of the government did not make substantial concessions to the liberals. Grey replaced Ripon as Lord Privy Seal with the Earl of Carlisle, who already sat in the Cabinet; the Marquis of Conyngham, who had been a pro-Catholic minister under Liverpool's premiership, succeeded Richmond. Graham's and Stanley's replacements were Auckland and Spring Rice, both protégés of Lansdowne, although Spring Rice, a Unionist Irish MP, moved in liberal Anglican circles and was known to support appropriation. Poulett Thomson became President of the Board of Trade, a post he already held *de facto*, with a seat in the Cabinet. The appointments of Spring Rice and Thomson were the only immediate concessions to the liberal Whigs. Grey had not originally intended to make any offer to Abercromby, who not only was one of the leaders of the revolt on Irish appropriation, but had also opposed the government on the Irish Coercion Bill the previous year. The clamour against the announced appointments, however, proved so great that on 9 June Grey offered him the Mastership of the Mint with a seat in the Cabinet.[30] On 20 June Ellice, the party manager and Prime Minister's brother-in-law, also took a seat in the Cabinet.

The events of July 1834, which resulted in Grey's own resignation, appeared to confirm his contention that the main

[28] Grey Papers C3/1B: Howick Jour., 22, 25 May 1834; Brougham Papers, MS 1662: Le Marchant to Brougham, n.d. [1834]; Aspinall, *Nineteenth-Century Diaries*, 379–80.

[29] *Hansard*, 3rd ser., xxiv (1834), 11–18.

[30] On Abercromby, see Grey Papers C3/1B: Howick Jour., 28 May, 9 June 1834.

threat to Whiggery came not from the Tories, but from the Radicals and Irish, and that the best defence consisted in a union of moderates against Radicalism. Grey believed that this second disruption of the government was the result of the Chief Secretary for Ireland's unauthorized concert with O'Connell. The Whig leader blamed Littleton and Brougham for persuading Wellesley to change his mind as to the merit of the public meetings clauses of the Irish Coercion Act due for renewal in the summer of 1834, and to advocate instead their removal in his letter of 21 June. This despatch produced confusion in the Cabinet since few ministers wished to act with Grey, and in defiance of the Lord Lieutenant's advice. On Monday, 23 June Littleton told O'Connell that he did not believe the Cabinet would consent to renew those clauses in view of the opposition to them of Littleton himself, Wellesley, Brougham, Althorp, Ellice, Abercromby, and Grant. Thus when Grey did move their renewal on 3 July in the House of Lords, O'Connell was understandably angry. On the following Thursday he consulted Littleton, who told him that he would indeed now support the Bill as proposed by Grey. Thereupon O'Connell moved in the Commons for the production of the Lord Lieutenant's official correspondence with Grey, his purpose being to make the Cabinet dissension public. On the Saturday Littleton tendered his resignation, followed on the Tuesday by those of Althorp and Grey.[31] In the reconstruction of the government which followed, Melbourne, who had become Prime Minister, persuaded Althorp and Littleton to stay at their posts, and dropped the public meetings clauses. Duncannon, who had extensive Irish connections, became Home Secretary, and E. J. Stanley, who in 1833 had voted in favour of the retention of Clause 147, became his new Under-Secretary. Mulgrave, who had been responsible for overseeing the abolition of slavery in Jamaica as Governor-General, an associate of Thomson and Abercromby, and a cousin of H. G. Ward, entered the Cabinet along with Hobhouse, who had been a liberal Chief Secretary for Ireland. It appeared that Grey's resignation had resulted in O'Connell's triumph.

[31] BL Addit. MSS 51728 (Holland House Papers), fos. 4593a, 4599a: copy, Wellesley to Grey, 21 June 1834, secret note by Wellesley, n.d. [?1835]; A. D. Kriegel (ed.), *The Holland House Diaries 1831–1840* (London, 1977), 255–60; Grey Papers C3/1B: Howick Jour., 9 July, 1834.

The events of the summer of 1834 did not consolidate the liberal victory won in the spring. Instead, they served to establish the ground on which the ensuing conflict would be fought, as well as to give a renewed impetus to the cause of the High Church and Grey-led old Foxite Whigs. The dismissal of the Whig government by the King in November 1834 provided an opportunity to renew the contest and to establish the terms of the Whig reunion which would be required to overthrow Peel's Tory administration. The followers of Stanley needed to convince potential adherents that their position on the Irish Church Bill was in accordance with Whig principles. The Foxite Whigs (joined by a number of liberal Anglican Whigs out of personal loyalty) needed to demonstrate that union against Radicals was more important than the Irish Church issue. Finally, liberal Anglican Whigs needed to show that their position on the Irish Church owed nothing to O'Connell, and that their acquisition of Radical support did not mean that they appeased the Irish to the detriment of the true interests of the country. The reward of the contest would be the right to determine the character of the next Whig government, for the one thing the contending parties agreed on was that, in its present form, Peel's government was unlikely to survive the meeting of parliament.

Following his resignation, Grey retired to Howick, more than willing to criticize his successors and advocate a policy of moderation. The dismissal of Melbourne's government provided the opportunity for the re-emergence of the Foxite politics of compromise. He wrote to Melbourne that he wished to see a government which asserted its just authority 'against the radicals and O'Connell'. He feared that the ensuing elections would result in great losses for the Whigs and gains for the Radicals. Initially he even sympathized with the Tories, commenting that Peel was the only person who was acknowledged 'as possessing the qualities necessary to a leader of the House of Commons'. The High Church and Orange appointments of the new ministry left him less sanguine, although he felt that the election results did not render the dissolution of Peel's administration inevitable as others had predicted. The advice he gave to the Whig leaders was to pursue a wait-and-see policy which, by allowing the Tories to act first, would not prematurely hinder a junction with Stanley. Grey recommended that the Whigs desist from any attempt to contest Manners Sutton's election to the Speakership at the commencement of the Session, or to propose an amendment to the Address from the Throne relating to the Irish Church. Above all he objected to any collusion with O'Connell and the Radicals. He wrote to Holland: 'I must distinctly avow the most uncompromising opposition to the Radicals and O'Connell. And it seems to me *worse* than a short-sighted policy to have any communication with them to obtain their support without considering the consequences to which it may lead.'[32]

Lord Holland, the Foxite elder statesman and close friend of Grey, shared this outlook. While, unlike Grey, he recognized the need to act quickly to establish some form of party organization on the eve of the new session, this was in order to restrain rather than excite violent opposition. Holland warned Mulgrave that the lessons of the elections in the West and the South was that there was 'no inclination to go either too fast or too far'; that in order to ensure the fall of the Tory ministry, it was necessary to produce an impression that 'Stanley and his followers can with honour and consistency make up their matters with us'. On the same day Holland wrote to Melbourne that 'the accession or the hopes of the accession of Stanley' to his party could alone enable him 'to form a ministry with the slightest prospect of stability'. According to Thomson, the Hollands were doing 'much mischief by their abuse of what they term Radical'.[33] Grey's two most influential agents in London were not these leaders of political society, but his son, Viscount Howick, who had been a junior minister under Stanley and Melbourne, and his son-in-law, Charles Wood, who, as a former Parliamentary Secretary to the Treasury, was nominally in a strong position to influence party organization. Their activities were constrained by the fact that Howick did

[32] BL Microfilm 859/3 (Melbourne Papers): Grey to Melbourne, 16, 18 Nov. 1834; BL Addit. MSS 51557 (Holland House Papers), fos. 35, 41, 43: Grey to Holland, 16 Nov., 19 Dec. 1834, 10 Feb. 1835; see also NLS MSS 15022 (Ellice Papers), fo. 49: Grey to Ellice, 22 Jan. 1835.

[33] Mulgrave Castle Archives, box M (Normanby Papers), fo. 369: Holland to Mulgrave, 24 Jan. 18[35]; BL Microfilm 859/3 (Melbourne Papers): Holland to Melbourne, 24 Jan. 1835; Mulgrave Castle Archives, box O (Normanby Papers), fo. 871: Thomson to Mulgrave, 30 Jan. 1835.

not arrive in London until 14 February, by which time the decision to contest the Speakership had already been taken. Consequently they found themselves in the position of having to resist initiatives. Nevertheless they took up the challenge. On 17 February Grey commended to Howick an association with Spring Rice, who had been passed over for the Speakership; on 19 February Howick and Spring Rice breakfasted together at Wood's house. Together the coterie planned a reconstructed administration, based on a coalition of moderate Tories, moderate Whigs, and the followers of Stanley.[34]

This they did despite holding liberal Anglican views on the issue of the Irish Church. Howick, indeed, was possibly more extreme in his wish to appropriate the surplus revenues than such a leading liberal Anglican as Russell, whose parliamentary tactics he opposed. At the meeting at Russell's on Sunday, 22 March to decide the form of words on the Irish Church resolution, Howick was for the most decided appropriation and objected to Russell's compromise as the worst of all. In a memorandum to Russell, Howick wrote: 'I think a bolder and more decided resolution ought to be adopted.' At the end of January, he explained his position to Grey, commenting apropos the failure of previous Irish Church measures: 'I think it was hardly to be expected that the property could be saved from total loss except by conceding to what I must consider the well-founded objection of the Irish people to its present application'.[35] In general outlook Howick found himself most in sympathy not with his father, but with the liberal Anglican Whigs. Somewhat to his surprise, Hobhouse was to note approvingly: 'From what I have seen of Lord Howick in Cabinet his views are in accordance with the popular portion of our ministry'.[36] Nevertheless, from July 1834 to April 1835 Howick subordinated such beliefs to a haughty defence of his family name and the assertion of Whig independence from O'Connell. His reason for doing so was his loyal anger at the

[34] Grey Papers, box 25 file 2: Grey to Howick, 17 Feb. 1835; Halifax Papers A8/1/1: Wood Jour., 19 Feb. 1835; Grey Papers C3/1B: Howick Jour., 19 Feb. 1835; NLI MSS 13379 (Monteagle Papers): Wood to Rice 24 Jan. 1835.

[35] BL Addit. MSS 61826 (Broughton Papers): Hobhouse Diary 23[2] Mar. 1835; PRO 30/22 1C (Russell Papers), fo. 167: memo. by Howick, n.d. [1835]; Grey Papers, box 24 file 2: Howick to Grey, 27 Jan. 1835.

[36] BL Addit. MSS 61826 (Broughton Papers): Hobhouse Diary, 29 Apr. 1835.

forced resignation of his father in July. He too resigned, and, before leaving England on 23 July to join his convalescent wife on the continent, he began (with his brother-in-law, Charles Wood) a newspaper campaign against Brougham as one of the leading conspirators in his father's downfall. He also attacked Littleton, and only restrained himself on Lord John Russell's assurance that this would provoke Althorp's resignation from the government. Once abroad, newspapers reports convinced him that Melbourne's government gave the impression of being run by O'Connell. In the course of these ten months, Howick, abetted by his brother, Captain Charles Grey, and by Wood, sought to defend his father's honour and policy. Hobhouse remarked: 'Howick and Charles Grey are making fools of themselves and doing all the mischief in their power to the opposition, they are angry at everything said in praise of Lord Melbourne as it was an implied censure of Lord Grey.'[37]

Spring Rice was the last senior member of this small faction (Brougham calculated they numbered '30 or 40 old Whigs').[38] Like his colleagues, he supported the principle of appropriation, as Russell made efforts to confirm when Abercromby was approached in late January 1835 in a final effort to persuade him to stand for Speaker. Rice wrote to Russell: 'There was an entire and perfect agreement between you and me respecting the principles on which we were ready to proceed' on the Irish Church. But, as with the Grey clan, as a Whig Irish MP, he feared O'Connell more than he supported these principles. The results of the 1835 elections reinforced his fears. To his confidant, Wood, he expressed a desire not to proceed precipitately and, by so dividing the Whigs, prevent a reunion with Stanley. Pessimism at the prospect of preserving what he termed 'rational Whiggism' led him to contemplate political retirement by becoming Speaker of the Commons, thus removing himself from the invidious position of having to decide between the Scylla of O'Connell and the Charybdis of Peel.[39]

[37] Grey Papers C3/1B: Howick Jour., 17, 19 July, 6 Oct. 1834; BL Addit. MSS 61826 (Broughton Papers): Hobhouse Diary, 22 Feb. 1835.
[38] BL Addit. MSS 51563 (Holland House Papers), fo. 115: Brougham to Holland [26 Dec. 1834].
[39] R. Russell, *Corresp. of Lord John Russell*, ii. 79–81; NLI MSS 546 (Monteagle Papers): Rice to Wood, 14 Jan. 1835, Rice to Spencer, 13 Jan. 1835, Rice to Lansdowne,

Howick and Wood both wrote to Spring Rice to dissuade him from this course, as did his patron Lansdowne: all were aware that his absence from the political circus would make it more difficult to achieve their object.[40] When Abercromby agreed to become the Whigs' candidate for the Chair, Spring Rice announced his intention of travelling to London only to vote for him, and then returning to his ailing wife at Hastings until Easter.[41] In the event he was persuaded to stay in London to cabal with Wood and Howick, and to acquiesce in putting aside the religious question and the liberal Anglican principles which he had supported since the 1820s. The task of the faction was to convince Stanley and Graham that their disagreement of May 1834 was of no consequence; that the provenance of their resignation lay not in principles but in trifles and mis-apprehensions.

When members of parliament began to assemble in London in mid-February 1835 in time for the new session of parliament, the followers of Grey were reasonably optimistic that a reunion could be effected. Howick called on Stanley on 20 February in his house in Carlton Terrace. That evening he noted in his diary: 'I was surprised to find that on the Irish Church he did not seem to me quite so impracticable as I had feared . . . I received the impression that if he had been properly talked to last year . . . he would not have taken the line he did.' On 23 February Wood also visited Stanley and suggested a compromise on the Irish Church question, which, Wood noted, 'seemed to strike him'. None the less little of consequence transpired until the beginning of March when this time Howick talked to Graham. He reported to his father that 'his conversation completely confirmed the impression that I had before received from what Stanley and the Duke of Richmond had said to me, that their resignation last year was quite as much the result of temper . . . as [due] to real differences of opinion'. On the following day Howick dined with Stanley, and the next week saw an exchange of memoranda and letters on the subject of

23 Jan. 1835, Rice to Kennedy, 9 Dec. 1834, Rice to Drummond, 16 Jan. 1835.

[40] NLI MSS 13379 (Monteagle Papers): Howick to Rice, 24 Jan. 1835, Wood to Rice, 24 Jan. 1835; W. M. Torrens, *Memoirs of William Lamb, 2nd Viscount Melbourne* (London, 1890), 335–6.

[41] Halifax Papers, box A4 fo. 130: Rice to Wood, 1 Feb. [1835].

the Irish Church.[12] These negotiations took place in an atmos-phere of urgency. There were rumours of ministerial changes and a Tory revolt on the malt tax; Hume was preparing what was in effect a vote of no confidence in the government by proposing to vote supplies for only three months; the Tories were about to introduce their own Irish tithe measure. It was also known that the party which Stanley had gathered about himself since the commencement of the general elections was discontented with his leadership.

The members of the Derby Dilly were comparatively few in number. Those giving adherence to Stanley at a meeting of supporters on 23 February 1835 totalled just 38 (Stanley had expected 40). When these are added to those marked 'certain' in Stanley's *catalogue raisonné* of those circulated inde-pendently by G. H. Vernon for an alternative meeting, a total of 44 results, excluding Stanley, but including Graham. This corresponds with Greville's two accounts of the meeting of 25 February in which he put the number of adherents at 45–50 and 'about fifty' respectively. Stanley unfortunately could not command these troops. No less than seven of those traced from the above composite list voted for the Whig candidate in the division on the Speakership, more than accounting for the Whig majority of just ten. Stanley's hopes of sustaining Peel in office were in vain. As the session proceeded, more drifted back to the Whig fold; by March Mulgrave had counted at least five defections. Those who remained exerted pressure on Stanley to aid the Whigs in turning out Peel's Cabinet. Charlton, the 'Dilly' MP for Ludlow, reported to Greville on 15 March, during the week of the negotiations with Howick, that at the most recent meeting of Stanleyites such supporters as G. F. Young, the MP for Tynemouth, had pressed Stanley to declare his want of confidence in the government; others considered supporting Hume's motion to vote supply for only three months.[43]

[12] Grey Papers C3/1B: Howick Jour., 20 Feb. 1835; Grey Papers, box 24 file 2: Howick to Grey, 10 Mar. 1835; Halifax Papers A8/1/1: Wood Jour., 23 Feb. [1835]; Bod. Film 110 (Graham Papers): Howick to Graham, 9 Mar. 1835 and see below.
[43] Derby Papers, box 120 bundle 1: list of MPs who gave their adherence on Wed. 23 Feb. 1835; Goodwood Papers, MSS 1570, fo. 9214: Stanley to Richmond, 22 Feb. 1835; Bod. Film 110 (Graham Papers): *catalogue raisonné* enc. Stanley to Graham, 23 Feb. 1835. [Note on the composite list: of the 44, only 41 may be traced—hence

Stanley also differed from many of his supporters in his attitude towards the surplus revenues of the Irish Church. Howick wrote to Graham on 9 March: 'Are you ignorant . . . that nine tenths of those who compose the Third Party by which you are surrounded differ from you upon this question?'[44] If this was exaggeration due to tactical licence, it was nevertheless substantially true. Stanley could muster only 29 to meet in the 'King's Head', Palace Yard, on the night prior to the commencement of the debate on Russell's Irish Church resolution.[45] This was an instance of the general divergence in religious attitudes of leaders and led. Of those who sat in the previous parliament, exactly half demonstrated Low Church attitudes in either voting in favour of Agnew's sabbatarian legislation (which Graham had refused to sponsor) or in supporting Buxton's attempt to restrict the duration of the apprenticeship scheme for negro slaves in the West Indies. Ten of the 36 adherents in the previous parliament acted on liberal principles, supporting either the admission of Dissenters to the universities or the emancipation of the Jews; two had even voted for the reinstatement of the controversial Clause 147 of the Irish Church Temporalities Bill.[46] The truth was that many of Stanley's supporters originally followed him as a defence against Radicalism. Greville, otherwise an adherent to the cause of a third party as a bulwark against democratic insurgents, confessed that he was 'lost in astonishment at the views they [Stanley and Graham] take on this subject', by which he meant the Irish Church.[47] Forced to choose between Stanley's High Churchmanship and Russell's liberal Anglicanism many Dillyites decided in favour of the latter, putting their religious

discrepancy between total and sum of those accounted for in divisions cited below. This is not a comprehensive list (e.g., excludes J. E. Denison) but the numbers if not always the names appear reasonably accurate in comparison with contemporary observation.] R. Fulford and L. Strachey (eds.), *The Greville Memoirs* (London, 1938), iii. 166–8; *Hansard*, 3rd ser., xxvi (1835), 56–61; Fulford & Strachey, *Greville Memoirs* iii. 170, 174; Grey Papers C3/1E: Howick Jour., 5 Apr. 1835.

[44] Bod. Film 110 (Graham Papers): Howick to Graham, 9 Mar. 1835.

[45] Fulford & Strachey, *Greville Memoirs* iii. 183. Auckland put number attending Stanley's meeting at 40, 10 of whom objected to his Irish Church policy. See NLS MSS 11793 (Minto Papers), fo. 69: Auckland to Minto, 30 Mar. [1835].

[46] *Hansard*, 3rd ser., xvii (1833), 1337–8; ibid., xviii (1833), 59–61, 1098–1102; ibid., xix (1833), 1081–2, 1219–20; ibid., xxii (1834), 928–9; ibid., xxiii (1834), 356–7.

[47] Fulford & Strachey, *Greville Memoirs*, iii. 41.

sentiments, if only temporarily, above their concern for the constitution. The Grey party's task was to press Stanley and Graham to be equally obliging.

Howick and Wood had further grounds for optimism in addition to the known inclination of Stanley's supporters. Since June 1834 the debate on the Irish Church had been conducted in a language of equivocation and ambiguity. It was unclear that the claims which the Stanleyites had made in public, during the passage of Littleton's Irish Tithe Bill through the Commons, would be adhered to in private, where the need to mark out an independent stance on the issue, in order to acquire support, would be less compelling. Although Stanley had denied that church property differed from any other kind, and had accused the Whig government of intending to rob and confiscate the property of the Irish Church, these claims had the appearance of rhetorical excesses. As the minister responsible for the introduction of Clause 147 of the Irish Church Temporalities Bill he had already given his *de facto* sanction to parliament's right to appropriate the surplus revenues of the Perpetuity Purchase Fund set up with the proceeds of diocesan lands. Retrospectively, Stanley had justified this position by drawing a distinction between this property and church property in general. He argued that since the Perpetuity Purchase Fund was a new value created by an Act of the legislature, it was fully disposable by that self-same legislature.[48] But this was a distinction the Whigs were also prepared to make when it suited them. The Whig Tithe Bill of the summer of 1834 had authorized the use of the Perpetuity Purchase Fund to replenish the Consolidated Fund for its advances to landowners, given to encourage the conversion of ecclesiastical tithes into a rent-charge. Althorp made it clear in defending the measure that the Cabinet regarded the Perpetuity Purchase Fund as different from other church funds because it was not 'the property of any individuals in the Church, or of any Corporation in the Church'.[49] In any case most politicians had begun to accept that the property of the Irish Church was held in trust. Peel himself recognized the

[48] *Hansard*, 3rd ser., xxiv (1834), 1159; Derby Papers, box 172/2: Stanley to R. V. Smith, 21 Dec. 1835.

[49] *Hansard*, 3rd ser., xxiv (1834), 1163.

need for parliament to appropriate the Irish Church funds as part of the reform of the church, if only to Anglican ecclesiastical projects.[50] As Brougham pointed out in the Lords, if the Stanleyites agreed with Peel that it was possible to redistribute property within the church by Act of Parliament, then it was absurd to deny on principle parliament's right to reallocate the surplus. Stanley could only maintain the principle of absolute non-interference by aligning himself with the ultra-Tories, and asserting that parliament had no more right to interfere even in the internal organization of the church than it had in the management of a private estate.[51] Not only were such views rapidly becoming anachronistic, they were also scarcely compatible with the leadership of what was professedly a moderating force in politics.

According to Stanley, the ground for establishing a church was its truth. He wrote that 'The State supports the Protestant Church because as the State it believes in the truth of the doctrine of that Church and deems it for the good of the whole community that these doctrines should be promulgated by the State and endowed with a provision permanently appropriated to that object'. The Dilly leaders feared that to establish a church on the ground of its utility as an agent of religious education implied that this utility would be ascertained by its popularity alone. The consequence would be the establishment of the Catholic Church in Ireland and the dissolution of the Union. In the Lords Richmond expressed his apprehension 'that the establishment of a Catholic in the room of a Protestant Church was contemplated'.[52] Certainly many of the Whigs wished to pay the Roman Catholic clergy from government funds. Russell, for example, committed himself to this view in a memorandum he wrote following his visit to Ireland in late 1833, and the Irish administration had made such a proposal in the autumn of the same year.[53] But it was not anticipated that a Catholic endowment should be funded to the detriment of the finances of the Anglican clergy. Stanley himself had agreed to such an endowment when, as Irish Secretary, the

[50] Ibid., 60.
[51] Ibid., 303.
[52] Bod. Film 110 (Graham Papers): memo. by Stanley, 12 Mar. 1835; *Hansard*, 3rd ser., xxiv (1834), 269.
[53] Ogden MSS 84: Russell's Irish Jour., 7 Sept. [1833]; above p. 75.

Cabinet had instructed him to convey to the Catholic bishops an assurance of the government's willingness to pay £120–130,000 per annum to the Catholic clergy. Likewise Gally Knight, a 'Dilly' supporter with a 'disposition to magnify every danger', argued that the Catholic clergy should be paid by the state.[54] The Whigs, furthermore, in order to maintain an open door to Stanley, repeatedly emphasized that the institution of a commission of inquiry to ascertain the numbers of the Established Church in each parish and benefice in Ireland was not an indication of their intention to endow the Catholic Church out of Irish Church funds. Grey, Lansdowne, Brougham, Althorp, and Spring Rice all stated in 1834 that the government had no intention of appropriating surplus funds to support the Catholic Church. Brougham on behalf of the government even explicitly disclaimed Paley's and Warburton's doctrine that the religion of the majority should be endowed.[55] Certainly it was not a logical entailment of the Whig-instituted Commission that the so-called principle of popularity should be applied to the Irish Church. The numerical assessment of church attendance could equally well be applied to ascertain the genuine existence of congregations, and so test the church's efficiency in order to improve rather than destroy the Establishment. In parishes where no congregation existed the government could suppress the benefice and use the funds so freed for the propagation of religious truth elsewhere. Stanley inclined to acquiesce in such a scheme. He confessed that he was prepared to suppress livings in 'cases of a mere nominal congregation as no doubt will appear on the Commissioners' Report'.[56] Stanley concurred with the Whigs that the absence of a congregation as established by the Commission justified the reallocation of ecclesiastical revenues without endangering the existence of the establishment.

Howick, instead of exploiting such ambiguities and appealing to non-ecclesiastical sources of union, attempted to resolve them. He thus highlighted and reinforced the differences

[54] Kriegel, *Holland House Diaries*, 112–3; Derby Papers, box 132 bundle 5: Gally Knight to Stanley, 24 Dec. 1834; Grey Papers, box 118 file 9: Denison to Howick, 3 Dec. [1835].
[55] *Hansard*, 3rd ser., xxiv (1834), 256, 293, 304, 754, 776.
[56] Derby Papers, box 171: Stanley to Ridley, 31 Dec. 1834.

between the parties. In his two memoranda of 9 March and 16 March 1835 he only confirmed the fears which hitherto the Whigs had spent much energy in dispelling. In this correspondence he set out the general principles on which he was prepared to act as regards the Irish Church in the naïve belief that Stanley would acquiesce in them. He stated that his defence of an established church was on the ground of its utility, as understood by the discredited Paley, and not on the ground of its truth, which, invoking the Reformation doctrine of private judgement, he claimed was beyond the capacity of the legislature to ascertain. He implied that the utility of the church depended on its acceptability to the general populace. He suggested that in Ireland the association of the Protestant Church with the Orange Ascendancy through the act of endowment had the effect of 'indisposing the people to the Creed . . . and of extinguishing in those who ought to have disseminated the restored faith that power of the holy zeal in the name of truth'. Therefore he asserted that 'the religion of the majority ought to be preferred'. He suggested this was the lesson of experience as proven in the legislature's support for the Catholic religion in Canada and the Mahometan and Brahminical in India. He concluded that ideally the Roman Catholic Church should be established in Ireland, but since this was impracticable the legislature should apply the surplus revenues of the Anglican Church to education as this would most conduce to a religious end.[57] Stanley commented: 'I can not see in Lord Howick's proposition the basis of any safe settlement or compromise. The principles involved seem to me most dangerous'.[58] On 18 March Graham closed the Irish Church correspondence with Howick. By so stating his principles, Howick had rendered reconciliation impossible; he had confirmed Graham and Stanley in their intention to oppose their former colleagues. The old Foxite plan of Grey, namely to effect the return of High Churchmen to the Whig fold by shuffling on the church question, was no longer practicable.

Even if Howick had not committed this blunder, it would

[57] Bod. Film 110 (Graham Papers): Howick to Graham, 9 Mar. 1835, memo by Howick, enc. Howick to Graham, 9 Mar. 1835, memo by Howick, 16 Mar. 1835.
[58] Bod. Film 110 (Graham Papers): memo by Stanley, 12 Mar. 1835, Graham to Howick, 18 Mar. 1835.

still have been unlikely that Stanley and Graham could have given their full support to Russell's Irish Church resolution. This, drafted on 22 March, sought to appropriate the surplus to purposes of general education. Certainly Stanley did not deny that education was an ecclesiastical duty. He wrote: 'I admit as a *subsidiary* Church purpose if there were an unappropriated Church revenue, Education in the principles of the Church . . .'. Moreover, as Chief Secretary, he had established a National School system in Ireland, open to both Catholics and Protestants, which included mixed religious education. But he had never found this system of general religious education very satisfactory. He claimed that 'It never was supported as the *best possible* education for Protestants taken separately; but as the *most Protestant* because the most scriptural education which could be given to Protestants and Roman Catholics jointly.' He therefore opposed the experiment by Liverpool corporation to introduce the Irish mixed system into its own schools.[59] Graham's support for the National System had also been qualified. He regarded it not so much as a good in itself as an agency of conversion to the Protestant cause. He wrote that 'its true defence and practical utility are to be found in this single circumstance, that while nominally it is a scheme embracing Catholics and Protestants, in reality it is a plan for educating the Catholic population in tenets more scriptural and less exclusive than the priesthood would consent to tolerate in any other form'. Graham did not believe that non-dogmatic, non-sectarian religious education was possible: 'Experience proves that agreement on fundamental articles of the Christian faith as the basis of a mixed scheme of general instruction is delusive'.[60] Ultimately such views were bound to come into conflict with those of a Prime Minister and government who believed that 'the main opinions' of the Catholic Church were 'essentially the same' as those of the Church of England.[61]

The Stanleyites asserted that their dispute with their former colleagues was over the true nature of Whiggery. They believed that their resignations from the government in 1834 were

---

[59] Bod. Film 110 (Graham Papers): memo by Stanley, 12 Mar. 1835; Derby Papers, box 172/2: Stanley to A. Hodgeson, 6 Aug. 1836. On the origins of the Irish system see ch. 6 below.

[60] Brougham Papers, MS 14198: Graham to Brougham, 24 Oct. 1841.

[61] Torrens, *Memoirs of William Lamb*, 375.

undertaken to maintain the integrity of Whiggism immune
from Radical contagion. Graham wrote to Stanley's father that
the principles on which he had resigned were 'not inconsistent
with those genuine Whig principles' which he had first
embraced on entering public life, and which included 'the firm
maintenance of the Established Protestant religion, the religion
of perfect freedom which the Revolution of 1688 bore triumphant over Popery and regal tyranny'.[62] The failure of the
Stanleyites to reunite with the Whigs led by Russell marked
the end of the Foxite Grey's notion of the Whig party as a
broad coalition against Radicalism. It also marked the end of
the Whig conception of the constitution as being primarily
Anglican. There was no longer any room for a Whig party led
by High Churchmen, and the 'Derby Dilly' disintegrated. On
1 July Stanley and Graham established themselves on the
opposition bench below Peel, joined by only five or six followers. Their regular party meetings ceased. At the opening of
the session of 1836 Stanley recognized he could no longer
influence politics in the way he had hoped, and he declined
to lead anything like 'the formal union of an intermediate
party'.[63] The path was clear for the Whigs to emerge as the
exponents of liberal Anglicanism.

After the dismissal of the Whig government in November
1834, the running of the party was left by default to the more
radically inclined party organizers. By the beginning of
December, Melbourne was in Derbyshire, Russell in Devonshire, Grey and Howick in Northumberland, and Palmerston
in Hampshire. In the middle of December, Thomson informed
Howick that only Mulgrave, Duncannon, and himself were
left in London to do anything about the forthcoming elections.
With the aid of Hobhouse, these three prepared lists at Cleveland Square, assisted in selecting candidates for the elections,
and helped to distribute the Whigs' limited financial resources.
In the New Year they met to plan tactics for the new session.
On 12 January Duncannon, Hobhouse, and Mulgrave met to
discuss the re-election of Speaker Sutton. They agreed that
Hobhouse should begin negotiations with the English Radi-

---

[62] Parker, *Life and Letters of Sir James Graham* i. 195–6.
[63] Fulford & Strachey, *Greville Memoirs* iii. 219–20; Derby Papers, box 172/2: Stanley
to G. H. Vernon, 2 Jan. 1836.

cals; on the following day he consulted Hume, and the following week he talked to Warburton. Meanwhile Duncannon and Hobhouse kept Melbourne informed of developments. On 18 January Thomson and Hobhouse agreed that they should assemble the new MPs a few days before the opening of the session by writing to each returned MP who had designated himself a Reformer at the hustings. At the same time Duncannon was in touch with O'Connell, and at the end of January Warburton sent O'Connell circulars summoning him to the meeting proposed by Cleveland Square.[64] Such action occurred in a political vacuum; the Whig leaders hesitated in their country houses. On 19 January Hobhouse wrote to Melbourne demanding leadership from 'wiser heads than those which now consult together in Cleveland Square'. On the following day the more conservative Holland urged Melbourne to assume the mantle of leadership and resolve some important tactical considerations, a request which was repeated two days later.[65] Meanwhile the Whig leadership had begun to assert itself. Melbourne wrote to Duncannon recognizing the need to engage in a fight over the Speakership, and Russell travelled to Bowood to consult Lansdowne on that issue. Pessimistic about the prospects for a resurgent moderate Whig party, Melbourne summoned Hobhouse and Thomson to Brocket Hall on 24 January to confer with himself and Russell on tactics.[66]

There, in between shooting and eating, the representatives of Cleveland Square outlined their plans. On the evening of 25 January Thomson and Hobhouse pressed upon Russell the expediency of co-operating with Warburton, the leader of the English Radicals, and O'Connell, the leader of the Irish, both

[64] Grey Papers, box 127 file 7: Thomson to Howick, 13 Dec. 1834; BL Addit. MSS 61826 (Broughton Papers): Hobhouse Diary, 17 Dec. 1834, 12, 13, 23 Jan. 1835; BL Microfilm 859/2 (Melbourne Papers): Duncannon to Melbourne, 16 Jan. 1835, Hobhouse to Melbourne, 19 Jan. 1835; Bessborough Papers, file 201: O'Connell to Duncannon, 6 Dec. 1834; W. J. Fitzpatrick (ed.), *Correspondence of Daniel O'Connell* (London, 1888), i. 520; BL Addit. MSS 47227 (Broughton Papers), fo. 163: O'Connell to Warburton, 2 Feb. 1835; Torrens, *William Lamb*, 342.

[65] BL Microfilm 859/3 (Melbourne Papers): Hobhouse to Melbourne, 19 Jan. 1835, Holland to Melbourne, 20 Jan. 1835.

[66] Bessborough Papers, file 182: Melbourne to Duncannon, 18 Jan. 1835; Torrens, *William Lamb*, 333; BL Addit. MSS 61826 (Broughton Papers): Hobhouse Diary, 24 Jan. 1835.

to be subordinate to Russell's overall command. Two days later Duncannon joined the party to urge the necessity of negotiating with O'Connell. They pressed this course of action not because they approved of 'the Liberator', but because they feared the consequences if the Whigs did not take the lead in opposing Peel's government. As early as the previous December Duncannon was urging both his friends and Melbourne that the dismissed Prime Minister should not abandon the leadership since he, uniquely, stood 'so high with the whole party, radicals and all'. Duncannon feared that the effect of the dismissal would be to increase the influence of such Radicals as Durham and O'Connell, and so to encourage 'the overthrow of Protestantism in Ireland and consequently strike a hard blow at the Church'. Accepting the fact of their strength, he suggested that such events could only be prevented if the Whigs agreed to work with the Radicals, and so moderate their influence. Whig leadership of the Radical forces was an unpleasant, but possible, act of necessity.[67] There were tensions within this Whig camp. Duncannon was prepared to conciliate those Whigs who opposed his means. Hobhouse noted that following a violent row with Howick on 18 February, Duncannon recommended 'keeping the peace'. Unfortunately not all members of the Cleveland Square party were quite so temperate. Both Thomson and Hobhouse, for example, thought Russell should exclude Howick from Whig inner counsels, and Hobhouse even threatened to cease participating in opposition Cabinets if Howick were to be present.[68] The Cleveland Square party was in danger of unnecessarily splitting the Whig party to the benefit of the Radicals.

At this late January country-house party in Hertfordshire, Melbourne and Russell rejected the Cleveland Square plan for party organization. Their problem was to formulate one of their own. Initially Russell had been sympathetic to Grey's line. Brougham reported that Russell had formed a resolution

[67] BL Addit. MSS 61826 (Broughton Papers): Hobhouse Diary, 25, 27, Jan. 1835; Mulgrave Castle Archives, box O (Normanby Papers), fo. 870: Thomson to Mulgrave, 25 Jan. 1835; BL Microfilm 859/2 (Melbourne Papers): Duncannon to Melbourne, 18 Dec. 1835; Mulgrave Castle Archives, box M (Normanby Papers), fo. 96: Duncannon to Mulgrave, 27 Dec. 18[34].

[68] BL Addit. MSS 61826 (Broughton Papers): Hobhouse Diary, 18 Feb., 13 Mar. 1835.

'to do nothing that Howick dislikes'. By February, however, Russell thought that the exiled Grey was out of touch with political developments. He explained to Melbourne: 'What Lord Grey says . . . is I think said in ignorance of the temper of the Commons, of the Country, nay of the Tories'.[69] Most of the senior Whig politicians accepted the need to proceed aggressively against Peel's government if they were to remain in control of the opposition. Palmerston wrote to Russell supporting a contest for the Speakership, and Spencer recommended that the Whigs propose an amendment to the Address from the Throne.[70] Russell acquiesced in such opinions, but he refused to have direct dealings with O'Connell. At the beginning of February Hobhouse informed O'Connell through the double mediation of Wellesley and Blake that Russell refused to communicate directly with Irish MPs. When O'Connell wrote to Russell pledging support, the latter composed a circumspect reply which Duncannon had to amend, lest it caused offence.[71] Russell's policy was deliberately ambiguous. He told Wood that his sympathies lay with the Grey family;[72] but many of his actions on particular issues were in accord with Cleveland Square. His task was to lead the Whig party without irreparably offending either wing. He thus refused both to seek reunion with Stanley (on account of the Irish Church issue) and to enter into a formal alliance with O'Connell. In the first few months reunion could be avoided by prudent inactivity, but Russell needed to be more assertive if he was not to acquire a reputation for collaborating with O'Connell.

The meeting at 12 noon, Wednesday, 18 February 1835 at 13 St James's Square, Lord Lichfield's London house, could not be avoided (the circulars had been sent to Whig, Radical, and Irish MPs before Russell had resolved upon a strategy). But its tone and significance had yet to be determined. Thomson and Hobhouse had originally intended that the meeting should confirm Russell in his leadership of a united opposition

---

[69] BL Addit. MSS 51563 (Holland House Papers), fo. 115: Brougham to Holland, 26 Dec. 1834; R. Russell, *Corresp. of Lord John Russell*, ii. 89.

[70] PRO 30/22 1E (Russell Papers), fo. 10; Palmerston to Russell, 22 Jan. 1835; R. Russell, *Corresp. of Lord John Russell*, ii. 76–8.

[71] Walpole, *Russell*, i. 220–2.

[72] Halifax Papers A8/1/1: Wood Jour., 14 Feb. 1835.

by having some one stand up in the course of the meeting to request Russell to issue summonses for future assemblies. Russell was also supposed to announce a specific date for further meetings. In this manner the Radicals and Irish were to acknowledge Whig leadership. When Wood informed Howick of this, the latter's immediate reaction was to consult Russell at his house in Queen Street, and to dissuade him from this course. Russell agreed to limit the business of the meeting to arranging the opposition's conduct in the debate on the Speakership. Wood persuaded Warburton to acquiesce in this restriction. Thus the Lichfield House meeting of 135 MPs had a significance contrary to the initial desire of Cleveland Square. It did not cement an alliance between O'Connell and the Whigs, but forestalled its occurrence. The event did not in itself guarantee Russell's control of Whig tactics; rather it announced the opening of a contest between members of the Foxite Grey's camp, led in London by Howick, who sought to restrain precipitate action in order to keep alive negotiations with Stanley, and those at Cleveland Square, who thought party unity could only be preserved by pursuing an active opposition. The effects of this contest were felt throughout the remainder of February and March. In a meeting of Whig leaders on 22 February, for example, a disagreement occurred over whether or not Hobhouse should support the Radical Hume's proposal to table a motion of no confidence in the government. The contest was not finally settled until the Whig leaders had to decide on the line they would take with respect to another of Hume's motions, this time to limit government supplies to three months, and the negotiations with Stanley had collapsed. Russell meanwhile preserved a fraught unity by skilfully hesitating between the two camps.[73]

On Tuesday, 3 March, Mulgrave, Thomson, and Hobhouse met at Russell's to discuss the propriety of holding a general meeting of the party and the proposed motion to vote the supply for only three months. Russell, conscious of Grey's opposition to any dealings with O'Connell, objected to both the motion and to the meeting. After the conference Hobhouse

[73] Grey Papers C3/1B: Howick Journ., 18 Feb. 1835; Halifax Papers A8/1/1: Wood Jour., 18 Feb. 1835; BL Addit. MSS 61826 (Broughton Papers): Hobhouse Diary, 18, 22 Feb. 1835.

and Russell visited Melbourne who concurred in placing a premium on Grey's co-operation.[74] Wood and Howick pursued a policy of delay as they knew that Stanley would oppose such a motion. At a meeting at Brooks's on the 5th they were able to persuade Hobhouse, Mulgrave, Morpeth, Carter (a leading back-bencher), and Russell to postpone any decision for a few days. On the 6th Wood lobbied Warburton and persuaded him that opinions should be canvassed before any decision was reached; on the 8th he had a long conversation with Rice who agreed that the opposition would lose the vote on supplies.[75] Meanwhile rumours of ministerial changes induced Russell and Melbourne to reverse their opinions and to support Hume's motion instead, virtually agreeing that Hobhouse should propose it. On the 9th Russell and Melbourne travelled to Woburn to consult Lord Grey who was staying there on his way from Northumberland to London. Acting unilaterally, Wood ordered Hobhouse not to send out the notes summoning MPs to a meeting on the 13th; but on the 10th Thomson and Mulgrave rejected this interference and issued the notices.[76]

The meeting at Woburn proved crucial. Although Russell was unable to placate the recalcitrant Grey, he once again altered his opinion and returned to London on the 10th pledged against the supply motion. He summoned a meeting for the 11th to discuss the issue. Two camps emerged: Mulgrave, Thomson, Hobhouse, and Spencer in favour of Hume's motion, Lansdowne, Spring Rice, Howick, and Wood against. Russell, judiciously ambiguous, represented himself as undecided. The upshot was that, as Hume had already tabled his motion, Hobhouse could not wrest it from him and so turn it into a proposal officially sponsored by the Whigs; nor could the Whigs' friends be expected to support the proposition of a Radical. Rather than permit such divisions being made public, the Whig leaders agreed to persuade Hume to withdraw his motion. Since the meeting called by Mulgrave and Thomson could not be de-summoned, despite the protests of Wood and Howick, they agreed to use this forum to dissuade Hume

[71] BL Addit. MSS 61826 (Broughton Papers): Hobhouse Diary, 5 Mar. 1835.
[75] Halifax Papers A8/1/1: Wood Jour., 2, 5, 6, 8 Mar. 1835.
[76] Ibid., 7, 9 Mar. 1835; BL Addit. MSS 61826 (Broughton Papers): Hobhouse Diary, 9, 10 Mar. 1835.

from proceeding. On the appropriately selected Friday 13th at Lichfield House, where 180 MPs had assembled, they succeeded in persuading Hume to withdraw his motion. Russell thus ensured that he was free from Radical domination. The Radical initiative to overthrow Peel's government (the supply motion) had been thwarted, and the liberal Anglican initiative (the Irish Church resolution) could proceed in its own course. At the same time, because of the protests of Howick and Wood, Russell could preserve his reputation for having Radical sympathies.[77]

At the Lichfield House meeting, O'Connell also made a plea to Hume to withdraw his motion and to support the Irish Church resolution then expected for the 23rd.[78] This request was not made because he considered Irish Church reform to be in Ireland's best interests. Indeed O'Connell was to display almost indecent haste in his wish to abandon the appropriation clause. As early as 2 July 1835 Mulgrave, newly appointed Lord Lieutenant of Ireland, wrote to his Chief Secretary, Morpeth, that the Irish MPs had 'by looking into the question found out that appropriation of the surplus would never be of much advantage to them'. Consequently, he suggested, they would be prepared to relinquish the clause if this would guarantee the safe passage through the Lords of the Irish Municipal Bill. In April the following year O'Connell volunteered to throw over the appropriation clause, and by the end of June he had given notice of a new plan for Irish tithes which altogether omitted that clause.[79] The Whig Cabinet met to discuss this move on 25 June when the ministers unanimously agreed to stand by the Irish Church resolution of April 1835. Hobhouse recorded: 'We all confessed that if O'Connell declares against appropriation there is an end of the administration for we would stand by our resolution & if we fall, fall with honour.'[80] Duncannon resolved to dissuade O'Connell

[77] Halifax Papers A8/1/1: Wood Jour., 10, 11, 12 Mar. 1835; BL Addit. MSS 61826 (Broughton Papers): Hobhouse Diary, [11], 12 Mar. 1835; Grey Papers C3/1B: Howick Jour., 11 Mar. 1835; Kriegel, *Holland House Diaries*, 282; SCRO MSS D260/M/F/5/26 (Hatherton Papers), ix. 65: E. J. Littleton Jour., 10 [Mar. 1835].

[78] Halifax Papers A/8/1/1: Wood Jour., 12 Mar. 1835.

[79] Carlisle Papers J.19.19, fo. 64: Mulgrave to Morpeth, 2 July [1835]; Mulgrave Castle Archives, box M (Normanby Papers), fo. 543: Morpeth to Mulgrave, 26 Apr. 1836.

[80] BL Addit. MSS 56558 (Broughton Papers): Hobhouse Diary, 25 June 1836;

from fulfilling his notice of intent. O'Connell acquiesced not because Irish appropriation was essential to his own policy, but because the Whigs had deemed it essential to theirs.

O'Connell's attitude was comprehensible: the Irish Church resolution was simply a flag of convenience under which he could lead his ratings to the Whig ship. In itself it was unlikely to confer benefit upon Ireland. Not only was there considerable doubt as to whether a surplus actually existed, but even the Whigs were less than sanguine in believing that a measure of appropriation would quell agitation. In January 1836 Mulgrave noted the existence of agrarian combinations 'arising from struggles to possess land' in a country where 'ejectment in the absence of any other provision' led to 'inevitable starvation'. By September he was advocating a moderate public works programme for the relief of Irish distress including the encouragement of fisheries and the improvement of agriculture. In February and March 1838 the Irish government began pressing for the appropriation of rent-charges to finance the construction of trade-inducing railways.[81]

O'Connell himself was primarily concerned with more self-interested matters. He had recommended the Repeal agitation in 1834 because he then feared that Grey intended to reintroduce the Coercion Bill with the public meetings clauses, the effect of which would have been to ban his political organization. In his October speeches for that year, however, O'Connell reserved his wrath for the Whigs' judicial appointments which he had unsuccessfully sought to influence. It was because Blackburne continued to hold the office of Irish Attorney-General against O'Connell's wishes, that he changed his political tactics, believing it to be a sign that the Whig government was reluctant to pursue an active policy of dismantling the Protestant Ascendancy as enshrined in the Irish legal system. He addressed his public letters no longer to Duncannon, the Home Secretary, but to Durham, who was then undertaking a Scottish speaking tour which culminated

Mulgrave Castle Archives, box M (Normanby Papers), fo. 546: Morpeth to Mulgrave, 25 June 1836.

[81] Carlisle Papers, MSS J 19.1.10, fo. 62: Mulgrave to Russell, 16 Jan. 1836; PRO 30/22 2C (Russell Papers), fo. 113: Mulgrave to Russell, 13 Sept. 1836; PRO 30/22 3A (Russell Papers), fos. 151, 224: Mulgrave to Russell, 21 Feb. 1838, Drummond to Russell, 20 Mar. 1838.

in the Glasgow dinner of 29 October 1834 and the announcement of his support for household suffrage, short parliaments,
and the ballot. Having once sought to embarrass the government, when the King dismissed the Whigs in November,
O'Connell again altered his tone. The Whigs, after all, were
more pliable patrons than the Tories. At a meeting in the
Dublin Corn Exchange he transformed himself into a con-
ciliator prepared to praise even Grey's ministry for its many
benefits. Support for the Whig party's known stance on the
Irish Church was one means by which O'Connell could
reaccommodate himself to the ministers he had spurned consistently for the past month. Indeed O'Connell had so alienated
the Whigs that as early as 2 September Russell had recommended
to Melbourne that, among measures to deal with the Irish
menace, the public meetings clauses of the Coercion Bill should
be reintroduced. Irish appropriation was necessary to
O'Connell as a means to revive a displaced sympathy, to put
himself once more in the position of court supplicant.[82]

The cause of the Whigs' obsession with Irish appropriation
is rather less clear. Certainly there were immediate tactical
advantages to be gained from its advocacy in 1835 since it
was a means to rally the support of both Whigs and Radicals
without appearing to compromise the principles of either
group. But this is not an explanation of why, as has been
demonstrated, a number of the Whigs (a combination of liberal
Anglicans and 'young' Whigs) had taken up the issue as early
as 1832; nor does it explain why they persisted with this issue
long after the Irish had lost interest in the subject. Appropriation remained a shibboleth for these Whigs until the 1837
election, and even after this release they still refused to rescind
the Irish Church resolution, as their successful opposition to
Acland's motion of May 1838 demonstrated. Russell and Melbourne appear to have adopted their policy towards the Irish
Church primarily out of conviction, even if the timing of their
public conversion was determined by the contingent advantages it brought. This perhaps was most clearly revealed in

---

[82] Fitzpatrick, *Corres. of Daniel O'Connell* i. 442, 488, 493; *Morning Chronicle*, 25 Nov.
1834; BL Microfilm 859/6 (Melbourne Papers): Russell to Melbourne, 2 Sept. 1834;
SCRO MSS D593/8/22/1/3 (Leveson–Gower Papers): Lansdowne to Sutherland, 29
Dec. [1834].

the winter of 1836 when, following the double rejection of the
Irish Tithes Bill by the Lords, the Whigs once again set to
the wearing task of considering their course. In an atmosphere
amounting almost to quiet despair at the government's
inability to persuade parliament to acquiesce in an Irish
measure, Duncannon, O'Connell's representative in the
Cabinet, proposed, as he put it, to do 'almost nothing'. He
suggested that the government should only introduce a Bill to
encourage voluntary conversion of tithes into a rent-charge,
and to omit appropriation altogether. This the Cabinet, led
by Melbourne, rejected. In the face of English hostility and
Irish indifference the Irish government suggested the more
radical plan of concurrent endowment. Morpeth's scheme was
to abolish tithes, raise a land tax and out of this revenue
support the Anglican, Catholic, and Presbyterian churches.
The Cabinet also rejected this scheme as being impractical.
Instead serious consideration was given to Russell's own
scheme which was to divide the Bill, one part authorizing the
conversion of tithes into a rent-charge, the other to establish
a land tax to be appropriated to non-Anglican purposes. The
Cabinet debate was not about the merits of appropriation:
this was the *sine qua non* of any measure. Rather it centred on
whether or not Russell's measure entailed the rejection of
appropriation, Spring Rice, Palmerston, Lansdowne, and
Russell denying, Howick, Thomson, Hobhouse affirming that
it did so. In the end the traditionalists won the argument and
preserved their sense of honour.[83] Both the debate and the
outcome revealed that the Whigs, independently of O'Connell
and immediate party gain, were committed to a reformation
of the Irish Church. The Cabinet division as to means disguised
a unanimity of purpose.

On the day Peel resigned office, a last ditch attempt at
reconciling Grey to the new Whig strategy took place. Having
himself failed to persuade his father to head a government,
Howick spoke to Lansdowne to initiate a joint letter from the
Whig leaders requesting Grey to resume office. Lansdowne,

[83] BL Addit. MSS 61827 (Broughton Papers): Hobhouse Diary, 24 Nov., 3 Dec.
1836; PRO 30/22 2D (Russell Papers), fos. 44, 108: Morpeth to Russell, 19 Nov.
1836; paper by Russell on Irish Tithes, 4 Dec. 1836; Mulgrave Castle Archives, box
M (Normanby Papers), fo. 851: Russell to Mulgrave, 4 Dec. 1836.

Melbourne, Holland, Palmerson, and Spring Rice all signed,
but Russell, attending his own wedding, was out of town and
conveniently unable to do so. A note from the King was
appended to this missive, but to no avail. Grey, aware of the
impossibility of pursuing his own strategy, refused to comply
and entered a graceless retirement.[84] It was a symbolic reminder that the liberal Anglican Whigs had triumphed over Grey.
Under Melbourne's and Russell's leadership a government
emerged committed to the appropriation of the Irish Church
surplus, but comparatively untainted by Radicalism. The new
Prime Minister excluded both Brougham (whom the Whigs
had made the public scapegoat for their dismissal in November
1834) and the Radical's hero, Durham. He also vetoed O'Connell's appointment and in November rejected Ebrington's
suggestion of entering into an understanding with him.[85] On
the other hand, Lansdowne, who had considered retirement
in May 1834, resumed office along with Spring Rice and
Howick, who had established themselves in the course of 1835
as political moderates as regards O'Connell, if not on the Irish
Church question. On 18 April Graham reported to Stanley
his disappointment that the Radicals were displeased with
Melbourne's appointments. Stanley himself gracefully
accepted (in part) Sir Harry Verney's conclusion 'in thinking
that in its component parts the Government is less Radical
than might have been expected'.[86] What transpired in 1834–5
was less a change in the Whigs from being a party of conservative reformism to one of Radicalism, than from being defenders of High Anglicanism to being exponents of liberal
Anglicanism. This was a change which such Whig leaders as
Russell and such back-benchers as Ebrington had brought
about. Melbourne's government, formed on the issue of the
Irish Church, did not so much mark the dominance of Irish
MPs as an end to the policy of Grey and Stanley. It marked
the acquiescence of old Foxites such as Holland and
Lansdowne, if they were to remain active Whig politicians, in

      [84] Grey Papers C3/1B: Howick Jour., 8, 11 Apr. 1835; Halifax Papers A8/1/1:
Wood Jour., 12 Apr. 1835.
      [85] L. C. Sanders (ed.), *Lord Melbourne's Papers* (London, 1889), 237; DCRO MSS
1262M FC 91 (Fortescue Papers): Melbourne to Ebrington, 10 Nov. 1835.
      [86] Bod. Film 110 (Graham Papers): Graham to Stanley, 18 Apr. 1835; Derby
Papers, box 171: Stanley to Verney, n.d. [Apr. 1835].

a policy of liberal reforms of the church. While nominally still occupying senior posts in the new administration, such politicians lost their positions of dominance in the cross-fire between Stanley and Russell. In political terms the emergence of liberal Anglicanism was now possible.

Neither the present nor the previous chapter has offered any conclusion about the personal as opposed to the political commitment of liberal Anglican politicians to the causes which they supported. Indeed in both chapters it has been acknowledged that the Whigs reaped considerable political benefits from such support, which they gave, in part, in anticipation of these rewards. It would thus be possible to re-write the previous two chapters in a cynical reductionist tone, suggesting that 'liberal Anglicanism' had no intrinsic interest since it was merely a means to achieve office. Certainly the political evidence available would make such an interpretation possible. The problem is whether it is possible to choose between two plausible accounts, the one suggesting that 'liberal Anglicanism' was a cynical ruse, the other that it was the product of personal commitment. The contention here is that such a choice is indeed possible, but that it cannot be made solely on the basis of the available political evidence. It is suggested that when the personal religious beliefs of liberal Anglican politicians are taken into account, it is more plausible to argue that these Whig politicians acted out of conviction rather than calculation. It is the purpose of the following two chapters to examine the nature of the religious belief of the proponents of the liberal Anglican political creed. In so doing, an attempt is made to defend the Whigs from the charge that they were all religious sceptics.

3

Personal Religion and Lives of Devotion

Two claims have been made concerning the Whigs' liberal outlook in ecclesiastical affairs: the first, that it was the product of religious indifference; the second that its intellectual origins lay in the Scottish Enlightenment rather than in Anglican thought. The first was the argument of the Whigs' contemporaries, and was used as a political jibe to excite fears about the security of the Anglican establishment. They suggested that Whiggish religious scepticism would make it easy for liberal governments to concede Radical demands for the destruction of the state's Anglican institutions. In 1832 Arnold reminded Brougham that the High Church party had joined the Evangelicals in order to raise 'the cry of Irreligion against the Government'; indeed, the Tory High Church peer, Lord Kenyon, viewed the party conflict of 1834 as a choice between 'vital Christianity' and 'infidelity'.[1] Historians, such as Professor Best, have been responsible for making the second claim. He argued that Whig Christianity was 'largely a blend of the classical precepts of morality and the moral sense of the Scottish philosophers', albeit made respectable by the addition of a few biblical exhortations.[2] It is necessary to consider these two claims in order to establish that the political adoption of a liberal religious rhetoric by liberal Anglican Whigs, most notably Russell, was not merely the outcome of expediency, but was also in keeping with their sense of the religious; that the liberalism, which these politicians embodied, involved not a rejection of, but a reflection upon Anglican theology and ecclesiology. In this chapter the personal religion of Whig Cabinet ministers is discussed, and it is shown that the younger generations of Whig politicians were not exempt from the

---

[1] Brougham Papers, MS 10271: Arnold to Brougham, 9 Apr. 1832; *Morning Chronicle*, 5 Dec. 1834.
[2] G.F.A. Best, 'The Whigs and the Church Establishment in the Age of Holland and Grey', *History*, xlv (1960), 107.

Victorian religious revival which affected their Tory counter-parts such as Shaftesbury and Gladstone, even if the Anglicanism to which they subscribed was of a different kind.

Assuming, as historians must, that religious faith is an historical fact, and not the disguised expression of some other, more deeply rooted, phenomenon,[3] it is not easy to assert with confidence that particular Whig politicians possessed a distinctive Anglican faith. This is not only because of the indeterminate nature of much of the available evidence, but also because it is difficult to know what it would mean for such a politician to have a religious faith. Our understanding of what constituted aristocratic Victorian piety is peculiarly limited. Perhaps because so many of the 'intellectual aristocracy' of this century have owed their origins to the Evangelical Clapham Sect of the last, it has become conventional to attribute the religious renewal of the nineteenth-century English aristocracy to the Evangelical movement. G. M. Young, in his influential essay of 1934, appeared to go so far as to identify Victorian history with the intellectual Odysseys of the lapsed-Evangelical editor of the *Dictionary of National Biography*, Leslie Stephen, and his apostatizing companions. According to Young 'Victorian history is the story of the English mind employing the energy imparted by Evangelical conviction to rid itself of the constraints which Evangelicalism had laid on the senses and the intellect; on amusement, enjoyment, art; on curiosity, on criticism, on science'.[4] The most common model of aristocratic Evangelical piety in the Victorian age is that of Lord Shaftesbury, the Tory paternalist, but it would be a mistake to regard this politician as the archetypal Anglican in politics. This is not simply because he was idiosyncratic in his religion (he had, for example, no experience of 'conversion'); nor because, as Dr Hilton has shown, the term 'Evangelicalism' covers a variety of religious and political outlooks, which cannot be subsumed in a consideration of one man.[5] It is primarily

[3] For a critical account of attempts to explain religious belief as the product of some other phenomenon, see D. Z. Phillips, *Religion without Explanation* (Oxford, 1976).

[4] See N. G. Annan, 'The Intellectual Aristocracy' in J. H. Plumb (ed.), *Studies in Social History: A Tribute to G. M. Trevelyan* (London, 1955), 241–87; G. M. Young, 'Portrait of an Age' in G. M. Young (ed.), *Early Victorian England* (Oxford, 1951), ii. 417.

[5] See G. B. A. M. Finlayson, *The Seventh Earl of Shaftesbury* (London, 1981); A. J. B. Hilton, 'The Role of Providence in Evangelical Society Thought' in D. Beales and

because the range of religious experience, which affected Anglican politicians in the nineteenth century, cannot be contained within the term 'Evangelical'.

In so far as historians have recognized this, it has only been to create a category of High Church politicians. In his Ford lectures, Kitson Clark noted: 'Evangelical Christianity had made its inroads into the nobility to be followed a little later by the Oxford Movement and the Catholic revival.'[6] The effect of such perceptions is that several historians have turned their attention to a Gladstone pursuing High Church causes in British politics.[7] But Gladstone, although abetted by such front-bench spokesmen as Roundell Palmer, Lord Chancellor in his first government, and J. D. Coleridge, who became Lord Chief Justice, found himself at odds not only with nonconformist back-benchers in the Liberal party which he led, but also with the Liberal leadership, which, on the whole, looked elsewhere for its spiritual ministrations. Dr Parry has identified this for the last quarter of the nineteenth century as the 'Rugby-Balliol' tradition.[8] The existence of such (and its designation by some as 'Broad Church'), however, was not acknowledged formally until the 1850s: by A. P. Stanley in the *Quarterly Review*, by W. J. Conybeare in the *Edinburgh Review*, and by J. H. Rigg in his book, *Modern Anglican Theology*.[9] Thus for the 1830s there is no acknowledged model of the religiously minded liberal aristocrat, against which any particular Whig might be assessed. To use existing Tractarian or Evangelical studies, on the other hand, would clearly be misleading. Consequently an assessment of whether the practices of any particular Whig signified the possession of religious commitment must begin with a consideration of the only model of behaviour available: that of their fathers and elders. A third category of Anglican piety must be established for the early nineteenth century.

In discussing Whig religious affiliations, it is important to

G. Best (eds.), *History, Society, and the Churches: Essays in Honour of Owen Chadwick* (Cambridge, 1985), 215–33.

  [6] G. S. R. Kitson Clark, *The Making of Victorian England* (London, 1962), 217.
  [7] See Shannon, *Gladstone* for bibliography.
  [8] Parry, 'Religion and the Collapse of Gladstone's First Government', 76.
  [9] [W. J. Conybeare], 'Church Parties', *Edinburgh Review*, xcviii (1853), 330; [A. P. Stanley]. 'Archdeacon Hare', *Quarterly Review*', xcvii (1855), 19; J. H. Rigg, *Modern Anglican Theology* (London, 1857), 31.

note the different groups of Whigs revealed by a prosopographical analysis of Whig Cabinet ministers for the years
1830 to 1841. These are established on the basis of age in
1830, the year of entry into parliament, the date of holding
political office, the political affiliation of family, place of education and religious adherence (the first three categories are
designed to establish the political generation of a Whig, the
last three the tradition in which he was brought up).[10] Such
an analysis indicates the existence of three generations, which
may be classed as that associated with the Ministry of All the
Talents of 1806–7, that with the years in opposition (particularly after 1818–19), and that of the resurgence of Whiggery
in the years of Catholic Emancipation (1829), the Reform Bill,
and government. These generations do not correlate directly
with age, since natural differences are displaced by attaining
and exercising office. For example, although Radnor and
Lansdowne were almost exact contemporaries, Lansdowne
accepted the Chancellorship of the Exchequer in the Talents
ministry, whereas Radnor refused the offer of a Lordship of
the Treasury. Not until after 1816 did Radnor's views gain a
widespread currency in the party. Thus he should be classified
as belonging to the second generation, while Lansdowne
should be classified with the first. Likewise, although Sir
George Grey and Sir Francis Baring were contemporaries of
Morpeth and Howick, they had more in common with Spencer
and Fortescue, and should be classified with these rather than
with the third generation. In this manner, the views which
are properly associated with one generation may have
outlasted that generation's span in active life. A further cause
of distortion was the influx into the Whig fold in 1830 of some
of the followers of the liberal Tory, George Canning. These,
such as Palmerston, did not always find their allies among
their Whig contemporaries, such as Russell, but often sought
them among an older generation. But this distortion is not
sufficient to render the notion useless in an analysis of the
party leadership in this period, which passed from generation
to generation, from that of Holland and Grey, rejuvenated by
Melbourne and Palmerston, to that of Spencer and Grant,
and so to that of Russell, Morpeth, and Howick: from sceptical

[10] See Table 1.

Personal Religion and Lives of Devotion

Table 1. A Prosopographical Analysis of Whig Cabinet Ministers 1830–41

Name	Age in 1830	Year of entering parliament	Office pre-1830	Office Post-1841	University	Family	Religion
Grey	66	1786	*	—	Cambridge	Whig	—
Holland	57	1796	*	—	Oxford	Whig	—
Carlisle	57	1795	*	—	Oxford	Whig	—
Abercromby	54	1807	*	—	—	Whig	?
Brougham	52	1810	—	—	Edinburgh	?Tory	Evangelical
Grant	52	1811	*	—	Cambridge	Canningite	—
Melbourne	51	1806	*	—	Cambridge & Glasgow	Whig-Canningite	—
(Radnor)	51	1801	—	—	Oxford & Edinburgh	Pittite	Evangelical
Lansdowne	50	1802	*	*	Cambridge & Edinburgh	Whig	—
Duncannon	49	1805	—	*	Oxford	Whig	?
Ellice	49	1818	—	*	Aberdeen	Commercial	—
Cottenham	49	1831	—	—	Cambridge	?	?High
Spencer	48	1804	*	—	Cambridge	Pittite	?Evangelical
Minto	48	1806	—	*	Edinburgh	Whig	Presbyterian
Ripon	48	1806	*	*	Cambridge	Canningite	High
(Ebrington)	47	1804	—	—	Oxford	Grenvillite	Evangelical
Palmerston	46	1806	*	*	Edinburgh	Tory	—
Auckland	48	1810	—	*	Oxford	Whig	?High
Hobhouse	44	1820	—	*	Cambridge	Whig	?Liberal
Spring Rice	40	1820	*	—	Cambridge	Whig	Liberal

Richmond	39	1812	—	—	—	Tory	High
Durham	38	1813	—	—	—	Whig	?
Russell	38	1813	—	*	Edinburgh	Whig	Liberal
Graham	38	1818	—	*	Oxford	Tory	High
Baring	34	1826	—	—	Oxford	Commercial	Evangelical
Normanby	33	1818	—	*	Cambridge	Tory	Liberal
Labouchere	32	1826	—	—	Oxford	Commercial	Evangelical
Thomson	31	1826	—	—	—	Commercial	?Liberal
Stanley	31	1822	*	*	Oxford	Whig	High
Grey (Sir George)	31	1832	—	*	Oxford	Whig	Evangelical
Macaulay	30	1830	—	—	Cambridge	Tory	?
Clarendon	30	1838	—	*	—	Tory	—
Howick	28	1826	—	*	Cambridge	Whig	Liberal
Morpeth	28	1826	—	*	Oxford	Whig	Liberal

* held office.

NB Although neither Ebrington nor Radnor were Cabinet Ministers, they have been included in this table since they were leading politicians within the Whig party at a time when the Whigs were out of office.

old Foxites, via Evangelical 'young' Whigs, to liberal Anglicans.[11] In the following consideration of these generations, the renegades of 1834 (Stanley, Graham, Richmond, and Ripon), and their High Anglican defence of the integrity of the Church of England, have been ignored. This chapter is concerned with the Whig leadership as it actually developed, not as it might have been.

While claiming to consider the religious attitudes of the Whig Party as a whole in the 'Age of Holland and Grey', Best referred in fact almost exclusively to such stalwarts of the Foxite faith as its begetter himself, Holland, Brougham, Bishop Bathurst as their representative cleric, and Melbourne as their borrowed leader. The purpose of Best's article was to show that a belief in the virtues of a tolerant Established Church need not be grounded on a religious faith, that unchristian Whigs might still defend a tolerant Anglican Church, albeit on arguments derived from non-Anglican premises. Although it is certainly true that a particular generation of Whigs in the governments of the 1830s possessed an irreverent, eighteenth-century, Enlightenment form of Christianity, the particular should not be allowed to stand for the whole. This early generation comprised such Whigs as Grey, Holland, the 6th Earl of Carlisle, Brougham, Lansdowne, Melbourne, and Palmerston. These men received their education at either an unreformed Cambridge (Grey was a friend of Thomas Adkin, with whom he frequented the White Bear Inn opposite Trinity College, popularly known as Adkin's College) or at a Scottish university preaching a variation of Thomas Reid's moral sense philosophy (Palmerston, up at Edinburgh University before proceeding to St John's College, Cambridge, boarded at the house of Dugald Stewart, Reid's eloquent exponent, and Professor of Moral Philosophy in the university).[12] With the exception of Brougham and the Canningites Palmerston and Melbourne, these Whigs all held office in the last Whig government of 1806 (which was also the occasion of Brougham's

[11] For a definition of 'young' Whigs see, Wasson, 'The Young Whigs' (Ph.D. thesis), for 'Liberal Anglicans' see, D. Forbes, *The Liberal Anglican Idea of History* (Cambridge, 1950) and below. See also political analysis contained in Chs 1 and 2 above.

[12] Trevelyan, *Lord Grey of the Reform Bill*, 9; K. Bourne, *Palmerston: The Early Years 1784–1841* (London, 1982), 12.

conversion to Whiggery). This brand of Foxite influence declined dramatically with the destruction of Grey's ministry in 1834. Carlisle and Grey retired to Castle Howard and Howick Hall respectively, and Brougham was excluded from Melbourne's second administration. Holland, still in office, confined himself to questions of foreign affairs when not ill with gout, while Melbourne complained that Fox's descendant was now a 'fatiguing old woman'.[13] According to Howick, Lansdowne had become a 'mere cypher', while Mulgrave accused him of being 'lazy'. His political stock, in any case, had fallen to a low point, as far as younger Whigs were concerned, as a consequence of his co-operation with Canning's liberal Tory government of 1827.[14] Only Melbourne and Palmerston retained their political authority, and, of the entire group, only Lansdowne and Palmerston were to hold office after 1841. When Palmerston became Prime Minister in 1855, he did so half a generation after most of Fox's immediate heirs had faded from the political scene.

Grey's biographer, Trevelyan, omitted to discuss his subject's religion. Despite having a Tory High Church bishop (who was addicted to laudanum) for a brother, and a High Church Archdeacon for a chaplain (Thorp, the first Warden of Durham University), this omission appears a reasonable indication of Grey's sense of the spiritual.[15] As a youth, he was noted for his 'violent temper and unbounded ambition' as well as his affair with the Duchess of Devonshire by whom he had an illegitimate child, Eliza Courtenay. As the leader of the Whig party he objected to the group which had gathered around his brother-in-law, Whitbread, which had adopted 'a new', and by implication improved, 'code of political morality and honour'.[16] His closest political ally and friend was the 3rd Baron Holland, who openly declared that he had never been to church in London in his life. At his death, the mother of

[13] Grey Papers C3/1B: Howick Jour, 23 Ap. 1835.

[14] Ibid., 15 July 1834; PRO 30/22 3B (Russell Papers), fo. 230: Mulgrave to Russell, 29 July 1838; Walpole, *Russell*, i. 136–7.

[15] J. Clarke, 'From Business to Politics: The Ellice Family 1760–1860', D.Phil. thesis, (Oxford 1972), ii. 291; Charles Thorp, *A Charge to the Clergy of the Archdeaconry of Durham and of the Officiality of the Dean and Chapter* (Durham, 1838), 1.

[16] Clarke, 'From Business to Politics', ii. 288; Trevelyan, *Lord Grey of the Reform Bill*, 12, 168.

Lord Clarendon, his Cabinet colleague, remarked that there
was 'nothing so shocking to one's feelings as the sudden death
of a person who had so avowedly lived without God in the
world'.[17] The diarist Greville remarked of Holland's West
London salon, Holland House, that 'Everybody knew that the
House was sceptical: none of them ever thought of going to
church and they went on as if there was no such thing as
religion.'[18] At Holland House, Fox's political heir supported
at various times an atheist as librarian (John Allen), a free-
thinker as wife, and a former Catholic priest, Joseph Blanco
White, whose spiritual excursus led, by way of the Noetic
Anglicanism of Oriel College, Oxford, to Unitarianism.[19] In
this latter phase, he received Lord Holland's confession that
his eighteenth-century rationalism had led him to doubt the
Trinity, which he proceeded to describe as 'revolting to one's
understanding' and 'a solecism in language'. Holland argued
that an unbiased critic would pronounce Unitarianism 'more
consonant with reason' than any other version of Christianity.
It had the added virtues of being 'less productive of fanaticism
and superstition and more conducive to the morality of
mankind and the well-being of society' than other Christian
sects; it was to be valued on account of its political benefits.[20]

It was, indeed, primarily as a politician that Holland valued
the Church of England, but, in what was supposed to be the
tradition of the eighteenth century, not so much as a means
of moral elevation as a source of jobs for Whig supporters.
Hobhouse noted less than a week after the resignation of
Wellington's government in November 1830 that Lady
Holland and John Allen were distributing the ecclesiastical
patronage of the Duchy of Lancaster (Holland's office in the
new government), and acting and thinking 'as if they were in
the days of the Pelhams and Walpoles, with perfect tranquility
and self-complacency'.[21] Holland, by virtue of his new post,
was near the centre of the ecclesiastical patronage network of
the government. He was a source of patronage in his own

[17] BL Addit. MSS 56560 (Broughton Papers): Hobhouse Diary, 2 Mar. 1839; H.
Maxwell, *Life and Letters of the Fourth Earl of Clarendon* (London, 1913), i. 213.
[18] Fulford & Strachey, *Greville Memoirs* v. 87.
[19] L. Mitchell, *Holland House*, 103, 232.
[20] Thom, *Revd Joseph Blanco White* ii. 129–30.
[21] Broughton, *Recollections of a Long Life*, iv. 72.

right, a position he shared with the Lord Chancellor and the First Lord of the Treasury, and acted as an adviser to his fellow patrons. It was characteristic of him that he used this position to find employment for political and personal friends. He had scarcely any understanding of contemporary theological learning. When, on Lord Radnor's suggestion, he recommended Thirlwall, a former Cambridge don, for a vacant bishopric, Melbourne replied that the fact was that Holland had 'only caught this name of Thirlwall . . . from another without the least knowledge of the man, of his writings, of his temper, disposition or anything about him'.[22] Likewise, when Holland recommended Shuttleworth, the Warden of New College and his sons' former tutor, for a place on the bishop's bench, Melbourne remarked that Holland 'did not care a damn for Shuttleworth but my lady's vanity and love of meddling would be pleased by his being made'.[23]

Shuttleworth was one of three whom Holland particularly desired to see as bishops, the other two being William Herbert and Sydney Smith.[24] The promotion of Herbert, who became Dean of Manchester in 1840, was in accord with Holland's predilections. Although a mild Evangelical, who preached the virtues of toleration, Herbert was better known as a distinguished naturalist, and for his contributions to classical and linguistic scholarship. Even more importantly, he was the brother of the 2nd Earl of Caernarvon, who had become a Tory after the passing of the Great Reform Act (Herbert himself had been a Whig MP before taking holy orders in 1819).[25] Sydney Smith had already received the Hollands' bounty in 1806, when he had accepted the Chancery living of Foston-le-Clay from the Whig ministry.[26] Despite an undoubted personal piety, and an excellent record as a parish clergyman at Foston where he had acted as 'village parson, village doctor, village comforter, village magistrate', his

[22] BL Addit. MSS 51558 (Holland House Papers), fo. 132: Melbourne to Holland, 25 Mar. 1837.
[23] Broadlands MSS MEL/RU (Melbourne Papers), fo. 242: Melbourne to Russell, 8 Apr. 1836.
[24] BL Addit. MSS 51548 (Holland House Papers), fo. 211: Holland to Grey, 3 Mar. 1837.
[25] *DNB, Burke's Peerage.*
[26] A. Bell, *Sydney Smith* (Oxford, 1980), p. 72.

theology was of the eighteenth rather than of the nineteenth century, from which perspective he had attacked the Methodists in the *Edinburgh Review* and the Anglican Evangelicals in the 'Peter Plymley' letters.[27] Smith's irreverence characteristically revealed itself in advising the 6th Countess of Carlisle, who attended his church at Foston and was the wife of a Whig Cabinet minister, on how to overcome her low spirits. His first injunction was 'live as well and drink as much as you dare'; it was not until his nineteenth, and final, exhortation that he urged: 'Be firm and constant in the exercise of rational religion'.[28] By such acts Smith acquired a reputation for irreligion. J. G. Lockhart, the Tory editor of the *Quarterly Review* and Sir Walter Scott's son-in-law, wrote of the Edinburgh Reviewers: 'I fancy the whole set were really most thorough infidels and S. Smith at the top of them in that respect as in all others'.[29]

Brougham, the Whigs' 'philosophical statesman' and a Scottish-educated Edinburgh Reviewer, was the only member of this generation to produce a work of theology. He presented a re-worked eighteenth-century natural religion to a nineteenth-century public.[30] When Lord Chancellor he wrote *A Discourse of Natural Theology* (1835) for the Society for the Diffusion of Useful Knowledge, a work which his friend, the Unitarian minister from Liverpool, William Shepherd, warned him could be used to show him up as 'a notable infidel'.[31] This work was not intended to be a treatise on natural theology as such, but an inquiry into the principles on which such a treatise might be written. It began with the claim that natural theology was a science, just as natural and moral philosophy were sciences: its truths could be discovered by induction.[32] According to Brougham, his work was only original in so far as it regarded the study of mind to be as valid a means of proving the existence of a First Cause as the study of matter (hitherto the concern of most natural theologians). He wrote affirmatively:

---

[27] Ibid., 71, 78, 102.
[28] N. C. Smith (ed.), *Selected Letters of Sydney Smith* (Oxford, 1981), 94.
[29] J. Clive, *Scotch Reviewers* (London, 1957), 149.
[30] [Spring Rice], 'Ministerial Plan of Education', 159; H. Brougham, 'A Discourse of Natural Theology' in *Collected Works* (London & Glasgow, 1856), vi.
[31] Brougham Papers, MS 34524: Shepherd to Brougham, n.d. [1835].
[32] Brougham, 'A Discourse of Natural Theology', vi. 7.

'the structure of the mind in every way in which we can regard it, affords evidences of the most skilful contrivance'.[33] In the manner of Paley and other eighteenth-century Christian apologists, Brougham attempted to come to terms with Hune's criticisms of natural religion, as expressed in his essays 'of miracles' and 'of a particular Providence and of a Future State'. This defence was to prove Brougham's downfall. His enthusiasm for natural religion led him to adopt positions which were not in keeping with orthodox Anglicanism.

The tenor of his remarks was to suggest that the arguments which Hume used to discredit the existence of miracles, and to limit the range of valid inferences from natural phenomena, were equally applicable to natural philosopy or science. But since no one doubted the truths of science, so no one should doubt the truths of natural religion. In his note, 'of Mr Hume's Sceptical Writings', Brougham did not attempt to refute all of Hume's arguments against natural religion. He did not, for example, deal with Hume's denial of the claim that an essentially unchanging order could be discerned in the world of nature (and thus that natural objects showed less evidence of being governed by design than did human artefacts). Brougham took as given the validity of the analogy between natural objects and human fabrications. Brougham's attack on Hume began with a consideration of the following sugges- tion. According to Hume, the existence of miracles contradicted the observation that natural laws were uniform in their operation. The question was whether it was more likely that natural laws were uniformly applied, or that they were occasionally broken by miraculous interruptions. Hume argued that the former was more plausible because the evidence available was of greater weight; the regularity of natural laws was subject to the repeated test of experience, whereas the evidence for the existence of miracles consisted solely in the testimony of deceased witnesses. Brougham claimed, by way of reply, that testimony was the evidence not only for our belief in miracles, but also for our belief in the uniformity of the laws of nature; since there was no difference in kind between the sort of evidence which supported both propositions, there was no a priori reason to believe one in

[33] Ibid., 41.

preference to the other. The question was which set of
testimonies was the more probable. Brougham ended with the
claim that the testimony in favour of miracles was overwhelming.[34] He also attempted a refutation of Hume's argument that
it was illegitimate to draw inferences about the omnipotence
of a First Cause from an analogy between man and the objects
of his design, and God and his creations. According to Hume,
if the analogy held, it only proved that God had created a
number of particular things, just as man had created a number of particular observable objects, and not everything.
Brougham contended, rather lamely, that if this reasoning
were valid, it would put an end to 'all scientific speculations'
and the generalizations on which science had built up its laws:
science had advanced in just the manner to which Hume
objected. It had formed universal propositions from particular
examples, on the assumption that what was true in a number
of cases would be true for all cases. Further, the value of such
an inferential science, according to Brougham, had been
proved; a science of theology, operating on the same rules of
inference, should be equally valuable.[35] David Brewster, the
Scottish scientist, welcomed the book in the *Edinburgh Review*
as an attack on scepticism by 'a deathless name', who would
'draw around our faith its mystic circle of light and
knowledge'.[36] Such a view overlooked the fact that Brougham's
reconciliation of Christianity and natural philosophy had
unchristian implications.

Brougham, enthusiastic about the utility of scientific
thought, made greater claims for natural theology than even
many of its eighteenth-century exponents had allowed. In short
he maintained that 'revelation cannot be true if Natural Religion is false, and cannot be demonstrated strictly by argument
or established by any evidence without proving or assuming
the latter'.[37] Natural religion alone, argued Brougham, was
both a necessary and a sufficient basis for Christianity; scriptural revelation only confirmed what the eye beheld. One proof
of this was Brougham's attempt to derive the doctrine of the

[34] Ibid., 152–5.
[35] Ibid., 155–8.
[36] [D. Brewster], 'Lord Brougham's Discourse on Natural Theology', *Edinburgh Review*, lxiv (1837), 302.
[37] Brougham, 'A Discourse of Natural Theology', vi. 130.

immortality of the soul from a study of the world of nature. This attempt revealed his thought to be heterodox. His argument was that the mind was immaterial and independent of matter; that the notion of annihilation was entirely derived from the decomposition of matter; consequently, the mind, being, unlike the body, simple in construction and so incapable of resolution or dissolution, could not decompose.[38] G. R. Gleig, who had been appointed to the chaplaincy of Chelsea Hospital in 1834 by Lord John Russell, attacked this claim in *Fraser's Magazine*. Gleig claimed that if the argument were true, Brougham was a pantheist; if mind was neither created nor destroyed, the Divinity was not the creator of all, external to the world, but must be implicit in the world. Second, Gleig argued that if Brougham was right, and the doctrine of immortality was a deduction of human reasoning, this was out of keeping with the notion of the Divinity as the supreme intelligence: divine scriptural revelation, in which the doctrine was also stated, was superfluous. Third, and most tellingly, Gleig claimed that, if immortality was an attribute of mind, it could not be the 'free gift of grace' which the Gospels said it was. Brougham's arguments were subversive of New Testament Christianity, which claimed that it was the death and Atonement of Christ which brought the promise of everlasting life to man. If Brougham's arguments were true, and immortality were simply an attribute of mind, then the Atonement was at best a superfluous event; at worst it was merely a fable.[39] Gleig concluded: 'We are thoroughly convinced that his lordship has hit upon the right objection to his theory when he hints that natural theology, as decked out by him, must "prove dangerous to the acceptance of revealed religion".'[40] In his defence of the reasonableness of Christianity, Brougham unwittingly revealed that his species of faith subverted a scripturally-based Anglicanism.

This Whig tradition of indifference masquerading as a form of rational religion was continued by three 'converts' to Whiggery: the Canningites Palmerston and Melbourne, and the 4th Earl of Clarendon, a former diplomat. According to

[38] Ibid., 65–89.
[39] [G. R. Gleig], 'Lord Brougham on Natural Theology', *Fraser's Magazine*, xii (1835), 375–93.   [40] Ibid., 382.

his son-in-law Shaftesbury, Palmerston did not know the difference between Moses and Sydney Smith. When Prime Minister, he relied on his natural son, William Cowper, and Shaftesbury, to supply him with ecclesiastical information.[41] As Foreign Secretary in the governments of the 1830s, the only ecclesiastical preferment he requested was that the Deanery of Winchester be granted to Garnier, with whom he dined and went shooting.[42] As for Clarendon, his biographer Herbert Maxwell searched in vain for his Anglican faith, and concluded his biography with this implicit indictment: 'Nowhere else can I find a more articulate expression of what I conceive to have been his guiding faith than in the profession of Spinoza, the Pantheist'.[43] Perhaps in reaction to his Evangelical uncle, the miserly 3rd Earl, Clarendon despised the religious enthusiasm which turned religious faith into a political affair. To his brother Edward, he wrote: 'I would not make use of religion for my own interests or convert the Bible into a poll-book as Sandon did or go hunting in fine carriages after crack preachers'.[44] In the only substantial letter on religion which Maxwell found, Clarendon urged his sister to cease her melancholia, stating his conviction that it was not 'God's intention that we should eternally have before our eyes another world and nothing else'.[45] Reputedly, Melbourne was equally lax in his religious observances,[46] but with Melbourne a transitional phase is reached. While personally he was more at home with eighteenth-century rationalism, as befitted a Glasgow-educated Whig, he was, nevertheless, soberly respectful towards the *Ecclesia Anglicana*. This was a paradox akin to that of his reputedly natural father, the Earl of Egremont, who, though said to have no religion of his own, consistently gave between a quarter and a third of annual income to philanthropic causes in the course of sixty years.[47]

The High Church party claimed that the Whigs sought to

---

[41] W. O. Chadwick, *The Victorian Church* (London, 1966), i. 469–70, 473; Finlayson, *7th Earl of Shaftesbury*, 376 *et seq.*

[42] Broadlands MSS D/7 (Palmerston Papers): Palmerston's Diary for 1835, 28, 30 Jan., 20 Feb. 1835.

[43] Maxwell, *4th Earl of Clarendon* (London, 1913), ii. 370.

[44] Ibid., i. 156. [45] Ibid., i. 53.

[46] Chadwick, *The Victorian Church*, i. 107; Grey Papers C3/1B: Howick Jour., 15 July 1834. [47] F. K. Brown, *Fathers of the Victorians* (Cambridge, 1961), 28–9.

Table 2. Whig Appointments and Translations to English Bishoprics 1830–41

Name	See		University	Anglican affiliation
	First appointment	Translation		
Maltby*	Chichester (1831)	Durham (1836)	Cambridge	Liberal
Carr		Worcester (1831)	Oxford	Evangelical
Allen	Bristol (1834)	—	Cambridge	High
Butler*	Lichfield (1836)	—	Cambridge	Liberal
Otter	Chichester (1836)	—	Cambridge	High
Longley*	Ripon (1836)	—	Oxford	Evangelical
Denison*	Salisbury (1837)	—	Oxford	Liberal
Stanley	Norwich (1837)	—	Cambridge	Liberal
Musgrave*	Hereford (1837)	—	Cambridge	Liberal
Bowstead*	Sodor and Man (1838)	Lichfield (1840)	Cambridge	Liberal
Davys	Peterborough (1839)	—	Cambridge	Evangelical
Pepys	Sodor and Man (1840)	Worcester (1841)	Cambridge	? High
Shuttleworth*	Chichester (1840)	—	Oxford	Evangelical
Thirlwall*	St David's (1840)	—	Cambridge	Liberal
Short*	Sodor and Man (1841)	—	Oxford	Evangelical

Key: * = involved in the movement for university reform.

change the church into an agency of government, and it has
certainly been the claim of one historian, writing in 'the Gore
tradition', that Melbourne appointed bishops on account of
their political affiliations.[48] This argument, however, does not
bear close scrutiny. Both Longley and Butler were nominated
for the sees of Ripon and Lichfield respectively, although
Melbourne was fully aware that they did not support the
government on the Irish Church question.[49] Holland, indeed,
commented: 'I hardly know how to account for Longley who
has never voted with us'.[50] Even Hampden, who was appointed
to the Regius Chair of Divinity at Oxford, and thus was
closely identified with the government, was not thought to be
a Whig in politics. Le Marchant, the Whig Secretary to the
Board of Trade, told Lord Holland: '*I* do not think him safe.
His politics are not with us'.[51] Melbourne appears to have taken
appointments to the episcopate seriously, as much on account
of their theological as their political implications, perhaps
because he was aware that the receipt of patronage could not
guarantee votes. 'I do not believe that the Clergy would have
been more favourable to us if we had more bishoprics to give',
he wrote to Mulgrave in 1835, 'I am convinced that the
influence of Patronage is very much overrated.'[52] Melbourne's
concern for the quality of his appointments led him to resist,
albeit in the end unsuccessfully, Shuttleworth's elevation to
the bishops' bench, 'not on account of his politics but because
he never appeared . . . to have much merit'; likewise he resisted
pressure from the Duke of Bedford to appoint Russell's step-
brother, Lord Wriothesley Russell, to a position of ecclesiastical eminence, describing him as 'a snuffling Methodist and a
foolish fellow'.[53] If his private secretary, the Cambridge-

---

[48] Chadwick, *The Victorian Church*, i. 121; M. J. Cowling, *Religion and Public Doctrine in Modern England* (Cambridge, 1980), 414; for influence of Chadwick's judge-ment see E. R. Norman, *Church and Society in England 1770–1970* (Oxford, 1976), 72; G. I. T. Machin, *Politics and the Churches in Great Britain 1832–1868* (Oxford, 1977), 88.

[49] Sanders, *Lord Melbourne's Papers* 506.

[50] Kriegel, *Holland House Diaries*, 344.

[51] BL Addit. MSS 51591 (Holland House Papers), fo. 132: Le Marchant to Holland, [26 July 1837].

[52] Mulgrave Castle Archives, box MM (Normanby Papers), fo. 43: Melbourne to Mulgrave, 5 Oct. 1835.

[53] DCRO MSS 1262M FC94 (Fortescue Papers): Melbourne to Fortescue, 31 Aug. 1840; BL Addit. MSS 51558 (Holland House Papers), fo. 132: Melbourne to Holland, 25 Mar. 1837.

educated son of the Lord Lieutenant of Ireland, is to be believed, this should be no surprise, since Melbourne was 'a great theologian', a man who decided upon 'principle' and brought 'abstract rules to bear on everyday cases'.[54] Certainly, when he was Prime Minister, Melbourne managed to read (and often in bed), among other authors, the Early Fathers, Newman the Tractarian, Whewell the Trinity College Peelite, Hare the liberal Anglican, and Thirlwall's translation of Schleiermacher's *Essay on St Luke*, a work of German biblical criticism.[55]

These were primarily intellectual interests, read, according to Sir Henry Taylor, poet and Colonial Office official, 'for entertainment more than for edification'.[56] It is not possible to infer from Melbourne's eclectic tastes that he differed from his contemporaries on the grounds of his support for the Established Church. For Melbourne, the Reformation's importance was that it signalled not the establishment of religious liberalism, but the removal of the church from Rome's dominion. To his private secretary, he wrote: 'I do not care a damn what they say of the religious part of the Reformation, but the political part of it I am for standing by to the Death'.[57] According to Melbourne, there was little to choose between the doctrines of the Roman and Anglican Churches. He confessed: 'I think there is so much of the truth of the Gospel mixed I dare say with errors in the Church of England form, in the Roman Catholic form and in the Presbytery form of Christianity as to justify a Christian in acquiescing in the establishment of any one of them.'[58] The consequence of Melbourne's doctrinal indifference was to make him an active opponent of religious enthusiasm, as manifested, for example, by the High Church Puseyites.[59] According to him, the essential articles of

[54] DCRO MSS 1262M FC96 (Fortescue Papers): Fortescue to [?William Wilson], 21 Sept. 1840.

[55] H. Taylor *Autobiography* (London, 1885), ii. 305; DCRO MSS 1262M FC94 (Fortescue Papers): Melbourne to Fortescue, n.d. [?1840]; Broadlands MSS MEL/RU (Melbourne Papers), fo. 243: Melbourne to Russell, 12 Apr. 1836.

[56] H. Taylor, *Autobiography* (London, 1885), ii. 305.

[57] Broadlands MSS MEL/CO (Melbourne Papers), fo. 42: Melbourne to Cowper, 9 Aug. 1841.   [58] Grey Papers, box 115 file 1: Melbourne to Howick, 21 Jan. 1837.

[59] Broadlands MSS MEL/CO (Melbourne Papers), fo. 43: Melbourne to Cowper, 9 Nov. 1841: Mulgrave Castle Archives, box MM (Normanby Papers), fo. 303: Melbourne to Normanby, 15 Nov. 1841.

religion were identical with the rules of society, and constituted the inculcation of social order. All that was necessary was belief 'that there was a God who would punish . . . that Jesus Christ had made atonement for the sins of the world and that it was displeasing to God and therefore wrong to murder and rob'.[60] This was a view of religion entertained by one who conceived of himself primarily as a man of property, and it was as a man of property that he performed his religious duties. On his Derbyshire estate he augmented the living of the vicar of Melbourne; he subscribed £200 for the repair of a church in Boothby, near Lincoln; he endowed the vicarage, aided the extension of church accommodation, funded the rebuilding of the chapel and helped purchase an additional burial ground in the parish of Greasley in the archdeaconry of Nottingham; but when requested by the Revd H. W. Plumptre for a subscription for the rebuilding of a church in Nottingham, he replied: '. . . I cannot give you any help towards the object which you have in view. Any assistance which I can render for such purposes must necessarily be confined to those parts of the country with which I am connected by property and which therefore appear to me to have a fair claim as far as I am concerned'.[61]

If Melbourne and Holland primarily shared a secular view of Christianity, the former none-the-less managed to appeal to Whigs of a younger generation. Baring, who became Chancellor of the Exchequer in 1839, wrote of his Prime Minister: 'I have been remarkably pleased with his whole tone with respect to patronage and the spirit in which he seems inclined to carry on the official part of his business; which is saying something, considering my former experience was almost entirely with Althorp', a conscientious Evangelical and former Chancellor of the Exchequer.[62] Melbourne was able to appeal across the generations, and so bridged the gap between the Foxites and those who changed the Foxite nature of the party.

[60] Sanders, *Lord Melbourne's Papers* 395.
[61] BL Microfilm 859/44 (Melbourne Papers): Fox to Melbourne, 15 Nov. 1838; BL Microfilm 859/13 (Melbourne Papers): Melbourne to Revd La Tour, 31 Dec. 1840; BL Microfilm 859/18 (Melbourne Papers): Wilkins to Melbourne, 28 July 1836; BL Microfilm 859/16 (Melbourne Papers): Melbourne to Revd Plumptre, 2 Apr. 1838.
[62] T. G. Baring (ed.), *Journals and Correspondence of Francis Thornhill Baring, Lord Northbrook* (London, 1905), i. 108.

The leader of this latter group of 'young' Whigs in Grey's Cabinet was Lord Althorp, who, in the 1820s, had attempted to preserve Whig independence by stressing the party's unique appeal to 'the people'. Radnor and Ebrington were precursors of this outlook, in so far as, in association with Whitbread's *enragés*, they had taken up such issues as anti-slavery, the corruption of government, and the suppression of 'the liberties of the people' in order to sever the Whig alliance with the Grenvillites, if never to enter into a fulsome alliance with Radicalism. Their successors in the government were such men as Sir George Grey, Sir Francis Baring, and Henry Labouchere. From the Canningites, they recruited Charles Grant, who had been brought up in the tradition of Wilberforce, the anti-slave trade campaigner.[63] They differed from the previous generation in being largely educated at Oxford and Cambridge and often distinguished academically. Althorp was placed first in his year at Trinity College, Cambridge, in 1801; Baring and Grey both obtained firsts; Charles Grant won a fellowship at Magdalene College. The coherence of this group was reinforced by intermarriage. Baring married George Grey's sister, while his own sister married Labouchere. Grey married into the Canningite Ryder family, to which Ebrington was related by marriage (he had married a cousin of Grey's wife).[64] These politicians tended either not to wield great political influence, or to retire early from the political fray. Sir George Grey was remembered best as an official with no political following, and, according to Le Marchant, Baring's manner was 'cold and his disposition reserved so he had few friends or political followers'.[65] Despite being offered the Lord Privy Seal in 1834, Radnor never held political office; Ebrington never sat in the Cabinet.[66] Althorp, the most conventionally successful in politics, retired in 1834 to cultivate his country estate on inheriting his father's earldom. All these politicians had an affinity for country life and country pursuits. George Grey was especially fond of hunting and

---

[63] See Wasson, 'The Young Whigs'. (Ph.D. thesis), *passim* and Table 1 above.
[64] See Fig. 1.
[65] M. Creighton, *Memoir of Sir George Grey* (London, 1901), p. 109; D. Le Marchant, *Memoir of John Charles, Viscount Althorp, Third Earl Spencer* (London, 1876), 490.
[66] R. K. Huch, *The Radical Lord Radnor* (Minnesota, 1977), 134.

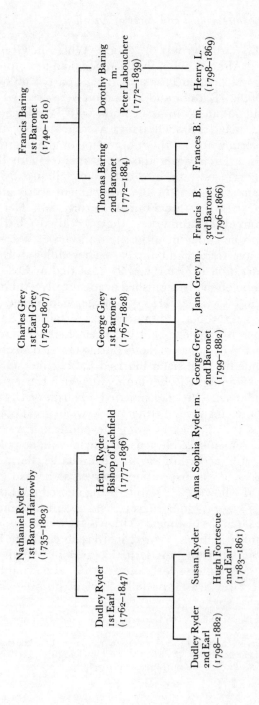

Ryder—Fortescue—Baring—Labouchere Connection

Althorp, as well as being devoted in his youth to racing and pugilism, was master of the Pytchley hunt from 1808 to 1817. Althorp, Ebrington, and Radnor were all interested in agricultural sciences: Althorp, for example, became President of the Smithfield Club for the improvement of livestock.[67]

These politicians primarily conceived of themselves as English country gentlemen in politics, possessed of an elevated understanding of their social duties and responsibilities. According to Edward Ellice, a Whig Chief Whip and Grey's brother-in-law, Althorp was 'an excellent illustration of the type of an English country gentleman gifted with a strong common sense, equal courage, firmness and independence'.[68] Baring explained at length to his son the importance of the country gentleman in English life, reminding him of his future obligation:

From them are selected [he wrote] the statesman, the members of Parliament, the magistrate. They are at the head of almost every undertaking, literary or charitable . . . by the constitution of England the government, the administration of the laws through the rural districts and the management of most matters are thrown into the hands of the class of men of property who generally go by the name of country gentlemen.[69]

What underlay such participation in English public life was a sense of Christian duty, of a debt owed to God for the blessings of Providence, which obliged them to be worthy stewards of whatever earthly lot the Deity had bestowed on them. Radnor expressed the importance of Christian stewardship in a family sermon:

Assuredly no man can suppose that a just God . . . will punish any rich man for the mere fact of his being rich, but the punishment is inflicted for not having made a good use of his riches; and any rich man may feel apprehension on that score that he has not made as good use of them as he might and ought, either that he has spent them in frivolous pleasures for himself when they might have been employed in acts of usefulness for others—or that he has thought

[67] Creighton, *Sir George Grey*, 138; Le Marchant, *Viscount Althorp*, 142, 145, 250; Huch, *The Radical Lord Radnor*, 164.
[68] Le Marchant, *Viscount Althorp*, 566.
[69] Baring, *Jour. & Corresp. of Lord Northbrook*, i. 192.

too much of himself and of his own qualifications and too little of the wants and necessities of his fellow creatures.[70]

These Christian impositions were of a peculiar nature. They were not only the product of a humanitarian philanthropy, but also of Evangelical convictions, of a religious faith which separated these politicians from the sceptical Foxites. This distinction can be seen in the differing reactions of Althorp and Brougham to the founding of London University. While the Foxite was a prime agent in the establishment of this place of higher learning, Althorp initially refused to subscribe, fearing it might be 'godless'. Likewise, although Brougham consulted Althorp during the composition of his *Discourse of Natural Theology*, the latter was unable to convince the former of the superiority of revelation over natural religion. Althorp, in particular, could not accept Brougham's contention that our immortality could be inferred from the immateriality of the soul. He asserted, contradicting Brougham, 'that although we can now prove the existence of the Deity, without the assistance of Revelation, we cannot prove our own immortality without such assistance'.[71]

These politicians accepted rather than rejected the Evangelical religion of their fathers. Francis Baring's father, Sir Thomas, subscribed to forty-seven societies associated with Evangelicals, acted as president of one, the vice-president of twenty-two, sat on the committee of four, and was a governor of six;[72] his brother, Charles, became a Palmerston-appointed Evangelical bishop. The Labouchere family resided near Clapham Common, the home of the Evangelical 'Saints', as did the Grants, whose eldest son, who became a Cabinet minister, attended an Evangelical-dominated Magdalene College, Cambridge.[73] Sir George Grey's parents (Earl Grey's brother

---

[70] BCRO MSS D/EPb F33 (Radnor Papers): Sermon No. 16, read 10 Mar. 1844 in London and July 1850 at Coleshill.

[71] Brougham Papers, MS 10381: Althorp to Brougham, 25 Mar. 1829; Le Marchant, *Viscount Althorp*, 547; Earl Spencer, *Letters of Lord Althorp* (privately printed, n.d.), 125–6; Althorp MSS H (Papers of 3rd Earl Spencer), box 13: Althorp to Brougham, 14 June 1835. These papers contain extensive correspondence between Althorp and Brougham on immateriality of the soul, and whether this constitutes conclusive proof of its immortality, on nature of instinct and relation to the operation of Providence, and on nature of Biblical inspiration.   [72] Brown, *Fathers of the Victorians*, 357.

[73] Ibid., 352, 390; on Magdalene see J. D. Walsh, 'The Magdalene Evangelicals', *Church Quarterly Review*, clix (1958), 499–511.

and Mary Whitbread, the sister of Samuel Whitbread, the Whig politician and brewer) were both devout Evangelicals, and the fathers of both Althorp and Radnor subscribed to Evangelical societies.[74] These parental pieties were passed on to the sons. Ebrington, when at Dublin Castle in his capacity as Lord Lieutenant, held prayers every morning at a quarter to ten; Radnor attended St George's Hanover Square, and composed sermons for delivery to his family and servants; Sir George Grey attended St Michael's, Chester Square, rigorously observed the sabbath (he only ever worked on a Sunday twice during his entire political career), read works of devotion, kept a commonplace book, and on Sundays spent in London visited the poor of St Giles.[75] But what these Whigs did not inherit were the parental politics. These second generation Evangelicals often came from Tory or Pittite households, although they associated themselves with liberals. Althorp was converted to Whiggery as a result of his friendship with Lansdowne at Trinity, Cambridge—a conversion akin to the transfer of allegiance which Macaulay made, also of an Evangelical family, from parental Toryism via Radicalism of a kind to Whiggery. Radnor also rejected his Pittite family background, and Ebrington's family had been Grenvillite.[76] Their infusion into the Whig party marked the reconstruction of the Whig alliance, which had been reduced to a Foxite rump at the ascendancy of Pitt. It was an infusion which disproves the claim (if disproof is needed) that Evangelical followers of Wilberforce tended to be Tories in politics.

In 1818 Althorp, following his wife's death, experienced something of a religious conversion. He took to reading the Bible and works of political economy, the first, in his words, 'to do myself good; the other to enable me to do good to others'. Thereafter he became obsessed with his prospects of salvation, understanding his activities almost exclusively in the light of his relationship with God. In the opening paragraph of a

[74] Creighton, *Sir George Grey*, 13; Brown, *Fathers of the Victorians*, 354, 356.

[75] DCRO MSS 1262M LI (Fortescue Papers), fo. 64: Fortescue to his grandmother, 6th Apr. 1839; BCRO MSS D/EPb C52 (Radnor Papers) John Peat to Radnor, 16 Jan. 1850; ibid., D/EPb F33 (Radnor Papers): sermons by Lord Radnor; Longford Castle Archives (Radnor Papers): Radnor to Folkestone, 15 Mar. 1853; Creighton, *Sir George Grey*, 73, 112, 133, 136.

[76] Le Marchant, *Viscount Althorp*, 110; Huch, *The Radical Lord Radnor*, 6; *Debrett's*.

fragment of autobiography, composed in 1834–5, he began: 'I have long known and endeavoured to impress upon my mind that there is only one object which is worthy of the ambition of a man of sense and that is to obtain the favour of God.'[77] He held that the only test of conduct 'which can safely be applied is the test of religion'.[78] It was to be this test which he attempted to apply to his conduct as a politician. When Ebrington tried to persuade Althorp to return to office in 1835, he refused with the claim: 'nothing but an imperative Religious Duty could induce me again to involve myself in the miseries of offices as nothing on this side of the Grave could possibly repay me for it'.[79] For Althorp, such a religious duty did not exist, since God did not distinguish between those who cultivated the national estate and those who cultivated their own, provided, of course, that both enterprises were conducted in accordance with His wishes. The reluctant politician reflected: 'I do not think I take a course displeasing to God in deciding that I will attend to my duties as the nominal owner of a great estate, rather than to those which men would call the higher duties of political life.'[80] Althorp became a model landlord, removed nude paintings from his country residence, wrote prayers, and read sermons to guests at Christmas house parties.[81] He summed up his faith to his former High Church tutor, Joseph Allen, for whom he secured a bishopric in 1834, as consisting in a belief, first, 'in an active reliance on the Goodness of God & in perfect resignation to his Will, secondly in Charity, towards Men in the Scriptural Sense of the word Charity, & thirdly in an humbleness of mind which estimates oneself as nothing & hopes for mercy only through the merits of Atonement'.[82]

The doctrine of Atonement (the reconciliation of man and God through the sacrifice of Christ) was also crucial to Sir George Grey's sense of religion. Mandell Creighton, later

[77] Le Marchant, *Viscount Althorp*, xv, 169.

[78] Baring, *Jour. & Corresp. of Lord Northbrook*, i. 114.

[79] DCRO MSS 1262M FC91 (Fortescue Papers): Spencer to Ebrington, 21 Feb. 1835.

[80] Baring, *Jour. & Corresp. of Lord Northbrook*, i. 114.

[81] Le Marchant, *Viscount Althorp*, 544, 547; Father Pius, *Life of Father Ignatius of St Paul* (Dublin, 1866), 93; Wasson, 'The Young Whigs' (Ph.D. thesis), 22.

[82] Althorp MSS H (Papers of 3rd Earl Spencer), box 12: Althorp to Allen, 25 Nov. 1835.

Bishop of London and, for a time, Grey's local rector at Fallo-
den, wrote in his memoir of the politician that 'the central
point of his [Grey's] own religious feeling was the Atonement
. . . which he felt to be absolutely necessary. The sense of sin
was ever present with him and he found in the Cross of Christ
the sense of forgiveness and reconciliation with God'.[83] Just
as Althorp contemplated political activity in the light of his
sense of religious duty, so Sir George Grey, half a generation
younger, considered his political enterprises, if somewhat more
positively, as 'labour in the service of God'.[84] Grey, perhaps
even more than Shaftesbury, was the Evangelical equivalent
of Gladstone. After graduating from Oriel College, Oxford,
he considered taking holy orders. In pursuit of this ambition
he spent a further two years at university studying theology.
Political service in Evangelical causes (significantly his first
government post was an under-secretaryship at the Colonial
Office under the direction of the Evangelical Charles Grant)
was, in part, a substitute for preaching, a service directed by
God. When Home Secretary, he reflected on his successful
handling of the mass Chartist demonstration of 1848, which
culminated in a rally on Kennington Common: 'I trust I do
feel really thankful for the merciful Providence which directed
and upheld me during that anxious time.'[85]

In the 1830s this Evangelical contingent sought ecclesiastical
preferment for two divines in particular: Thomas Vowler
Short, who became Bishop of Sodor and Man in 1841, and
Charles Thomas Longley, who became Bishop of Ripon in
1836 and later Archbishop of Canterbury.[86] Short's father had
tutored Baring before he went up to Christ Church, and Short,
a distant relation of Baring, in his turn tutored him and his
cousin, Henry Labouchere, at Christ Church.[87] Baring's father,
by way of a reward, had presented Short to the living of Kings

---

[83] Creighton, *Sir George Grey*, 134.

[84] Ibid., 23.

[85] Ibid., 82.

[86] BL Microfilm 859/1 (Melbourne Papers): Baring to Melbourne, 23 Aug. 1840;
BL Microfilm 859/16 (Melbourne Papers): Radnor to Melbourne, 11 July 1835. Of
five clergymen mentioned in this letter he claimed only to have substantial personal
knowledge of Longley. BL Addit. MSS 51566 (Holland House Papers), fo. 192:
Radnor to Holland, 22 June 1835.

[87] Baring, *Jour. & Corresp. of Lord Northbrook*, i. 1, 8; Christ Church MSS XLB. 1:
Payments to Tutors, 1813–1821.

Worthy in 1826.[88] The liberal Anglican Archbishop of Dublin, Richard Whately, described Short as a man of 'third rate talents', but stressed by way of compensation his high moral character and good sense as a parish minister, when replying to Melbourne's demand for advice on his suitability for a bishopric.[89] It was, indeed, as a practical rather than intellectual Christian that Baring recommended his elevation to the bench, an appointment also designed to please Sir George Grey and Labouchere.[90] Baring noted that Short was 'in earnest on Religion—I mean Religion not Theology', and that he had been the only subscriber to the 'Bible Lives' in the Christ Church Common Room.[91] In 1836 Short moved to the see of Ripon from the large London parish of St George's, Bloomsbury. There he had gained for himself a reputation for being an excellent parish priest. He had instituted an evening service, Sunday School, a lending library, weekly lectures, and (a classical sign of Evangelical Low Churchmanship, because it involved parishioners in an activity often thought to be the exclusive preserve of the clergy) a Visiting Society. He made these improvements public in his manual for parochial clergymen, *Parochialia*.[92]

Radnor was the prime promotor of C. T. Longley's claims to ecclesiastical preferment, on whose behalf he wrote to both Holland and Melbourne.[93] Although Radnor sponsored other divines, it was only Longley whom he knew personally, and whose moderate Evangelicanism was in accord with his own religious outlook. (When Radnor built a new church at Folkestone, the south coast resort which he developed, he presented to it a moderate Evangelical named William Powell.)[94] Longley had married the daughter of the Evangelical Whig and political economist, Sir Henry Parnell; according to Radnor he was a 'great friend' of another Evangelical peer, Lord Darnley.[95]

[88] Christ Church MSS: T. V. Short's Commonplace Book.

[89] Broadlands MSS MEL/WH (Melbourne Papers), fo. 2: Whately to Melbourne, 27 Jan. 1836.

[90] BL Microfilm 859/1 (Melbourne Papers): Baring to Melbourne, 2 Sept. 1840.

[91] Ibid.

[92] T. V. Short, *Parochialia* (London, 1842), 19–21, 108.

[93] See n. 86, above.

[94] BCRO MSS D/EPb C45 (Radnor Papers): corresp. with and respecting the Revd William Powell.

[95] Torrens, *2nd Viscount Melbourne*, ii. 180; BL Addit. MSS 51566 (Holland House

Longley, like Short, had been a Student of Christ Church, but in 1829 had resigned his Studentship to become Headmaster of Harrow (where, incidentally, he taught Ebrington's son, who in 1841 became Melbourne's private secretary).[96] Longley had advised Radnor in the preparation of the Oxford University Bill of 1835, which enabled Radnor to recommend him to the Whig government as that rare phenomenon, an Oxford man favourable to the abolition of subscription to the Thirty-Nine Articles on matriculation at the university.[97] Both Longley and Short acquired reputations as university reformers, and it was in the hope that they would be liberal (although not partisan) that they were appointed to the bench.

This Evangelical toleration was not predicated so much on an understanding of the difficulty of knowing in what theological truths consisted, as on a belief that such worries were comparatively unimportant. It was not so much an intellectual as a practical stand, the outcome of a distinctively Evangelical comprehension of the relationship of man and God. The crucial role which this relationship played in the Evangelical scheme of salvation, the essentials of which were faith in God and in His gift of redemption for our sins through the atoning sacrifice of Christ, humility before Him, and repentance for our own sinfulness, meant that for many Evangelicals theological disputes beyond this personal apprehension of the heart simply did not matter. We have seen how Sir George Grey, for example, cared only for the doctrine of the Atonement. His biographer recalled that 'on all other points concerning theology he was exceedingly tolerant of diversities of opinion'.[98] Likewise the Evangelical Bishop of Chichester, Shuttleworth, thought theology was 'not the substance of religion but its mere accidental outworks'.[99] Further, since this central

Papers), fo. 192: Radnor to Holland, 22 June 1835; *Church of England Biographies*, (2nd ser. London, n.d.), 183.

[96] DCRO MSS 1262M FC98 (Fortescue Papers): Longley to Ebrington, 4 Dec. 1844.

[97] Pusey House MSS, chest B draw 3 (Radnor Papers), fo. 9: Longley to Radnor, 30 Dec. 1834; BL Microfilm 859/16 (Melbourne Papers): Radnor to Melbourne, 11 July 1835.

[98] Creighton, *Sir George Grey*, 134.

[99] P. N. Shuttleworth, *The Last Three Sermons Preached at Oxford in 1839 and 1840* (London, Oxford, & Cambridge, 1875), 62.

doctrine was apprehended not so much by the mind as by the heart, doctrinal disputes revealed not so much that the truth was uncertain, as that the heart was unsound. They were indicative of the sin of pride and a restlessness of spirit. William Herbert, who became Dean of Manchester, wrote that secession was 'often the offspring of a secret pride, of a notion that we are wise and better than the community which is quite at variance with the humility of a true Christian'.[100] Intolerance towards others was also a failure to recognize that everybody was a fellow-traveller on the journey towards salvation. It was an implicit denial of man's common humanity established in the light of God. George Davys, Queen Victoria's Evangelical tutor, who became Bishop of Peterborough, asked rhetorically:

Do we act towards one another as if we knew that we were fellow-travellers on the same journey, and that, at the end of our course, we shall be received, not according to the rank and station which we have held during the journey, but to the manner in which we have conducted ourselves, and the dispositions which we have exercised?[101]

Although Evangelical tolerance of this kind was based on an understanding of the route to salvation, it did not mean that Evangelicals of this period were unsympathetic towards the more rationalist defences of Christian doctrine which were current, especially among liberal Anglican Whigs such as Russell and Morpeth. Even though most Evangelicals would have agreed with Shuttleworth that the fundamental biblical truths of Christianity were such that a 'simple and pure mind' could apprehend them without the aid of an educated theologian,[102] they were not entirely dismissive of attempts to prove that such beliefs were also reasonable. Radnor, for example, was happy to nominate Hampden and Arnold for bishoprics, both of whom were associated with attempts at perfecting a method of rightly interpreting scripture. Labouchere, who had been at Winchester with Thomas Arnold, read Stanley's adulatory life of the Victorian headmaster 'with great admiration for his character and energy', although he confessed to a

[100] W. Herbert, *Works* (London, 1842), i. 344.
[101] G. Davys, 'Danger of Delay in Religion', *Original Family Sermons* (London, 1833), i. 101.
[102] Shuttleworth, *The Last Three Sermons*, 64.

distrust of his judgement.[103] Such sympathies should not come as a surprise. These Evangelical Whigs practised their religion before the growth of a more fundamentalist Evangelicalism and the rise of Tractarianism, both of which had the effect of ossifying Evangelical belief in the form now commonly associated with Victorian England. Low Churchmanship, a belief in the plenary inspiration of the Scriptures, a literal interpretation of the Bible, the necessity of conversion were all characteristics of an Evangelicalism which achieved its dominance in the 1840s and 1850s. Before then, in Whig circles at least, the views of such Evangelicals as Charles Simeon or Daniel Wilson were more common. These clergymen managed to combine a moderately high view of the church (Simeon, for example, taught a doctrine not so dissimilar from baptismal regeneration[104]) with a toleration of other forms of Christian worship on the assumption that diverse sects were agreed on fundamental truths. Wilson, for example, when Bishop of Calcutta, endorsed a form of Sunday family prayers at the Martinière School, which combined elements from the Anglical liturgy, the Catholic missal, and Armenian prayers.[105] In view of this, it was perhaps not surprising that Evangelical and younger Whigs of the third generation should co-operate on church reform. George Pryme, for example, the Simeonite MP for Cambridge, co-operated with Spring Rice on the repeal of university tests. Edward Stanley, the Whig Bishop of Norwich, defending the government's scheme of elementary education in 1839, referred, if not altogether accurately, to Bishop Wilson as the originator of the distinction between 'general' and 'special' religious education, on which Russell's proposal rested.[106] The boundaries between liberal Anglican and moderate Evangelical were not always easy to define.

The third generation of liberal Anglican Whig politicians presented the phenomenon of Foxite sons rejecting the mores of their fathers. By birth they were metropolitan Whigs, but by inclination they followed the leadership of country Whigs

[103] BL Microfilm 859/16 (Melbourne Papers): Radnor to Melbourne, 11 July 1835; Nottingham Univ. MSS Os C (Ossington Papers), fo. 117: Labouchere to Denison, 9 Jan. 1845.

[104] G. W. E. Russell, *A Short History of the Evangelical Movement* (London, 1915), 53.

[105] J. Bateman, *Life of the Right Revd Daniel Wilson, DD* (London, 1860), ii. 34–5.

[106] On Pryme, see Ch. 5 below; *Hansard* 3rd ser. xlviii (1839), 1290.

such as Althorp and Ebrington. This was the generation of
politicians who achieved political maturity in the late 1830s,
led by Russell, virtually Prime Minister by 1839, Morpeth,
and Howick, the sons of the 6th Earl of Carlisle and the 2nd
Earl Grey respectively, and, according to Holland, 'the most
rising young men of the day'.[107] They were joined by men such
as Spring Rice, acting the cautious elder statesman, Hobhouse,
the former Radical now turned moderate, Duncannon, and
Mulgrave, a former Canningite. The difference between the
fathers and sons was mutually recognized. Holland, remarking
on the religion of Morpeth and Howick, said: 'they are both
very serious. I am afraid to talk before them'. Morpeth, from
his younger, more sober perspective, commented that
Holland's posthumously published *Memoirs* contained 'no
principle more lofty than Whiggism, no virtue more perfect
than Charles Fox', who possessed 'too little morality and too
much faction'.[108] Morpeth also considered his father's favourite
preacher, Sydney Smith, to be 'altogether short of completely
great or good'.[109] Mulgrave gave a fictional account of this
generational disparity in his novel *The English At Home*. In this
he contrasted the immoral Lord Ratoath, brought up in the
'French school', with his illegitimate son, Ernest Willoughby,
who had received his education from the 'orthodox moralists'.
Ratoath's moral failure was to 'mistake one century for
another'.[110] Russell, Howick, Hobhouse, and Duncannon were
all members of the 'watchmen', who in 1827 preferred the
independence of the Whigs and the leadership of Althorp to
a coalition with Canning.[111] This marked a break with the
orthodox Foxite leadership as represented by Holland and
Lansdowne, who, with the notable exception of the haughty
Grey, had looked primarily to a political realignment of
Toryism to secure an entry to government. In the 1830s these
younger Whigs became the prime beneficiaries of the collapse
of the coalition with Canning, the disintegration of the Tory
Party, and their preservation of a measure of Whig independence and popularity.

[107] Kriegel, *Holland House Diaries*, 347.
[108] BL Addit. MSS 56560 (Broughton Papers): Hobhouse Diary, 2 Mar. 1839;
Lascelles, *Journals kept by Earl of Carlisle*, 211–3.
[109] Ibid., 18.   [110] [Phipps], *The English at Home* i. 121, ii. 8.
[111] Wasson, 'The Crisis of Whig Leadership'.

With the exception of Russell, these Whigs, unlike their
fathers, but like their mentors, were educated exclusively at
Oxford or Cambridge, and at two colleges in particular: Trinity
College, Cambridge, and Christ Church, Oxford.[112] They also
resembled their mentors in being for the most part academically serious. Morpeth, for example, gained a first-class degree
in classics and won university prizes for Latin and Greek verse;
Hobhouse was the Hulsean Prize winner at Cambridge in
1808. This was in part the reflection of their attendance at
institutions which had emerged from the reputedly slothful
atmosphere of eighteenth-century university life. Trinity had
begun to reform itself by the late eighteenth century, initiating
the tutorial system and annual college examinations by 1790,
and introducing an entrance examination in 1810;[113] an influx
of Evangelically inclined students such as Pryme (the first
Cambridge Professor of Political Economy) and Sedgwick, the
geologist, and their election into college fellowships, had begun
to produce an academically distinguished college. Christ
Church, likewise, under the direction of Dean Jackson and his
successors, had begun to establish itself as the producer of
highly educated office-holders in church and state such as Peel
and Gladstone, both with double firsts, and Lloyd, Peel's tutor
and Bishop of Oxford. In accordance with such an education,
and the contemporary fashion for religion, these liberal Anglican Whigs demonstrated pieties which their fathers did not
possess.[114]

Hobhouse had been brought up a Unitarian, but, by way
of Westminster School and Trinity College, acquired a temperate Anglicanism, which, despite his association with Byron,
did not desert him. Indeed, in 1819 he advised the poet against
the publication of *Don Juan* on account of its blasphemy.[115] In
his journal for the 1830s he recorded his attendance at church,
and on his wife's death in 1835 he turned to the Bible for
consolation.[116] Howick also recorded his attendance at church

[112] Hobhouse, Rice, Mulgrave, and Howick all attended Trinity, Duncannon and
Morpeth Christ Church.
[113] W. W. Rouse Ball, *Notes on the History of Trinity College, Cambridge* (London,
1899), 137, 143, 148.
[114] W. J. Baker, *Beyond Port and Prejudice* (Orono, Maine, 1981), 19.
[115] Zegger, *John Cam Hobhouse*, 38; Broughton, *Recollections of a Long Life*, ii. 110.
[116] BL Addit. MSS 61826 (Broughton Papers): Hobhouse Diary, 26 Oct. 1834, 3,
9, Apr. 1835.

(usually Spring Gardens Chapel or St James's) and in the journal he kept with his wife he noted when he took the sacraments. He reserved Sundays for devotional reading (Wilberforce's *Christianity*, Paley's *Sermons*, Keith on *Prophecy*), and criticized himself when the sabbath was ill-spent.[117] Rice led his family in prayer and scripture readings, and, when resident in Mansfield St, Mayfair, kept a family pew at his local church. He kept up with contemporary theological writing such as Gladstone's *The State in Its Relations with the Church* and Shuttleworth's *Scripture not Tradition*. Such reading was not merely of intellectual interest. His daughter ended her engagement to Henry Taylor, then a clerk at the Colonial Office, on the ground of his irreligion. Taylor recorded that it was not until he had submitted a *confessio fidei* to Rice's scrutiny that the engagement was restored.[118] Morpeth wrote Christian verse, often attended two sermons on a Sunday, and rarely missed church. His attendance upon preachers was remakably catholic. On one day he noted in his diary: 'I have gone through . . . nearly the whole cycle of religious opinion—low Anglican, Presbyterian, High Anglican and Jesuit.' In social exchanges he was as much struck by the sober as the frivolous. After a dinner at which the very Low Church Baptist Noel had explicated Bible passages and prayed, Morpeth remarked that 'It was not a usual sequence of a London dinner, but one liked it very much.'[119] Mulgrave was equally keen in the display of fashionable sobriety. His novel *The English in France* contained an attack on French mysticism, on the work of Constant and Cousin, and a statement on the importance of revelation. He wrote: 'The truth that mortals are to receive and worship must not be the work or the discovery of their own hands . . . it must be revealed to them in some more imposing, some more commanding way . . . it must take the

[117] Grey Papers C3/1B: Howick Jour., 9 Feb., 16 Mar., 12, 26 Oct. 1834, 22 Feb., 6 Dec. 1835.

[118] NLI MSS 551 (Monteagle Papers): Rice to Alfred, 24 Sept. 1835; John Rylands Library Eng. MSS 1187 (Monteagle Papers), fo. 159: Rice to C. Spring Rice, 30 Apr. [1837]; NLI MSS 533 (Monteagle Papers): Rice to Whately, 15 Nov. 1838; NLI MSS 543 (Monteagle Papers): Rice to Macaulay, 22 Dec. 1838; Taylor, *Autobiography*, i. 220.

[119] [Howard], *The Vice-Regal Speeches and Addresses Lectures and Poems of the Late Earl of Carlisle, KG*, ed. J. J. Gaskin (Dublin, London, and Edinburgh, 1865), ix, lxxxvii; Lascelles, *Journals kept by Earl of Carlisle*, 32, 61, 70, 72.

private, the divine path to the heart . . .'.[120] When on a visit
to the Earl of Bessborough's Irish estates, Creevey noted that
Duncannon attended the local Anglican Church (the rector
being the Archdeacon of Ossory), had transformed the village
of Piltown into a haven of civilization which nothing in England
could surpass, and entertained the local Catholic priest at his
dinner table.[121] Although Russell had never been confirmed,
this fact did not, according to his second wife, prevent him
from taking communion,[122] or indeed otherwise restrain him
in his religious worship. His grandson, the 2nd Earl Russell,
who went to live at Pembroke Lodge in 1876, noted that 'the
atmosphere of the house was religious'. The day always began
with morning prayers and Sundays were marked by attendance
at church in nearby Petersham. Russell's religious attendance
in London, when living at Chesham Place, was the subject of
a pamphlet war in the 1850s, following his 1851 attack on
ritualism, since he had the opportunity to attend both a
ritualist church (St Paul's, Knightsbridge) and a Low-Angli-
can chapel. In fact, according to his biographer, he attended
both. Certainly Morpeth noticed him at Belgrave Chapel,
Pimlico, along with Thomas Musgrave, a former Fellow of
Trinity, liberal reformer and Archbishop of York.[123]

These religious devotions should not be mistaken for
Evangelical sobriety. Although there were exceptions to
Evangelical bans on gambling, horse-racing, and card-playing
(William Wilberforce, for example, had played cards and in
1841 Lord Shaftesbury attended Ascot), by and large, even
among the more liberal Evangelicals G. W. E. Russell recollected from his aristocratic childhood, these bans were enforced,
along with condemnations of opera, theatre, and balls, and a
strict observance on the sabbath.[124] Yet these were not rules
of conduct, which these younger Whigs felt obliged to obey.
Rice's son-in-law, Henry Taylor, described him as 'a man of
light heart and happy nature', his house at Petersham characteristically being 'full of poetry'. Rice's ambition (which

---

[120] [Phipps], *The English in France* iii. 234.
[121] Maxwell, *The Creevey Papers*, ii. 173, 175.   [122] Wapole, *Russell*, ii. 468–9.
[123] J. F. S. Rusell, *My Life and Adventures* (London, 1923), 30, 34, 50, 334; W.
Thorpe, *A Review of the Revd. J. E. Bennett's Letter to Lord John Russell* (London, 1850);
Lascelles, *Journals kept by Earl of Carlisle*, 145.
[124] G. Russell, *Evangelical Movement*, 133–7.

shortage of funds put out of his reach) was to follow Holland's lead in maintaining a salon which would have united politics and literature.[125] Morpeth frequently played whist, croquet, cricket, and had a passion for dancing. Lord Ronald Gower remembered that 'Whatever the game or frolic "Uncle Morpeth" was the merriest.'[126] Even Howick did not object to the opposition Cabinet in 1835 meeting on a Sunday, nor did he carp at Sunday visiting. He also went to the theatre, seeing Kean play Hamlet in 1838 and a production of *London Assurance* at Covent Garden in March 1841.[127] The religion which these Whigs possessed was broad and tolerant. At his election in 1830 Morpeth referred to the existence of religious principles to which all could subscribe, namely 'the worship of a common Creator, the doctrines of a common Gospel and the faith of a common Cross'.[128] Rice, writing to J. W. Blakesley, likewise agreed that, as far as education was concerned, it was true that 'the common truths of Christianity may be disengaged from the peculiar tenets and distinct professions' of particular sects.[129] He did not hesitate to send his sons to attend lectures at the ecumenical London University.[130] Such actions were not signs of indifference or lack of consideration, but the product of a particular affiliation, of beliefs associated with a liberal school of divines centred around the colleges of Oriel at Oxford, and Trinity at Cambridge, and numbering among its members such theologians as Arnold, Whately, Thirlwall, and Peacock.

In his diary Morpeth recorded his reading of Arnold's *History of Rome, Essay on the Interpretation of Scripture, A Fragment on the Church,* and *Sermons.* On finishing Dean Stanley's *Life of Thomas Arnold* he wrote enthusiastically: 'I could not have liked a book more: the predominant feeling has been but selfish. Oh, why was I not brought up under him or as that could not be, why

---

[125] Taylor, *Autobiography,* i. 210–11; John Rylands Library Eng. MSS 1187 (Monteagle Papers), fo. 202: Rice to C. Spring Rice, 27 Oct. 1840.

[126] Gower, *My Reminiscences* (London, 1895). 83.

[127] Grey Papers C3/1B: Howick Jour., 1, 22 Mar. 1835; *ibid.* C3/3: Howick Jour., 21 Feb. 1838; ibid. C3/7: Howick Jour., 12 Mar. 1841.

[128] Gaskin, *Vice Regal Speeches etc., of Earl of Carlisle,* 249.

[129] TCC Addit. MSS a.244 (Blakesley Papers), fo. 82: Rice to Blakesley, 16 Nov. 1839.

[130] John Rylands Library Eng. MSS 1187 (Monteagle Papers), fo. 14: C. Spring Rice to S. Spring Rice, n.d. [1835–6].

could I have not known more of him? It might have led me into too much idolatry of him . . .'.[131] When the Whigs were in office Morpeth supported Arnold's candidacy for the Wardenship of Manchester. Russell also aligned himself with Arnold's religious outlook in his *Recollections and Suggestions*, and identified himself with the views of Arnold fils and Milman, the Broad Church Dean of St Paul's, in the preface to his *Essays on the Rise and Progress of Christianity*.[132] Russell's idea of 'a good Xtian bishop' was Edward Stanley, the Bishop of Norwich and father of the Broad Church Dean of Westminster, who pressed for Arnold to be given ecclesiastical preferment, and was one of his greatest admirers and supporters; his son wrote Arnold's life.[133] Rice also praised Arnold, referring to him as one 'in whose principles we place the greatest confidence and for whom we entertain the utmost respect'. He formed a friendship with another Oxford liberal, Baden Powell, who was his house guest in 1839, and entertained two others, Richard Whately and his pupil, Nassau Senior, to dinner.[134] Other liberal Oxford divines who moved in Whig circles included Milman, who entertained Morpeth and Rice at his table, and Hampden, amongst whose supporters in 1836, during the controversy surrounding his appointment to the Regius Chair of Divinity, Morpeth was reckoned to be one of the strongest.[135] Next to Arnold, however, it was probably Whately who exercized the strongest fascination for these politicians. Morpeth noted in his diary with regard to the Archbishop of Dublin that he had 'certainly never heard a preacher with whom it was more impossible to disagree', and, when Whately died, Morpeth desired Fitzgerald, the Bishop of Killaloe, as his successor (he was known colloquially as 'the Archbishop's shadow'). Mulgrave, when Lord Lieutenant, in a similar fashion, took

[131] Lascelles, *Journals kept by Earl of Carlisle*, 3, 11, 12, 22.

[132] J. Russell, *Progress of the Christian Religion in Europe*, v, viii; *idem, Recollections and Suggestions*, 140.

[133] Broadlands MSS MEL/RU (Melbourne Papers), fo. 45: Russell to Melbourne, 10 Sept. 1837; A. P. Stanley (ed.), *Memoirs of Edward and Catherine Stanley* (London, 1879, 80–81).

[134] NLI MSS 534 (Monteagle Papers): Rice to Arnold, 5 Nov. 1838; BL Addit. MSS 51573 (Holland House Papers), fo. 87: Rice to Lady Holland, 1 Sept. 1839; Whishaw, *The Pope of Holland House*, 270.

[135] Lascelles, *Journals kept by Earl of Carlisle*, 43; Hampden Papers, fo. 63: Dibden to Hampden, 30 Apr. 1836.

the unusual step of appointing an Englishman, Whately's chaplain, Dr Dickinson, to the see of Meath.[136]

Trinity was the Cambridge equivalent of Oriel. Rice had been a friend since his college days of the Fellow of Trinity, liberal divine, and mathematician, George Peacock, and he offered to nominate him to a series of preferments, including the deanery of Ely, the principalship of Haileybury, and the mastership of Trinity.[137] Peacock was tutor to Rice's son, Stephen, and through the filial connection, Rice met another Trinity Fellow and Apostle, J. W. Blakesley, whom Rice nominated for the headmastership of Rugby and who later became Dean of Lincoln.[138] Rice's association with the borough of Cambridge as its MP brought him into contact with other liberals who helped at elections. When he returned to Cambridge for his by-election in June 1834, on his elevation to the Cabinet, he dined with Empson, Musgrave, and Romilly, all Fellows of Trinity.[139] Connop Thirlwall, another Trinity don, knew Howick from when they had both been members of the London Debating Society. When he removed to the living of Kirby Underdale in 1834, he entered the society of Yorkshire Whiggery in so far as Sir Francis Wood, the father of Charles Wood, the Whig politician, was the local landed proprietor.[140] Sedgwick, the geologist and liberal, originally from Yorkshire, worked for Morpeth in the 1835 election.[141] Trinity, indeed, became something of an educational centre for Whiggery during this period. Not only Rice, but also Ebrington, Radnor, and Sydney Smith sent their sons there, and Lansdowne asked Peacock to arrange tutors for his.[142]

These divines were also the recipients of Whig ecclesiastical preferment. Sedgwick obtained a canonry at Norwich, Peacock

[136] Lascelles *Journals kept by Earl of Carlisle*, 262; Fitzpatrick, *Richard Whately*, i. 249.

[137] NLI MSS 13382 (11) (Monteagle Papers): Peacock to Rice, 17 Apr. 1836; NLI MSS 13392 (6) (Monteagle Papers): Peacock to Rice, 9 May 1839; NLI MSS 532 (Monteagle Papers): Rice to Hobhouse, 18 Aug. 1837.

[138] NLI MSS 13393 (6) (Monteagle Papers): Lord Stanley to Rice, 26 July 1842.

[139] J. P. T. Bury (ed.), *Romilly's Cambridge Diary 1832–1842* (Cambridge, 1967), 59.

[140] C. Thirlwall, *Letters Literary and Theological* (London, 1881), 129; J. C. Thirlwall Jr., *Connop Thirlwall* (London, 1936), 87.

[141] J. W. Clark and T. M. Hughes, *Life and Letters of the Revd Adam Sedgwick* (Cambridge, 1890), i. 441.

[142] On the 3rd Earl Fortescue, see *DNB*; Peacock Papers, MSS 2, fo. 30: Radnor to Peacock, 2 June 1835; ibid., MSS 1, fo. 127: Lansdowne to Peacock, 24 May 1828; ibid., MSS 2, fo. 64: Smith to Peacock, 2 Sept. 1834

the deanery of Ely, Thirlwall the see of St David's, and Musgrave that of Hereford. Hare, another former Fellow of Trinity, in 1840 was considered for a bishopric, and James Bowstead, a Fellow of Corpus closely associated with the Trinity Whigs in their campaigns to remove university restrictions on Nonconformists, became Bishop of Sodor and Man in 1838.[143] Arnold, if never given the ecclesiastical preferment these Whigs desired, was appointed nevertheless to a fellowship at London University and became Regius Professor of Modern History at Oxford. Hampden, considered for a bishopric in 1835, gained the Regius Chair of Divinity at Oxford in 1836.[144] Whately became Archbishop of Dublin in 1831. Russell, when Prime Minister, expressed a distinctive preference for such divines in his ecclesiastical appointments. He translated Musgrave to York and appointed Hampden to Hereford. He gave the see of Norwich to Hinds, Whately's former chaplain and Vice-Principal of St Alban Hall, Oxford, and the newly created see of Manchester to Arnold's Trinity-educated assistant at Rugby, James Prince Lee. Milman received the deanery of St Paul's in 1849 and Tait, Arnold's successor as headmaster of Rugby, became Dean of Carlisle.[145]

The politicians also attempted to involve the divines in the machinery of government itself. This involvement marked the receipt of favours not granted to other clergymen in this period, and thus is an indication of one way in which the government acquired the reputation for religious liberalism. Peacock and Arnold drew up the code for the new college in Van Dieman's land on behalf of the Colonial Office, and Arnold was involved in composing some of the text books used by the Irish National Board of Education. Baden Powell composed a defence of the government's 1839 education proposals, Arnold in the *Edinburgh Review* defended the appointment of Hampden to the Oxford Regius Chair of Divinity, and Nassau Senior submitted proposals concerning the surplus funds of the Irish Church to the consideration of the Cabinet. Hampden advised Radnor, and through him the government, on the Oxford

[143] On Hare, see Broadlands MSS MEL/RU (Melbourne Papers), fo. 120: Russell to Melbourne, 28 Aug. 1840.

[144] On Hampden as a candidate for a bishopric, see Sanders, *Lord Melbourne's Papers*, 496.

[145] Chadwick, *The Victorian Church*. i. Ch. 4 *passim*.

University Bill of 1835, and gave Russell advice on the creation
of new theological professorships at Oxford as eventually
proposed in the Dean and Chapters Act of 1840. Peacock
supplied Rice with information on university reform in 1837.[146]
Whately, above all, proved the most influential ecclesiastical
politician. He advised the government on ecclesiastical preferment and acted as its agent when sounding out Hampden on
the possibility of becoming a bishop, or attempting to persuade
Arnold to remain a Fellow of London University. He advised
the government on Irish Poor Laws and Irish education (he
sat on the National Board and was its most important
propagandist in Ireland). Perhaps his most decisive legislative
achievement was when he forced the government to redraft the
Irish Church Bill in 1835, in order to ensure that the surplus
funds, which were to be appropriated to educational purposes,
did not depend on the fluctuating fortunes of the Irish Church.
Arnold wrote of the government: 'In Church matters they
have got Whately and a signal blessing it is that they have
him and listen to him.'[147] Whately, and with him the liberal
Anglican tradition, was placed at the heart of the government's
church policy.

While, therefore, it is right to suggest that Foxite Whigs
could happily acquiesce in Radical demands for the reform of
the Anglican Church because they had no substantial religious
beliefs to affront, it would be wrong to apply this argument
to younger Whigs who were the predominant exponents of
policies designed to liberalize the national establishments of
nineteenth-century Britain. Those young Whigs who
developed a liberal Anglican doctrine in politics, and who rose
to political prominence in the mid-1830s by means of their

[146] TCC Addit. MSS a.77 (Whewell Papers), fo. 133: Hare to Whewell, 8 March
[1842]; Pusey House MSS, chest B draw 3 (Radnor Papers), fo. 18: Hampden to
Radnor, 21 May 1835; BL Microfilm 849/12 (Melbourne Papers): Hampden to
Russell, 28 Feb. 1840; NLI MSS 13386 (5) (Monteagle Papers): Peacock to Rice, 3
Feb. 1837; B. Powell, *State Education considered with Reference to Prevalent Misconceptions
on Religious Grounds* (London & Oxford, 1840); T. Arnold, 'The Oxford Malignants
and Dr Hampden', *Edinburgh Review*, lxiii (1836), 225–39; S. Leon Levy, *Nassau W.
Senior 1790–1864* (Newton Abbot, 1970), 98; *Parl. Papers* 1837, viii. i. 45.

[147] Hampden Papers, fo. 17: Whately to Hampden, 16 Oct. 1835; NLI MSS 13390
(1) (Monteagle Papers): Whately to Rice, 5 Nov. 1838; E. J. Whately *Richard Whately*,
79, 110, PRO 30/22 1E (Russell Papers), fo. 223: Melbourne to Russell, 22 Oct.
1835; A. P. Stanley, *Life and Correspondence of Thomas Arnold, DD* (6th edn., London,
n.d.), 212.

timely advocacy of policies which sceptical Foxites opposed, possessed not merely an undefined religious sympathy, but definite and distinctive religious beliefs. The question which is addressed in the following chapter is whether or not such beliefs mattered; whether or not there was a connection between the religious affiliation and the liberal policies. It is shown, by studying the theological and political doctrines of their more articulate clerical friends, that there was indeed a connection between their religious outlook and their political beliefs. The practical political consequences which these liberal divines derived from their Christian thinking were consonant with the church policies of the Whig governments. This resulted in a fruitful collaboration between these dons and politicians on the question of university reform, an issue which illustrated, as Chapter 5 indicates, in what practical ways they envisaged incorporating Dissent into national establishments.

4

The Theological Origins of
Liberal Anglicanism: Oriel Noetics and
Trinity Liberals

THE liberal Anglican clerics, whom the Whigs praised and patronized, possessed an impressive range of intellectual and theological preoccupations. No attempt will be made, in the discussion which follows, to provide a full account of their Promethean activities. To do so would be to make a contribution, at the very least, to the study of theology, political economy, history, philosophy, philology, classics, and the natural sciences. These early Victorian clerics were not nice observers of those academic distinctions which now separate one discipline from another. What follows, however, is not the comprehensive account of their thought which they deserve, but a description of the intellectual route by which they arrived at political positions, akin to those of their lay patrons. Only such of their concerns as were pertinent to the relations of both church and state to Dissent will be treated here. In intellectual terms this means their understanding of revelation, and hence biblical exegesis; of the standing of the church's creeds and formularies with regard to the truths of Christianity; of ecclesiastical authority and of the importance of tradition. Disproportionate space will be devoted to those theologians who wrote specifically on these topics. Such an imbalance may appear to diminish the importance of those (mainly Cambridge) theologians, such as Peacock, a mathematician and later Dean of Ely, and Sedgwick, Woodward Professor of Geology, whose contributions to the problem of Dissent were primarily practical. No such diminution is intended. It is only the unfortunate consequence of sketching the published doctrines of these divines in so far as they were of importance to liberal politics and politicians.

To consider these divines as a group may be considered controversial. Certainly they did not exist as a party in the Tractarian sense. They had no manifesto, equivalent to the *Tracts for the Times*, nor a political organization akin to the Corpus committee. In part, this was due to accidents of time and place. Almost a generation separated the youngest from the oldest Noetic. Consequently, pursuing their careers at different ages, they tended to find themselves scattered in moments of crisis. When, for example, Hampden was appointed to the Reguis Chair of Divinity at Oxford in 1836, Davison, the Oriel Noetic, had already died; Copleston was Bishop of Llandaff; Whately resided in Dublin as Archbishop, and Arnold occupied the Headmaster's house at Rugby. Only Hawkins, the Provost of Oriel, Hampden himself, and Powell, Savilian Professor of Geometry, were left to contest the opposition at Oxford. At Trinity College, Cambridge, there was also a diaspora of liberals in the course of the 1830s, with the result that Hare, the German scholar and later Archdeacon of Lewes, Thirlwall, who became Bishop of St David's, and Musgrave, later Bishop of Hereford, moved to preferments outside the university. Thus it would have been difficult to concert action in anything like the Tractarian fashion. These liberals did not exist as a college within a college, but were members of that greater society of Oxford and Cambridge which existed beyond city walls, and which, in the absence of other major educational institutions, so dominated Victorian England's public life. These liberals were members of an invisible club, the rules and purpose of which are to be inferred from private correspondences and informal associations, and not from any publicly transcribed regulations.

These liberal friendships were the products of intellectual influence and sympathies, consolidated, sustained, and extended through a series of interlocking societies: school, college, and club. Hinds, Whately's chaplain in Ireland and later Bishop of Norwich, Hare, and Thirlwall were at Charterhouse together; Hare met Arnold through his brother, Augustus Hare, both being members of the Attic Society; Hare, Thirlwall, Arnold, and F. D. Maurice, the apostle and Broad Churchman, dined together as members of the John Sterling Club; Thirlwall and Arnold were among the founders of the

London Philological Society.[1] A shared interest in the promotion of scientific studies led Sedgwick, Peacock, and Whewell, the scientist, philosopher, and Master of Trinity, to be members of the Cambridge Philosophical Society, while the desire to reform Cambridge mathematics led Herschel, the Johnian astronomer, Peacock, and Babbage, the Peterhouse mathematician, to found the Analytical Society.[2] Through their association with the Cambridge Conversazione Society, Hare and Thirlwall were able to influence new generations of undergraduates such as Maurice, John Sterling, essayist and poet, J. W. Blakesley, the Dean of Lincoln, and Stephen Spring Rice, the son of the Whig Chancellor of the Exchequer. Intellectual debt was a major cause of the friendships established. Sedgwick taught Musgrave, Peacock, and Hare; Whately acknowledged Copleston, the Provost of Oriel, as his intellectual mentor, and he, in his turn, taught Senior, the political economist, and Hinds, and strongly influenced Arnold and Hawkins.[3] Intellectual debt further extended the influence of these liberals into the mid-nineteenth century. At Rugby, Arnold taught A. P. Stanley, who became Dean of Westminster, who was then tutored by Hare before going up to Balliol. Hare taught James Prince Lee, the first Bishop of Manchester, before Arnold secured his services as an assistant master at Rugby.[4] Such a partial unravelling of the connecting threads gives only a brief indication of the nature of the associations between nineteenth-century liberals. Nevertheless, it demonstrates something of the closed, self-referential nature of the Victorian intellectual world.[5]

As is the case with many clubs, it would be wrong to assume that membership implied an identity of views and interests. In politics, these liberals were not uniformly Whiggish in a

[1] N. M. Distad, *Guessing At Truth* (Sheperdstown, 1979), 102; P. Allen, *The Cambridge Apostles* (Cambridge, 1978), 182, 186–7, 193; H. Aarsleff, *The Study of Language in England 1780–1860* (Princeton, 1967), 211–12.

[2] Clark & Hughes, *Revd Adam Sedgwick* (Cambridge, 1890), i. 206; M. M. Garland, *Cambridge Before Darwin* (Cambridge, 1980), 20, 23; Cannon, 'Scientists and Broadchurchmen', 72.

[3] Allen, *The Cambridge Apostles*, 10 and *passim*; Clark & Hughes, *Revd Adam Sedgwick* i. 121; E. J. Whately, *Richard Whately*, 15, 236; Oriel MSS Db 182 (Hawkins Papers): Whately to Hawkins, 11 Oct. 1831; Stanley, *Thomas Arnold*, 377.

[4] Distad, *Guessing At Truth*, 103, 127.

[5] Annan, 'The Intellectual Aristocracy'.

partisan sense. Whately claimed that he had 'always been exempt from Whiggery and Toryism & such like infirmities'.[6] Copleston, an adviser to the Whigs on matters of ecclesiastical patronage, was 'a most decided Tory', if of the more liberal, Grenvillite school; Hare, despite his earlier association with the Whig party, by 1840 had become 'decidedly Conservative'.[7] These liberals were neither intellectually nor politically monolithic. Arnold opposed the removal of civil disabilities for Jews, which Whately supported.[8] Hawkins privately believed Hampden's Bampton Lectures contained 'many things very rash', and 'as they stand, unsound', although this did not prevent his compiling a vindication of Hampden's opinions.[9] Dickinson, Whately's chaplain in Dublin, in 1833 clashed publicly with Arnold on the principles of church reform.[10] These liberals, moreover, concerned themselves with different areas of religious debate. Sedgwick and Baden Powell preoccupied themselves primarily, although not exclusively, with scientific pursuits and the defence of an orthodox natural theology. Thirlwall and Hare began as classical and philological scholars; the latter, by way of studying German theology and Coleridge, concluded with a defence of Christianity, based on an understanding of the transcendent relationship between man and God. Whately, Hampden, and Arnold, in their turn, were chiefly interested in employing historical and linguistic skills to mount a rational defence of revealed religion.

Even if this internal diversity had not existed, two considerations, fundamental to an understanding of these liberals, would have prevented the transformation of this club into a partisan group. Certainly, internal diversity alone is not a sufficient explanation of their failure to act in a Tractarian fashion. (There were, for example, substantial differences between the leading Tractarians themselves, as their subsequent careers testify. Keble remained fundamentally a

---

[6] BI Addit. MSS 51965 (Holland House Papers), fo. 108: Whately to Miss Fox, 4 Dec. [1841].

[7] E. Copleston, *Remains; With an Introduction by R. Whately* (London, 1854), 28; BL Microfilm 859/7 (Melbourne Papers): Melbourne to Russell, 27 Aug. 1840.

[8] Stanley, *Thomas Arnold* 274; R. Whately, *A Speech in the House of Lords on a Bill for the Removal of Certain Disabilities* (London, 1833).

[9] Oriel MSS Db 413 (Hawkins Papers): Hawkins to Whately, 18 Feb. 1836.

[10] C. Dickinson, *Observations on Church Reform* (Dublin, 1833).

non-juror, Pusey became an Anglo-Catholic, and Newman's intellectual disquiet was only finally silenced by the embrace of the Church of Rome.) The first of these restraints was that the liberals, unlike the Tractarians, did not regard their fellow Anglicans as their domestic enemies. On the contrary, since these liberals were inspired by the need not to attack but to defend Anglicanism, High Churchmen were welcome fellow-travellers in the process of Anglican renewal.

It is debatable, indeed, whether it makes much sense to draw a distinction between liberals and High Churchmen in the years before the Whig governments of the 1830s. It was only in that decade, in response to Whig tamperings with the church, particularly in Ireland, that the church parties associated with the Victorian era began to assume their distinctive form. Until then, the defence of Anglicanism was a collaborative enterprise, a source of union rather than a cause for dispute. The close connections which existed between various persons, who retrospectively acquired the reputation for being antagonists, is indicative of this. Newman revealed this most notoriously in his *Apologia*, in which he acknowledged the importance of the teaching of Hawkins for his doctrine of tradition, and of Whately for his anti-Erastian views. This was not so much unique as illustrative. In 1825 and 1826, Pusey travelled to the German centres of liberal theology, Göttingen and Berlin, and returned an enthusiast for the new criticism, which he advocated in his first published, if subsequently repudiated, work, an attack on H. J. Rose.[11] Hampden, for his part, held a curacy at the High Church centre of Hackney, and in 1825 gained the editorship of the High Church *Christian Remembrancer*. Baden Powell, in his earlier years, was a frequent reviewer for the *British Critic*.[12] The legacy of such associations can be seen, for example, in the initial reaction of Thirlwall to the Tractarians. In his Charge for 1842, the *Tracts for the Times* were welcomed as part of the current renaissance in theological learning. Thirlwall looked on the existing controversy with more 'hope' than 'alarm'. Perhaps, by way of

[11] J. H. Newman, *Apologia Pro Vita Sua* (London, 1966), 35, 37; H. C. G. Matthew, 'Edward Bouverie Pusey', *Jour. of Theological Studies*, new ser. xxxii (1981), 106, 108.
[12] H. Hampden (ed.), *Some Memorials of R. D. Hampden, Bishop of Hereford* (London, 1871), p. 15; Corsi, 'Baden Powell' (D.Phil. thesis), 27, 104.

explanation, it should be recollected that Thirlwall, isolated in rural Wales from the rows at Oxford, could afford to take a more tolerant view than his Noetic counterparts such as Baden Powell. But even he claimed, in his published discussion of Tractarian doctrine, that he had no other object in writing than 'that of promoting *inquiry*'.[13]

The second, and this time intellectual, restraint on the liberals forming themselves into an organized church party was their ultimate aim of comprehension. The liberals saw themselves as combating that great 'evil' of post-Revolutionary Europe, religious scepticism. Hinds, for example, believed that it was 'urgently important' to reiterate the external evidences of Christianity, given 'the advance of free-thinking and scepticism'. Whately addressed his early Anglican apologetics primarily to 'those who regard Christianity with *indifference*'. Both theologians were concerned to demonstrate the authenticity and necessity of revelation.[14] The vehicle for this reassertion of Christianity was to be the Anglican Church, viewed as the church of the nation. They wished to gather into its pews all those professing a Christian faith. Arnold expressed their view in characteristically bald fashion, when he suggested that, to 'check' unbelief, 'nothing would be so efficient as a well organized and comprehensive National Church acting unitedly and popularly, and with adequate means upon the whole mass of the population'.[15] With such an aim in view, preaching toleration became second nature. It would have been hypocritical for the liberals to have constituted themselves a church within the church, after the alleged fashion of the Tractarians. The High Churchmen, of course, were to argue that it was a weak faith which could accommodate diverse doctrinal beliefs, while pretending to proclaim the one Truth. But as long as the liberals refused to recognize the contradiction, it was impossible for them to consider the Tractarians as their enemies, as it was to anathematize Nonconformists. All were

[13] C. Thirlwall, *A Charge to the Clergy of the Diocese of St David's by Connop, Lord Bishop of St David's* (London, 1842), 37, 39; B. Powell, *A Supplement to Tradition Unveiled* (London & Oxford, 1840), 1.

[14] S. Hinds, *An Inquiry into the Proofs, Nature, and Extent of Inspiration, and into the Authority of Scripture* (Oxford, 1831), 45–6; R. Whately, *Essay on Some of the Peculiarities of the Christian Religion* (Oxford, 1825), ix.

[15] T. Arnold, *Principles of Church Reform*, (4th edn., London, 1833), 87.

putative adherents of the same comprehensive and national Christianity.

The Noetics were possibly the last English representatives of a school of Christian apologetics which had its origins in Locke's *An Essay concerning Human Understanding* (1689). In this work, while he denied that the idea of God was innate, Locke argued that 'having furnished us with those Faculties, our minds are endowed with, he [God] hath not left himself without witness: since we have Sense, Perception, and Reason, and cannot want a clear proof of him, as long as we carry ourselves about us'.[16] With this assumption, much eighteenth-century apologetic writing was a demonstration of the evidence for God's existence. These were two kinds, the natural and the written or revealed, and the demonstrations sought to show, first, that the existence of God (and of a future state) could be inferred from the contemplation of nature; second, that the Scriptures were an authentic record of God's Providence, and especially of the ministry of Christ. Further, theologians attempted to show that there was no contradiction between these two types of Christian evidence: that the God of Nature and the God of the Bible were identical and equally intelligible to human reason. This, indeed, was one argument of Locke's own essay on *The Reasonableness of Christianity* (1695). In this work he attempted to prove, among other things, that there was no contradiction between the historical fact that divine revelation was granted to only a few and the doctrine of God's universal benevolence, which was derived from studying nature.

The Noetics looked to two eighteenth-century divines in particular as their precursors: William Paley, the Archdeacon of Carlisle, and Joseph Butler, Bishop of Durham. The Paley of these liberal Anglicans was not the moral philosopher, whose utilitarianism they deplored, but the author of *A View of the Evidences of Christianity* and of the *Natural Theology*. Whately, Paley's nineteenth-century editor, commented in a lecture that the Archdeacon of Carlisle's writings were 'less read . . . than they deserve to be'; it was 'worthwhile' to study nature and revelation 'with the aid of such a guide as Paley'.[17] This was

---

[16] J. Locke, *An Essay concerning Human Understanding* (Oxford, 1979), 619.

[17] R. Whately, *Dr Paley's Works: A Lecture* (London, 1859), 5, 9.

partly because such divines as Whately felt intellectually
stranded in the mid-nineteenth century cross-fire between, on
the one side, the Tractarians and Evangelicals, and, on the
other, the 'Mythics' and 'Naturalists' (to use Whately's
terminology), those German-inspired theologians who reduced
the Scriptures to the level of parables, or who explained away
miracles as natural phenomena. Paley was an eighteenth-
century guide to a *via media* of reason and light, which led
between routes either to infidelity or to irrational, although
traditional, faith.

Paley's chief virtue, as far as the Noetics were concerned,
was that in his two popular works he had mustered almost all
the eighteenth-century weaponry there was in defence of the
separate authenticity of biblical and natural revelation. He
had left little for the Noetics to add. More importantly, Paley
accepted the form, if not the substance, of Hume's attack on
the evidences of Christianity. That is to say, he had accepted
Hume's assumption that the authenticity of the Scriptures was
a question of probability, but reached the counter-conclusion
that the Bible was a highly plausible document. Paley attempted to vindicate Christian doctrines without abandoning the
rhetoric of rational disputation. In this he was not unique; in
1736 Butler had written in his defence of revelation that 'probability is the very guide of life'.[18] But Butler had written before
Hume had published his first *Philosophical Essays concerning
Human Understanding* (1748), which included his famous essay
'Of miracles'. It was up to those who defended Christianity
in the second half of the eighteenth-century to come to terms
with Hume's scepticism. Paley commenced his vindication on
the generally accepted assumption that the world of nature,
with its signs of divine contrivance, was an imperfectly understood revelation. Thus he believed it was unnecessary to show
that man needed an additional revelation. At the same time
he asserted that God was not likely to leave man in a state of
ignorance. Paley therefore concluded that it was very probable
that God had made further revelation; the question was
whether the Scriptures, as handed down to man, constituted
a true account of that revelation. He provided the evidence
that it was. This included proof of the reliability of its witnesses,

[18] J. Butler, *Works*, ed. W. E. Gladstone, (Oxford, 1896), i. 5.

of the historical authenticity of the biblical texts, of the unique-
ness of the events, and of other equally salient circumstances.
Acknowledging that the truth of Christianity depended on 'its
leading facts', Paley claimed that 'we have evidence which
ought to satisfy us'.[19]

Some of the Noetics wrote simply in accordance with this
design of Paley. They added to, or elaborated, the 'auxiliary
evidences' of Christianity which Paley had suggested in his
Evidences. Thus Davison's *Discourses on Prophecy* (1824), in
demonstrating the fulfilment of Old and some New Testament
prophecies, provided corroborating proof that Christianity was
a revelation from God. The argument was that successful
predictions of a kind, which could not ordinarily be foreseen,
constituted evidence 'that neither Fate nor Man are masters
of the world'. Hinds, likewise, in writing *The History of the Rise
and Early Progress of Christianity* (1828), elaborated Paley's ninth
auxiliary evidence, namely 'The Propagation of Christianity'.[20]
Of course neither Noetic author was a mere echo of his
eighteenth-century forbear. Davison famously adumbrated
his doctrine of progressive revelation to explain differences
between the moral code set out in the Mosaic law, that of the
prophets and that of the Gospel, declaring that God's revealed
will was 'enlarged from time to time, with respect to the sense
of his law'; while Hinds, in discussing the history of primitive
Christianity, also passed comment on the true nature of the
church, on the assumption that 'much of the character' which
a Christian asserted for his church depended on a 'true
representation of the Rise of Christianity'.[21] Nevertheless,
despite these variations, such work was in accordance with
the scheme of Christian apologetics already well established
when Paley published his work. Indeed, nowhere was this
more apparent than in Whately's first published work, *Historic
Doubts Relative to Napoleon Buonaparte* (1819).

In this work Whately attempted an ironical refutation of
Hume's essay on miracles, in order to support Paley's claim
that 'in miracles adduced in support of revelation, there is not

[19] W. Paley, *A View of the Evidences of Christianity in Three Parts* (London, 1859), 386.
[20] J. Davison, *Discourses on Prophecy* (London, 1824), 83; S. Hinds, *The History of the Rise and Early Progress of Christianity* (London, 1828); Paley, *Evidences of Christianity*.
[21] Davison, *Discourses on Prophecy*, 62; Hinds, *Early Progress of Christianity*, x.

any such antecedent improbability as no testimony can surmount'.[22] On the assumption that Napoleon's exploits were as much infractions of the laws of nature, established by experience, as were miracles, Whately proceeded to argue that it was just as possible to doubt witnesses to contemporary events as it was to doubt those to divine revelation. He suggested that those who had faith in the former, but disbelieved the latter, were 'unduly prejudiced against whatever relates to religion'.[23] If such doubts were to be held consistently, argued Whately, nothing would be believed outside immediate experience, no testimony would ever be admitted as accurate. Consequently, anybody who adopted such a position would have to argue that he had no reason to believe that either Christ or Napoleon committed those acts attributed to them. But if it were accepted that Napoleon had existed, and had performed 'impossible' acts, then it was just as probable that Christ had performed miracles. The course of Christ's life was no more improbable than that of Napoleon's.

Bishop Butler was responsible for inspiring the form of Whately's argument. In discussing the possible existence of miracles, Butler had claimed that there was 'a presumption of millions to one, against the story of Caesar, or of any other man', before sufficient proof was provided. He then asked, with particular regard to miracles, 'what can a small presumption, additional to this, amount to . . . ?', in order to make the point that the presumption against miracles was no more different in kind than that with respect to any unusual event.[24] It should be no great surprise that a Noetic such as Whately turned to Bishoip Butler as his guide in an argument which elaborated one of Paley's evidences. Whereas Paley was chiefly a popular summarizer of late eighteenth-century Anglican apologetics, Butler had been one of its principal agents. Paley wrote only one work of great originality, the *Horae Paulinae*, his skills being largely expository; Butler, on the other hand, in the *Analogy of Religion* (1736), produced a work, the methodology of which was to serve as a model for many of the Noetics' own theological exercises. Hampden went so far

---

[22] Paley, *Evidences of Christianity*, 32.
[23] R. Whately, *Historic Doubts relative to Napoleon Buonaparte* (London, 1819), 39.
[24] Butler, *Words*, i. 217–8.

as to claim that he had 'endeavoured to exemplify' the 'spirit' of Butler's *Analogy* in all that he had written. At Oxford, moreover, he had been 'mainly instrumental in introducing the works of Bishop Butler into the course of reading for Academical Honours'.[25]

The importance of Butler's *Analogy* was that it proved a connection between natural religion and revelation. In effect, it used 'natural religion' as an auxiliary evidence for the truth of written revelation, and argued that the author of the two divine dispensations (Nature and Scripture) was the same person. Butler accepted as a well-attested fact that the world of nature was God-given. He went on to argue that 'if there be an analogy or likeness between that system of things and dispensation of Providence, which revelation informs us of, and that system of things and dispensation of Providence, which experience together with reason informs us of, i.e. the known course of nature; this is a presumption that both have the same author and cause . . .'.[26] Not surprisingly, Butler concluded that such an analogy did indeed exist. Part I of the *Analogy* was devoted to showing that the scriptural doctrine of a future life could also be inferred from the contemplation of nature. In Part II, Butler indicated that the difficulties involved in written revelation were similar to those found in experience. For example, if it were protested that the Scriptures contained many things surprising to reason, then Butler replied that this was no different from the study of nature. The 'acknowledged constitution and course of nature', he wrote, 'is found to be greatly different from what, before experience, would have been expected'. Likewise, to the objection that a truly benevolent God would not have bestowed the gift of scriptural revelation on a priviledged few, Butler answered this was simply in keeping with the natural distribution of gifts. God, he remarked, dispenses his gifts 'in such variety, both of degrees and kinds, amongst creatures of the same species, and even to the same individuals at different times'.[27] Since these difficulties did not constitute objections to viewing

[25] R. D. Hampden, *Introduction to the Second Edition of the Bampton Lectures of the Year 1832* (London, 1837), 37.

[26] Butler, *Works* i. 10.

[27] Ibid., i. 224, 380.

nature as a divine revelation, they could not be legitimate objections to considering Scripture in a similar fashion.

Butler's work was notoriously obscure. Hampden set himself the task, in his *An Essay on the Philosophical Evidence of Christianity*, of disproving that charge. The work was inspired by a publicly confessed admiration for the *Analogy* and a desire to explain the full force of the argument which Butler had developed. The consequence was that while Butler had disdained to explain the nature of analogical reasoning ('This belongs to the subject of Logic'), Hampden spent much of his essay in explaining precisely that. He dealt at length with the grounds for the analogy between nature and revelation, the force and implications of the argument, and its peculiar attractiveness— as he saw it—as a defence of scriptural truth. But the theological substance of the book was identical to that of Butler. He frequently quoted Butler in the course of the work to indicate that such doctrines as that of a future life and of retribution could be derived from a proper analysis of the natural world. The last section of Hampden's essay dealt with objections to the use of the analogy with nature. Significantly Hampden demonstrated that it did not detract from 'the commanding authority of the written word'. He argued that the system of natural theology was imperfect, that its conjectures were only 'the shadows which foretell the rising of the sun of revelation'.[28] It was necessary to study the Scriptures if God's Providence was to be comprehended fully. This claim was central to the Noetics' apologetic task. For whatever the significance of Butler's additional proof of scriptural truth, the Noetics preoccupied themselves primarily with the interpretation of the Bible. It was this task which gave the Noetics their intellectual distinction, and which ultimately was to prove their downfall.

Neither the appeal to Paley, nor to Butler, places the Noetic enterprise in its true historical context, since neither theologian was primarily concerned with interpreting the Bible. In this regard they are not accurate guides to nineteenth-century liberal theology. In the *British Critic* for 1799, a reviewer referred to the absence of writings on 'the *institution of theology* . . . in a manner adapted to the present state of opinions, and

---

[28] Ibid., i. 7; R. D. Hampden, *An Essay on the Philosophical Evidence of Christianity* (London, 1827), 79, 87, 249, 250.

literary and intellectual habits'. A generation later, the review commended Whately's *Essays on Some of the Difficulties in the Writings of St Paul*, suggesting that he was 'labouring in the same course' as that of John Hey, a former Norrisian Professor of Divinity at Cambridge, who was 'almost the founder of a new and better school of Scriptural criticism and exposition', a generation before. Arnold believed that Hey's commentary on the Thirty-Nine Articles was 'the best and fairest' of any that he knew, while Hampden was happy to cite Hey's work in his *Essay on the Philosophical Evidence of Christianity* (1827), referring to Hey's 'valuable remarks' on analogy and his comments on the regularity of nature.[29] What Hey began, and the Noetics completed, was the incorporation and codification of advances in biblical scholarship undertaken in the eighteenth-century. In his *Lectures in Divinity* (1796), Hey offered advice on how to interpret the Bible correctly, arguing that 'All sayings of Scripture' were best understood with reference to 'the circumstances in which they are used'. He suggested that a knowledge of such matters as Antiquities, History, and Geography were necessary prerequisites for accurate interpretations. 'Right notions' or 'canons of controversy' were required, if religious truth was to be defended without hurting 'the general interests of religion'. Articles of religion should be distinguished from systems of theology, their intention being 'to find a *remedy* for some actual error'. As such, they could become 'a *dead letter*, merely by improvement in the forms used in other churches'. Although Hey was against the repeal of the Test and Corporation Acts, he suggested that 'the Church should be enlarged', endorsing the scheme for comprehension proposed in 1689, which allowed for 'the most perfect toleration to opinion and worship, that could be given'.[30]

The liberal Anglicans merely repeated many of the notions which Hey had stated. As will be seen, in some respects Whately's

[29] *British Critic*, xiv (1799), 496; ibid., new ser., v (1829), 384; Stanley, *Thomas Arnold*, 229; R. D. Hampden, *Philosophical Evidence of Christianity*, 6–7 n, 62 n; H. F. G. Swanston, *Ideas of Order* (Assen, 1976), 24. Swanston differs from account given here, claiming Hampden's 'works were not at all in the Hey manner', but it should be stressed Swanston is primarily concerned with their respective uses of analogical arguments.

[30] J. Hey, *Lectures in Divinity* (Cambridge, 1796), i. 73, 74, 390; ibid., ii. 83, 87, 155.

work was simply a reiteration of Hey's. His essays on St Paul and on the peculiarities of the Christian religion repeated Hey's strictures on interpreting the Bible; Whately's Bampton Lectures, his work on the errors of Romanism, and his manuals on logic and rhetoric extended and revised Hey's canons of civilized debate; Copleston's and Whately's attacks on Calvinism were but the published versions of criticisms Hey had made privately. With regard to the Simeonites, Hey had declared: 'I should be very glad to be of use in checking in any degree the eagerness for running into the inextricable perplexities of Calvinism . . .'.[31] But what the Noetics possessed, and Hey did not, was the ability to give a theoretical gloss to their practical work. The Noetics developed a new theory of biblical exegesis, while Hey merely stated the art of scriptural interpretation as he found it. In a polemical and occasionally boisterous fashion, the Noetics dug into the eighteenth-century seam of rationalist Christianity, until, in the eyes of many, it became exhausted. In order to understand the achievements of the Noetics, it is necessary once again to turn to Bishop Butler and his fellow eighteenth-century Christian apologists.

In the *Analogy*, Butler taught the dangers involved in speculative reason. He insisted that 'reason' was not the source of knowledge, but simply the capacity to know or understand 'experience'. Only by contemplating the world as it was, and not as we would like it to be, could we obtain true theological knowledge. As Hampden described Butler's prescription, 'he calls upon us to abandon our theories,—to curb our imaginations,—to lay aside our prejudices,—and to come, as athletes, bared for the conflict of severe inquiry into the truth, to the consideration of what the constitution *in fact is*'.[32] In his introduction to the *Analogy*, Butler explicitly rejected the work of those 'who indulge in vain and idle speculations, how the world might possibly have been framed as it otherwise is'.[33] Understanding the world of nature was not an activity of abstract reason, but simply a matter of apprehending the facts of nature, as they presented themselves, without forethought or prejudice.

[31] CUL Add. 5864, fo. 120: Hey to Plumptre, 25 May 1812.
[32] R. D. Hampden. *Philosophical Evidence of Christianity*, 282.
[33] Butler, *Works*, i. 12.

Given that the only possible knowledge of the world was knowledge through experience, it next needed to be asked, what sort of knowledge this was. Even before Butler's published work, there had been a long debate, conducted along similar lines, as to what sort of knowledge of God man possessed from contemplating the natural world. The difficulty was that in ascribing to God such attributes as benevolence or foreknowledge, it might be taken to mean that God was benevolent and prescient in a human sense. If this was meant, then God could not be divine; if it was not, then there was no reason to describe God after that fashion. Archbishop King had attempted to solve this difficulty in his *A Discourse on Predestination* (1709). He argued that we know nothing of the essential nature of God; we know only his works which we observe. Thus when we ascribe to Him certain faculties as a consequence of our experience, we do so not because we believe that God possessed those faculties in human form, but because we observe a similarity between God's acts and the acts of those who possess such faculties. We infer that God possesses analogous, not identical, qualities.[34] Our knowledge of God from experience, as Hampden wrote, is 'confessedly relative', which is to say 'we acknowledge His intellectual and moral attributes by conceiving principles in Him, corresponding to the principles in ourselves which produce moral and intellectual effects'.[35] According to these divines, knowledge from experience was of facts relative to the observer.

This was a position which nineteenth-century liberals such as Copleston, Whately, and Hampden endorsed. But they went further than their eighteenth-century models and argued that there was no substantial difference in kind between knowledge derived from nature and that derived from the Scriptures. In the sense outlined above, both were analogical. Hampden offered proof of this in his *Essay*. He suggested that this conclusion could be inferred from the fact that divine knowledge in the Scriptures was addressed to human faculties. God employed 'human ideas and language' as his instruments

---

[34] See E. Copleston's account in *idem, An Enquiry into the Doctrines of Necessity and Predestination* (London, 1821), 116 ff., and W. King, *A Discourse on Predestination With Notes by Revd Richard Whately* (Oxford, 1821), *passim.*

[35] R. D. Hampden, *Philosophical Evidence of Christianity*, 16–7.

of communication; the knowledge thus imparted was dependent on the 'modes of thought which we have acquired in the course of our natural education'; it was taught 'by ideas which are already part of the stock of human knowledge'.[36] Consequently it was impossible to know God in anything but human terms; man was always ignorant of the divine essence. Copleston had previously stated the same view in his *Inquiry*. 'God is revealed to us not as he is *absolutely* in himself', he wrote, 'but *relatively* to ourselves . . . the terms employed are such as clearly indicate not his nature and essence but the duties which belong to us arising out of that relation'.[37]

From this argument it followed that the Scriptures were to be studied in the same way as nature. There was no distinction in kind to be made between the evidence of the natural world and that of the history of Christianity. Both were 'conversant about the phenomena of nature'. They were only to be distinguished 'in respect of the subject-matter' of their respective collections of facts. Thus there was no distinction to be made between the methodology of theology and the other sciences. No human science, claimed Hampden, could give 'an acquaintance with the essential nature of the subjects'; it could only aspire to teach 'an accurate and comprehensive knowledge of the particular facts in that department of nature which is the field of its investigation'.[38] Given that the Scriptures were a collection of facts as was the world of nature, then the rules of induction should be applied equally to both. Hampden argued for the possibility of a scientific inductive theology. In the introduction to the second edition of his Bampton lectures, he wrote that 'the same rule of proceeding applies to Theology and Science . . . we must study the Sacred Records as we study Nature. The method of Induction is to be used here as there'.[39]

Hampden was optimistic as to the success of the inductive method in establishing an incontrovertible religious orthodoxy. He claimed that 'if we follow the method of Induction and confine ourselves to Facts, excluding all hypotheses, we shall

---

[36] Ibid., 20, 22, 23.

[37] E. Copleston, *Necessity and Predestination*, 102.

[38] R. D. Hampden, *Philosophical Evidence of Christianity*, ii, 25.

[39] *Idem*, 'The Scholastic Philosophy considered in Its Relation to Christian Theology', *The Bampton Lectures for 1832* (2nd edn., London, 1837), xlviii–ix.

arrive at absolute Truth'.[10] Apart from a naïve nineteenth-century faith in positivism, two provisos should be mentioned to explain Hampden's claim. The first is Hampden's definition of a scriptural 'fact'. In this term he included not only the doings of Christ but also His sayings: religious truths were as much matters of fact as the actual historical event of the Crucifixion. He claimed, in his defence, that facts were 'WHATEVER IS,—Universal as well as particular Truths, whether founded on Experience or on the Authority of Divine Revelation . . . Nothing was further from my thoughts than to say that Christianity is made up wholly of mere Events and has no Doctrinal Truths in it'.[41] In this manner, Hampden included in his definition of a scriptural 'fact' all that was considered to be essential to Christianity. He observed: 'The whole revelation contained in them [the Scriptures] so far as it is revelation, consists of matter of fact.'[42]

Hampden's second proviso concerned what he meant by 'excluding all hypotheses'. He believed that induction could teach only a certain kind of religious truth, namely that which concerned ourselves and our condition in this life. To proceed to an understanding beyond this, to attempt to establish truths concerning the nature of God, or indeed the origin of the world, from an examination of the Bible was to indulge in dangerous hypothetical speculation. It was a presumptuous undertaking, in which reason assumed the role which only experience should occupy. Thus Hampden, in keeping with his fellow Noetics, emphasized the limits to the knowledge which revelation could provide. He wrote that we should regard the Scriptures 'as engaged in revealing to us the moral of our present circumstances, and not as an attempt to delineate to us "things which eye hath not seen, not ear heard, neither hath it entered into the heart of man to conceive" '.[43] Whately endorsed the suggestion that revelation had only a particular and limited purpose. It was 'not for the increase of our speculative knowledge', he wrote, 'but for our instruction in what is needful to be known' for 'our serving God and conforming our lives

[10] Ibid., xlix.
[41] Ibid., xl–xli.
[42] R. D. Hampden, *Observations on Religious Dissent* (2nd edn., Oxford, 1834), 13–4.
[43] *Idem, Philosophical Evidence of Christianity*, 164.

to his commands'. The information which the Scriptures imparted concerning 'the regulation of our character and practice' while leaving 'our curiosity unsatisfied'; it could not, and did not, provide such knowledge as geological theories.[44] Arnold, in a similar fashion, stressed the importance of what he termed 'accommodation', namely the fact that biblical commands were addressed to particular human needs. He wrote: '. . . most true is it that the Scriptures contain in every case what we want, if we know how to look for it; but the greatest wisdom which we need is this very thing, to know how to look for it aright'.[45]

Such a search, then, if it was to be successful, required that presumption be abandoned, so that neither the hypotheses of speculative reason nor distorting passion interfered with the disinterested contemplation of Scripture. The establishment of rules or guides to induction constituted a significant part of the Noetic enterprise. Whately undertook this task in his Bampton Lectures for 1822, entitled *The Use and Abuse of Party Feeling*. These were essentially an account of the state of mind required by enquirers after religious truth. They were a prescription for avoiding the destructiveness of those who were unnecessarily partisan in religious debate. He attributed party spirit to such causes as ambition, love of novelty, and love of disputation; these three vices, he claimed, had given rise to three specific unorthodox sects: Methodism, Unitarianism, and Calvinism. At the same time he prescribed psychological attitudes, which ought to be adopted if disputation was to be productive. These included admonitions to make allowances for differences of taste and temper, to avoid imputing bad motives and using party phrases.[46] These themes he developed in later works. In his essay *On the Love of Truth*, he suggested tests of psychological self-examination, to see whether or not Christians were pursuing the truth selflessly. The absence of such conditions among Catholics, he used to explain their theological errors. In *The Errors of Romanism*, Whately traced the existence of contentious Catholic dogma to their origins

[44] R. Whately, 'The Use and Abuse of Party Feeling', *The Bampton Lectures for 1822* (Oxford, 1822, 182; *idem, Peculiarities of the Christian Religion*, 196, 199.
[45] T. Arnold, *Sermons, Chiefly on the Interpretation of Scripture* (London, 1845), 279–80.
[46] Whately, *Bampton Lectures for 1822*, 45–7, 252–6.

in human nature. 'The errors of the Romanists', he concluded,
. . . will be found to be the natural and spontaneous growth
of the human heart; they are . . . not so much the effects as
the cause of the Romish system of religion.' These human
failings he identified as the love of superstition in preference
to reason, the disposition to take something on trust rather
than establish its truth for oneself, the desire for unobtainable
knowledge, the preference for the expedient rather than the
true argument, the unwarranted belief in infallibility, the love
of persecution, and, finally, the weakness for trusting in a
name.[47] Whately concluded his attempt to establish the
psychological requirements for a successful examination of the
Scriptures by enjoining a spirit of toleration. His modest aim
was 'to seek out a middle course . . . between narrow-minded
bigotry . . . on the one hand and careless indifference on the
other'.[48]

Given that the truths of Scripture were conveyed relative
to man, they were conveyed in a historically specific fashion.
They were couched in the language and ideas of the Middle
East of two thousand years ago. If restraints on human
presumption were necessary, if man were to learn by experience alone, so was a knowledge of the circumstances in which
divine revelation occurred. Such a knowledge was developed
by using historical, philological, and philosophical tools.
Arnold wrote to the Prussian diplomat and theologian, Bunsen:
'O how heartily do I sympathize in your feelings as to the
union of philological, historical and philosophical research, all
to minister to divine truth'; more soberly he noted that 'The
intellectual means of acquiring a knowledge of the Scriptures
in themselves are, I suppose, Philology, Antiquities and Ancient
History'.[49] Historical knowledge was required in order to establish in what circumstances God addressed man, and so to
discern the divine lesson apart from its particular application.
Philology was a means of appreciating the meaning of God's
message without confusing the historical words, in which it
was expressed, with the objects or divine truths which it

[47] *Idem, Essays on Some of the Difficulties in the Writings of St Paul* (London, 1828),
12–13, 22–31; *idem, The Errors of Romanism traced to their Origin in Human Nature* (London,
1830), 10, 12–19.

[48] *Idem, Bampton Lectures for 1822,* 64.

[49] Stanley, *Thomas Arnold,* 236, 360.

conveyed. Philosophy or logic was a requirement for sound reasoning, a guard against importing fallacious arguments into scriptural exegesis.

The Noetics contributed to the development of these exegetical aids. Whately wrote the *Elements of Logic* (1821), which became an Oxford Schools book; in the preface he announced his belief that 'the adversaries of our Faith would . . . have been on many occasions more satisfactorily answered and would have had fewer openings for cavil, had a thorough acquaintance with logic been a more common qualification than it now is'.[50] Arnold contemplated, though he never completed, a commentary on the Testaments designed to separate the historical statements of fact from the divine. He wrote to Whately that such a commentary would be useful in order 'to make people understand where God spoke to their fathers and where he speaks to them; or rather—since in all he speaks to them, though not after the same manner—to teach them to distinguish where they are to follow the letter and where the spirit'.[51] In this task of exegesis the Noetics were joined by their fellow liberals at Trinity College, Cambridge. It would be a mistake, however, to assume that they did so with altogether similar views.

The Trinity school of liberal theologians, unlike the Oriel Noetics, did not trust to inductive reason alone as the basis of their faith. Hare, later Archdeacon of Lewes, most famously denounced the rule of reason, which he believed to be the delusion of the age, in his 1828 sermon, *The Children of Light*. He insisted that 'if we are to pass from darkness into light, we must have another, an unearthly superterraneous source' of knowledge. This, he argued, was 'that true light, which lighteth every man who cometh into the world' and will 'burst through the dark cloud which sin casts over it'.[52] This theme received its most fulsome expression in a series of sermons entitled *The Victory of Faith*. In these, Hare argued that faith was not an intellectual affirmation of the truths of Christianity, nor a system of philanthropical morality, but an 'inwrought conviction' whose main witness was 'the heart of the believer

---

[50] R. Whately, *Elements of Logic* (London, 1827), xxviii.

[51] Stanley, *Thomas Arnold*, 187.

[52] J. C. Hare, *The Victory of Faith and Other Sermons* (Cambridge, 1840), 213, 215, 220.

himself'. Faith, not being of the sensuous external world, was a peculiar attribute of man; it was 'that power or faculty in man which gives substance and reality to such things as are not objects of sight and fills him with a lively assurance of the things he hopes for'.[53] Other Trinity liberals held this notion, namely that man possessed a unique faculty peculiarly adapted to the reception of divine truth. Blakesley, for example, believed that the divine nature of the Bible was not to be established by an impersonal theological science; it was to be apprehended by 'the individual conscience'. This view he repeated in a sermon entitled *Christian Evidences*, a description which he suggested should be applied 'to such personal experience as this indwelling Power produces in the individual Man'.[54]

Such Platonic mysticism, reworked through Christianity, was largely the legacy of Coleridge, albeit mediated through Hare. In 1817–18 Hare had attended some of Coleridge's lectures in London and, in the early 1820s, he began to attend soirées at the Grove, Hampstead, where he met the poet. At Trinity, Hare was to teach Plato.[55] But even more importantly, this doctrine of an 'indwelling Power' was a safeguard against a rationalist-induced scepticism. This was a position Hare argued in his memoir of John Sterling, a friend and pupil. Sterling's problem in life was 'the same as the great problem' of the age, namely how 'to reconcile faith with knowledge, philosophy with religion, the subjective world of human speculation with the objective world in which God has manifested Himself'. Much to Hare's disquiet, Sterling became estranged from Anglicanism after reading such works of German critical theology as Strauss's *Leben Jesu*. Hare thought it 'a book which a person can hardly read without being more or less hurt by it. If we walk through mire some of it will stick to us'. The lesson he drew from Sterling's life was not that such critical enquiries should be abandoned, but that faith was the necessary and impregnable position from which such campaigns in the domain of the enemy should be conducted. These

[53] Ibid., 24, 60.
[54] J. W. Blakesley, *Conciones Academicae: Ten Sermons preached before the University of Cambridge* (London, 1843), 144.
[55] Distad, *Guessing At Truth*, 39, 44.

Cambridge critics recognized that Christianity needed to be reconciled in some degree with 'the postulates of the intellect', because, in the nineteenth century, this was the only effective form which Christian apologetics could take. Hare wrote in his memoir of Sterling that 'such work must be done. The men of our days will not believe, unless you prove to them that what they are called on to believe does not contradict the laws of their minds, and that it rests upon a solid, unshakeable foundation.'[56] Because they diminished the importance of rational Christianity as a foundation for belief, these Cambridge theologians were able to indulge in rational biblical criticism with impunity.

This Blakesley did explicitly in his sermons. He claimed that there was no need for such criticism to undermine belief; the critic was not so much searching for faith as looking for fresh evidence for an existing belief. Biblical or historical revelation was merely one source of such evidence (and this not the most important), to be placed alongside the moral and experiential. Blakesley urged that Noetic tools of criticism should be brought to bear on this historical evidence in order to verify the authenticity of the canonical Scriptures. Further, by considering the laws of language and the conditions imposed when the Scriptures were written, it would be possible to demonstrate that contemporary faith was the same as that delivered to the saints.[57]

Blakesley's mentors at Trinity, Thirlwall and Hare, both made important contributions to the development of methods of exegesis. This they did by publicizing not so much the philosophy as the technical biblical criticism of the German theologians. Thus they were responsible for translating Schleiermacher's *Essay on St Luke* and Niebuhr's *History on Rome*. What characterized Schleiermacher's *Essay* was the notion that the Scriptures were not in themselves inspired, but rather contained within them records of revelation, written in a language contemporary to their occurrence. Schleiermacher wrote on the assumption that the compiler of the Gospel was not in receipt of continual emanations of the divine

[56] J. C. Hare (ed.), John Sterling *Essays and Tales* (London, 1848), i. ccxxi, cxxxiii, ccxxx.
[57] Blakesley, *Conciones Academicae*, 144–5, 150–53, 160.

spirit; he was the arranger and digester of the testimonies of those who had witnessed such events.[58] Niebuhr's importance, likewise, lay in his refusal to accept myths literally, and in his attempt to establish their truth critically. In his *Vindication of Niebuhr*, Hare wrote approvingly: 'it is very possible in Germany . . . to unite a fervent faith in Christianity . . . with considerable doubts and scruples about the historical value of certain passages in Scripture'.[59]

Thus Oxford united with Cambridge in developing techniques of biblical criticism. In the early 1830s, Thirlwall and Hare founded the *Philological Museum*, a journal designed 'to raise the interest of educated persons for ancient literature and the various subjects connected with it'. They aimed to introduce to England German philological methods, the novelty of which lay in the notion that the definition of words was not fixed by their association with particular things, but by the culturally varying usage of people.[60] Hare solicited contributions for this enterprise from Arnold, who, though declining, did so on the ground of insufficient expertise rather than from disagreement with the aim of the project. Arnold, indeed, was a great admirer of Hare. On receiving a collection of Hare's sermons, published in 1840, Arnold wrote: 'It is a great delight to me to read a book with which I can agree so generally and so heartily'.[61] Perhaps the best indication of their common sentiments was the liberals' friendship for Chevalier Bunsen, the friend and pupil of Niebuhr. In the mid-1830s it was Bunsen's aim to effect by means of liturgical reform a union between the different Protestant confessions. He had composed a general liturgy for that purpose as well as his *Essay towards a General Evangelical Hymn and Prayer-book*.[62] Thirlwall termed this exercise 'the application of philology to the various branches of theology', and in this undertaking

[58] F. Schleiermacher, *A Critical Essay on the Gospel of St Luke* (London, 1825), v–vi.

[59] J. C. Hare, *A Vindication of Niebuhr's History of Rome from the Charges of the Quarterly Review* (Cambridge, 1829), 59.

[60] TCC MSS O.15/44 (Thirlwall Papers), fo. 1: Thirlwall to Bunsen, 10 Oct. 1833; Aarsleff, *The Study of Language*, 145–7; J. Burrow, 'The Uses of Philology in Victorian England', R. Robson (ed.), *Ideas and Institutions of Victorian Britain* (London, 1967), 180–204.

[61] Distad, *Guessing At Truth*, 77; Stanley, *Thomas Arnold*, 400.

[62] Lambeth Palace MSS 2164 (Whately Papers), fo. 10: Bunsen to Whately, 25 Jan. 1834.

Bunsen received the support and close friendship of Hare, Thirlwall, Arnold, and Whately.[63]

These liberals, believing that their techniques of biblical exegesis could establish the essential truths of Christianity, looked forward to the day when a common Christianity and a comprehensive church would exist. Arnold stated his own 'firm belief' that 'every difference of opinion among Christians is either remediable by time and mutual fairness or else is indifferent'; while Hampden asserted: 'Most certainly then do I believe that there is but one Catholic faith—one invariable standard of orthodox truth; and that all departures from this consequently are errors of doctrine and corruptions of faith'.[64] These theologians anticipated an era when religious party strife would cease, and Christians would collaborate in a common cause. After all, Dissent, Hampden suggested, was nothing but a 'difference of opinions arising out of the different conclusions drawn by different minds out of the same given elements of Scripture'; consequently, 'all who acknowledge the divine authority of Scripture are made more unanimous in reality than they profess themselves to be'.[65] The liberal techniques of interpreting Scripture were the prerequisites for a tolerant, enlightened, rational, and true Christianity, one which proved that such qualities did not necessarily imply a tempering of faith or an indifference to religious truth. In the 1820s such an outlook met with a favourable response; by the 1830s it came to be associated with a partisan liberal government which, undeservedly, acquired a reputation for heterodoxy. As the theologians became more explicit about the particular form their religious toleration took, so they were increasingly seen as subversive of the very othodoxy they had initially defended.

In the 1820s these liberal theologians applied their inductive method to a consideration of those theologies which rivalled orthodox Anglicanism: Unitarianism, Calvinistic Evangelicalism, enthusiastic Dissent, and Roman Catholicism. Their argument, at its most extreme, was that Anglicanism

[63] C. Thirlwall, *Letters Literary and Theological*, 103; Burrow, 'The Uses of Philology', 194; Lambeth Palace MSS 2164 (Whately Papers), fo. 10: Bunsen to Whately, 25 Jan. 1834.

[64] Stanley, *Thomas Arnold*, 263; H. Hampden, *R. D. Hampden*, 268.

[65] R. D. Hampden, *Observations on Religious Dissent*, 4–5.

was the only logical outcome of their methodology; all other doctrines were the product of wrongful applications of reason to revelation. Not surprisingly, since this conclusion reinforced the prejudices of those in the mainstream of Anglicanism, High Churchmen were as sympathetic to this approach as the liberals. The liberals, indeed, drew on the work of High Churchmen to reinforce their arguments. Baden Powell, for example, admitted that he was greatly in debt to the work of the High Church Bishop of Durham, van Mildert, in writing *Rational Religion Examined* (1826). He 'afforded the main design, in conformity with which the present remarks have been put together'. Powell's work was the archetypal Anglican apology of this kind. 'The search after religious truth', wrote Powell, was to be conducted on 'the principles [on] which Bacon laid the foundation, and Newton and his successors reared the superstructure of physical truth.' The Scriptures were to be considered as facts arranged in a system which was unknown to man. Because of this, the knowledge which could be derived from them was partial and incomplete; revelation was full of 'difficulties and obscurities'. Thus the rule of rational interpretation consisted 'simply in avoiding such a sense [of the Scriptures] as shall be at absolute variance with itself, or with some equally asserted and evidenced truth'. Since it was uncertain as to how the facts of Scripture related to each other, no humanly derived theological doctrine could afford to be contradicted by any scriptural fact. Powell claimed that this rule of interpretation was 'the ground of faith and the rule of doctrine professed by the Church of England' because 'the Scripture alone is admitted to be the standard and depository of the truth'.[66]

Other doctrines were to be discounted in so far as they deviated from this rule. The Roman error lay in the fact that their faith depended on the existence of a depository of faith in addition to the Scriptures, namely the tradition of the church. But there was insufficient evidence to prove that this further depository was the gift of God. As a consequence the Romanist surrendered himself 'to the dominion of servile superstition'. The enthusiastic Dissenter committed the

---

[66] B. Powell, *Rational Religion Examined: Or, Remarks on the Pretensions of Unitarianism*, (London, 1826), 9, 28, 36, 37.

mistake of believing he possessed a peculiar capacity to interpret revelation; he was falsely persuaded 'of his own peculiar
illumination by the gift of the Holy Spirit'. In his case, reason
was forced to submit to imagination. The Unitarian erred in
making 'the primary truths of Natural Religion' the judge of
'the general authority of Revelation'. He presumed to make
an arbitrary theory the judge of scriptural evidence, and was
so forced into the error of discarding certain passages in the
Bible as false, an act akin to disbelieving his own experiences.
He discarded 'all rational respect for authority, all common
estimation of evidence'. While pretending to reason, the Unitarian acted unreasonably.[67]

While Powell concentrated his fire on the Unitarians, his
fellow Noetics wrote more fully on the Evangelicals. Copleston
in his *Enquiry into the Doctrines of Necessity and Predestination*
showed that there was no contradiction between a belief in
freewill and in divine foreknowledge. The latter doctrine did
not imply, as the Calvinists suggested, the rejection of the
former. Copleston's pupil, Whately, also attacked the Calvinist
notions of election, as well as the antinomian doctrine that
Christ made all righteous by his sacrifice. Arnold argued in a
similar fashion in his sermons.[68] Most controversially of all,
the Noetics were strong opponents of sabbatarianism. In
Thoughts on the Sabbath, Whately showed that the Mosaic law
was no longer applicable in Christian kingdoms; sabbath
observance rested on custom and example rather than on scriptural command.[69] In his essays, Whately also rescued the texts
of St Paul from the clutches of the Evangelicals. He subjected
them to interpretation after the liberal Anglican fashion and
demonstrated that it was a misuse of them to treat them as
justifying Calvinism. Whately argued that his aim, to quote
Paley, was 'to relieve Christianity of a weight that sinks it '.[70]

Retrospectively this exegesis gained in importance. In the
1830s, when faced with High Church opposition, the liberals
used the writings of St Paul as their scriptural defence. St Paul
became the archetypal liberal Anglican. In a volume of

[67] Ibid., 41–47, 56.
[68] Copleston, *Necessity and Predestination, passim*; R. Whately, *Writings of St Paul*,
Essays III, VI; T. Arnold, *Sermons* (London, 1829–34), i. Sermon XII.
[69] R. Whatley, *Thoughts on the Sabbath* (London, 1830).
[70] *Idem, Writings of St Paul*, 173.

sermons published in 1834, Arnold declared that 'the only latitudinarianism to be met with in these Sermons, is of a kind of which St Paul has set the example'. In a similar fashion, in a sermon preached at Rugby, he informed his assembled pupils that St Paul's words 'were to be our guide forever. Therefore in him there is not only Christian truth, but it is free from the mixture of human foolishness and error'.[71] The Noetics' St Paul was the leader of the proselytizing, Gentile church: tolerant, undogmatic, scriptural. His goal was to achieve a Christian unity of spirit.[72] More importantly, St Paul lived before the corruption of scriptural truth. This had begun, according to the liberals, with the doctrinal disputes of the Early Fathers and the predominating influence of the Church of Rome. Whately credited St Paul with foreseeing the causes of religious strife, a subject which Whately had discussed in his Bampton Lectures. He also claimed St Paul had been the first to point out the dangers of particular human passions as causes of religious discord, just as he had also indicated the importance of such qualities as gentleness and patience as prerequiesites for Christian toleration. St Paul's writings, according to Whately, were 'a principal bulwark of the Gospel', which had been neglected unjustly.[73]

By the 1830s, following the repeal of the Test and Corporation Acts and Catholic Emancipation, liberals began to consider the creeds and formularies of the Church of England, that is to say, Anglican dogma. On the assumption that the truths of Christianity were facts, Hampden, in his Bampton Lectures for 1832, attacked scholastic theology. In his definition of scholasticism he appeared to include, as Pusey pointed out, not only the peculiar speculative theology of the Schoolmen, but also 'the whole period wherein the Christian faith was established and its language on the main Articles fixed by means of the Councils of the universal Church'.[74] Hampden suggested that such theology was mistaken because it argued deductively. That is to say, it regarded biblical statements not as facts, but as hypotheses akin to mathematical axioms, and

---

[71] Arnold, *Sermons*, iii. v; *idem, Sermons, on Scripture*, 273.

[72] *Idem, Sermons*, i. 85–7, iii. v; Whately, *Bampton Lectures for 1822*, 137.

[73] Ibid., 74, 149; R. Whately, *Writings of St Paul*, 46.

[74] [E. B. Pusey], *Dr Hampden's Theological Statements and the Thirty-Nine Articles compared.* (Oxford, 1836), x.

treated these as the first terms of a deductive proof. But if it was accepted that the Bible was a human record of things, then the scholastics' error was understandable. They had mistaken the historically relative name for the object, and so had constructed a theology on an infirm basis: their doctrines depended on a humanly invented signifier and not the divine truth signified. Consequently creeds and formularies (the deductions from such hypotheses) could never be unquestionable and absolute. They were permeated with human interpolations and thus fallibilities. Hampden wrote: 'the doctrinal statements of religious truth have their origins in the principles of the human intellect. Strictly to speak in the scripture itself, there are no *doctrines*. What we read there is matter of fact'.[75] Theological opinion, therefore, was 'necessarily mixed up with speculative knowledge'.[76] According to Hampden, formularies and creeds, being historical statements of doctrines, were a mixture of truth and error, designed to meet the exigencies of a particular age, rather than to be eternal statements of divine truth. At best they were 'a collection of negation; of negations . . . of all ideas imported into Religion beyond the express sanction of Revelation'; at worst, they encouraged unfounded speculations.[77] In any case, they could never be superior to scriptural truth which was the essence of Christianity. 'Religion', wrote Hampden, 'consists of those truths which are simply contained in the Divine Revelation with the effects, dispositions and actions suggested by them. Theological opinion is the various result of the necessary action of our minds on the truths made known to us by the Divine word.'[78]

The consequence of this view was the advocacy of toleration towards religious Dissent. Given that the facts of religion comprised the essence of revelation, and that Dissent primarily involved disagreements about creeds and formularies, such Dissent as existed was not about the essential truths of Christianity, but about human interpretations. It was a mistaken religious zeal which led a partisan to defend such doctrines

[75] Hampden, *Bampton Lectures for 1832* 374.
[76] *Idem, Observations on Religious Dissent* 22.
[77] *Idem, Bampton Lectures for 1832*, 377.
[78] *Idem, Observations on Religious Dissent*, 18–19.

as though they were fundamental truths, and to attack those who disagreed as heretics. In his pamphlet *Observations on Religious Dissent*, Hampden first publicly advocated the removal of religious tests as a requirement of matriculation at Oxford. He declared: 'I do not scruple accordingly to avow myself favourable to a removal of all tests', and, by so doing, he expressed his preference for an education open to all Protestants.[79] It was a reform akin to the developments which had taken place in other national institutions. Arnold had advocated a similar reform in his pamphlet *Principles of Church Reform* (1833). In this work he had suggested that there were principles of Christianity common to all sects. For the purpose of comprehension, he advocated a reform of the creeds and formularies of the Anglican Church comparable to the proposals of the late seventeenth century. He was 'anxious to see a truly national church which uniting within itself all Christians who deserved the name . . . would leave without its pale nothing by voluntary or involuntary godlessness'. He stated as his motives the fear of unbelief and the then necessity to check the progress of irreligion. In view of the prevalence of the latter, the gain of church unity would outweigh any losses incurred. According to Arnold, 'the widest conceivable difference of opinion between the ministers of such a Church would be trifling compared with the good of their systematic union of action'.[80] By the 1830s, as a consequence of applying their inductive theology to the Church of England, these liberals began to adopt contentious stances on matters of public concern. What had commenced as a conservative defence of Anglicanism against various heterodoxies, ended as a plea for progressive change. These theologians began to put the religious case for liberal reforms.

Such advocacies met with the dismay of those Anglicans who saw them as yet further attempts at eroding within the constitution the position of the Anglican Church and Anglican doctrines. High Churchmen reacted by rejecting the methods of biblical interpretation which they had condoned in the 1820s. They designated them as signs of a secularizing liberalism. These High Churchmen, many of whom were to

[79] Ibid., 35–6.
[80] Arnold, *Principles of Church Reform*, 29, 79, 87, 92–4.

become Tractarians, attacked what they saw as the corrupting effects of Noetic principles, rather than the personal religion of individual Noetics. They identified the methods, which the liberals employed, as the prime cause of degeneracy. Pusey, for example, in his pamphlet of 1836, concentrated his fire on characteristically Noetic notions such as Hampden's assertion of the limited character of revelation and his definitions of scriptural facts and scholasticism. He argued that the real debate was 'not about one or other doctrinal error', but about 'opposite systems', where 'one must ultimately destroy the other'.[81] In response, the Tractarians developed an alternative method of interpreting Scripture. In doing so they had recourse to the notion of a divinely ordained tradition of interpretation, of which the priests of the church were the custodians. Instead of interposing a critical method between reader and text (induction), they interposed a given critical reading, its truth being dependent on its presumed descent from the Apostles. This reading was formulated in the creeds and Articles of the church. The priests, whose authority rested on their being the direct successors of the Apostles, were distinguished from the laity on account of the special powers of scriptural interpretation which their ancestry entitled them to claim. This direct challenge to the Noetics led the liberals to consider the standing of the church and its officers. Once more the result was their advocacy of liberal positions.

The liberals' case against the Tractarians first began with a denial that Christianity possessed a divine government on earth. This was a prerequisite of the Tractarian claim that the priests, as the bearers of the apostolic tradition, were God's appointed agents on earth. The denial was predicated on the notion of the existence of two divine dispensations, namely the Jewish and the Christian. The Jewish state had been theocratic in its most literal sense, that is it had been under God's direct rule, subservient to His commands as mediated by His appointed officers on earth. The Christian Kingdom was the converse of this; it was not of this world but of the world to come. Therefore it was not to have any representatives in this world, nor any incipient institutional organization. Faith was not a matter of obedience to the priestly ordered forms and

[81] [Pusey], *Dr Hampden's Theological Statements and the Thirty-Nine Articles*, viii.

regulations of a church (these, not being enjoined by the Scriptures, could not be the manifestation of divine rule on earth), but to 'the inward motives and dispostions of the heart'.[82] Those who claimed the contrary, so the Noetics argued, were guilty of confusing the two dispensations. The Noetics originally used this argument to show that the Roman Catholic notion of the priesthood was Jewish or pagan and not Christian.[83] They also used it to discredit Evangelical sabbatarianism, and to defend the church from the attempts of secular authorities, as they saw them, to turn it into an instrument of government, undertaken on the assumption that church and state performed the same divinely ordained role.[84] It was now used to diminish the authority of the church itself. Thus Hinds distinguished between the authority of the Scripture, which was 'analogous to the authority of a law or of the charter of a civil constitution', and the authority of the church, which was but a power 'for the purpose of administering the Scriptural laws of Christ's Kingdom on earth'.[85] The Tractarians were guilty of confusing the two.

The Noetic case was established by a biblical exegesis, which was conducted in accordance with the inductive method. Whately, for example, in his anti-Tractarian *The Kingdom of Christ*, analysed the two trials of Christ (the one before the Jewish Council for blasphemy, the other before Pilate for inciting rebellion), in order to establish what Christ meant by his claim that His Kingdom was not of this world. He argued that the Jewish Council condemned Christ for blasphemy: He had falsely claimed to be the son of God. Pilate, on the other hand, acquitted Him, because he recognized that Christ did not pose a threat so much to secular authority as to the Jewish religion. From this, Whately deduced that Christ's words meant that He claimed a spiritual and not a temporal control over his followers. Other interpretations, though possible, were irrelevant, if they were ones 'which could not have been so understood at the time, or which would have been utterly foreign to the occasion'. The historical context was everything.

[82] R. Whately, *The Kingdom of Christ* (London, 1841), 44.

[83] R. Whately. *Peculiarities of the Christian Religion*, 281–5.

[84] R. Whately, *Thoughts on the Sabbath*; [R. Whately], *Letters on the Church by an Episcopalian* (London, 1826), ch. 1.

[85] Hinds, *Inquiry into Inspiration and the Authority of Scripture*, 177.

Such interpretations Whately described as evasions rather than understandings of the Scriptures.[86] Whately insisted that the essence of Christianity was to be found in the Scriptures and not in any temporal institutions.

Second, the liberals attempted to demonstrate that the tradition which the Tractarians claimed to be apostolic did not in fact correspond to that of the Primitive Church. Arnold, in his posthumously-published *Fragment on the Church*, considered the works of the early Christian fathers: Barnabas, Hermas, Clemens of Rome, Ignatius, and Polycarp. He concluded that the Tractarian notion of the priesthood could not be found in them. He analysed Ignatius's exaltation of the episcopate in strictly historical terms, as an expedient measure designed to preserve the church from immediate evils. His conclusion was that Ignatius was 'laying down no general and perpetual principle, but speaking to the Christians of Smyrna of his own time, with reference to their own particular bishop'.[87] In an unpublished paper read to the Apostles, Blakesley claimed that the idea of a secret oral tradition, which did not depend on the Scriptures as the ultimate standard of Christian faith, originated not with the orthodox Fathers of the church, but with the gnostic heretics who rejected large portions of both New and Old Testaments. Irenaeus and Tertullian, in order to refute these heretics on their own terms, had recourse to an argument based on the existence of an ecclesiastical tradition: it was only to such an argument that the heretics would listen. According to Blakesley, this argument arose simply out of 'the necessities of the case'; it was only 'an emergency', and there was nothing 'in the circumstances to justify the *insulation* of it for ever as an independent authority of any importance'. These Early Fathers, he argued, provided no grounds for tradition being regarded as authoritative as Scripture.[88]

Apart from arguing that the Tractarian doctrine was both unhistorical and unscriptural, the liberals also condemned it as undermining the Protestant justification of faith. They argued that faith without reason was no different from mere

---

[86] R. Whately, *The Kingdom of Christ*, 30.

[87] T. Arnold, *Fragment on the Church* (London, 1844), 100.

[88] TCC Addit. MSS a.243./17 (Blakesley Papers), fos. 48–52: unpublished paper by J. W. Blakesley.

superstition; what distinguished Christianity from other religions was that the appeal to reason confirmed its truth. Thus
Powell argued that if it was true, as the Tractarians claimed,
that the early church Fathers possessed miraculous gifts identical to those of the Apostles, then there was no clear distinction
'between the apostles and their successors to the present day'.
Consequently, there was no clear depository of Christian
evidences to which appeal could be made in the event of a
doctrinal dispute. Christians were dependent on emotion, not
reason, for their adherence to particular doctrines. 'All test of
distinct evidence being abandoned, and all appeal to reason
discarded', wrote Powell, 'the only substitute is a mere vague
feeling or sentiment, common to all religions, true or false.'[89]
Hawkins went so far as to suggest that Christians not only
had a right, but also a duty, to exercise private judgement,
that is to exercise reason in judging the truth of Christianity.
The meaning of faith included 'the exercise of our Reason and
Judgement', while revelation did not ask for 'our assent to any
truth contradictory to reason'.[90] The liberals, in counteracting
Tractarianism, reasserted what they saw as true Protestant
doctrines. They denied both that the priests were divinely
ordained agents of God's government and that they were the
custodians of an inspired traditional Christianity. They
reaffirmed the assumption on which the Noetic method itself
was predicated, namely every one's right to judge the truth
of Christianity for themselves.

Nevertheless, this did not mean that the liberals were
advocates of religious anarchy. According to Whately, the
importance of the English Reformers was that they had not
succumbed to the intellectual freedom which the Reformation
had granted; they had not altered the church's doctrines simply
out of a love of innovation. They had displayed a commendable
'rationality' in keeping 'steadily in view their original object
of. rejecting what had been mischievous *innovations* of the
Romanist and *restoring* the church of Christ to its original
purity'.[91] Further, the Reformers, in recognizing the continued
need for catechetical instruction, also recognized the need for

[89] B. Powell, *Tradition Unveiled* (London, 1839), 67.
[90] E. Hawkins, *The Duty of Private Judgement* (Oxford, 1838), 13, 14.
[91] Whately, *Bampton Lectures for 1822*, 78.

an ecclesiastical tradition as a guide to interpretation.[92] But
this was the 'unauthoritative tradition' which Hawkins had
expounded in his famous dissertation on the subject. It
recognized the utility of oral or traditional instruction as a
preparation for the reception of the Scriptures, but it also
recognized that such instruction might be both fallible and
corrupt. Above all, it recognized that the proofs of Christian
doctrine and the substance of divine truth existed only in the
Bible.[93]

Thus, while opposing the Tractarians as offending liberal
canons of scriptural interpretation, the liberals accommodated
a notion of tradition within their theological system. The error
of the Tractarians was not that they were the advocates of
tradition, but that, in advocating a notion of authoritative
tradition, they erected a double barrier to the pursuit of religious truth. They demanded that a churchman should not only
believe the Christian truths found in the Bible, but that he
should also believe a particular account of them. This doctrine
Whately named the doctrine of double-reserve, and he accused
its proponents of gross impiety, since they placed a third party,
the church, between man and God. Such an assent to Christianity, based on a trusting faith in human infallibility rather
than the independent exercise of reason, Whately argued, was
barbaric, akin to the faith of Hindu thugs.[94] Tractarian tradition was not so much a guide to, as a substitute for, true or
reasoned faith.

Likewise, a rejection of the notion that the Kingdom of
Christ achieved an institutionalized form on this earth did not
entail a rejection of any notion of a church. Whately recognized
that Christianity was a social religion, one that was not only
a system of doctrines, but also a combination of men. The
church had to meet the requirements of any corporation if it
was to survive; it had to reserve for itself the power to appoint
officers, to draw up a body of rules and to admit and exclude
members. These were human and transient requirements, as

---

[92] E. Hawkins, *A Dissertation upon the Use and Importance of Unauthoritative Tradition*
(London, 1889), 21.

[93] Ibid., 14–5.

[94] E. J. Whately, *Richard Whately*, 165–7, 194; R. Whately, *The Kingdom of Christ*,
158–9; Oriel MSS Db 252 (Hawkins Papers): Whately to Hawkins, 22 Apr. 1843.

recognized, albeit negatively, by God's dispensation. Revelation did not prescribe any details of church government. Whately argued that these had been deliberately withheld so that 'other Churches, in other Ages and Regions might not be led to consider themselves bound to adhere to several formularies, customs and rules that were of local and temporary appointment'.[95] An ecclesiastical organization, therefore, could not usurp the functions of a Christian society whose ruler was God. It could not guarantee the remission of sins, or decree admission to the Kingom of Heaven. Arnold thus distinguished between the Christian religion and the Christian church. By religion he meant 'that knowledge of God and of Christ, and that communion of the Holy Spirit, by which an individual is led through life'; such knowledge was derived from the Scriptures and manifested itself in a personal relationship with God. By the church, he meant 'that provision for communicating, maintaining and enforcing this knowledge by which it was to be made influential'; the church was an agent for teaching and not for mediating between man and God.[96] The church's institutional role was to induce social cohesion and to spread the Gospel; it could never be an incipient Kingdom of Christ.

This diminishing of the importance of the church led to a revaluation of the relations between church and state. Arnold argued that since the church did not possess divinely ordained powers, there were no grounds, in the long run, for its independence from the state. Its aim was not to mediate between man and God, but to effect a practical improvement in the moral lives of men by teaching the truths of Christianity. Thereby men's hopes, fears, and affections were to be altered. 'The immediate object of Christianity' was 'to produce in men a moral and spiritual improvement'. At the same time, Arnold dissented from the view that the business of the state was simply the protection of property. He attacked Macaulay's view of the state as existing only to secure the material means of existence; the purpose of the state should be to secure the happiness of its citizens in the highest sense. Thus, since the aims of the church and of the state were identical, Arnold

[95] R. Whately, *The Kingdom of Christ*, 51–9, 75, 80–1.
[96] Arnold, *Fragment on the Church*, 3–4.

suggested that the church should be the state. 'The natural and fit state of the Church', wrote Arnold, 'is that it should be a sovereign society or commonwealth.' An unchristian state was simply an inferior form of government, one which sought 'man's highest happiness with mistaken views'; its pursuit of the true object of the state was not 'according to knowledge'. Christianity, indeed, being a universal religion, was additionally suited to serve as the foundation of a state. According to Arnold, the states of ancient Greece fell because they restricted citizenship to a particular race; the consequence was a 'narrow minded bigotry'. Christianity, being independent of race, showed how 'civilization could be obtained without moral degeneracy'. Christian states could be exempt from the Greek cycle of growth and decay.[97]

Whately disapproved of this identity between church and state. He thought, wrongly, that Arnold's scheme was similar to Hooker's, the only real difference between Arnold and the Tractarians being over the terms of communion: both parties agreed that political society was 'ordained'. Hawkins believed that Arnold's *Principles of Church Reform*, taken as a whole, was 'wretched'.[98] In his anonymously published *Letters of an Episcopalian*, Whately inclined towards disestablishment and the separation of church and state. He agreed with Arnold that the church possessed no powers beyond those accredited to it, but proceeded to argue that if it acquired the support of a secular government, it was in danger of becoming tainted with Judaic aspirations. He wrote that all interference of the church in secular affairs, and of the state in religious affairs, was at variance with the character of Christ's spiritual kingdom. Whately suggested that an alliance between church and state gave the impression that religion was only a state contrivance for maintaining order. At the end of his *Letters of an Episcopalian*, Whately called for all 'to strive earnestly and steadily to *separate the Church* from the every way pernicious alliance with the state'.[99]

[97] T. Arnold, *Fragments on Church and State* (London, 1845), 28, 58, 65; *idem, Fragment on the Church*, 10; *idem* (ed.), Thucydides, *Peloponesian War* (8th edn., Oxford, 1874), iii. part i, xiii.
[98] BL Microfilm 859/34 (Melbourne Papers): Whately to Melbourne, 7 Feb. 1836; Oriel MSS Db 412 (Hawkins Papers): Hawkins to Whately, 4 Feb 1833.
[99] [R. Whately], *Letters on the Church by an Episcopalian*, 89, 110, 190.

This difference in outlook between Arnold and Whately should not be exaggerated. In the short run, in terms of the proposals for reform of the 1830s, it mattered relatively little. Whately's pro-disestablishment tract, after all, had been published anonymously. When he was elevated to the bench in 1831, he did his best to uphold the dignity of his office. The most he ever demanded from the Whig government was the reintroduction of Convocation, or some similar body, so that the church retained control over its spiritual affairs.[100]Likewise, Arnold's dream of a union of church and state remained Utopian. It depended on the unrealized goal of comprehension. Church and state were to be united not by excluding, but by incorporating all the Christian elements within the existing nation. Until church and state were united, Whately and Arnold were happy to join forces in pressing for toleration as a prelude to further reform. In politics, with the exception of whether or not Jews were to be accorded full civil rights, Arnold and Whately had more or less identical liberal opinions. Moreover, whether the church was to be united with the state or not, both accepted the need for the morality of the country to be Christian. Christianity was the guarantor of civilization's progress, whatever the religious identity of the government.

In his *Introductory Lectures on Political Economy*, Whately argued that divine intervention was the cause of man's progress from barbarism to civilization. He suggested further that man's duty and his real interest coincided: religion, or rather Christianity, was important for the amelioration of mankind. This he illustrated by claiming that the religious impulse to discourage wars and abolish slavery was conducive to national prosperity; likewise, the diffusion of Christianity balanced the ill-effects of the division of labour, namely the contraction of the worker's faculties and consequent debasement of the mind.[101] Cambridge theologians such as Hare also associated Christianity with the well-being of the country. Hare attributed the decadence of Rome to the fact that Epicurean materialism and utilitarianism had supplanted its ancient faith. The

---

[100] Ibid., *A Speech on a Bill for the Removal of Certain Disablilities*, 17; Grey Papers, box 12 file 5, fos. 16, 18: Whately to Grey, 25 Aug., 19 Sept. 1832.
[101] R. Whately, *Introductory Lectures on Political Economy* (London, 1831), 135–6, 183–4, 205–6, 217.

progress of England, on the other hand, was to be attributed to the advancement of Christianity. 'Whatever may be the difference between this [the present] and the face of England two thousand years ago when vast forests and swamps and morasses spread from sea to sea . . .', he claimed, 'is altogether owing to the power and workings of Faith.' Addressing the undergraduates of Oxford University, he urged: 'England expects every man to do his duty', by which he meant that they could avert national calamities only with 'zealous hearts and holy lives'.[102] In this manner, liberal theologians linked Christianity with nationalism. But this was a liberal, all-comprehensive nationalism, because the nation comprised not only Anglicans but all Christians. 'I call this United Kingdom as yet a Christian nation', Arnold wrote, 'although it be neither Episcopal nor Presbyterian.'[103]

This belief in the contribution which Christianity made to the success of the nation was important, from the liberals' view, in ensuring continued state funding of Christian projects. These liberals, unlike many Tories, recognized the right of the state to interfere in the temporalities of the church. Whately first acknowledged this right as a consequence of his theory of the two jurisdictions: the temporal and the spiritual. He argued that the church's primary concern was with spiritual affairs. As archbishop, he held that 'The spiritual welfare and efficiency of our Church is *our* special concern'. At the same time, he recognized that the temporal domain was the special concern of the state. It had a right to interfere in the finances of the church, even if it had no authority to control men's consciences.[104] But this right did not mean that the state could withdraw its support from the church at will.

One major function of the clergy, in addition to the cure of men's souls, was to act as 'a sort of nucleus of civilization'.[105] This function depended on a historical fiction, which had received its fullest expression in the work of Coleridge. He suggested that a fund or 'nationalty' had been established for the maintenance of a permanent order or class, which would

[102] Hare, *Victory of Faith*, 99, 127.
[103] Arnold, *Fragments on Church and State*, 54.
[104] R. Whately, *Charges and Other Tracts* (London, 1836), 37, 60–1.
[105] Ibid., 318.

preserve the civilization of the country. Thereby its future
prosperity would be ensured. The custody of this fund had
been entrusted to the Church of England, as a consequence
of recognizing Christianity's contribution to English civilization. The condition of the trust was that the church continued
to exist as a national church, by which was meant not 'the
Church of Christ' or propagator of religious truth, but the
repository of the national civilization. As soon as the church
ceased to perform this function, the fund might be withdrawn
and entrusted to some other body more capable of performing
the same task.[106] Because liberals argued that a close causal
connection existed between Christianity and the progress of
civilization, they suggested not only that the 'nationalty' had
been donated rightly to the Church of England, but that it
should continue to be associated with a Christian body. Thus
there were limits, in liberal eyes, to the interference of the
state. Further, because the liberals claimed that the fundamental truths of Christianity were independent of any particular
dogma or sect, they could acquiesce in the state's reallocation
of funds from the Church of England to another religious body.
Within this restraint, state interference was acceptable. It
would not contribute to the decline of Christianity which was
so important to the well-being of the nation.

Thus in the 1830s, although they began as the exponents
of Anglican orthodoxy, these theologians emerged as the
supporters of liberal causes. The possibility of Anglican
comprehension and religious toleration—as shown in their
support for the admission of Dissenters to universities—
was predicated on their belief that doctrinal disputes were
essentially trivial. Their notion of the two dispensations
reduced the institutional significance of the Anglican Church,
and, in the followers of Whately, resulted in the desire to
withdraw the religious from involvement in the political,
to concentrate on inward spirituality rather than outward
display. While they denied the essential role of the church as
the vehicle for saving souls, these liberals turned their attention
to a consideration of the contribution which Christianity made
to the foundation of this world's civilization. This entailed the

[106] S. T. Coleridge, *On the Constitution of Church and State* (London, 1839), xvii, 46–7,
48.

recognition that the prosperity of the state depended on the sustenance of a religion of a non-dogmatic, but also orthodox, kind. These ideas were consonant with the positions which liberal politicians avowed with regard to such religious issues as the admission of Dissenters to universities, the withdrawal of institutionalized religion from the mechanisms of the state and the foundation of a non-dogmatic religious education. They are also an indication that these political stances involved a reflection on Anglicanism, and not its rejection. In so reflecting, these liberal divines and politicians provoked the anger and opposition of Tory politicians and Anglican Churchmen, ranging from the Duke of Wellington to the Regius Professor of Hebrew at Oxford University. How they did so, is the subject of the next two chapters.

5

The Liberals and University Reform:
From Clergymen to Politicians

THERE was little novel in the renewed demand of the Dissenters
in the 1830s for university reform: the exclusion of Nonconformists from the degrees of the ancient universities had been a
long-standing grievance. The demands of the Protestant
Dissenting Deputies drawn up in 1833 and the Bills of 1834
and 1835 had their precedents in the Feathers Tavern Petition
of 1772 and Hoghten's Relief Bill of 1773. But what had
changed were the political circumstances in which they pressed
their cause. First, the repeal of the Test and Corporation Acts
had formally acknowledged the political role of Dissenters:
they were new and potentially powerful constituents of the
political nation. Second, the Whigs had courted Dissent as
part of their electoral strategy in the years of opposition. The
Whig party's ability to satisfy Dissenting demands was as
much a requirement of political tactics, as it was an indication
of the truth of the liberals' claim that they were judicious
'friends of the people'. The question at issue in the 1830s was
less whether the Whigs would attempt to concede Nonconformist demands for university reform (the passing of the 1832
Reform Act in effect had decided this), than the manner of
the concession. It is the argument of this chapter that this was
determined by liberal Anglican rather than Dissenting opinion.
The question of university reform was remarkable for the political connections which were made between the liberal clergymen in the universities and the Whig politicians—political
alliances which were to reaffirm the already extant religious
and intellectual sympathies.

University liberals and liberal politicians joined forces on
the issue of university reform. It was a question on which
liberal dons directly sought the aid of Whig politicians in order
to pursue their ideal of a liberal education, and the politicians
in their turn took up the issue as a vehicle for their religious

liberalism. The prime contest was over the admission of Dissenters to degrees and so to the privileges which such qualifications conferred. Although at Cambridge Dissenters were allowed to matriculate, they could not obtain a BA without declaring that they were members of 'the Church of England as by law established'; nor could they obtain an MA, BD, or a doctorate in Law, Physic, or Divinity without subscribing to the three Articles of the 36th Canon. At Oxford a Dissenter could not ever matriculate without subscribing to the Thirty-Nine Articles. The new London University (1826) was specifically founded in order to offer higher education to members of all sects, but since it did not possess a Royal Charter until 1835 it was unable to confer degrees. At Durham University (1832), students had to conform to the discipline of the Church of England.[1] The repeal of the Test and Corporation Acts thus presented the paradox of admitting Dissenters to the political nation, while continuing their exclusion from the national provision for higher education. The contest in the 1830s occurred over what form that provision should take: whether religious diversity and doctrinal purity should be preserved by the maintenance of sectarian institutions, or whether a truly national establishment was a practical possibility. The liberals argued in favour of the latter. In so doing they found themselves required to demonstrate that such an education was not harmful to that other great national establishment, the Church of England.

The immediate impetus to the liberal agitation of 1834 was the Cantabrigean fear that the exclusion of Dissenters from the ancient universities would result in their decline as centres of intellectual excellence. An important Dissenting grievance was that their inability to obtain a degree curtailed their ability to pursue a course of professional education in law and medicine. The possession of an Oxford or Cambridge BA enabled an attorney to reduce his training by two years and allowed a doctor to become a Fellow of either the College of Physicians or Surgeons. The Tory solution to this problem

---

[1] NLI MSS 13377 (21) (Monteagle Papers): summary respecting religious tests in the University of Cambridge; W. R. Ward, *Victorian Oxford* (London, 1965), p. 91; H. Hale Bellot, *University College, London, 1826–1926* (London, 1929), 56; C. E. Whiting, *The University of Durham* (London, 1932), 41.

was to induce a change of regulations in the professional bodies. The liberal concern was that this would result in the emergence of scientific faculties outside Oxford and Cambridge and, in particular, give added prestige to London University. Dr Hewett, who vetoed a petition to be proposed to the Senate of Cambridge against the abrogation of tests, explained that his action as 'the appointed guardian of the Medical Faculty' was motivated by the fear that 'if the University were to act in the spirit of exclusiveness . . . the inevitable and not un-merited result would be the separation ere long of the Faculty of Medicine from the University'. Dr Haviland, the Regius Professor of Physic at Cambridge, in his turn, expressed his concern that if the College of Physicians received a Charter enabling it to confer medical degrees, the effect would be 'to exclude every hope of the further promotion of medical studies: which effect would be injurious to the interests of the univer-sities'.[2] Unable to secure internal reform the Cambridge liberals took their cause to Westminster. The petitions presented in the Lords and Commons in March 1834 praying for the abrogation of religious tests were a direct consequence of the Caput's vetoing attempts in the previous Michaelmas and Lent terms to bring the Dissenters' case before the Senate.[3]

After the Senate had resolved to petition the crown to be heard by counsel on the subject of the proposed Charter for London University on 12 March 1834, several liberal members of Cambridge University met in Professor Hewett's rooms and decided to present a petition to both houses of parliament to pray for the removal of tests. Sedgwick, Woodward Professor of Geology and Fellow of Trinity, was the prime organizer of this attempt. On 14 March he wrote to the MP for Cambridge, Spring Rice, who had also been an undergraduate at Trinity and now held office, that he was 'cooking up a *petition to Parliament* for the abrogation of all religious tests'. Sedgwick requested him to 'drum up some of our good Cambridge liberal friends to give us a lift out of our present illiberal slough with which our lights are half put out and even half choked'. Two

---

[2] CUR MSS 118 (Abolition of Tests), fo. 10: Reasons of Dr Hewett for throwing out Grace, 16 Apr. 1834; [J. Haviland], *A Letter to the Members of Senate on Graduates in the University of Cambridge* (Cambridge, 1833), 4. For identification of names in the text consult Table 3.

[3] *Hansard*, 3rd Ser., xxii (1834), 499.

Table 3. Fellows (and former Fellows) of Oxford and Cambridge Colleges cited in the text of Chapter 5 ???? ???? referred to elsewhere

Name	Dates	University	College	Status	Misc. appointments	Party
Ainslie, G.	1793–1870	Cambridge	Pembroke	Master	1836 V-C	?
Blakesley, J. W.	1808–1885	Cambridge	Trinity	Fellow	1872 Dean of Lincoln	Whig
Blomfield, C.	1786–1857	Cambridge	Trinity	(Fellow)	Bp. of London	Peelite
Butler, S.	1774–1839	Cambridge	St John's	(Fellow)	HM Shrewsbury; 1836 Bp. of Lichfield	Whig
Chevallier, T.	1794–1873	Cambridge	Pembroke	(Fellow)	1835 Prof. of Maths, Durham Univ.	
Churton, E.	1800–1874	Oxford	Ch. Ch.	—	Rector of Crayke	Tory
Collison, F. W.	1814–1889	Cambridge	St John's	1838 Fellow		Anglo-Catholic Tory
Conybeare, W. D.	1787–1857	Oxford	Ch. Ch.	—	1844 Dean of Landaff	Anglo-Catholic Tory
Corrie, G. E.	1793–1885	Cambridge	St Catharine Hall	Fellow	1838 Norrisian Prof. of Divinity	Whig
Crick, T.	1801–1876	Cambridge	St John's	Fellow		Tory
Eden, C. P.	1807–1885	Oxford	Oriel	Fellow	1839 President	?Tory
Empson, W.	1791–1852	Cambridge	Trinity	—	1824 Prof. of Law, Haileybury	Tractarian Tory
Evans, R. W.	1789–1866	Cambridge	Trinity	Fellow	1856 Archdeacon of Westmoreland	Liberal
Gaisford, T.	1779–1855	Oxford	Ch. Ch.	Dean	Reg. Prof. of Greek	Tory
Geldart, J. W.	1785–1876	Cambridge	Trinity Hall	Fellow	Reg. Prof. of Civil Law	Tory
Graham, J.	1794–1865	Cambridge	Christ's	Master	V-C 1840; 1848 Bp. of Chester	?
Hall, F. R.	1788–1866	Cambridge	St John's	(Fellow)	Rector of Fulbourn?	Liberal
Hamilton, W.	1788–1856	Oxford	Balliol	—	1836 Pro. of Logic & Metaphysics, Edinburgh	Liberal
Haviland, J.	1785–1851	Cambridge	St John's	Fellow	1817 Ref. Prof. of Physic	Liberal
Hawkins, E.	1789–1882	Oxford	Oriel	Provost		?Liberal
Hewett, C.	1786–1841	Cambridge	Downing	Fellow	Downing Prof. of Medicine	Liberal
Hildyard, J.	1807–1886	Cambridge	Christ's	Fellow	—	?Liberal

Table 3 (*continued*).

Name	Dates	University	College	Status	Misc. appointments	Party
Howley, W.	1766–1848	Oxford	New College	—	Ab. Canterbury	Tory
Jenkyns, R.	1782–1854	Oxford	Balliol	Master	V-C 1824–8	Tory
Marriot, G.	1811–1858	Oxford	Balliol & Oriel	Fellow of Oriel	1850 Vicar, St Mary's	Tractarian Tory
Musgrave, T.	1788–1860	Cambridge	Trinity	Fellow	1837 Bp. of Hereford; 1847 Ab. of York	Liberal
Peacock, G.	1791–1858	Cambridge	Trinity	Fellow	1836 Lowdean Prof. of Astronomy; 1839 Dean of Ely	Liberal
Perry, C.	1787–1891	Cambridge	Trinity	Fellow	1847 Bp. of Melbourne	Evangelical
Pryme, G.	1781–1868	Cambridge	Trinity	Fellow	Prof. of Polit. Economy; 1832–41 MP Cambridge	Liberal
Pusey, E. B.	1800–1882	Oxford	Ch. Ch.	Canon	Reg. Prof. of Hebrew	Anglo-Catholic Tory
Rolfe, R. M.	1790–1868	Cambridge	Trinity & Downing	(Fellow of Downing)	MP 1832–50; Melbourne's Solicitor-General; Lord Chancellor 1852	Liberal
Romilly, J.	1791–1864	Cambridge	Trinity	Fellow	Univ. Registrar	Liberal
Rose, H. J.	1795–1838	Cambridge	Trinity	—	1833 Prof. of Divinity, Durham Univ.	High Church Tory
Sedgwick, A.	1785–1873	Cambridge	Trinity	Fellow	1818 Woodwardian Prof. of Geology; 1834 Canon of Norwich	Liberal
Selwyn, W.	1806–1875	Cambridge	St John's	Fellow	1855 Lady Margaret Prof. of Divinity	Tory

Shuttleworth, P. N.	1782–1842	Oxford	New College	Warden	1840 Bp. of Chichester	Whig
Symons, B. P.	1785–1878	Oxford	Wadham	Warden	V-C 1844–8	Evangelical
Thorp, C.	1783–1862	Oxford	Univ.	(Fellow)	1833 Warden of Durham Univ.	High Church Tory
Turton, T.	1780–1864	Cambridge	St Catharine Hall	Fellow	Reg. Prof. of Divinity; Dean of Peterborough; 1845 Bp. of Ely	Tory
Van Mildert, W.	1765–1836	Oxford	Queen's	(1813 Reg. Prof. of Divinity)	1826 Bp. of Durham	High Church Tory
Whewell, W.	1794–1866	Cambridge	Trinity	Fellow	1838 Knightsbridge Prof.; 1841 Master of Trinity	Peelite
Wordsworth, C.	1774–1846	Cambridge	Trinity	Master		Tory
Wynter, P.	1793–1871	Oxford	St John's	President	V-C 1840–4	?Tory

( ) quondam.

NB All offices named refer to posts held during the 1830s unless otherwise stated.

days later George Peacock, also a Fellow of Trinity and a friend of Rice since his Trinity days, promised him a copy of the petition. Meanwhile Musgrave, Fellow of Trinity, informed Brougham of the petitioners' cause; on 19 March Sedgwick and Musgrave briefed Grey, who was to present the petition to the Lords.[4] When the Prime Minister and Spring Rice presented the petitions in the Lords and Commons, they did so in effect endorsing the liberals' cause as the government's own. At the same time the Lancashire unitarian GWF Wood began to prepare a Bill to the same effect and on 17 April, in the course of the adjourned debate on the Cambridge petition, he secured the leave of the House to bring in a Bill.[5]

Given the temporary disintegration of its political alliance with Dissent, the government was well-disposed to the attempts of university liberals to secure the admission of Dissenters to their educational establishments. There was, however, an obvious political danger in allowing a Dissenter to propose a measure of university reform. Since the beginning of 1834 particular groups of Dissenters had declared in favour of disestablishment and the separation of church and state.[6] A measure of reform in the interest of Dissent was therefore liable to the charge that it was intended as a stage in the overthrow of the Church of England. The liberals attempted to convince opponents that unlike militant Dissent, they sought neither an end to religion as the basis of national institutions, nor the destruction of Anglicanism. As regards the universities, the liberals tried to confine their proposed reform to the public establishments alone in order to exclude the private and essentially Anglican colleges from legislative interference. To this end they attempted to modify the Dissenter Wood's Bill.

Prior to the printing of the Bill on 21 April, Wood had agreed to alterations suggested by Musgrave, who feared that the original preamble was of 'too sweeping and violent a complexion'. After conferring on 11 April with Peacock, Sedgwick, and Romilly, the University Registrar and a Fellow

---

[4] Clark & Hughes, *Revd Adam Sedgwick* i. 418–9; NLI MSS 13377 (11) (Monteagle Papers): Peacock to Rice, 16 Mar. 1834; Brougham Papers, MSS 47353: memo by Musgrave, 20 Mar. 1834; CUL Addit. MSS 7652 IG (Sedgwick Papers), fo. 78: Grey to Sedgwick, 17 Mar. [1834].

[5] *Hansard*, 3rd ser., xxii (1834), 927.

[6] On the Whig alliance with Dissent, see Ch. 7.

of Trinity, Musgrave requested that the right of admission should be restricted to those of 'good moral character', of 'competent knowledge' and 'willing to conform to the regulations established by the executive authorities of the several colleges'. These modifications were duly incorporated.[7] On 20 April, still concerned that colleges were under threat, Peacock asked Rice to request Robert Rolfe, MP, lawyer, and former student at Trinity, to enquire if the Bill as now framed granted the Dissenters a right to demand admission to any particular college against the wishes of that institution.[8] Presumably as a result of Rolfe's opinion, Rice wrote to Musgrave pointing out a discrepancy between the petition and the Bill, namely that the former explicitly stated the desire to uphold all existing college statutes and rules, while in the latter this position was unclear. Rice informed the Trinity don that he would move a clause in committee to make the Bill commensurate with the petition. Consequently Musgrave saw Wood, and both wrote to Sedgwick: the Trinity liberal to inform of his interview, and the Unitarian to agree to the removal of the ambiguous reference to the colleges which he had previously acquiesced in adding. Although Wood confessed that he was unable to amend the Bill himself since it was now committed to the charge of the House, he promised to raise no objection to any amendments proposed in committee.[9] Such negotiations were testimony to the fact that Wood's measure was primarily in the hands of the government and the Cambridge liberals. They indicated that reform was to be framed not according to Dissenting, but to liberal Anglican predilections.

Indeed, in pressing for the abrogation of religious tests, these liberals made deliberate attempts to dissociate themselves from militant Dissent. In a series of letters published in Baines's *Leeds Mercury*, Sedgwick defended Cambridge against the attacks made on it by a former undergraduate, turned Congregationalist, R. M. Beverley. In his concluding letter, published on 2 June, he denied that Nonconformist agitation had resulted in the liberal reform movement. He wrote that

[7] NLI MSS 13377 (8) (Monteagle Papers): Musgrave to Rice, 13 Apr. 1834; Bury, *Romilly's Cambridge Diary*, 54.

[8] NLL MSS 13377 (10) (Monteagle Papers): Peacock to Rice, 20 Apr. 1834.

[9] CUL Addit. MSS 7652 IG (Sedgwick Papers), fos. 83, 84, 81: Rice to [?Musgrave], 29 Apr. 1834, Musgrave to Sedgwick, 29 Apr. 1834, Wood to Sedgwick, 29 Apr. 1834.

Beverley 'flatters himself that it was the publication of his letter which induced Professor Pryme to offer a grace for abolition of certain academic tests. But let not his vanity deceive him or any one else in such a question as this. The subject has been thought of for many years . . . '. Likewise in an open letter to the Bishop of London, who opposed the abolition of tests, Sedgwick was at pains to stress that his object in promoting the petition was not to give the Dissenters *qua* Dissenters a right of admission to the university. '*A man is not to come up as a Dissenter*', he wrote, 'he must conform to discipline and we give him a degree without exacting subscription.'[10] This notion that the admission of Dissenters would not fundamentally alter the nature of the universities was taken up by other liberal pamphleteers as an integral part of their advocacy of the liberal cause. F. R. Hall, a Fellow of St John's and Rector of Fulbourn, desired Dissenters to sign a declaration that as long as they were *in statu pupillari* they would not attempt to proselytize in the university, 'nor speak nor write against the doctrines and disciplines of the Church of England'.[11] In parliament too it was stressed that the abolition of tests would not result in the sudden transformation of the country's institutions from being Anglican to being Nonconformist. The Dissenter from Leeds, Edward Baines, 'took it upon himself to state that it was not the wish of the Dissenters in the smallest degree to interfere with those institutions which were devoted to the support of the established religion of the country'.[12] If such avowals were the result of the dialectical need to convince doubting Anglicans who formed parliamentary majorities, they nevertheless imposed upon the advocates of this liberal cause an obligation to provide a distinctively liberal justification for their activities, one that was offensive neither to devout Anglicans nor to Nonconformists.

The assertion that the justification for their measure was not the need to appease Dissent but the necessity to preserve intellectual excellence, did not render the liberals' proposal any less contentious: many did not recognize this as the historic

---

[10] A. Sedgwick, *Four Letters to R. M. Beverley* (n.p. 1834), iv. 11; CUR MSS 118 (Abolition of Tests), fo. 43 copy, Sedgwick to Bishop of London, 27 Apr. 1834.

[11] F. R. Hall, *A Letter to R. M. Beverley Esq.* (Cambridge, 1834), 53–4.

[12] *Hansard*, 3rd ser., xxii (1834), 628.

function of the universities in the first place. Sir Robert Inglis, the member for Oxford University who succeeded Peel in that responsibility, attacked the notion that the universities of England were 'lecture-shops'. He asserted that they were 'places of discipline and moral constraint' which, in educating 'the rising generation of English gentlemen', provided the means for 'the preservation of this country'. This education was founded on the teaching of a doctrinal religion which would either be adulterated by the admission of Dissenters, or at the very least be disturbed by a partisan strife: dogmatic Anglicanism was the very fount of an English education.[13] Conservatives assumed that the traditional role of the universities was to be bulwarks of the Established Church. As proof, they pointed to the fact that universities proved the only training available for the Anglican clergy. The Duke of Gloucester, the Chancellor of Cambridge, declared that it was founded for 'the education of persons of the Church establishment and especially for the education of those who were destined to be the clergy of that establishment', while Dr Philpotts, Bishop of Exeter, claimed the universities were 'two great seminaries for instruction in the national religion'.[14]

By contrast, the liberals contended that the universities were national institutions founded primarily for the benefit of the citizenry of the country; that as such they should include Dissenters since recent legislation had acknowledged their existence as a component of the nation. They asserted that this was also the historical role of the universities until subverted by acts of the same overweening monarchs who had precipitated the Great Rebellion and the Glorious Revolution. Liberals depicted themselves as restoring ancient laws and customs, as reintroducing the ancient constitution, which the Stuarts had usurped, as it applied to higher education. The history of the statutes of Cambridge University, as rehearsed by the Whigs, was that no restrictions on the admittance of Dissenters to degrees existed in the by-laws of the university or *Statuta Antiqua*, but were introduced as a consequence of a letter from James I. This had demanded that no one should graduate unless he subscribed to the three articles of the 36th

---

[13] Ibid., 688.
[14] Ibid., 982; ibid., xxv (1834), 879.

Canon which contained the Thirty-Nine Articles; a second letter from the King desired that the restriction be extended to include MAs.[15] Dr Ainslie, the Master of Pembroke, produced a pamphlet setting out 'the whole facts of the case'. Sedgwick, basing his argument on evidence thus supplied, complained that the restrictions had been 'imposed in a manner informal and unprecedented'.[16] In this sense liberals merely demanded the correction of abuses which the Revolution had overlooked. The restoration of the university system, however, as demanded by the liberals, did not only mean the admission of Dissenters to degrees. It also entailed the release of the ancient universities from the control of the colleges. These, it was argued, had subverted the role of the universities as national institutions by confining their operations to the purposes for which halls of residence had been privately endowed.

The Tories refused to recognize a distinction between the colleges and the universities, and so could argue that the admission of Dissenters to the latter would undoubtedly endanger the character of the former. In this there was a practical truth since the colleges possessed a monopoly as halls of residence. Such a distinction, however, was necessary to the liberal case since colleges as private corporations could not be reformed by parliament and, as private foundations, also possessed the right to exclude whomsoever they chose. Liberals therefore could not argue that the universities were essentially national establishments if they were understood to be merely aggregations of colleges. This Sir William Hamilton, the Edinburgh liberal philosopher and scientist, acknowledged in his articles published in the *Edinburgh Review*. He argued that as a consequence of the Laudian statutes the heads of the private corporations or colleges at Oxford had illegally subverted the public trust bestowed on them; they had illicitly ensured that the aims of the university and the colleges were conterminous. He suggested that although universities were supposed to be national schools, Oxford was no longer established for 'the

[15] Ibid., xxii (1834), 501: A. Sedgwick, 'Letter to the Resident Members of the Senate', *Cambridge Chronicle'*, 11 Apr. 1834.

[16] [G. Ainslie], *An Historical Account of the Oaths and Subscriptions required in the University of Cambridge on Matriculation* (Cambridge, 1833), 1; A. Sedgwick, 'Letter to the Resident Members of the Senate', *Cambridge Chronicle*, 11 Apr. 1834.

benefit of the nation', but only for 'the benefit of those in community with the English Church'. He suggested, along with Whately, that the solution to this problem was the restoration of the faculties free from collegiate dominion. Arnold in 1834 likewise recognized that the best way to obviate Dissenters' objections to the existing university system was to restore the government of the university to the university officers, namely the Professors and Doctors of the various faculties 'without any reference to the colleges'. In this way it would be possible to transform the universities into genuinely national institutions—by which Arnold meant open 'to all to whom I would open Parliament'.[17] According to the liberals, the Tory defence of the *status quo* was the product of an intellectual confusion, namely the failure to distinguish between the public and private ends contained within the one institutional form. Once this was recognized, the truth of the petitioners' claim was self-evident, namely that the university was 'a lay corporation', 'invested with certain civil privileges and on that account, resting on no secure foundation which is not in harmony with the social system of the State'.[18]

One solution to the problem of competing sects, which wished to secure the rewards of a university education, might have been to found sectarian universities of equal status, but of different membership. This the liberals specifically rejected. They wished instead to incorporate differing parties within the one institution as a consequence of recognizing what they had in common. Liberal politicians, aware of sectarian disputes in Ireland, feared the creation of a fractured polity in England. Spring Rice, the leading Unionist MP, warned the House that if Dissenters did not participate in the acknowledged national establishment, they would 'be left no option but that of withdrawing themselves into circles and establishments of every kind formed on dissentient principles and separating them on all points from their fellow citizens'.[19] According to such liberals, one function of national institutions was the

[17] [W. Hamilton], 'The Universities and Dissenters', *Edinburgh Review* ix (1835), 434; BL Addit. MSS 34589 (Butler Papers), fo. 64: Arnold to Butler, 7 May 1834; Grey Papers, box 12, file 5, fo. 45: copy Whately to Lansdowne, n.d. [1834].
[18] CUL MSS UA/UP (1834), fo. 394: copy of Petition to Parliament to emancipate Degrees in Arts, Law, and Physick from Religious Tests.
[19] *Hansard.* 3rd ser., xxiv (1834), 669.

inculcation of a sense of nationality which included all members of a civil polity. In his work *On the Principles of English University Education* Whewell, a Peelite don of liberal inclinations, wrote of the beneficial effects of students living in a community. He argued that 'a common participation in a liberal education' put students on a footing of equality and mutual respect; that an important consequence of a university education was to produce in a student the feeling 'that he *is* an Englishman', to give him a knowledge of the principles on which his fellow citizens regulated their lives, and so to acquire 'a sympathy with their objects'.[20] A liberal university was not only a national institution because it was in harmony with the social system of the state, but because it was also designed to be an agent of civic peace.

In its attitude towards Durham University in the 1830s, the government endorsed this view of the university as essentially a national establishment. The Chapter of Durham Cathedral had founded the university in late 1831 as a defensive device to ensure that its surplus funds would not be appropriated to secular purposes in the course of the anticipated reform of the Anglican Church. It was essentially a High Church enclave, with both Newman and Keble co-opted on to its governing body and H. J. Rose as its first Professor of Divinity. Students at Durham were subject to the same tests as at Cambridge, that is they had to subscribe to the Thirty-Nine Articles on graduation, while as undergraduates they had to conform to the discipline of the church. The regulations established for degrees in Arts required a candidate to demonstrate proficiency in examinations on Christian Evidences, Bible history, the four Gospels, the Acts in Greek, and the Thirty-Nine Articles.[21] In the mid-1830s the university sought a Charter from the government to issue degrees, an application which coincided with a redistribution of ecclesiastical revenues and the removal of the palatinate jurisdiction from the see of Durham. The university also pressed for an increased endowment by means of attaching cathedral stalls to particular offices and requested that Durham Castle be held in trust by the bishop on behalf of the university. The purpose behind such

[20] W. Whewell, *On the Principles of English University Education* (London, 1838), 87–8.
[21] Whiting, *University of Durham*, 31, 32, 43.

requests was to prevent the university being reduced to a theological seminary through a shortage of funds produced by the reduction in episcopal incomes which the Ecclesiastical Commissioners had recommended.[22]

The dons of Durham University made these applications with the expectation that the Whigs would demand the admission of Dissenters as the *quid pro quo* of agreement. As Jenkyns, the Professor of Divinity, wrote to Thorp, the Warden of the university: 'It is plain they will attempt to force dissenters on us.'[23] They were not disappointed. Lord Grey warned Thorp that although he would consent to agitate on the university's behalf for a further endowment, the government would demand 'the abandonment of the principle of exclusion'—by which he meant 'that Dissenters should be admitted not only to the benefit of the education which the university will afford, but also to the attainment of honours which it may confer'.[24] Howick forwarded Grey's request to Spring Rice, now Chancellor of the Exchequer, with the proviso that any favour shown 'should be made to depend upon the admission of Dissenters to its honours'.[25] In the end the government was forced to withdraw this condition. The Bishop of Durham persuaded the Home Secretary, Lord John Russell, to agree to the unconditional issue of the Charter by arguing that van Mildert, who had founded the university, had done so with an understanding then obtained that the government would not compel the admission of Dissenters.[26] As Jenkyns had predicted at the beginning of the campaign, the government, adhering to 'the doctrine of Lord Althorp as expressed in his speech on the Durham Bill in 1832', was forced to grant the Charter 'out of policy'.[27] But although the government issued the Charter, the Whigs did not abandon their intention of making the university accessible to Dissenters. Temple Chevallier, the Professor of mathematics, noted that Russell accompanied the concession 'with an intimation that he will use all

[22] Ibid., 54, 65, 74; *Parl. Papers 1837*, xli. 50; NLI MSS 13382 (12) (Monteagle Papers): Thorp to Rice, 2 Apr. 1836; Thorp MSS, fo. 212; draft Thorp to Melbourne, 26 Feb. 1836.   [23] Thorp MSS, fo. 235: Jenkyns to Thorp, 28 Mar. 1836.
[24] Thorp MSS, fo. 229: Grey to Thorp, 22 Mar. 1836.
[25] NLI MSS 13382 (5) (Monteagle Papers): Howick to Rice, 24 Mar. 1836.
[26] Thorp MSS, fo. 292a: Maltby to Thorp, 15 May [1837].
[27] Jenkyns MSS VB, bundle 11: Jenkyns to H. Hobhouse, 26 Apr. 1836.

his efforts to remove here and elsewhere the obstacles which oppose his dissenting friends from being made gentlemen'.[28] The Home Secretary sought alternative ways of ensuring that Durham University became a national institution.

In late December 1837, the government issued a royal warrant empowering the University of Durham to issue certificates indicating that its students had completed a course of instruction which met with the approval of the university of London. The government's aim was to allow non-Anglicans studying at Durham to take London University degrees. The Senate of Durham took exception to the warrant on the reasonable ground that, as it was not issued as the result of an application made by the Warden and Senate, but as the consequence of a private agreement between Lord John Russell and the Bishop of Durham, it threatened the university's independence; in particular, it appeared to place the university in a subordinate position to London University. Thorp was especially alarmed by a letter received from Dr Arnold in which he treated Durham as connected with London University, in a fashion akin to King's or University College. 'It is not at all in our thoughts to be joined to London even on a footing of equality, still less as a subordinate', Thorp complained.[29] The university authorities consequently sought and obtained an assurance from the government that there was no intention on the Whigs' part of prescribing any course of instruction for the students of Durham University.[30] After these negotiations, which altogether took little more than a year, the Senate eventually agreed to issue certificates of attendance, while the government persuaded London University to alter its regulations in order to accept such certificates as sufficient qualification for a London degree. The spirit of the original warrant was adhered to if not its letter. Although Russell was compelled to compromise, he ensured none the less that members of all Christian sects could attend the university with benefit. He thus ensured the transformation of the university from a sectarian to a national establishment.[31]

[28] Chevallier MSS 1, fo. 21: Chevallier to Corrie 27 May 1837.
[29] Thorp MSS, fo. 312: Thorp to Maltby, 8 Apr. 1838.
[30] Thorp MSS, fo. 314: Maltby to Thorp, 24 Apr. 1838.
[31] *Parl. Papers 1837–8*, xxxvi. 261–4; *ibid.*, xxxviii. 36; *Parl. Papers 1840*, xl. 61, 81–2, 90–2, 97–9.

Comprehensive, however, did not also mean secular. George Peacock, who became Dean of Ely in 1839, proposed in his work on university reform to maintain the examination for all Arts students at Cambridge in one of the four Gospels, a portion of a Greek and Latin author, and Paley's *Evidences of Christianity*.[32] His aim was to develop an education which combined theological, classical, and scientific learning. These liberals regarded religion as an important constituent of the education of the upper classes, but they recommended its inclusion less on the ground of its intrinsic truth than as an important element in civilized society. As Whately wrote: 'To say that a man can gave gone thro' a course of liberal education in this country totally ignorant of the outlines of Xn. History is to imply not merely than the Xn. Religion is *untrue* or bad, but that it is *insignificant* and unworthy of serious attention except from those who have a fancy for it.'[33] According to these liberals, Christianity should be taught in a scheme of national education because it was an essential component of the nation's civilization or culture. This understanding enabled liberals to refuse to recognize a contradiction between their twin assertions that a university was both a national lay corporation and a place of religious education. In his letter to the *The Times* stating seventeen reasons why the prayer of the petition from Cambridge University should be adopted, Sedgwick could quite unreservedly accept as his first premise that the university was 'a place of sound learning and religious education': the two were inseparable.[34]

In government the Whigs sought to ensure that religion was the foundation of higher education. Unlike many voluntaryist Dissenters, they did not see the establishment of secular national institutions as the solution to the problem of competing religious sects. When the government's attention was directed towards London University as a centre of national education, the Whigs attempted to christianize it. University College, London, if by default as much as by design, was essentially a secular institution. It was founded on the principle

---

[32] G. Peacock, *Observations on the Statutes of the University of Cambridge* (London, 1841), 161.

[33] NLI MSS 13390 (9) (Monteagle Papers): Whately to Arnold, 5 Jan. 1838.

[34] CUL MSS UA/UP (1834), fo. 395: extract from *The Times*.

that it would have no religious tests which would act as a barrier to any sect of the British citizenry. Its attempts to provide some form of theological instruction, conceded as a result of pressure from moderate Dissenting and Evangelical supporters, had proved a failure. In 1827 the Council of the University declared that it had 'found it impossible to unite the free admission to persons of all religious denominations with any plan of theological instruction or any form of religious discipline', although it had insisted that the boarding-house keepers on its register should ensure that their lodgers regularly attended a place of worship. In 1828 even this regulation was abandoned.[35] Although defenders of the university excused this irreligion (as compared with the universities of Oxford and Cambridge) on the ground that as a non-residential centre of higher education, it was entitled to leave the teaching of religion to the discretion of students' parents or guardians, this was a less than satisfactory defence. It implied that religion was a contingent rather than essential component of education.[36] Since 1833 the Council of the University had been pressing for authority to issue degrees. In that year a Charter had received the sanction of the law officers, but had met with the refusal of the Great Seal as a consequence of memorials presented by Oxford and Cambridge, and the Colleges of Physicians and Surgeons. Hearings had taken place before the Privy Council in April and May 1834, but the government had taken no further step before its dismissal in November.[37]

The timing of Whig action was dependent upon its attempts to secure the admission of Dissenters to Oxford and Cambridge, and so to remould the ancient universities as centres of national education. While the energies of the liberal leaders were directed towards the latter aim, their support for a Charter for London University waned. The defeat of Wood's Bill in the Lords on 1 August 1834 did not mean that the Whigs has as yet abandoned the measure. In the middle of August, Melbourne established a Cabinet committee consisting of Russell, Holland, Mulgrave, and Hobhouse to produce measures for the relief of Dissenters' grievances. At the begin-

[35] Bellot, *University College, London*, 56, 57.
[36] e.g., Tooke in *Hansard*, 3rd ser., xxvii (1835), 280: NLI MSS 533 (Monteagle Papers): copy Rice to Doyley, 15 Dec. 1835.
[37] Bellot, *University College, London*, 226–246; *Hansard*, 3rd ser., xxvii (1835), 280.

ning of September, Radnor (who had introduced Wood's Bill
in the Lords) sent Holland a draft Bill to introduce a minimum
age requirement for taking oaths and subscribing to the
Articles. Holland sent copies of this Bill to his fellow committee
members Russell and Hobhouse. In October, Holland began
a correspondence with Shuttleworth, the Warden of New
College. By the end of the month the government had gathered
sufficient information to come to a final decision, but its dismissal in November prevented any such scheme from coming to
fruition.[38] Although the exigencies of opposition left little time
for university reform, the issue was not left buried.

On 6 March 1835 Radnor moved in the Lords for returns
respecting the oaths taken at the universities. He and Holland
also collaborated on a series of reform resolutions to be laid
on the table of the House. Meanwhile Radnor also consulted
Sir William Hamilton, the author of articles in the *Edinburgh
Review* advocating university reform. Such activities prompted
Oxford to initiate its own measure, and on 16 March the
Hebdomadel Board agreed to propose to convocation a declaration in lieu of subscription. Radnor's response was to
postpone his own action since the university was now employed
in the task of reform.[39] The Board's proposal, however,
provoked a furious pamphlet war, as Heads of Houses such as
Symons, Warden of Wadham, and Hawkins, Provost of Oriel,
defended the measure against the attacks of Pusey, Marriott,
Eden, and others. The claims of the latter party that the declaration was evidence of the rise of German scepticism and
latitudinarianism at Oxford, that it ran counter to the tradition
of the university, and that it encouraged laxity and carelessness
of thought proved sufficiently strong to defeat the proposed
statute in Convocation on 20 May.[40] The immediate effect of

[38] BL Addit. MSS 51677 (Holland House Papers), fos. 150, 154: Russell to Holland,
17, 24 Aug. 1834; Pusey House MSS, chest B draw 3 (Radnor Papers) fos. 5, 6:
Holland to Radnor, 4, 11 Sept. 1834; BL Addit. MSS 51597 (Holland House Papers),
fos. 128, 130: Shuttleworth to Holland, 2. 11 Oct. 1834; BL Addit. MSS 51677 (Holland
House Papers), fo. 168: Russell to Holland, 21 Oct. 1834; BL Addit. MSS 47224
(Broughton Papers), fo. 81: Holland to Hobhouse, 26 Oct. 1834.

[39] Pusey House MSS, chest B draw 3 (Radnor Papers), fos. 145, 16 Hamilton to
Radnor, 16 Mar. 1835, draft Radnor to Hamilton, 21 Mar. 1835; OU Archives MSS
WPj. 24.5: Minutes of Hebdomadal Meetings 1833–41, 16, 23 Mar. 1835.

[40] [B. P. Symons], *A Letter upon Subscription to the Thirty-Nine Articles at Matriculation*,
(Oxford, 1835); [E. Hawkins], *A Letter to the Earl of Radnor upon the Oaths Dispensations*,

the defeat was to divide the Oxford liberals into those such as Shuttleworth, who still favoured internal procedures of reform, and those who now desired to take the cause to Westminster. Hampden, Principal of St Mary Hall, wrote to Radnor expressing his hope that the peer would 'Persevere and eventually succeed' in his 'restoration of the University to its ancient method of proceeding'.[41] Radnor once more entered the fray and, with Hampden's aid and Holland's advice, drew up a Bill for the abolition of subscription which was printed at the beginning of June. On 20 June the Hebdomadal Board agreed to petition against the Bill on the ground of its interference in the internal administration of the university; on 14 July Radnor's Bill was defeated in the Lords on its second reading. Three days later the government announced the issue of a Charter establishing London University: the ministers once more turned their attention to London as the centre of a liberal national education.[42]

However, the Charter which the government granted was not identical to that requested on behalf of the university by Tooke, Treasurer of the London University and President of the Royal Society of Arts, on 26 March 1835. Instead of incorporating the institution as then established, the government proposed to issue two Charters. The first was to be issued to London University, which was now to be constituted a college and therefore unable to confer degrees, and the second was to establish a metropolitan university which would have the power to grant degrees to students from existing chartered colleges and from such colleges as would thereafter be created by Royal Charter.[43] In so doing the government incorporated the Anglican King's College, founded as a religious rival to the secular University College, within the new university. It thus

---

and Subscription to the XXXIX Articles at the University of Oxford (Oxford 1835); [E. B. Pusey], *Questions respectfully addressed to Members of Convocation on the Substitute for the Subscription to the Thirty-Nine Articles at Matriculation* (Oxford, 1835); [C. P. Eden], *Self-Protection: The Case of the Articles By Clericus* (Oxford, 1835); [C. Marriott], *Meaning of Subscription* (Oxford, 1835).

[41] Pusey House MSS, chest B draw 3 (Radnor Papers), fo. 22: Hampden to Radnor, 2 June 1835.

[42] Ibid., fo. 21: Holland to Radnor, 2 June 1835; OU Archives MSS WPj.24.5: Minutes of Hebdomadal Meetings 1833–41, 20 June 1835; *Hansard*, 3rd ser. xxix (1835), 534; Bellot, *University College, London*, 246.

[43] Ibid.

recognized the importance of religious teaching in the educational system. The Whigs conferred further honour on King's by appointing its first principal, William Otter, to the see of Chichester on Maltby's translation to Durham in 1836. Perhaps even more importantly, the government appointed Thomas Arnold, whose aim was to Christianize the new establishment, a Fellow of the university. Arnold had already, if unsuccessfully, attempted a comparable task in his dealings with the Society for the Diffusion of Useful Knowledge, on the committee of which sat many of the founders of London University, such as Brougham, Abercromby, and Russell.[44] In his new task Arnold had the cautious support of Spring Rice, the Chancellor of the Exchequer, who warned the liberal theologian that if they pressed for all examinations in Arts to include theological matters they 'should fail'; but that examinations in classics 'embracing as they must the principles of moral science—history—and political philosophy not only admit but demand . . . all that recognition of the religious principle' which Arnold could require.[45]

Arnold accordingly originated in the sub-committee of classics of the Faculty of Arts the proposal that 'as a general rule the candidates for the degrees of Bachelors of Arts shall pass an examination either in one of the four Gospels or the Acts of the Apostles in the original Greek; and also in Scripture History'.[46] His object was 'to admit all Christians to degrees, and none but Christians'.[47] This proposal, supported by the Bishops of Chichester, Durham, and Norwich, was passed to the Faculty of Arts at the end of November 1837. An attempt was made there to prevent the proposal from going forward, but was defeated by one vote. The Faculty resolved instead to request the Senate to inquire of Her Majesty's ministers whether it was within the legal competence of the university to institute such an examination.[48] This decision reflected a division within the newly formed institution between those

[44] H. Smith, *The SDUK 1826–46 A Social and Bibliographical Evaluation* (Halifax NS, 1974), 46; SDUK MSS 28: Arnold to Tooke, 18 June 1831; T. W. Bamford, *Thomas Arnold* (London, 1960), 30.

[45] NLI MSS 551 (Monteagle Papers): copy Rice to Arnold, 29 Sept. 1835.

[46] *Parl. Papers 1840*, xl. 223.

[47] Jenkyns MSS VA, bundle 3: Arnold to Jenkyns, 30 Mar. 1838.

[48] Ibid.; NLI MSS 13390 (2) (Monteagle Papers): Empson to Rice, n.d. [1838].

from University College who wished to maintain a primarily secular establishment in order to admit all classes of citizens including Jews, and those from King's College who wished to turn the university into an Anglican institution more akin to the two ancient universities. It was Arnold's task to convince both parties that Christian did not mean exclusively Anglican. Russell's reply on behalf of the government was ambiguous. He did not deny the competency of the university to establish such an examination, but expressed his concern at the disquiet the proposal had aroused among those who were professedly friends of 'religious liberty'. He hinted at the possibility of a voluntary examination as a compromise.[49] Whately meanwhile advised Arnold on tactics, suggesting he should contend for a knowledge of Christian history 'as an essential part of a course of liberal education'. Arnold, for the most part agreeing with such sentiments, passed the letter on to Rice.[50] Fortunately when the Faculty of Arts met on 7 February 1838, Russell's compromise of a voluntary theological examination was adopted without a division. William Empson, a former Fellow of Trinity, wrote to Rice, 'we are in smooth waters again'.[51] In July the Senate approved the terms of the voluntary examination drawn up by a sub-committee of the Faculty of Arts established for that purpose. The examination was to consist of Hebrew texts of the Old Testament and the Greek texts of the New, the Evidences of Christianity (Paley's *Evidences* and Butler's *Analogy*) and Scripture history. It was resolved 'that no question shall be put to any candidate bearing upon any doctrinal point disputed between Christians and Christians; and that no question shall be put as to require an expression of religious belief on the part of the candidate'.[52]

Although Arnold resigned his Fellowship in November 1838, this should be taken not so much as an indication of failure, as the consequence of his idiosyncratic nature and over-eagerness to achieve what only patience could yield. Arnold admitted to Rice that his resignation was not prompted by the

[49] *Parl. Papers 1840*, xl. 54.

[50] NLI MSS 13390 (9) (Monteagle Papers): Whately to Arnold, 5 Jan. 1838, Arnold to Rice, 15 Jan. 1838.

[51] *Parl. Papers 1840*, xl. 224; NLI MSS 13390 (2) (Monteagle Papers): Empson to Rice, n.d. [1838].

[52] *Parl. Papers 1840*. xl. 71, 229.

Senate's refusal to introduce a compulsory examination. His initial reaction to that decision had been to resolve 'to make so much' of the voluntary examination, 'that the degree of BA without it should be considered incomplete'. But he felt that the intention of the authorities of King's College to discourage their students from taking this examination in preference to their own collegiate test, rendered the voluntary examination a 'dead letter'. Arnold feared 'that Christianity' would be 'considered as an indifferent matter in the most extensive of all our National Institutions for Education', that the university would be 'wholly divested of any mark or character of Christianity'.[53] Rice and Whately, for their part, thought this judgement premature. Whately urged Arnold to stay, on the ground that 'his staying in would make the difference of the whole institution being or not being such as he should wish', and requested Rice to write after a similar fashion. Rice suggested that in accepting a voluntary theological examination the university had asserted the principle that 'religious study' was both a 'necessity' and an 'advantage'; that in a time of 'unhappily divided opinion', the course of the proposed study was 'the only path' open to them. He argued further that a compulsory examination was a retrograde measure akin to the Act of Uniformity which they both abhorred, and that religious conviction in any case was unlikely to be produced by compulsion.[54]

Indeed the true nature of religious conviction was a subject on which these liberals dwelt at some length in pressing for university reform. According to these liberals, religious belief was an apprehension of the conscience, an inwrought conviction and not therefore a matter of the observance of outward forms. Their objection to compulsory oaths as requirements of entry to places of learning was in part the product of a scepticism which doubted that they were efficient tests of sentiment. Thirlwall asserted 'that religion . . . cannot be instilled into men against or without their will . . .'[55], while the attempt

---

[53] NLI MSS 13390 (1) (Monteagle Papers); Arnold to Rice, 1 Oct. 1838; Jenkyns MSS VA, bundle 3: Arnold to Jenkyns, 30 Mar. 1838; Stanley, *Thomas Arnold*, 332.
[54] NLI MSS 13390 (1) (Monteagle Papers): Whately to Rice, 5 Nov. 1838; NLI MSS 534 (Monteagle Papers): copy Rice to Arnold, 5 Nov. 1838.
[55] TCC Addit. MSS a.213 (Whewell Papers), fo. 177: Thirlwall to Whewell, n.d. [Sept. 1834].

to do so was more than likely to produce doubt. The consequence was that compulsory tests in practice were ineffective
as measures of belief. When used in this fashion they had, as
Peacock observed, a tendency to diminish 'the reverence with
which they should always be regarded'.[56] The misguided
nature of these tests was a point the liberals attempted to drive
home in parliament. Radnor challenged a common defence of
the Oxford test at matriculation, namely that it was a means
of demonstrating a general assent to Anglicanism rather than
an adherence to, and so an understanding of, particular Anglican doctrines. He commented that in so far as the Thirty-Nine
Articles were not actually meant to be understood, they could
not furnish an adequate criteria by which to judge whether a
person was a Dissenter or Muhammadan; that in any case
they were ineffective since in practice Dissenters were not
excluded from attending Oxford (and thus the value of such
oaths was diminished); that other signs of religious belief, such
as attendance at chapel, were more reliable indicators.[57] The
liberal objection to religious tests was not solely that they were
designed to exclude, but also that they were an inadequate
means of demonstrating a true religious faith.

The Tories denied the liberal assumption—embodied in
such measures as the London University Voluntary Theological Examination—that combined religious instruction was
possible without being offensive. Christopher Wordsworth, the
Master of Trinity, complained that religious instruction
without controversy comprised only 'the beggarly elements of
a negative and deistical Christianity'; agreement on religious
doctrines was the product of 'indifference'. He wrote: 'The
religious feeling of these societies must it is clear languish from
this compromise. It must fade and die.'[58] Turton, Dean of
Peterborough and Regius Professor of Divinity at Cambridge,
cited Doddridge's Dissenting Academy at Northampton as a
disastrous experiment in combined instruction which resulted
in 'a vagueness and indecision of language in the discourses

---

[56] Peacock, *Statutes of the University of Cambridge*, 77.

[57] *Hansard*, 3rd ser. xxix (1835), 500.

[58] C. Wordsworth, *On the Admission of Dissenters to the University of Cambridge. A Letter to the Rt. Hon. Viscount Althorp MP.* (Cambridge, 1834), 28, *idem. A Second Letter etc.* (Cambridge & London, 1834), 51, 52.

of the young ministers . . . which made it a matter of uncer-
tainty whether they really had any positive opinions at all, on
some of the most momentous points that can occupy the attention of mankind'.[59] In their theological writings, Oxford divines
such as Whately, Hampden, and Arnold had already sketched
the possibility of elucidating a common Christianity. In
Cambridge the liberals attempted a more practical demonstration in which they pointed to the acceptance by both
Dissenters and Anglicans of the existing arrangements for
theological instruction in the university. In so doing they
underscored their claim that the formal admission of Dissenters
would not significantly alter the character of the universities.
Thirlwall, a Fellow of Trinity, most notoriously addressed this
question in his public letters to the Dean of Peterborough of
May and June 1834. They were to result in his resignation
from the college and his removal to a living in Yorkshire, one
of the last acts of preferment conferred by Brougham on behalf
of the outgoing Whig government.

In his *Letters* Thirlwall concentrated on the religious instruction offered by the colleges and, in particular, on that of his
own college. This was understandable since the university
lectures given by the theological professors at Cambridge were
voluntary; it was on the subject of the university as a domestic
and therefore collegiate institution that the debate was
conducted. Thirlwall claimed that, according to the Master
of Trinity, those students who wished to enter the church
could not expect to receive a formal education to meet their
needs, but would be expected to pursue such a course of studies
by means of private reading. He suggested further that colleges
did not act as 'missionary institutions' in which heathens were
converted to Anglicanism, but that collegiate authorities
assumed, on the contrary, that students had imbibed the main
principles of religion at a previous institution. He stated that
college theological lectures, since they were confined to such
subjects as portions of the New Testament and Paley's
Evidences, could not provide a rigorous course of theological
instruction; that such subjects in any case were treated in a
literary and historical, as well as a doctrinal, manner. Indeed

[59] T. Turton, *Thoughts on the Admission of Persons without regard to their Religious Opinions
to Certain Degrees in the Universities of England* (Cambridge to London, 1834), 10.

he contended that college examinations in theological subjects primarily concerned questions of grammar, chronology, geography, history and antiquities. From this he concluded that the theological instruction offered might 'very properly be admitted into a liberal plan of education' which had 'no reference to any particular profession'; that they were designed to communicate certain kinds of knowledge which an undergraduate 'as a gentleman and a scholar' ought to possess. The teaching of Trinity College was offered as testimony of the practical possibility of a comprehensive religious education. Not surprisingly such an offering provoked a storm of controversy.[60]

William Selwyn, former Fellow of St John's and Canon of Ely, replied in a pamphlet containing extracts from various college examinations in Divinity. These he claimed demonstrated 'a system of instruction' which comprehended 'the most sacred truths of Christianity, as maintained in the formularies and Liturgy of the Church'.[61] At the end of May, R. W. Evans, a Fellow and Tutor of Trinity, issued a statement respecting current lectures given by himself in the college on the subject of the New Testament, to the effect that these lectures had as much doctrinal as philological content.[62] Whewell, in a published reply to his colleague Thirlwall, asserted that in such lectures opinions were expressed 'as from Churchmen to Churchmen'.[63] An internal college dispute had been made public. On 26 May the Master of Trinity, opposed to the admission of Dissenters, requested Thirlwall to resign his office of assistant tutor. On 28 May Thirlwall responded by issuing a circular letter to all Fellows to establish how far they were in accord with the propriety of the Master's conduct, a letter which produced a protest to the Master, drawn up the following day, from a number of liberal dons.[64]

[60] C. Thirlwall, *A Letter to Thomas Turton DD* (Cambridge, 1834), 6–7, 16–17, 23, 24, 26–27.

[61] W. Selwyn, *Extracts from the College Examinations in Divinity for the Last Four Years.* (Cambridge, 1834), x.

[62] CUR MSS 118 (Abolition of Tests), fo. 66: R. W. Evans, 'A Statement respecting the Lectures at Present given on the Subject of the New Testament in Trinity College Cambridge', (Cambridge, 1834).

[63] W. Whewell, *Remarks on Some Parts of Mr Thirlwall's Letter on the Admission of Dissenters to Academical Degrees* (Cambridge, 1834), 20.

[64] CUR MSS 118 (Abolition of Tests), fo. 67; Bury, *Romilly's Cambridge Diary*, 58–9.

As the second reading of Wood's Bill to abrogate tests approached, Sedgwick returned to the publicist's task and produced an open letter to all Members of Senate, which repeated his claims of 11 April that no college lectures in divinity for the past thirty years had contained anything offensive to the tenets of any Dissenter. Sedgwick discredited Evans's evidence by stating that his lectures had not been commissioned by any regular college board nor made compulsory; he denied that didactic theology played 'a prominent and essential part' in an Arts degree. He claimed that the statutes of Trinity, explicit in all other respects, made no provision for any lectures in theology.[65] Thirlwall replied to his critics in a second letter which contained the assertion that 'all Dissenters have to wish is that no alteration should be made on their account in this part of our system' as the condition of their entrance to Trinity.[66]

The liberal ability to comprehend Dissenters in a Christian education depended on the distinction they drew between religion and theology, the former a union of fundamental beliefs and practice, the latter a professional intellectual discipline of doctrinal and often contentious substance. In his *Edinburgh Review* articles Hamilton stressed the importance of distinguishing between the liberal instruction in a university given to all in the preliminary or general Faculty of Arts, and the 'professional instruction' given to train to 'certain special dexterities' candidates for the clergy.[67] Parallel with the advocacy of a broad religious education went the desire to institute theological instruction as a professional course leading to qualifications akin to those already existing in law and medicine. Such a course was to be confined to post-graduates. It was thereby intended to remove dogmatic theology from a liberal education, and so to make possible combined religious instruction. Theology was to become the subject of a new specialized education. Peacock in his work on university reform detailed at some length proposals for the professional education of ordinands at the university. He recommended regular and

---

[65] CUR MSS 118 (Abolition of Tests), fo. 71; *Cambridge Chronicle*, 13 June 1834.

[66] C. Thirlwall, *A Second Letter to the Revd Thomas Turton DD* (Cambridge, 1834), 33.

[67] [W. Hamilton], 'Admission of Dissenters to the Universities', *Edinburgh Review* lx (1834), 212, 220.

systematic courses of lectures to be given annually on the doctrine, liturgy, and articles of the Anglican Church, on Hebrew, biblical criticism, ecclesiastical history, the Early Fathers, and moral philosophy. Candidates for holy orders, he suggested, should be examined by the several theological professors, a joint certificate should be issued to successful candidates to replace the certificate then issued by the Norrisian Professor alone and accepted by the episcopate as proof of worth. He hoped that the adoption of such a system would raise the general standard of theological attainments in the university.[68] The cause of professional theological instruction was taken up by other Cambridge-educated liberals such as Samuel Butler, the headmaster of Shrewsbury, and James Hildyard of Christ's College, Cambridge.[69] An address to the episcopate signed, amongst others, by such liberals as the Earl of Burlington (Chancellor of London University), Morpeth (Chief Secretary for Ireland), Arnold, and W. D. Conybeare, the geologist, likewise pressed for a reformed course of theological instruction. They suggested that at present such instruction was 'too general and vague' to be of much use to a Christian minister, but that a course of special theological instruction should be available to prospective ordinands which they could take voluntarily as part of their degree course. Participation in this course would then be a necessary qualification for ordination.[70] The preparation of the Dean and Chapters Bill provided the occasion for the government to act.

In the promotion of separate, but improved, theological instruction, the liberals were aided by the shared interests of both Evangelicals such as Simeon, Buxton, and Andrew Agnew, and High Churchmen such as Gladstone and E. B. Pusey.[71] A common desire for Anglican renewal resulted in cross-party support for such proposals. In their second report the Ecclesiastical Commissioners recommended that in the

[68] Peacock, *Statutes of the University of Cambridge*, 168–70.
[69] S. Butler, *Thoughts on Church Dignities* (London, 1833), 10; J. Hildyard, *Five Sermons* (London, 1841), viii–xxi.
[70] OU Archives MSS NW 21.5.2: 'Address to the Most Reverend and Right Reverend Fathers in God, the Archbishops and Bishops of the United Church of England and Ireland'.
[71] Ibid.; E. B. Pusey, *Remarks on the Prospective and Past Benefits of Cathedral Institutions in the Promotion of Sound Religious Knowledge and of Clerical Education* (2nd edn., London, 1833).

case of Christ Church Cathedral, in view of its connection with Oxford University, the number of its canonries should be reduced not to four, but to six, and that the Lady Margaret Professor of Divinity should be annexed to a stall there. Meanwhile a memorial from the Dean and Chapter of Ely pressed that they also should retain six canonries, and that two or three should be annexed to university offices 'connected with the advancement of sacred learning'.[72] Shortly prior to the second reading in the Commons of the Dean and Chapters Bill of 1840, Hampden, the Regius Professor of Divinity at Oxford, wrote to Russell requesting that a new chair in either Biblical Criticism or Ecclesiastical History be founded at Oxford and annexed to a Christ Church stall as an alternative to the Lady Margaret professorship, since the latter, as a result of being elected by members of the university, often acted as a political rival to the government-appointed Regius.[73] Accordingly Russell announced on 6 April 1840 two additional stalls for Christ Church and recommended that they be attached to professorships of Ecclesiastical History and Biblical Criticism (proposed in committee on 15 June); on 29 June he consented to the annexation of two professorships to stalls at Ely, requested from the promotion of 'religious education and instruction'.[74] Gaisford, the Dean of Christ Church, wrote to the Archbishop of Canterbury that 'whenever this scheme is perfected we shall have in truth a faculty of theology in active operation . . . We shall have the means of instruction and also be enabled through the Professors acting together as a board to discriminate the worthy from the unworthy.'[75]

In view of the government's proposals, Gaisford began discussing with Howley, the Archbishop, the terms of the proposed chairs. They both agreed that the professorships should not be confined to lecturing, but should have a greater involvement in theological teaching. Howley expressed his belief in the government's willingness to co-operate, and at the beginning of the Michaelmas term the Hebdomadal Board established a subcommittee to consider changes in divinity

---

[72] *Parl. Papers 1836*, xxxvi. 23; *Parl. Papers 1837*, xli. 55–6.
[73] BL Microfilm 859/12 (Melbourne Papers): Hampden to Russell, 28 Feb. 1840.
[74] *Hansard*, 3rd ser., liii (1840), 591; *ibid.*, liv (1840), 1203; *ibid.*, lv (1840), 217.
[75] OU Archives MSS NW 21.5.1: Gaisford to Howley, 17 Oct. 1840.

studies. By March 1841 Howley had gained the acquiescence
of Wellington, the Chancellor of the University, and the
committee had proposed regulations which Gaisford transmit-
ted to the Archbishop. Howley advised that the bishops should
not be consulted since this would promote controversy.[76] By
Easter 1841 the Hebdomadal Board had formally approved
the plan of instituting chairs in Ecclesiastical History and
Pastoral Theology, each professor to deliver a course of
lectures, give professional instruction and examine their pupils.
The two new professors and the two existing (the Regius and
the Lady Margaret) together with the Regius Professor of
Hebrew, were to constitute a Board to examine students who
had attended six courses of lectures in at least six terms following their obtaining a BA. Successful candidates would then
be granted a certificate or, as Hawkins wrote in November,
'something to that purpose'.[77] The general election of 1841
produced a hiatus, but by the autumn Howley had approached
Peel, and the negotiations commenced once again with the
new Prime Minister's approval.[78] The passage of the new
Statutum de Disciplina Theologica was delayed by wranglings
between Pusey and Hamden—a minor skirmish in the Tractarian War—but by late spring 1842 the two new chairs were
finally established.[79] Conservatives had instituted at Oxford
what liberals had maintained, namely that theological instruction as a preparation for the clergy was a separate task from
that of providing a general undergraduate education. Dogmatic and theological was distinguished from liberal yet religious
education by institutional means.

Cantabrigean efforts to institute a professional theological
education were rather more hesitant, perhaps because the
senior members of the university allowed the liberals to initiate
reform rather than seizing the opportunity themselves as
Gaisford had done at Oxford. Plans for a professional theolog-

[76] OU Archives MSS NW 21.5.1: Howley to Gaisford, 29 Oct. 1840, 12 Feb. 1841,
Gaisford to Howley, 21 Nov. 1840, 23 Feb. 1841. See also Wynter Papers: Bod. MSS
Dep. d.4., fos. 120 ff.
[77] TCC Addit. MSS a. 206 (Whewell Papers), fo. 15: Hawkins to Whewell, 20
Nov. 1841.
[78] OU Archives MSS NW 21.5.1: Howley to Gaisford, 11 Dec. 1841.
[79] Bod. MSS Dep. d.3 (Wynter Papers), fos. 110, 12, 14, 16: Pusey to Wynter, 20
Mar. 19, 27 Apr. 1842, Hampden to Wynter, 27 Apr. 1842.

ical examination had been mooted early in 1841 by Hildyard and Peacock (both liberals) and the Evangelical Charles Perry, but an actual move towards such reform in the university was delayed until April when Dr Graham, the liberal Master of Christ's, who, as Bishop of Chester, acquired a reputation for too great a tolerance of Dissent, published his intention to propose a Grace to Senate on the topic.[80] In his statement, he claimed that the course of study leading to the BA consisted principally 'in the cultivation of Mathematical Science and Classical Learning' prefatory to the 'prosecution of the peculiar studies of the liberal professions'; that the university provision for the 'Profession' of clergyman was inadequate; that to remedy this defect the period of study required for a BA should be abridged in order to allow time for the postgraduate study of theology. Students who had voluntarily undertaken this course would be examined by a Board consisting of the Regius, Lady Margaret, and Norrisian Professors of Divinity, and the Regius Professors of Hebrew and Greek.[81] This plan proved offensive to High-Churchmen and liberals alike. Collison, a member of the Anglo-Catholic Cambridge Camden Society, objected to the removal of theological teaching from under-graduate courses, and Crick, the President of St John's, feared it would lead to 'the degradation of sound learning—the substitution of Theology for education in Church principles—the weakening of the ties that attach men to the University'.[82] J. W. Blakesley, the liberal Fellow of Trinity, objected to the shortening of the BA course as a curtailment of a liberal general education. He desired instead the introduction of a plan of theological instruction 'without danger to the scientific and literary character of the Academical course'.[83] This almost universal disapprobation led Graham to withdraw his Grace, but the liberals did not relinquish the initiative; in May Blakes-ley brought forward a Grace of his own to appoint a Syndicate to consider the question of a 'theological examination'. This, however, was thrown out by the Senate on 26 May.[84]

[80] Peacock, *Statutes of the University of Cambridge*; Hildyard, *Five Sermons*; C. Perry, *Clerical Education* (London, 1841); Cam. Univ. Papers, MSS 12 fo. 579.
[81] Cam. Univ. Papers, MSS 12, fo. 579; CUL MSS DC 8550.
[82] Cam. Univ. Papers, MSS 14, fos. 326, 327.
[83] Ibid., fo. 323.
[84] Cam. Univ. Papers, MSS 12, fo. 586; Cam. Univ. Papers, MSS 14, fo. 341.

Although the liberal attempt had failed, the issue was still of sufficient concern to other parties to induce further action. The Bishop of London, Blomfield (formerly of Trinity), was concerned that some measure should be undertaken in the light of Oxonian plans. There was also a general fear that theological instruction might be lost to recently established diocesan colleges such as Chichester.[85] Negotiations accordingly took place in the ensuing months which led to the establishment of a Syndicate on 29 November to consider what steps should be taken by the University 'to provide a more efficient system of Theological Instruction'—thus omitting any direct reference to a postgraduate theological examination. The Vice-Chancellor, the Masters of Jesus, John's, and Trinity, the Regius, Norrisian, and Margaret Professors of Divinity, and the Regius Professors of Civil Law and Greek were all appointed to serve on it; Graham, most pointedly, had refused to be a member.[86] The report published on 14 March did not so much represent a High Church victory as a judicious compromise with the liberals. Dr Corrie, the Norrisian Professor, and Dr Turton, the Regius Professor of Divinity, succeeded in persuading their fellow Syndics to improve the course of undergraduate theological instruction by adding Old Testament history as a subject for the Previous Examination; and the shorter Epistles of the New Testament, the history of the Christian Church from its origin to the Council of Nicaea, and the history of the English Reformation as subjects for questionists who were not candidates for honours. Turton's attempt, however, to have law and medical students sit a theological examination previous to taking their degrees was foiled by Haviland and Geldart, the Professor of Law. A voluntary theological examination for candidates intending to take holy orders, to be held after the graduation, was instituted against the wishes of Dr Corrie (though on Turton's insistence), who as a consequence refused to sit on the proposed Board of Examiners. Thus it was possible for a liberal such as Hildyard to welcome the Syndicate's report, even if it did

[85] M. Holroyd(ed.), *Memorials of the Life of George Elwes Corrie* (Cambridge, 1890), 156–7.
[86] Cam. Univ. Papers, MSS 14, fos. 478, 665; Cam. Univ. Papers, MSS 15, fo. 29; Cam. Univ. Papers, MSS 12, fo. 655.

not accord precisely with his original wishes.[87] On 11 May the plan for the theological examination received the Senate's approval, and in October the first theological examination was held in Cambridge.[88] As was the case at Oxford, reforms which initially found their most vociferous proponents in liberals achieved their institutional form as a consequence of action by conservatives.

The appointment of the liberal reformer Hampden to the Oxford Regius Chair of Divinity brought a stream of abuse on the Whig government, an attack which revealed the ideological distinctiveness of its ecclesiastical preferences. On Tuesday, 9 February 1836, following the Sunday on which Hampden had been offered the chair, the Archbishops of Canterbury and York visited Downing Street to protest at the appointment. On the same day Cantuar put his protest in writing in a letter to Melbourne. On the Thursday, Edward Pusey's brother, Philip, forwarded to Melbourne via Howick a copy of the letter from the Oxford Heads of Houses objecting to the appointment. He offered to put a halt to the petition of Oxford MAs in exchange for the withdrawal of Hampden's nomination. Howley presented the address of the Caput to Melbourne on 13 February; the Prime Minister received a copy of Newman's pamphlet on the 16th. Meanwhile Oxford liberals had also been active in attempting to influence the government. Both Copleston and Whately wrote to inform Melbourne of Hampden's orthodoxy before the crucial Cabinet meeting of 13 February. The Cabinet met in all three times to discuss the appointment. At a Cabinet dinner at Lansdowne's on Wednesday, 10 February, they resolved to defer judgement until they had received the King's opinion. This arrived in the affirmative in time for a second Cabinet on the 13th. As a result of that meeting Melbourne wrote to Hampden confirming his new post. From then on through the ensuing storm Melbourne, with the aid of Copleston, defended Hampden against assorted Tractarians and Evangelicals at Oxford, and against the King (who had since changed his mind) at Brighton. The Cabinet of 15 February merely

[87] Holroyd, *George Elwes Corrie*, 180–3, 187; Cam. Univ. Papers MSS 15, fo. 29.
[88] CUL Misc. Coll., MSS 54: note on covers of 'Theological Examinations 1843–73'.

confirmed Melbourne in his resolve. He explained to the King that he defended the appointment since the agitation 'seriously impinges upon the rights of private judgement and free enquiry which are the foundations of the Protestant faith, and it saps the great principle of Toleration the great glory of this age . . . Finally it seriously endangers the real interests of the Church of England into which it introduces division and schism.'[89]

Hampden's appointment was a potent symbol of the union which occurred between liberal dons and politicians on the issue of university reform. Hampden had strongly and publicly been associated with the movement supported by the government to admit Dissenters to the university. The High Church Henry Wilberforce had suggested that the Oxford scheme had originated first in Hampden's pamphlet on Dissent which he described as 'the manifesto of the party by whom the proposal is introduced'; he proceeded to cite Blanco White, Arnold, and Samuel Hinds as leading members.[90] The agitation against this leader of 'the liberal party', as these Oxford theologians were popularly designated, was thought to be politically motivated, or as the *Globe* noted on 29 April: 'There can be no doubt that a large proportion if not a majority of those members of convocation who have taken part in the various proceedings against Dr Hampden at Oxford are influenced rather by political than religious zeal'.[91] Arnold also attributed the attack on Hampden to his support of the proposal to substitute a declaration for subscription to the Thirty-Nine Articles at matriculation.[92] The pamphleteers concentrated their fire on Hampden's theology, thus highlighting the religious principles which underlay the liberal measure, and acting in accord with Hampden's own claim that in his

[89] BL Microfilm 859/35 (Melbourne Papers): Melbourne to King William IV, 15 Feb. 1836, Howley to Melbourne, 9 Feb. 1836, Howick to Melbourne, 11 Feb. 1836: BL Addit. MSS 56558 (Broughton Papers): Hobhouse Diary, 13 Feb. 1836; BL Microfilm 859/35 (Melbourne Papers): Gilbert to Melbourne, 16 Feb. 1836, Whately to Melbourne, 7 Feb. 1836; Broadlands MSS MEL/WH (Melbourne Papers), fo. 1: Whately to Melbourne, 22 Jan. 1836; BL Addit. MSS 56558 (Broughton Papers): Hobhouse Diary, 10, 13, 15, 17 Feb. 1836; Hampden Papers, fo. 29: Melbourne to Hampden, 13 Feb. 1836.

[90] [H. Wilberforce], *The Foundation of the Faith Assailed in Oxford: A Letter to His Grace the Archbishop of Canterbury*, (London, 1835), 14, 23, 24, 26, 29, 31, 34.

[91] [Anon.] *State of Parties in Oxford from the Public Prints* (Oxford, 1836), p. 9.

[92] [T. Arnold], 'The Oxford Malignants and Dr. Hampden', *Edinburgh Review*, lxiii (1836), 228.

pamphlet he had put forward the 'religious grounds' for abolition.[93] Pusey accused him of advocating 'a philosophical
system' which was 'at variance with the Christian faith';
Churton suggested he was guilty of 'reviving the German
theory of Rationalism', and an anonymous author claimed
that his principles would 'pave the way to Socinianism and
other avowed forms of Infidelity'.[94] The government's appointment was thus a symbolic endorsement of the liberal theology
which lay behind these liberal political causes. The Hampden
controversy firmly associated the liberal government with the
liberal theologians in the public mind. This public display was
merely the outward mark of private relations of friendship and
intellectual sympathy.

[93] Pusey House MSS, chest B draw 3 (Radnor Papers), fo. 18: Hampden to Radnor,
21 May 1835.
[94] [E. B. Pusey], *Dr Hampden's Past and Present Statements compared* (Oxford, 1836),
22; Churton, *A Letter to an Edinburgh Reviewer on the Case of the Oxford Malignants of Dr.
Hampden* (London, 1836), 5; [Anon.], *A Non-resident MAs Self-Vindication for attending
to Support the Vote of Censure on Dr Hampden's Writings* (Oxford, 1836), 9–10.

6

The Liberals and Elementary Education

BY the 1830s, the need to provide elementary education for the poor was acknowledged by both Whig and Tory politicians. When debating Russell's proposed scheme of 1839, Peel used the opportunity to declare: 'I, for one, am deeply convinced of the absolute necessity, and the moral obligation, of providing for the education of the people', while the High Church Tory, T. D. Acland, despite opposing the liberal plan, suggested that 'if any class of her Majesty's subjects were excluded from the benefits of education', a specific plan should be brought forward.[1] In this period there was no shortage either of plans or of advocates. What distinguished these educational partisans was not so much the pedagogic technique they advocated as the kind of religious education they proposed. This was a traditional rivalry which had its origins in the contest between the primarily Dissenting British and Foreign School Society founded in 1808 and the Anglican National Society established in 1811. The educational techniques employed by both societies were virtually identical, being simply variations of the monitorial system or learning by rote. Admittedly, the foundation of the Central Society for Education in 1836 marked a new departure in both the means of educating and the religious education to be provided. One of its prime functions was to propagate Fellenbergian techniques in opposition to the monitorial system, and thus many of its publications were devoted to criticizing the two older societies for not dovetailing their lessons to the psychological development of the child. But by the late 1830s and early 1840s both the National Society and the BFSS had responded to these admonitions. In 1838 the National Society had established a Committee of Inquiry and Correspondence to institute such reforms, and from 1840 the BFSS began modifying its monitorial system until it was finally abolished in 1847. Neither society, however, responded

[1] *Hansard*, 3rd ser., xlv (1839), 309; ibid., xlviii (1839), 570.

to the Central Society's call for united but secular education, a call which gave the Central Society its political significance. Thus all three competing educational interest groups were rivals primarily in a religious sense, representative of deeply-held religious sentiments as much as educational concerns. The liberal government in proposing reforms found itself in the invidious position of having to choose between differing conceptions of the role religion should play in a child's development. In choosing, the Whigs inevitably aroused strong prejudices.

Those writing the history of English education have tended to be too concerned to distinguish between elementary education in the interests of the poor and education imposed in the interest of the ruling elite, to discuss fully the nature of the choice made by the Whigs. Silver, for example, in *The Concept of Popular Education*, primarily concentrated on distinguishing between the 'education-as-insurance, rescuing-from-revolution, schools-rather-than-prisons trend', exemplified by governments regardless of party affiliation, and the kind of education sponsored by the Owenites which subverted the status quo. Hurt in *Education in Evolution* offered a history of English education as the struggle between 'the forces of obscurantism' (the supporters of the church) and the moderately enlightened proponents of a state education system which was primarily intended to help to 'prevent the social unrest of the day from escalating into widespread revolution.'[2] In stressing the 'social control' function of education above all else, these historians state a truism. It is, after all, unlikely that politicians would have established an education system intended to lead to their own overthrow and the disintegration of the social order. As a consequence, these historians have paid less attention to important differences in party views about the society which it was sought to control. Admittedly the most recent work on education in the 1830s did not consider Whig measures exclusively in the context of social unrest, but this is virtue by omission. Dr Paz writes not so much as a

[2] H. Silver, *The Concept of Popular Education* (London 1965), 210; J. Hurt, *Education in Evolution* (London, 1971), 22, 38. See also R. Johnson, 'Educational Policy and Social Control', *Past and Present*, lix (1970), 119: 'The suggestion is that the early Victorian obsession with the education of the poor is best understood as a concern about authority, about power, about the assertion (or re-assertion?) of control'.

student of education *per se* as an historian of 'administrative
processes' contributing to the 'revolution in government'
debate about the extension of state influence in the 1830s. In
the course of a detailed narrative, he convincingly
demonstrates that Whig rather than Tory or Radical politicians
and administrators were responsible for the legislative initiative of 1839. Yet he deliberately eschews the tasks of elucidating
in an extended fashion the significance of the issues in contention and of placing Whig proposals within a broader understanding of Whiggery.[3] It is the purpose of this chapter to
indicate the vision of British society which the Whigs
advocated in drafting their educational plans. By placing Whig
proposals in the context of developments in Whig thought, it
may be seen that on educational reform liberal Anglicans
exercised their greatest influence and received their most
notable set-back.

Liberal Whig politicians viewed education as the agent for
establishing the liberal Anglican state. According to the liberal
Anglican ideal, each individual school, rather than the education system taken as a whole, was to act as a crucible of social
harmony by accepting within its walls the divergent groups
of the recently enlarged political nation, and by imparting to
the pupils a common sense of morality. Each school was to
be an institutional proof that politically warring factions were
in fact both reconcilable and compatible. In the 1830s this
entailed a demonstration of the similarities not between rich
and poor, nor between the indigenous and the foreign, but
between the Anglican and the Dissenter, the Protestant and
the Catholic, that is between the religious groups newly admitted into the polity. Since it was generally accepted that religion
had to be the foundation of any education, this demonstration
was dependent on the accepted existence of principles of Christianity common to all sects. Compatibility in the classroom
was not to be the consequence of avoiding the cause of sectarian
divisions. Secular education would only have solved the
problem at the expense of failing to provide a sound education.
If, however, the invention of non-sectarian Christianity solved
the apparent contradiction of providing a uniform education

[3] D. G. Paz, *the Politics of Working-Class Education in Britain 1830–50* (Manchester, 1980), viii.

for a religiously diverse population, it did so at the risk of offending both God and man. In advocating their educational measures, liberals had to counter the arguments of those who prided themselves on both their religion and their pragmatism. High Anglicans, militant Nonconformists, ultramontane, and Irish Catholics protested that common Christianity could only be taught at the expense of religious belief: doctrine and faith were inseparable. On this assumption they suggested that the impartial educational provision which the liberals advocated would in practice become partisan. Such schools would become, according to prejudice, the vehicles of subversive Catholicism, proselytizing Protestantism, voluntaryist Dissent, or intolerant Anglicanism. The liberal experiment was first attempted in Ireland. Thus it is with the National Board, established while Stanley was Chief Secretary in 1831, that an account of the liberal Anglican ideal in practice must begin.

It is perhaps a measure of the liberals' eventual failure, and of their opponents' triumph, that the Irish National School system has suffered retrospectively from considerable obloquy. Irish nationalist Catholics viewed the school system as a Protestant plot, designed to secure a transfer in the allegiance of Catholics from the priest to the English state, so sacrificing the true interests of both the great mass of the Irish people and of Roman Catholicism. Dr John MacHale, the Archbishop of Tuam, believed that the government was 'labouring to effect by fraud and wiles what past ones could not achieve by force and to supersede the authority of the local pastors and to place the entire education of the people in bodies over which they may exercise absolute control'.[1] In the 1830s MacHale sought a papal condemnation of the system; by the 1850s, in order to appease increased Catholic agitations, the Board agreed that if the 'Scripture Extracts' (the primary source of non-denominational religious instruction) were read in the classroom, they were not to be read as part of the ordinary school business as had occurred hitherto. This in effect was a condemnation of the non-sectarian education undertaken by the Board for the previous twenty years and,

---

[1] E. Larkin, 'The Quarrel among the Roman Catholic Hierarchy over the National System of Education in Ireland, 1838–41', R. B. Browne (ed.), *The Celtic Cross* (West Lafayette, Ind., 1964), 124.   [2] *Parl. Papers 1852–3*, xciv. 466–7.

not surprisingly, Richard Whately, its liberal Anglican architect, resigned in protest. Such actions merely confirmed what many Anglicans had charged, namely that the Irish system was an underhand means of giving a subvention to the Roman Catholic Church. A. G. Stapleton, who had undertaken a tour of inspection of National Schools in 1850 under the auspices of the Church Education Society, reported in 1854 that the schools under Roman Catholic patrons were 'in no sense "mixed" schools', that there was no impediment to 'extensive instruction in the doctrine and practice of the Roman Catholic Church'. Two-thirds of all National Schools came into this category. Indeed in 1854 only 48 out of 4,602 schools were run jointly by Protestant and Catholic patrons.[6] In view of the development of, in effect, a denominational educational system, it is not surprising that its architects glossed their earlier support in sectarian language. In 1852 Whately mistakenly claimed to Senior that 'The education supplied by the National Board is gradually undermining the vast fabric of the Irish Roman Catholic Church.'[7]

If Ireland did prove the graveyard of this liberal aspiration, as of so many others, the outcome should not be allowed to prejudice an understanding of its inception. The Irish Board of Education was heralded as an attempt at putting the liberal Anglican ideal into practice. Russell referred to it as an 'experiment' in a 'united system of education' which had met with 'great success', and Whately described it in 1838 as an 'experiment' in non-denominational scriptural instruction which, he claimed, had achieved 'unexpected success'.[8] Stanley, in introducing his scheme to the House on 9 September 1831, offered it as a solution to the problem of 'how religious, moral and literary instruction could best be imparted . . . and how companionship and kindly feeling could at an early age be best promoted between Catholics and Protestants'.[9] The Chief Secretary for Ireland proposed to end the government grant to the Protestant Kildare-Street Society and to place the sum of £30,000 p.a. thus released at the disposal

[6] *Parl. Papers 1854*, xv. i, 34, 525.

[7] Whately, *Richard Whately*, ii. 245.

[8] *Hansard*, 3rd ser., xlv (1839), 277; NLI MSS 13390 (9) (Monteagle Papers): Whately to Arnold, 5 Jan. 1838.

[9] *Hansard*, 3rd ser., vi (1831), 1250.

of the Lord Lieutenant, but under the direction of a Board to be composed of both Protestants and Catholics. The Board would allocate grants to schools, superintend a model school and edit and print books for the literary instruction of the pupils. Stanley originally proposed that the education provided would be combined literary and separate religious instruction.[10] By the time the letter of instruction had been sent to the chairman of the new board, the Duke of Leinster, this had been significantly altered to 'combined moral and literary and separate religious instruction'.[11] The Board also proposed to include in its list of books 'such portions of Sacred History or of religious and moral teaching as may be approved by the entire Board'.[12] Thus the Irish sytem as finally constituted provided for a form of non-denominational religious instruction. Although this was not intended 'to constitute a perfect and sufficient Religious Education', it was a move towards encouraging non-sectarian Christian teaching.[13] Spring Rice remarked apropos the proposal to appropriate the surplus revenues of the Irish Church to the National School system that 'We can teach them in our schools if we cannot teach them in the Churches & the one is the road to the other': for liberal Anglicans the education offered in such schools was not a travesty of Christianity.[14]

While it is unclear who was responsible for the alteration, it is certain that the responsibility did not lie with Stanley. Whately recalled that when 'Lord Stanley founded the Education Board' he had 'no such thought' as to introduce instruction in the Christian Scriptures.[15] James Carlile, the Presbyterian member of the Board of Education until his resignation in late 1838, informed Morpeth that the Scripture lessons 'formed no part of the original plan proposed to us by the Government'. He proceeded: 'It was indeed with some difficulty that I prevailed on Lord Stanley to consent to the use of such lessons', a claim repeated publicly in *The Times* seventeen years later.[16]

[10] Ibid., 1258.
[11] D. H. Akenson, *The Irish Education Experiment* (London, 1970), 119.
[12] R. Whately, *Scriptural Education in Ireland* (London, 1832), 26.   [13] Ibid.
[14] NLI MSS 550 (Monteagle Papers): Rice to Northampton, 26 June 1834.
[15] NLI MSS 13390 (9) (Monteagle Papers): Whately to Arnold, 5 Jan. 1838.
[16] Carlisle Papers, MSS J19.1.13, fo. 23: Carlile to Morpeth, 17 Aug. 1836; *The Times*, 2 Aug. 1853.

The immediate inspiration behind the introduction of the Scripture extracts thus appears to have been the need to appease Presbyterians, who opposed the National Board at its outset on the ground that it offended the Protestant principle of permitting unrestricted access to the Bible throughout the school day.[17] But once this concession had been made by the Irish Office, the liberal Anglicans took up the cause of non-denominational religious instruction in Irish schools with undisguised enthusiasm. Arnold assisted Carlile in preparing the latter part of the Acts of the Apostles and in 1837 revised the remainder for a second edition of the Gospel of St Luke and the Acts of the Apostles to be circulated in the National Schools.[18] Whately wrote a work on Christian Evidences for publication and distribution by the Board. Indeed the Archbishop of Dublin became the leading Anglican advocate for the Irish system, defending it against attacks from the clergy of his own diocese. He reconciled himself to criticism of his involvement in the experiment with the thought of the many thousands of Irishmen who, as a result of the education received, would be able 'to read the Scriptures' and so be introduced 'to the study of the Sacred Books'.[19]

If Presbyterian pressure forced Stanley to attempt the experiment in non-sectarian education, the outcome was more in keeping with liberal Anglican than Presbyterian views on Irish education. Irish Presbyterians, as represented by the Synod of Ulster, were not formally reconciled to the National system until 1840, whereas the proposals of 1831 were sufficiently in accord with the views of such politicians as the Unionist Spring Rice to induce the latter to put forward his own claim for the honour of being the scheme's inventor. To Lord Northampton he remarked: 'You know the scheme of general Education introduced by Stanley when Irish Secretary. The scheme was mine . . .'.[20] Rice's support for the Irish system was personal as much as political. He ordered National Board books and school requisitions for the schoolroom which he

[17] T. O'Raifertaigh, 'Mixed Education and the Synod of Ulster 1831–1840', *Irish Historical Studies*, ix (1955), 284.

[18] *Parl. Papers 1837*, viii. i, 45.

[19] R. Whately, 'National Education in Ireland'. *Charges and Other Tracts* (London, 1836), 129.

[20] NLI MSS 553 (Monteagle Papers): Rice to Northampton, 14 Mar. 1836.

had constructed on his estate at Loughill, County Limerick, and sent one of his schoolmasters to the model school in Dublin which included a course of lectures 'on the method of teaching a common Christian doctrine'.[21] In an article published in the *Edinburgh Review* in 1825, Spring Rice had anticipated the development of combined religious instruction. He concluded his discussion of the education of the Irish poor with the suggestion that 'One common system for all, whether Protestant or Catholic' was 'infinitely preferable to separate and exclusive schools.' He expressed his conviction that 'certain extracts might be made from the Scriptures . . . which would give no offence to pious Catholics' and cited experiments in France and Italy as proof. While he disclaimed education as a 'cure' for 'every possible disease', he nevertheless thought that government had a duty to provide a national scheme of instruction or, as he put it, 'a wise, a comprehensive and truly liberal system of Education'.[22] The Irish education system found its strongest Protestant adherents among the liberal Anglicans.

The identification of the Whig government with the Irish National system revealed itself most clearly in the crisis of 1838–41 concerning the Roman Catholic hierarchy's support for the use of the *Scripture Extracts* in Board schools. In five open letters to Lord John Russell published between February and May 1838, the Roman Catholic Archbishop of Tuam, MacHale, denounced the National system and in so doing divided the Catholic hierarchy: the Catholic Archbishop of Dublin, Dr Murray, was a prominent member of the Board. Murray responded to MacHale's attack by attempting both to secure the support of members of the Catholic episcopate and to inform the Prefect of Propaganda at Rome, Cardinal Fransoni, and the principal of the Irish College, Dr Cullen, of the exact terms of the National system. By October Murray had also joined in the press campaign. But Rome did not act to quell the dispute so much as exacerbate it by delay. Propaganda only referred the objections of its theologians to the *Scripture Extracts* to Dr Murray and the Irish bishops. The struggle continued for the next two years as Rome vacillated

[21] NLI MSS 543 (Monteagle Papers): Rice to Kelly, 4 Oct., 1838; P. MacSuibhne, *Paul Cullen and His Contemporaries* (Naas, 1961–77), i. 233.

[22] [T. Spring Rice], 'The Education of the Irish Poor', *Edinburgh Review*, xliii (1825), 222–4.

in the face of two warring parties. The Pope finally came to an equivocal decision in January 1841 which permitted each bishop to exercise his discretion in allowing National Schools in his diocese. The issue was thus temporarily resolved. This conflict between nationalist, ultramontane Irish Catholics and an older generation of Catholic ecclesiastical politicians, more used to seeking political bargains with English politicians, has been narrated elsewhere.[23] What has not been demonstrated before is the support which the Whig government gave to the National system and to the faction led by Dr Murray in their period of adversity.

The British government was kept informed of activities in Rome by Lord Clifford, whose father-in-law was Cardinal Weld, and of Catholic politics in Ireland by A. R. Blake, a Catholic Education Commissioner and Chief Remembrancer. The Whig party attached considerable importance to the maintenance of the Irish education system. When in July 1839 Ebrington, the Lord Lieutenant, received a letter from Melbourne informing him that The Prefect of Propaganda had condemned the National system, he conferred with Dr Murray at Dublin Castle. Murray's response was to write to Rome immediately, expressing his readiness to travel there to state his views. He also asked Ebrington to write a letter stating his good opinion of the effects of the education system. The Lord Lieutenant obliged by writing to Murray the following day requesting him to do his utmost 'to deprecate on the part of the Court of Rome a step [i.e. an adverse judgement] so sure to retard the advance of our common Christian faith as well as of those habits of morality and order which have been already derived from the national system of education'.[24] The Irish government extended what facilities it had at its command to Dr Murray in his bid to quell the judgement from Rome. At the beginning of September 1838 the Pope agreed to receive two deputies from the parties in dispute on the education question. Morpeth, the Chief Secretary,

---

[23] Larkin, 'The Quarrel over the National System of Education in Ireland'; P. C. Barry, 'The Holy See and the Irish National Schools', *Irish Ecclesiastical Record*, xcii (1959), 90–105; D. A. Kerr, *Peel, Priests, and Politics* (Oxford, 1982), 59–64.

[24] Carlisle Papers, MSS J19.1.23, fo. 77: Ebrington to Morpeth, 6 July 1839; DCRO MSS 1262 M/LI (Fortescue Papers), fos. 70, 76: Morpeth to Ebrington, 30 June 1839, copy Ebrington to Murray, 7 July 1839.

requested Granville, the British ambassador at Paris, to give a letter of introduction to the Internuncio at Paris on behalf of Dr Murray's representatives. Granville also obtained a letter of introduction to the French ambassador at Rome, and Soult, the French Prime Minister, wrote to the ambassador by diplomatic courier 'to assist Mr Ennis in the object of his mission'.[25] The previous August, Blake had requested Ebrington to supply the means (£200–300) to send two representatives to Rome on Murray's behalf.[26] Thus there was some truth in the claim of MacHale's biographer and apologist that Dr Murray, like all Archbishops of Dublin until 1886, was 'under the influence of the vice-regal court in Dublin'.[27]

The Whigs supported the Irish system for two reasons. The first was that it became the touchstone of Whig Irish policy, proof positive that the Whigs had succeeded in securing the loyalty of the Irish Catholics to the rule of the British state by conciliatory rather than coercive means. Ebrington wrote to Murray that if Irish Catholics accepted a papal judgement condemning the Irish education system, and so subscribed to 'a Right of despotic interference', they were 'unfit for any place of trust connected with the Government of the British Empire'.[28] If Irish Catholics withdrew from the education system in which all sects in the nation participated on equal terms, the argument ran, they were in effect withdrawing from full membership of the state. Second, the Irish system had to be maintained since its success was evidence of the feasibility of Whig proposals for educational reform in England. The crisis in the Irish system occurred just as the Whigs in February 1839 announced their tentative proposals for a national system in England which included an attempt to establish a non-sectarian model school. Throughout the discussion on Russell's plans the success or failure of the Irish system was debated as indicating both the practicality and the desirability of the

[25] Carlisle Papers, MSS J19.1.24, fos. 92, 112: Granville to Palmerston, 28 Oct. 1839, Granville to Morpeth, 8 Nov. 1839. Ennis was one of two priests sent by Archbishop Murray to Rome to present the case in favour of the National Board of Education.

[26] Carlisle Papers, MSS J19.1.24, fo. 15: Ebrington to Morpeth, 3 Aug. 1839.

[27] B. O'Reilly, *Life of John MacHale* (New York & Cincinnati, 1890), i. 416.

[28] DCRO MSS 1262 M/LI (Fortescue Papers), fo. 106: Ebrington to Murray, 9 Oct. 1839.

1839 scheme. Graham, for example, stated as one cause of his opposition to the government's measure that the Irish 'mixed system' had been a failure; Wyse, the Catholic Irish MP and educational reformer, defended the liberal plan on the ground that the Committee of the Privy Council, which was to be in charge of the distribution of grants to English schools, was no more objectionable than the National Board in Ireland.[29] Analogies between the English proposals and the Irish system could not help being drawn. Indeed in the debate on Russell's scheme, the current Chief Secretary, Morpeth, was put up by the government to defend the Whig measure against the attacks of the former Chief Secretary for Ireland, Stanley.[30]

Considerable pains have been taken by Dr Paz to deny the similarity between the Irish and English systems. He has rightly indicated the differences in detail between the two schemes, namely that the English board was to consist exclusively of members of the government while the Irish Board had fewer ministerial connections, that in the Irish system only extracts from the Scriptures were read while it was proposed to make the complete Bible available in the English model school, and that an Anglican chaplain was to be appointed to the English model school while no such appointment was made to the Irish schools.[31] But these differences may be excused in terms of differing circumstances. If in Ireland members of the Catholic Anglican hierarchies could be appointed to the Board, this could not be done in England: there was no Catholic hierarchy. If the unabridged Scriptures were to be read in English schools, this was a reflection of the fact that in England the major religious contests and the population were both predominantly Protestant. The differences were caused because the chief problem in Ireland was the need to reconcile Catholics to the British state, while in England the aspiration was primarily to establish Protestant Dissent as a respected component of the nation. The lack of identity between the two plans did not mean they lacked a common aim. In both schemes, whatever the means, the end was to educate together religiously diverse groups in order to

[29] *Hansard*, 3rd ser., xlviii (1839), 531, 650.
[30] Ibid., 59–68.
[31] Paz, *Politics of Working-Class Education*, 88.

provide them with a sense of identity. It was certainly this liberal Anglican ideal which provoked the fiercest criticisms of the government's plans in the Commons. Inglis, the Tory MP for Oxford, attacked Russell's proposals for a 'joint and comprehensive system of education' as 'a fallacy and an impossibility', and the Bishop of London, Blomfield, opposed the attempt 'to comprise in one system of religious education whatever class or denomination existed in the country' as leading to 'indifference, and generalities, and in the last [place] to irreligion'.[32]

Certainly whatever was novel about Russell's plans of 1839, it was not that they involved state intervention in education. Government involvement in educational provision had begun as early as 1813 when the first grant to the Dublin Society (later the Kildare-Street Society) had been made; royal letters instructing the clergy to preach charity sermons on behalf of the National society had been issued since 1823; building grants to both the National and British and Foreign School Societies had commenced in 1833. Nor was Russell's proposal to give separate grants to the National Society and the BFSS for the establishment of their own normal schools an especially noteworthy educational development. The need to improve not merely the quantity but also the quality of education had already been acknowledged by the government. In 1835 the Commons had approved a grant of £10,000 for the construction of normal schools to train teachers (a sum which had not been spent). What was controversial in the proposals of 1839 was the government's desire to institute a national inspectorate and to establish and run a model school of its own under the direct supervision of the Education Committee. As Spring Rice remarked, the previous government scheme left 'two essential principles' unprovided for, namely the 'inspection of schools' and a means 'to ascertain the qualifications of teachers'.[33] Russell's proposals were designed to meet these wants.

The prime importance of these two innovations was symbolic. The model school was intended as a particular demonstration that non-sectarian religious instruction was feasible. It was an indication of the possibility of including all

---

[32] *Hansard*, 3rd ser., xlv (1839), 288; ibid., xlvii (1839), 757.
[33] [Spring Rice], 'Ministerial Plan of Education', 160.

Christian citizens, regardless of sectarian affiliation, within the one institution. It was to be a national institution because all members of the political nation as established by the constitutional revolution of 1828–32 might attend with impunity. Russell at the end of his introductory speech remarked that he believed 'that the most simple rules of religion and habits of morality might be taught to children, without raising those great points of theoretical difference by which the country had been so long agitated', and therefore in the model school religion was 'to be combined with the whole matter of instruction and to regulate the entire system of discipline.'[34] The government held out the prospect of aid to schools with a system of combined religious instruction by means of a proposed amendment to the regulations concerning grants for building. In a minute of the Education Committee a resolution was recorded 'not to adhere invariably to the rule which confines Grants to the National Society and the British and Foreign School Society' and so to permit their award to schools conducted on model-school lines.[35] It was to be one of the functions of the inspectorate to inform schoolmasters of educational innovations and successes. They were to be ambassadors for combined instruction conveying information which demonstrated the practicality of non-sectarian education. Their task, as stated in the minute of the Committee, was 'to convey to the Conductors and Teachers of Private Schools in different parts of the country knowledge of all improvements in the art of teaching', as well as to report on the state of schools in receipt of government aid, and on the progress of education in the country.[36] In what was still to be a diverse and disparate elementary education system, the inspectorate was to form an element of continuity and to operate as an agent of uniformity. In order to appreciate the full significance of these proposals in terms of the emergence of liberal Anglican Whiggery, it is necessary to consider the liberal alternatives which the government rejected.

In the mid-1830s the leading Whig educationalist outside the government was Brougham, the former Lord Chancellor. Attempts to clarify his educational stance are fraught with

---

[34] *Hansard*, 3rd ser., xlv (1839), 284; *Parl. Papers 1839*, xli. 259.
[35] Ibid., 261.   [36] Ibid.

difficulties. His maverick personality and Machiavellism resulted in inconsistencies both in and between his diverse proposals as he attempted to appease various interest groups. After being dropped from the Whig Cabinet in 1835, personal malice towards his former associates became a dominating motive. In the course of 1837–8, having 'foreborne three years', Brougham began leading a campaign against the government on the ballot, Canada, education, and the slave trade. In his own defence he wrote to his friend, the Liverpool Unitarian William Shepherd: 'I have backed them to the uttermost as long as they retained their principles. I only leave them where they abandon reform'.[37] By October 1838 Russell considered Brougham 'factious, false, malignant, insulting'.[38] With this caveat, Brougham's educational outlook may be sketched by sifting consistency from inconsistency in his involvement in various schemes for educational reform from the 1820s onwards. These ranged from his first Bill of 1820 and his support for the Society for the Diffusion of Useful Knowledge and London University to his proposed resolutions of 1835, his Bill of 1837, and his articles in the *Edinburgh Review*. It will be clear that Brougham was essentially a rationalist of the Scottish Enlightenment. In rejecting Brougham's proposals, the liberal Whigs were to this extent also rejecting a tradition of Scottish Whiggery.

Towards the religious question—the central problem of educational reform in the mid-1830s—Brougham showed marked indifference if not apathy. His approach to this contentious issue was determined by what was acceptable politically, and in consequence his solution changed rapidly. In his 1820 plan for the establishment of a system of parochial schools, Brougham provided that the school curriculum should be decided by the local Anglican clergyman who would also have to approve the Anglican schoolmaster.[39] But if Brougham was willing to acknowledge the political influence of the Anglican Church in 1820, by the time of the foundation of London University, he advocated the virtues of excluding the teaching

[37] Brougham Papers, out-letters to Shepherd, fo. 20: Brougham to Shepherd, 30 Jan. 1838.
[38] Mulgrave Castle Archives, box M (Normanby Papers), fo. 922: Russell to Normanby, 17 Oct. 1838.
[39] J. Murphy, *Church, State, and Schools in Britain 1800–1970* (London, 1971), 12.

of theology altogether in order to prevent the institution from acquiring a denominational character. In the *Edinburgh Review* he stated that each sect 'must provide that branch of instruction apart, either at home or in private seminaries'.[40] During the 1830s he proved equally flexible on this issue. His solution to the problem of religious disputes arising in his proposed rate-aided schools, as set out in the *Edinburgh Review* of April 1837, was to institute 'local option', that is the power of the rate-payers of each area to decide the kind of religious education to be offered in the schools. 'The plan in question', he wrote, 'is so framed as to prevent any creed or observance being imposed, which the bulk of the community disapprove, in any given district.'[41] Between the postponement of his Bill in June 1837, however, and its reintroduction in December of the same year, he had altered this proposal. The Bill now required the reading of the Bible in all schools aided and sanctioned by the Education Board, permitting only Roman Catholic and Jewish children to withdraw from such lessons.[42] Afraid of losing support for his measure on the ground of its irreligion, Brougham conformed to demands to ensure that the education offered was fundamentally Christian.

The consequence was that Brougham's Bills were not clearly identified with any of the major education parties of the day. Following the publication of the amended Bill in December 1837, James Simpson of the secularist Central Society of Education wrote to Brougham suggesting that attendance at Bible-reading sessions should be made 'optional to *all* whose parents intimate in writing that they prefer home or pastoral instruction'.[43] Simpson himself, a founder of the Edinburgh modern infant school, advocated the institution of a national school system on secular lines, and commited the task of religious education to 'the clergy of the different denominations'.[44] Brougham's amendment, together with a number of other alterations, had been, in part, a response to the criticisms

[40] [H. Brougham], 'London University and King's College', *Edinburgh Review*, xlviii (1828), 238.

[41] [H. Brougham], 'National Education', *Edinburgh Review*, lxv (1837), 264.

[42] [H. Brougham], 'The Education Bill', *Edinburgh Review*, lxvi (1838), 444.

[43] Brougham Papers, MS 15920: Simpson to Brougham, 12 Dec. 1837.

[44] Brougham Papers, MS 15370: J. Simpson, 'A Second Letter to the Most Noble the Marquis of Lansdowne' (n.p., 1839).

he had received from Henry Dunn, the secretary of the British and Foreign School Society. In a letter sent to Brougham in September, among other proposals, Dunn insisted that the government should not leave the religious education in schools optional, but that its content should be limited by law in order to guard against the teaching of both sectarianism and 'transcendental trash'.[45] In November Dunn pointedly reminded Brougham that the Manchester Society for Promoting National Education had passed a resolution endorsing the reading of the Bible in schools, as advocated by the BFSS. He informed Brougham, on behalf of the society, 'that public opinion is with us'.[46] Brougham's first Bill of 1837 had clearly met with severe criticisms from the BFSS. Likewise his proposals enjoyed only lukewarm support from the government. If in August 1837 Russell thought Brougham's Bill launched 'a very safe and sound plan for Education', as the months proceeded, so his enthusiasm waned. By late November he was clearly sceptical. Russell no longer felt 'confident' that the religious clauses would work well, though he would be prepared to accept them if necessary, and he opposed Brougham's scheme of making the parish the local unit for the levy of an education rate in the absence of a municipal or local authority.[47] In the following summer, the Whig government moved to formulate its own measure.[48]

What finally killed the Whig administration's support for Brougham's Bill were the clauses which were distinctively his invention, namely those which introduced an educational qualification for the franchise empowering the raising of a local rate. This proposal followed fast upon Russell's declaration of November 1837 in his speech on the Address that the government would not contemplate any further instalment of electoral reform; it was part of Brougham's attempt to court the Radicals.[49] If Brougham's interpolation in his second Bill of 1837 was politically motivated, it was nevertheless in keeping with his Edinburgh rationalist views. The educational qualifi-

[45] Brougham Papers, MS 9572: Dunn to Brougham, 6 Sept. 1837.
[46] Brougham Papers, MS 9574: Dunn to Brougham, 20 Nov. 1837.
[47] Brougham Papers, MSS 14432, 14004: Russell to Brougham, 24 Aug., 25 Nov. 1837.
[48] Brougham Papers, MS 13632: Allen to Brougham, 14 Aug. 1838.
[49] Fulford & Strachey, *The Greville Memoirs* iii, 401, 404–6.

cation for the franchise was to be established by attendance
for at least a year at a literary or scientific association such
as a Mechanics' Institute, or by membership of an Inn of
Court or of Chancery, or by obtaining a certificate of attendance at any school subject to the visitation of the Central
Board of Education.[50] The purpose of his franchise was to
provide an incentive for the working-classes to educate
themselves as well as to enhance the status of such educational
institutions as already existed. Brougham looked forward not
to the establishment of a property-owning, but of a school-
attending democracy. In his article on the 'Diffusion of
Knowledge', Brougham envisaged the working population of
the country as a sort of extended society of literary men with
independent minds. He praised Pestalozzi for teaching that
'no man, be his station ever so humble or his life ever so
laborious, ought to be without knowledge, nay without
science'.[51] This was (albeit somewhat distorted) a reflection
of the Scottish 'ideal of the democratic intellect' as described
by George Davie and embodied in the Scottish university
system, which had produced Brougham and which he naturally praised. What was distinctive about the Scottish education
system, as Jeffrey and others claimed, was that 'the many'
had access to learning. Jeffrey wrote that the Scottish system
'enables relatively large numbers of people to get . . . that
knowledge which tends *to liberalise and make intelligent the mass
of our population*'.[52] But the body of 'democratic knowledge'
which Brougham suggested should be made accessible to all
was of a highly restricted nature.

According to Brougham, the democratic diffusion of
knowledge was the guarantee of civilization's survival. He
argued that the collapse of the ancient world was the result
of its being divided into only two camps, the Romans and the
Barbarians: this induced complacency among the Romans and
hence made them vulnerable to attack. When the empire fell,
so did civilization. But in the modern world there were a
number of independently civilized countries, the populations
of which constituted the repositories of accumulated wisdom.

[50] [Brougham], 'The Education Bill', 442.
[51] *Idem*, 'Diffusion of Knowledge', *Edinburgh Review*, xlvii (1828), 118–34.
[52] G. E. Davie, *The Democratic Intellect* (Edinburgh, 1961), xix, 27, 39–40.

Thus, 'Useful knowledge, practical experience, virtuous principles are no longer deposited exclusively in a few heads which may be struck off or consigned to a few leaves of papyrus which may be lost or consumed; but are spread among countless numbers of men and of printed books, beyond the power of any revolution short of a universal deluge to destroy.'[53] Such thoughts were commonplace in the early nineteenth century. Brougham's view was distinctive because he believed that the improvement of mankind was not dependent on accumulated wisdom in general, but on scientific knowledge in particular.[54] The knowledge which Brougham wished to diffuse democratically was limited to that necessary for maximizing the material benefits of an otherwise impoverished existence. If Adam Smith believed that the survival of the country required the continued existence of common moral sentiments and Russell held that the stability of a country was the product of its religion, then Brougham and the Edinburgh Reviewers asserted that its progress was the consequence of practical and technical knowledge. As Davie has observed, Jeffrey, Brougham's fellow-Edinburgh Reviewer, put forward the notion that 'popular science' was all that was required to enable the population to appreciate the meaning and purpose of society.[55] As a consequence Brougham primarily associated himself with educational projects which were practical, scientific and secular.

This was most clearly demonstrated in Brougham's support for the Society for the Diffusion of Useful Knowledge. Not only was he 'the only chairman the society ever had', but his pamphlet, *Practical Observations upon the Education of the Poor*, dedicated to the founder of the London Mechanics' Institute, George Birkbeck, was in effect the manifesto for the SDUK's formation. In this work, which set out the means whereby cheap publications 'to encourage and promote knowledge' could be made available 'among the poor', he looked forward to 'seeing formed a Society for promoting the composition, publication and distribution of cheap and useful works'; the

[53] [H. Brougham], 'Establishments at Hofwyl', *Edinburgh Review*, xxxii (1819), 502.
[54] *Idem*, 'Diffusion of Knowledge', 126.
[55] G. E. Davie, *The Social Significance of the Scottish Philosophy of Common Sense* (Dundee, 1973), 15.

SDUK was such a society.[56] It excluded from its publications any works on religion and concentrated primarily on practical subjects. Brougham himself wrote *Objects, Advantages, and Pleasures of Science* as an introduction to the Society's *Library of Useful Knowledge*.[57] In the concluding article of the Society's *Quarterly Journal of Education*, the anonymous author wrote of the education of the poor: 'Such men should be especially encouraged to contemplate the surrounding objects of nature and to study the most simple laws of mechanics and chemistry'; they should receive instruction in 'the most general laws of animal physiology', on the principles of which 'the preservation of health' depends and in 'the general laws which govern the production and distribution of wealth' in order to make them 'profitable members of that society in which they must live'.[58] The elementary education for the poor which Brougham advocated was directly related to improving their material lot rather than changing their position in society. Brougham welcomed the formation of the SDUK as a means whereby 'the common people' might 'improve their understanding and better their hearts' but, most importantly, 'mend their circumstances' in studying 'some branch or other of Natural Philosophy'.[59]

Brougham's interest in religious issues was marginal. His concern was merely to demonstrate that the scientific education which he advocated did not contradict the principles of Christianity. His *Practical Observations* ended with the claim that science did not undermine religion. 'The time is lost and gone', he insisted, 'when bigots could persuade mankind that the lights of philosophy were to be extinguished as dangerous to religion'.[60] Likewise, at the conclusion of an article on the 'Scientific Education of the People', he asserted that 'a pure and true religion has nothing to fear from the greatest expansion which the intellect can receive by the study either of matter or of mind'.[61] Brougham's concern for Pestalozzian

[56] H. Smith, *The SDUK 1826–1846*, 7; H. Brougham, *Practical Observations upon the Education of the Poor* (16th edn., London, 1825), 2, 10.

[57] *Idem, Objects, Advantages, and Pleasures of Science* (London, 1830).

[58] [Anon.] 'Education', *The Quarterly Journal of Education*, x (1835), 328–9.

[59] [H. Brougham], 'SDUK', *Edinburgh Review*, xlvi (1827), 243.

[60] Brougham, *Education of the Poor*, 32.

[61] [H. Brougham], 'Scientific Education of the People', *Edinburgh Review*, xli (1824), 122.

techniques for the development of character was also limited. In his article on Fellenberg's schools at Hofwyl run on Pestaloz-zian lines, Brougham was careful to restrict his praise to endorsing the principles espoused rather than the practice displayed. 'We by no means intend to assert', he wrote, 'that an attempt should be made to carry them into effect on a large scale; especially in the populous and above all manufacturing and commercial districts', precisely those areas most in need of elementary education.[62] In any case what most appealed to Brougham about the education of the poor was that it bestowed dignity upon their low social position rather than offering them an elevated sense of their individual worth. 'The pupils of the *school of industry* are not raised above their station; but their station, dignified and improved, is raised to them', he wrote of Hofwyl.[63] Brougham's interest in education was largely practical and utilitarian, and it was this which marked the difference between himself and the liberal Anglicans. While the latter looked towards a common Christian education to remove sectarian divisions of social origin, Brougham, indif-ferent towards religion, saw in education a practical means by which the poor might improve their welfare at the same time as being reconciled to a low status in life. For the liberal Anglicans, society was founded on a Christian ethic; for Brougham and like-minded Edinburgh rationalists, it was founded on the development of scientific principles of progress. The opposition between the two was highlighted in the addres-ses of the liberal Anglican Morpeth to the Brougham-inspired Mechanics' Institutes. To an audience at the Lincoln Insti-tution Morpeth asserted that civilization attained its full development when 'liberal and refined accomplishments' distinguished every family. He urged his audience 'never to lose hold of religion' since it was 'the source among mankind of all that is large, of all that is lovely, and that without it all would be dark and joyless'.[64] It was not an argument Brougham was accustomed to propose.

The alternative, which the liberal Anglicans also rejected

[62] *Idem*, 'Mr Fellenberg's Establishments at Hofwyl', *Edinburgh Review*, xxxi (1818), 164.
[63] *Idem*, 'Establishments at Hofwyl', 497.
[64] G. W. F. Howard, *Lectures and Addresses in Aid of Popular Education* (London, 1852), 122–4.

and which was embodied in the Central Society of Education, defined itself in part in opposition to Brougham's technical-based instruction. Sarah Austin who, along with the CSE, looked towards the Prussian system as the model for systems of national education throughout the world, confessed that she cared 'comparatively little—less perhaps than his Lordship [Brougham] about the diffusion of technical art or of that general information as it is called, which *does* leave "the nature of man" pretty near untouched'. She regretted that Brougham could not appreciate the distinction between education as proposed by Fellenberg and instruction as undertaken in the monitorial system.[65] The CSE also expended much energy in attacking the two great societies, the National and British, for a similar failure to appreciate the educational principles of Fellenberg. B. F. Duppa, the Secretary of the Society, included an extended attack on the BFSS and National Society in his article on 'Industrial Schools for the Peasantry'. He criticized the societies for not 'connecting the knowledge acquired with the probable pursuits of life', for failing to provide 'any instruction in a useful art' and for not adopting 'any systematic plan' for 'the formation of habits of virtue'.[66] Thomas Wyse suggested that the BFSS's and National Society's schemes of education failed because their systems referred 'much more to a certain series of applications' rather than 'the being to which they are to be applied'. They presupposed 'no study of the infant mind'.[67] The CSE dedicated itself to the propagation of a Fellenberg-inspired education which like that of Pestalozzi used methods based on the psychological processes of children.[68] Fellenberg was an honorary Fellow of the society, as well as contributing to its publications, and B. F. Duppa of the CSE acted as his agent in London.[69]

The point of the CSE critique was to suggest that both the BFSS and the National Society were too concerned to propagate particular religious views to pay sufficient attention to

[65] S. Austin, *On National Education* (London, 1839), i, 93–4.

[66] B. F. Duppa, 'Industrial Schools for the Peasantry', *Central Society of Education First Publication* (London, 1837), 174.

[67] T. Wyse, 'Education in the United Kingdom', *CSE 1st Pub.*, 58.

[68] On Fellenberg see W. A. C. Stewart & W. D. McCann, *The Educational Innovators* (London, 1971), i. 141–6.

[69] K. Guggisberg, *Philipp Emanuel v. Fellenberg* (Bern, 1953), ii. 469–70.

the welfare of their pupils in both a material and a spiritual sense. In an anonymous article on 'Schools for the Industrious Classes', the fact that the voluntary schools had been established as a means of ecclesiastical attack or defence was cited as a ground for questioning whether the education offered there was 'best adapted for fitting a youth for the active duties of life as well as preparing him for a life to come'.[70] The CSE in this sense stood for an alternative education to that Scripture-based instruction offered by the voluntary societies, one more concerned with the needs of man than his duties towards God. This is not to suggest that all members of the CSE were secularists. Thomas Wyse, the founder of the CSE maintained that there was no place like a school to teach 'unadulterated Christian benevolence', while Horner, the factory inspector and an annual subscriber to the society, insisted that it was 'a fundamental principle' that religion formed 'an essential part' of school business.[71] But in the political debates on education during the 1830s, the leading members of the CSE such as Duppa, Wyse, and James Simpson, acquired the reputation for promoting secularism as their solution to the problems of competing sects in elementary schools. Wyse acknowledged in his book on educational reform that where Christian teaching could not be confined to generalities, different persuasions should be separated, or the reading of Scriptures should be left 'to separate or out-of-school hours'.[72] Colquhoun, the Scottish Protestant MP, admitted to a difficulty in characterizing the Central Society, but claimed that Duppa believed it to be necessary 'to separate secular from religious instruction' and that Simpson wished to ban the Bible from the school.[73]

Simpson, the editor of the society's publications, set out his solution to the religious problem in a public letter to Lord Lansdowne. This was based on the distinction he drew between secular and religious education as a consequence of his belief in the existence of separate types of knowledge. Secular education was concerned with the improvement of the human

---

[70] [Anon] 'Schools for the Industrious Classes', *CSE Second Publication* (London, 1838), 344.

[71] T. Wyse, *Education Reform* (London, 1836), 267; V. Cousin, *On the State of Education in Holland*, trans. L. Horner (London, 1838), xxxiv.

[72] Wyse, *Education Reform*, 264–5.

[73] *Hansard*, 3rd ser., xlviii (1839), 546–7.

faculties and embraced all that man might learn 'without Scriptural aid'; religious education Simpson took to consist only in what 'God had been pleased to reveal in his Holy Scriptures'. He asserted that the 'facts and reasonings' of one branch of instruction could not 'be intermixed or in any way controlled by those of the other', and he included in secular education 'knowledge of ethics or morality'. He thus suggested, controversially, that it was possible to teach morality without Christianity. 'I have confidence in maintaining', he wrote, 'that there is a morality for secular study and exercise.' On this basis it was possible to exclude the teaching of religion from combined secular instruction, and by confining religious instruction to separate hours, to absolve proposers of schemes for national education from the need to come to terms with competing religious sects. Simpson recommended committing 'that important department of education the religious . . . [to] the clergy of the different denominations'; religious controversy would be excluded from schools or their managment by excluding religion. In so doing, Simpson looked forward to the establishment of a new, essentially secular morality parallel to the church-given Christian morality.[74] This position was, if novel, not altogether unusual. In the *Quarterly Journal of Education* for 1833, an anonymous author claimed that in the current age 'religious discipline' had been abandoned, but had not 'been replaced by a substitute'. The problem of the age was how to form 'moral habits' in such circumstances.[75]

Unable to comprehend the fears of voluntary societies that a government-imposed national system might damage particular religious interests, the Central Society emerged as the leading advocate of a strong, centralized, and secular education system. Duppa objected to Brougham's Bill of late 1837 for placing education in the hands of the politicians since this would impose upon members of the Board 'a vacillating and uncertain character'. He also objected to Brougham's suggestion that local rate-payers should be responsible for the local boards on the ground that they would be the most opposed 'to the education and moral elevation of the humblest classes'.

[74] Brougham Papers, MS 15370: Simpson, 'Second Letter to Marquis of Lansdowne', *passim*.
[75] [Anon.] 'Public Instruction', *The Quarterly Journal of Education*, vi (1833), 57, 64.

Duppa concluded that Brougham's Bill, which stressed the importance of local variations, 'would not be found to work'.[76] Wyse complained that the great defect of English education was its 'total want of a national organisation'. He particularly desired the establishment of a 'Parliamentary Commission' with a minister of instruction at its head with 'minutely defined but comprehensive powers, extended to every branch of education'.[77] Characteristically, he undertook to defend the Prussian system of education from charges that its introduction to England would be a 'dangerous innovation', an example of 'foreign despotism' and 'ministerial interference with civil and religious liberty'.[78] In offering such a defence, Wyse clearly identified himself and his proposals as tending towards the centralization of government. The CSE's parliamentary campaign reached a climax in June 1838 when Wyse proposed a motion for an Address to the Crown requesting the appointment of a board of Commissioners of Education.

The motion was defeated on 14 June by a mixture of Whigs and Tories in a small House.[79] The Whig government thus formally rejected the propositions of the Central Society. Russell as Home Secretary replied to Wyse, in effect setting out the terms of any future education measure which would obtain Whig support. He stated as his premise that it was the duty of the state to make people aware of 'their religious and moral duties' and to this end agreed that it was the duty of parliament and the state 'to further and encourage education' in the country. He made it abundantly clear that the government would not support 'united secular but separate denominational instruction'. Religion was to be the foundation of any education scheme sponsored by the Whigs. Russell also expressed his concern for the quality as well as the quantity of the instruction to be offered.[80] Spring Rice in his speech looked forward to the establishment of combined religious instruction, concluding, in the event quite erroneously, that the National

---

[76] B. F. Duppa, 'Lord Brougham's Bill for Promoting Education in England and Wales', *CSE 2nd Pub.*, 151, 155, 158.

[77] Wyse, 'Education in the United Kingdom', *CSE 1st Pub.*, 62; *Hansard*, 3rd ser., xlv (1839), 299.

[78] T. Wyse, 'Prussian Education', *CSE Third Publication* (London, 1839), 376.

[79] *Hansard*, 3rd ser., xliii (1838), 738–9.

[80] Ibid., 730, 732, 733.

Society and the BFSS 'were daily approximating towards each other', and anticipating that 'the great mass of Dissenters would be ready to consolidate their schools with the establishment if the Church catechism were taught on Sundays only'.[81] In the face of increasing parliamentary interest in the question of education, the Whig government began to act. On 11 August Russell received a delegation from the BFSS, and Allen, one of the delegates, reported to Brougham that Russell 'seems to be convinced that the time is come for the introduction of some great measure and that it ought to be based on liberal principles'.[82]

The Whigs who initiated the education proposals were primarily the liberal Anglicans Russell and Spring Rice, with the cautious guidance of Lansdowne, who also assumed responsibility for the measure in the Lords. Melbourne objected to the government's taking up education reform, while Palmerston appears to have shown no interest in Russell's proposals. The ministers who defended the measure in the Commons were Russell, Spring Rice, Morpeth, and Howick, all younger Whigs and liberal Anglicans. Indeed it was Russell, Spring Rice, and Lansdowne whom Hobhouse recorded in his diary as especially urging the necessity of doing something on the education question at the Cabinet summoned on 23 November to discuss the agenda for the forthcoming Session.[83] Paz has hinted that the chief influence on Russell in forming his plans was the British and Foreign School Society, and J. D. Alexander has claimed that 'Russell was attempting to legislate the BFSS programme'.[84] In so far as this judgement relates to Russell's support for the British Society's solution to the problem of religious education, it is correct. Russell wrote to Allen in August 1838 apropos a memorial received from the BFSS, that the government entirely concurred in the principle stated therein that 'the Holy Scriptures should be read and taught in schools, such instruction to form part of the usual order of occupation in the school . . . but that the children of Catholics and Jews might . . . be absent at such

---

[81] Ibid., 735.

[82] Brougham Papers, MS 13632: Allen to Brougham, 14 Aug. 1838.

[83] BL Addit. MSS 56560 (Broughton Papers): Hobhouse Diary, 23, 26 Nov. 1838.

[84] Paz, *Politics of Working-Class Education*, 78, 80; J. L. Alexander, 'The Committee of Council on Education', 414.

times' and that Dissenters should not be compelled to learn formularies.[85] Although the government did not make this principle the condition of awarding grants, since in the course of 1838 it had abandoned any scheme to establish a new national system as an alternative to that of the voluntary societies, it did propose to adopt this principle in its Normal School. Russell and the BFSS were agreed on the importance of religious instruction as the basis of education and on the possibility of imparting such without regard to sectarian doctrines. Henry Dunn, the secretary of the BFSS, stated in his pamphlet on national education that Christianity should form the foundation of a national system, because the prevalence of the Christian religion ensured the survival of the state. Government, he wrote, 'cannot keep society together without enactment in support of public morals . . . and since no one will pretend that it should revert to Paganism or Judaism or Mohammedianism, it can only act by assuming the truth of Christianity and the authority of the Bible'. Moreover the introduction of the Bible in schools, he argued, need not favour one sect over another since, given the possibility of separating 'truth from a human system, religion from the science of theology', it was possible to teach the Bible without teaching dogma.[86]

But on other issues the government and at least that section of the BFSS led by Henry Dunn parted company. Dunn was essentially a voluntaryist, sceptical if not of state aid then certainly of state interference and dominance. He argued that voluntary contributions to education would decline in proportion to the increase in grants of public money. As a consequence he held that extended government interference was by no means an 'unmixed good'.[87] Dunn, more so perhaps than other leading members of the BFSS such as the Quaker William Allen, saw the society as the representative of orthodox Protestant Dissent rather than a truly national society containing representatives of all Christian sects. He was as eager as High Churchmen to crusade against Unitarianism in order to demonstrate the society's fundamental orthodoxy. He claimed

[85] PRO 30/22 3B (Russell Papers), fo. 250: Russell to Allen, 13 Aug. 1838.
[86] H. Dunn, *National Education, the Question of Questions* (2nd. edn., London, 1838), 30–7. [87] Ibid., 18.

that in 'British' schools 'the doctrines of Trinity and Atonement' were never compromised, nor was 'a single text or word
of Scripture' omitted 'in order to meet the views of any class
of objectors'.[88] He therefore wished to preserve the standing
and integrity of the organization he represented and so,
perhaps suprisingly, he endorsed the scheme proposed by the
High Church *British Critic* to appoint a Minister of Public
Instruction primarily as a connecting link between government
and country, rather than as someone entrusted with the task
of replacing a voluntary by a national system. This divergence
from the government manifested itself most clearly on the
question whether or not a Normal School should be established
under the direct superintendence of a Board of Education.
Allen informed Russell that the BFSS had expressed considerable doubts as to the capacity of any Board of Education
'satisfactorily [to] discharge the duties involved in the Moral
and Religious training of young persons as teachers', although
he suggested that the Board might fund trainee teachers. Dunn
in his 1838 pamphlet critized Brougham's Bill for, *inter alia*,
empowering Education Commissioners to establish Normal
and others schools '*to any extent and on any principles* they please'.[89]
Yet the government pressed ahead with its scheme to establish
a Normal School while permitting the Education Committee
to determine its nature. It was a tentative gesture towards a
state rather than a voluntaryist-determined system of national
education, a move away from the duopoly which Dissenters
such as Dunn were happy to maintain.

In his autobiography James Kay claimed that the government's proposal for a Normal School was his own.[90] But it is
far more probable that it originated with Russell and the Whig
government. Certainly Russell was considering the question
of Normal Schools as early as August 1838, two months before
Kay sent his unsolicited letter to the Home Secretary urging
the setting up of a Normal School. Moreover Kay looked to
such a school to supply teachers for workhouse schools in

[88] H. Dunn *A Reply to the Misrepresentations of the Revd Francis Close* (2nd end. edn.,
London, 1839), 3.
[89] PRO 30/22 3A (Russell Papers), fo. 314: Allen to Russell, 14 Apr. 1838; Dunn,
National Education, the Question of Questions, Appendix p. iii.
[90] B. C. Bloomfield (ed.), *The Autobiography of Sir James Kay-Shuttleworth* (London,
1964), 59.

particular rather than for elementary schools as a whole. As he himself later admitted, his attention at that time was concentrated on pauper schools. He recollected: 'I was not thinking of education beyond that sphere.'[91] Thus this move towards a national system was the Whigs' own. Nevertheless the appointment of Kay to be the first Secretary to the Education Committee of the Privy Council and his involvement in drafting Whig plans from 1839 onwards, marked a second important difference between the aspirations of the government and the beliefs of the followers of Dunn within the BFSS. Dunn claimed that the Bible was 'the universal text book'. No work, he argued, was better able to promote intellectual development or contained so much useful knowledge and so many facts. The Bible was not simply a work of revelation, but was also 'the basis of all practical virtue'.[92] A regulation of the BFSS, therefore, excluded all books and lessons for reading and instruction of a secular character from their schools: in the presence of the Bible they were superfluous.[93] Indeed not until 1840 were non-scriptural lessons introduced into the Borough Road school.[94] The Whigs, on the other hand, while recognizing that religion formed the basis of any instruction, did not desire to confine education to this basis alone.

The Minutes of the Education Committee for 13 April 1839, probably drafted by Kay, specified that in addition to instruction in religion, there should be 'instruction in industry as a special department of the moral training of the children'; it was clearly envisaged that the Bible would not constitute the only source of education.[95] Kay explained the intentions of the government in a pamphlet published in 1839 in the course of the political controversy surrounding the government's proposals. As a statement of the motives behind the Whig measure, the work should perhaps be treated with some caution since it was designed specifically to appease Tory opposition: 'It is astonishing to us', Kay exclaimed, 'that the party calling themselves Conservative should not lead the van

[91] Ibid., 57; NLI MSS 534 (Monteagle Papers): Rice to Russell, 27 Aug. 1838; PRO 30/22 3B (Russell Papers), fo. 350: Kay to Russell, 29 Oct. 1838.

[92] Dunn, *National Education, the Question of Questions*, 43–8.

[93] PRO 30/22 3B (Russell Papers), fo. 10: Martine to Russell, 5 May 1838.

[94] H. B. Binns, *A Century of Education* (London, 1908), 160.

[95] *Parl. Papers 1839*, xli, 260.

in promoting the diffusion of . . . knowledge.' But as an account of the kind of education proposed it may be presumed to be accurate. Kay stated that religious instruction alone was insufficient; in addition 'the people should know how their interests are inseparable from those of the other orders of society'.[96] He brought to bear on his educational projects the examples of schools for the poor established by Fellenberg and run by his pupil Vehrli. The lessons of the Swiss schools, as understood by Kay, was that 'the formation of character' should always be kept in mind as 'the great aim of education'. The 'intelligence' of the child should be enlightened in order that he should better understand his duties and capacity for action, the capacity being 'determined by the cultivation of habits appropriate to the duties of the station which the child must occupy'. Consequently the children of the poor should be encouraged in 'steady and persevering' manual labour as well as in religion, that is in instruction in 'industry'. Kay's training school at Battersea included lessons in book-keeping, the elements of mechanics, design drawing, and singing—since 'school songs' were 'an important means of diffusing a cheerful view of the duties of a labourer's life'. For each class of society, he believed that there was an appropriate education. The Whigs were concerned to ensure not only that the poor were religious, but that they were as capable as aristocratic liberals of performing their 'duties' in exchange for their own 'privileges'.[97]

Spring Rice in his defence of the government set out the grounds of the education measure. Education, he urged, was in 'the social interests of mankind', a means to avert 'imminent dangers' to the social system. More importantly, it was a way of promoting the 'intellectual wealth which forms the capital of our moral nature'. Not only were our 'fellow men' to be made 'better subjects', they were also to become 'better Christians'.[98] The Christian basis of a united society was recognized in the establishment of a system of education which would be

[96] J. Kay-Shuttleworth, 'An Explanation of the Intentions of HMG entitled "Recent Measures for the Promotion of Education in England"', *Four Periods of Public Education* (London, 1862), 232, 233.

[97] *Idem.*, 'First Report on the Training of School at Battersea to the Poor Law Commissioners, January 1, 1841', *Four Periods of Public Education*, 298, 343, 344, 353, 354. [98] [Spring Rice], 'Ministerial Plan of Education', 179.

acceptable to the various denominations of the country. The liberal Anglican Whigs in formulating their proposals rejected the schemes of both of the Scottish rationalist Brougham, who understood education to consist in the diffusion of technical knowledge, and of the secularist CSE, which sought to replace instruction in the Bible with the teaching of a secular morality in the classroom. While these Whigs concurred with the BFSS in the belief that lessons in a common Christianity were a practical possibility, they differed from that organization in their desire to erect an education system under the direct control of the state and so gradually to abandon dependence on voluntary contributions. The Whigs also developed a concern for the moral welfare of the student as well as his Christian orthodoxy, a concern which the BFSS did not begin to appreciate until the early 1840s. Thus it would be untrue to argue that the Whig government legislated on Dissenting or British and Foreign School Society lines. The government's proposals of 1839 were liberal in that they sought to provide an education open to all; Anglican, in that the education offered was to be Christian if of a non-dogmatic kind; Whig, in so far as they anticipated the construction of a new national establishment in the form of a national system of education. In these respects, the scheme of 1839 was quintessentially liberal Anglican.

Not surprisingly it received the support of the Noetic Baden Powell. In a pamphlet published in 1840 he described the government's proposals as 'wise and enlightened measures', although he regretted the fact that political circumstances had necessarily imposed limitations on their extent.[99] He had praised in particular what he saw as the fundamental principle of the 1839 suggestions, namely that they upheld 'the free support of education among all sects alike, always based on religion'.[100] In his pamphlet Powell attempted to discuss the education question 'not with reference to the support of a party . . . but with regard to the grand and stable principles of right and of truth'.[101] In the event his conclusions were akin to those of the Whigs. Like the liberal Anglican politicians he objected to using the Bible as the sole school-book as was the practice

---

[99] B. Powell, *State Education Considered*, 74, 80.
[100] Ibid., 72.   [101] Ibid., 3.

in BFSS schools. But in a similar fashion he believed that education which was not grounded on religion was not worth the name. 'It may be truly maintained', he commented,' . . . that all real education ought to be *based upon religion*.' He proceeded to suggest that '*some* general religious instruction common to all' might be imparted, and he even conceded the possibility of devising a general formulary, although he believed that 'the present state of religious opinion' would hardly permit its introduction. Although he did not hold that such general religious instruction was 'sufficient', he contended that it was at least 'good', even if additional 'full, systematic and precise' denominational instruction was required.[102] In the course of the pamphlet he opposed confining education to the control of the church, suggested that the legislature had the right to interfere in the matter and opposed granting funds exclusively to sectarian schools, be they Anglican or Dissenting.[103] The work concluded with a paean to the virtues of comprehensive religious education worthy of Russell himself. 'It enlightens and it unites,' Powell declared, 'it gives rational intelligence and national strength; it attaches men to the state as enlightened subjects, and binds them together as Christian brethren.'[104]

To the extent that the Whigs could unite the varied components of the liberal alliance around their proposals, they were successful in legislating for the country. Wyse of the Central Society was prepared to support the government's measure as 'a forward step' although he argued that it was not in itself an adequate remedy for the problem in hand; Brougham expressed his 'extreme satisfaction' at the course taken by the government although it was his opinion that the government had not gone far enough; Charles Buller, the Radical, made a plea that the Bill should be supported although he too thought it was imperfect; Baines, the Leeds Dissenter, declared that the London Dissenting Deputies had resolved in favour of the plan.[105] Only four liberal MPs voted against the government on 20 June, three of whom were to move to the Protectionist or Conservative side of the House in the course of the

---

[102] Ibid., 13, 17, 25, 33–4, 53.   [103] Ibid., 39–42, 43–4, 67–8.   [104] Ibid., 83.
[105] *Hansard*, 3rd ser., xlv (1839), 291; *ibid.*, xlvii (1839), 763; *ibid.*, xlviii (1839), 554, 751.

1840s.[106] Outside parliament, the Whig–Radical *Morning Chronicle* took up the liberal Anglican cause, declaring that 'a proper system of National Education would ensure the instruction in all the Christian duties; for the books used would necessarily be selected on the principle of inculcating what all Christians are agreed on'. 'We trust', it concluded, 'that the Ministers will persevere in the scheme'.[107] But the liberal alliance was to find itself only one party in the country. Despite their claim to legislate in the interest of the nation, they found their proposal, however tentative, stridently attacked by an irate Tory opposition. Between the announcement of the liberal plans on 12 February and the debate in the Commons which commenced in June, the Whigs, defeated on their Jamaica Bill, had resigned office only to resume it following the inability of the Queen and Peel to agree terms. The Whigs were only too aware of the narrowness of their parliamentary majority and the limits to their national support. On 1 June Russell told the Cabinet that opposition to the education scheme had made it necessary to give up the plan. On 4 June he announced to the Commons that the government no longer intended to proceed with the establishment of a Normal School and that the funds to be voted would be divided between the National Society and the BFSS.[108] In the spring of 1840 the government conceded the church's right to appoint the inspectors of its schools.[109] The political limits to liberal Anglicanism had been reached.

In the Lords the High Church Blomfield attacked the Whig plan as 'the heaviest blow' yet struck on the Church of England; in the Commons Edward Litton, the Irish Protestant, opposed the plan for 'mingling up in one common school the children of the Socinian, the members of the Church of England and of the Roman Catholics' and so destroying 'all true religion'; the Evangelical Ashley considered the Whig scheme to be 'hostile to revealed religion itself' since the distinction drawn between fundamental truths of Christianity and dogma, he

[106] The four were G. J. Heathcote, Hon. A. F. Kinnaird, Lord A. Lennox, and W. Long. See *Hansard*, 3rd ser., xlviii (1839), 681–6.

[107] *Morning Chronicle*, 22 June 1839.

[108] BL Addit. MSS 56561 (Broughton Papers): Hobhouse Diary, 1 June 1839; *Hansard*, 3rd ser., xlvii (1839), 1381.

[109] Paz, *Politics of Working-Class Education*, 102.

suggested, did not exist 'in the nature of things'. Peel objected
to the government plan as introducing a scheme of education
from which the dignitaries of the Church of England were
excluded, since they were not to have a place on the proposed
Education Committee. He considered that the consequence of
implementing the government's proposals would in effect be
the state's maintenance of non-Anglican sects.[110] The Tories
appreciated the need for government to provide financial aid
for education, but objected to the introduction of a govern-
ment-run system which would necessarily subvert the Church
of England's authority. The constitutional revolution of 1828–
32, as they recognized, had made it politically impossible to
ensure that the religious education offered by the state would
be exclusively Anglican. Anglican Tories therefore desired the
continuance of the existing voluntary systems, both Anglican
and Dissenting, each to be run by their respective voluntary
societies supplemented by the pecuniary aid of the state. The
Tories wished to resist all government interference in the kind
of education to be provided. Wellington made his position
explicit in relation to the diocese of Winchester and to his
bishop, the Evangelical Charles Sumner, who had established
a Diocesan Education Society in 1839. Wellington gave his
opinion that the Society should neither submit its schools to
government inspection nor receive financial aid from the
government which might justify state interference. He wrote
to Sumner: 'As an individual I must decline to take part in
any meeting which may have for its objective to raise subscriptions for establishing schools; unless on the condition that such
Diocesan Associations shall engage that they will not receive
aid from the fund at the disposal of the Committee of the Privy
Council.'[111]

In education policy the Tories disputed the two chief tenets
of the liberal Anglicans, namely that dogma could be separated
from Christian truth and that as a consequence a truly national
system of education could be founded. They argued that
doctrine was of the essence of religion and that as a consequence, in a religiously diverse political nation (given that
religion was to be the foundation of instruction), a single

---

[110] *Hansard*, 3rd ser., xlvii (1839), 758, 1389; *ibid.*, xlviii (1839), 276, 277, 672, 677.
[111] G. H. Sumner, *Life of C. R. Sumner, Bishop of Winchester* (London, 1876), 267.

national system of education was a chimera—hence their continued support for voluntaryism. In this they were not alone. 1839 marked the high point of liberal unity. Thereafter the true diverse nature of the liberal coalition revealed itself. Fearful that the Anglican Church, especially in a period of Tory rule, would dominate any national system of education, the Dissenters became increasingly reluctant to surrender control of their schools to a national government. In January 1841 the committee of the BFSS demanded from the Whigs terms equivalent to those granted to the National Society, only to be refused. By December 1843 agreement was reached with a now Tory government.[112] In any case not all Dissenters had gone along with the government's proposals. In June 1839 two Dissenting deputies had proposed a motion to petition against the education plan on the grounds 'that education must be the result of voluntary effort and management'.[113] The truth was that liberal Anglican doctrines could only accommodate one section of Dissenters, those who were prepared to subordinate demands for disestablishment to practical concessions granted by the Whigs. There were limits to liberal Anglicanism as much within the liberal coalition as without. The final chapter deals with these limits in examining the relations between various sections of the party as seen primarily through the issue of anti-slavery. It is demonstrated that the coalition on which the liberal Anglicans depended was highly unstable, constraining as much as encouraging their legislative initiatives.

[112] N. Ball, *Her Majesty's Inspectorate 1839–1849* (London, 1963), 49–58; Binns, *A Century of Education*, 130–2.

[113] Guildhall Library MSS 3083 (Minutes of the Protestant Dissenting Deputies), ix. 370, 376: 17 June 1839.

7

The Limits of Liberal Anglicanism: The Liberal Coalition and the Anti-Slavery Movement

THE political success of liberal Anglicanism was dependent on its ability to appeal to other groups within the liberal firmament. It sustained itself with the aid of a coalition of like-minded Anglican and Dissenting groups. When the Whigs came to power in 1830, they had the support of such Evangelicals as T. F. Buxton, Dr Stephen Lushington, and Andrew Johnston; of orthodox Dissenters such as the Wesleyan John Wilks, the Independent Edward Baines, and the Quaker Joseph Pease; of Unitarians such as William Smith and Mark Philips; of Catholics such as O'Connell, R. L. Sheil, and Thomas Wyse. Such aid was vital since the liberal Anglicans were but one section, and that not obviously the most numerous, of the liberal coalition. In parliamentary terms the importance of Irish Catholic Support in the formation of the government of 1835 has already been demonstrated.[1] No less politically (if not numerically) significant was Buxton's support for the appropriation of the surplus revenues of the Irish Church to 'general education'. It was a living testimony that the Whig proposal, itself adopted on Buxton's suggestion,[2] was not derogatory to the spirit of Anglicanism. In electoral politics the support of Dissent was yet more important. As Anstey has calculated, the Nonconformist population in England in the 1830s numbered a little over half a million, but constituted approximately one-fifth of the post-1832 electorate.[3] These votes, being unevenly distributed about the country, were regionally more important than this national figure would immediately suggest. The Wesleyans, for example, although

---

[1] See ch. 2.　　　　　　　　　　　　　[2] *Hansard*, 3rd ser., xxvii (1835), 770.
[3] R. Anstey, 'Religion and British Slave Emancipation', D. Eltis and J. Walvin (eds.), *The Abolition of the Atlantic Slave Trade* (Madison, Wisconsin, 1981), 51, 53.

8.4 per cent of the total electorate, were only 3 per cent of the voters of Bury, but 12.7 per cent of those in Rochdale. In England the Dissenting vote was concentrated in the industrializing counties and had its greatest influence in the new urban boroughs such as Manchester and Leeds. The Wesleyans, for example, a little over two-fifths of the total English Nonconformist population, were to be found predominantly in Lancashire, Yorkshire, and the Potteries.[4] In view of the slump in the Whig agricultural vote in the counties in the course of the 1830s, the political role of these industrial boroughs, and so of the Dissenting vote, was to expand. As the 1841 election showed, the Whig party paid increasing attention to these areas of support, knowing that rural districts were lost to them. The 'free trade' cry of that year appealed to the large populous boroughs at the expense of the counties, the Whigs winning an overwhelming majority of the boroughs with electorates over 2,000.[5]

This coalition with Dissent, however, was fundamentally unstable, not least because Dissent was divided against itself. Particular Nonconformist denominations did not possess a uniform political affiliation. The Wesleyan leadership, as embodied in Jabez Bunting, the so-called 'pope' of Methodism, was predominantly Tory, a view expressed in the weekly newspaper, the *Watchman*, founded by a group of wealthy Lancastrian bankers and merchants.[6] On the other hand, the mass of the Wesleyan electorate ignored the pleas of their leaders and tended to vote liberal. The *Wesleyan Chronicle*, analysing returns from twenty-nine cities and boroughs and seven counties in the 1841 election, noted that almost three-quarters of the Wesleyan electorate had plumped for supporters of the existing government. Even given the Whig bias of the newspaper (it excluded the more Tory cities of Liverpool and Manchester from its consideration), the results were strikingly indicative of the Connection's inability to command the political loyalty of its members.[7] Likewise Catholic Irish, if less severely divided than the Methodists, were by no means

[4] Ibid.

[5] R. Blake, *The Conservative Party from Peel to Churchill* (London, 1972), 46. For a more extensive analysis of the 1841 election, see below.

[6] D. Hempton, *Methodism and Politics in British Society 1750-1850* (London, 1984), 182–3.   [7] Ibid., 204–6.

a homogeneous voting bloc. Outside the north, where their minority status enforced a denominational allegiance, Catholic voting was not always predictable. In Tralee, for example, in 1835, a quarter of those who preferred the Tory candidate were Catholic.[8] The more important division was within the liberal camp, between those Catholics prepared to co-operate with the Whigs and those whose enthusiasm for the repeal of the 1801 Act of Union did not diminish. Admittedly, after the *rapprochement* between O'Connell and the Whigs in 1835, the distinction between Whigs and Repealers for a while became blurred such that in 1839 the Whig government offered O'Connell the Mastership of the Rolls. None-the-less it remained an important undercurrent as the Whigs sought to attract Catholics at the expense of the Repeal movement. In 1837, for example, Thomas Drummond, the Irish Under-Secretary, had carefully distributed election subsidies to liberal candidates who were firmly in favour of the Union.[9] The Whigs knew that in courting Nonconformist sects, they were not attracting the Nonconformist vote *tout simple*.

Whig efforts in this direction were further hampered by the fact that mutual hostility between the denominations meant that the Whigs could only cultivate one group at the expense of another. The most striking example of this was with respect to the antipathy which existed between Wesleyans and Catholics. The more the Whig government was seen to appease Catholic interests, not only with regard to the appropriation clause and the attempt to settle the Irish tithe problem, but also with respect to its education policy in England and the possibility of state support for Catholic schools, the less Wesleyans felt inclined to vote Whig. In Manchester in the 1839 by-election the Wesleyans swung behind the Tory candidate on a 'no popery' cry, even if, to the good fortune of the Whigs, the phenomenon was not so strikingly repeated in the 1841 general election.[10] Equally important, in English politics at least, was the struggle which occurred in the 1830s for the leadership of Protestant Nonconformity between the orthodox Dissenters and the Unitarians. Until the middle years of the

[8] K. Hoppen, *Elections, Politics, and Society in Ireland 1832–1885* (Oxford, 1984), 38.
[9] Ibid., 258.
[10] D. A. Gowland, *Methodist Secessions* (Manchester, 1979), 131, 133.

decade, it had been the Unitarians who had taken the lead in agitating for the relief of Dissenters' grievances. Until 1830, the leading Dissenter in parliament was William Smith, a Unitarian and, until 1832, the chairman of the Protestant Dissenting Deputies;[11] until 1834 only two orthodox Dissenters sat in the Commons. From the mid-1830s, aware of their increasing strength in the country and buoyed up by the Evangelical revival's attack on rationalist Christianity, Baptists and Independents fought to gain control of Dissent's representative institutions, forcing the Unitarians out of the Protestant Dissenting Ministers and Deputies in 1836. The political consequence was a reluctance on the part of Trinitarian Dissent to support Whig Unitarian candidates at elections. This was true of Molesworth's candidacy for the representation of Leeds in 1837, and partly explains Wesleyan dissatisfaction with Robert Grey, who stood for Manchester in 1839.[12] What such rivalries meant was that the Whigs had to develop the ability to ally with whatever Nonconformist group was in the ascendant.

To a considerable extent this was dependent on the Whigs' own religious outlook. Political co-operation in part was the product of mutual sympathy. As might be expected from their rationalist religious views, the Foxite generation of Whiggery primarily associated with the Unitarianism of Belsham and Aspland, and it was through these Unitarians that the old Whig alliance with Dissent was organized. Lord Holland, for example, in 1834, the year in which Nonconformist organizations turned against the government, communicated directly with Edgar Taylor, the legal adviser to the Unitarian Association, and Robert Aspland, the founder of the Unitarian *Monthly Repository*. According to Manning, Taylor was also responsible for conducting negotiations between the government and the Protestant Dissenting Deputies.[13] Brougham's connections with provincial radicalism and Dissent included Joseph Parkes, the Birmingham Unitarian solicitor who

[11] See R. W. Davis, *Dissent in Politics 1780–1830: The Political Life of William Smith MP* (London, 1971), *passim*.

[12] D. Fraser, 'The Fruits of Reform: Leeds Politics in the Eighteen-Thirties', *Northern History*, vii (1972), 103; Gowland, *Methodist Secessions*, 131.

[13] R. B. Aspland, *Memoir of Revd Robert Aspland of Hackney* (London, 1850), 534–5; B. L. Manning, *The Protestant Dissenting Deputies* (Cambridge, 1952), 82.

became a Whig election manager, and William Shepherd, the Liverpool Unitarian minister.[14] The major Unitarian demand was for the reform of the marriage laws for which they pressed in 1824, 1825, and 1827, and on which issue the Whig government first acted in February 1834. The Congregationalist *Eclectic Review* noted sourly that Grey's government only took political risks in dealing with Unitarian grievances, one of which, the abolition of university tests, was a matter 'in which the great body [of Nonconformists] felt least interested'.[15] Foxite compliance with unitarian demands should not be surprising: Unitarians were often as conservative as Grey himself. They insisted that they were not voluntaryist, posed no threat to the Established Church and did not desire the separation of church and state. Most saw no objection to receiving the Regium Donum from the government, while the Boards of both Baptist and Independent Ministers passed resolutions against its continued acceptance. Equally important, Unitarians preferred discussion and private negotiation to radical and popular agitation as their means of political influence. In April 1833, for example, Robert Aspland even considered it unwise to present a public memorial to the government praying for the redress of grievances.[16] Retrospectively the *Eclectic Review* of 1839 characterized the Unitarians as 'satisfied, or unwilling to hurry or incommode the government',[17] a way of proceeding which the Congregationalist Richard Beverley referred to in 1837 as 'treachery'.[18]

Unfortunately for the Foxites, they realized too late that pleasing Unitarianism was not the same as pleasing religious Dissent at large. In 1834, the Whig government suffered a painful reminder that the liberal coalition was an unstable alliance. While a cautious approach to reform might have satisfied timid Unitarians, it did not satisfy the bulk of Nonconformity, which in 1834 desired a more expeditious method.

[14] J. K. Buckley, *Joseph Parkes of Birmingham* (London, 1926), 135; Brougham Papers: corresp. with W. Shepherd.

[15] M. J. Cullen, 'The Making of the Civil Registration Act of 1836', *Jour. of Eccles. History*, xxv (1974), 39–40; *Eclectic Review*, 4th ser., v. (1839), 20.

[16] K. R. M. Short, 'The English Regium Donum', *English Historical Review*, lxxxiv (1969), 69–70; Guildhall Lib. MSS 3086 (United Committee Minutes), i. 40: 29 Apr. 1833.   [17] *Eclectic Review*, 4th ser., v (1839), 15.

[18] Congregational Lib. MSS II.c.22 (Wilson Papers): Beverley to Wilson, 3 Mar. 1837.

The government's unpopularity was signalled in the country in February 1834 by the defeat of the Attorney-General in the Dudley by-election, the result of Dissenting opposition. The following month a mass meeting of Nonconformists took place in Manchester in order to upbraid the government. George Hadfield, a solicitor in the city, prophesied: 'The conduct of the government is the subject of very general condemnation which will soon shew itself throughout the country in the same way that Sir John Campbell [the Attorney-General] has already felt it at Dudley.'[19] Nor did the Nonconformists regard the government's legislative response to this state of affairs as adequate. Neither the Marriage Bill of late February nor the Church-Rate Abolition Bill of April met with Dissenting satisfaction. The consequence was that a public meeting of Dissenting Deputies in May, held in London to protest at the Whigs' proposals, resulted in resolutions demanding the separation of church and state.[20] At the same time as Grey's government was successfully losing the support of English Dissent, it also succeeded in alienating the sympathies of O'Connell's followers. The decision of the government to renew the Coercion Bill, and in particular the public meetings clauses, angered the Irish leader. O'Connell referred to the Whigs in private as 'The scoundrels!!!', and grimly reflected: 'My experiment has been perfectly successful. I have shewn that the most energetic anxiety to conciliate the British Government and British Parliament is totally useless.'[21] In public he commenced another Repeal campaign.

It was not until the change in the leadership of the Whig party in 1834–5 that the liberal coalition was fully reassembled. This brought to prominence Whig leaders who were used to dealing directly with orthodox Dissent and who possessed a religious outlook much more sypathetic to the Evangelicalism which had challenged Unitarianism's leadership. C. P. Thomson, for example, who became President of the Board of Trade in Melbourne's administration, frequently communicated with the Dissenters of Manchester whom he represented

---

[19] *Morning Chronicle*, 1 Mar. 1834; W. R. Ward, *Religion and Society*, 132; Congregational Lib. MSS H.a.10: Hadfield to Wilson, 3 Mar. 1834.

[20] *Morning Chronicle*, 9 May 1834.

[21] Fitzpatrick, *Corresp. of Daniel O'Connell*, i. 442.

in parliament. If in part this was due to an electoral dependency (Hadfield asserted that 'The Dissenters undoubtedly returned him for this borough'), it meant, nevertheless, that the Nonconformists had a direct channel of communication with the government. By 1836 Hadfield was writing: 'I have the ear of a Cabinet Minister who is anxious to hear from me.'[22] Russell, in particular, was the Dissenters' political hero (the Wesleyans excepted). In 1831 and 1835 the Dissenting Deputies raised funds for Russell alone of all liberal politicians in order to secure his return to parliament, noting on the latter occasion that 'it is of the greatest importance to the cause of civil and religious freedom that Lord John Russell's re-election for South Devonshire should be secured'.[23] The accession of liberal Anglican Whigs such as Russell to positions of political eminence meant that the disaffected looked more favourably on the reconstructed liberal ministry. Hadfield noted in October 1834 that 'It seems the new Government wish to make friends with us', while by September of the following year O'Connell was privately boasting: 'The prospects for Ireland brighten. I am beginning to think that I shall be a Cabinet Minister next Session, with the rule of matters in Ireland officially committed to me.'[24] If this last contained more than an element of Hibernian exaggeration, it was, for all that, a notable expression of content.

Orthodox Dissenters shared the enthusiasm of young Whigs for liberal Anglican theologians. Reviewing Whately's work on the origins of 'Romish Errors', the *Eclectic Review* welcomed him as a powerful 'auxiliary' and commented that all the truths which he has in so masterly a style illustrated and defended, have long been the prevailing and characteristic opinions of the great body of Protestants holding the congregational Polity'. The journal also greeted Hampden's Bampton Lectures on scholastic philosophy as 'significant and auspicious': 'Let Mr Hampden pursue his course.' Of Hampden's appointment in 1836 to the Regius Chair of Divinity at Oxford,

[22] Congregational Lib. MSS H.a.10: Hadfield to Beverley, 7 Nov. 1833; ibid., Hadfield to Wilson, 27 Sept. 1836.
[23] Guildhall Lib. MSS 3083 (Minutes of the Dissenting Deputies), viii. 30: 3 May 1831; ibid., viii. 263–4: 28 Apr. 1835.
[24] Congregational Lib. MSS H.a.10: Hadfield to Wilson, 13 Oct. 1834; Fitzpatrick, *Corresp. of Daniel O'Connell*, ii. 38.

the *Eclectic* believed that it 'cannot fail to have a beneficial influence'. The review also recommended Arnold's *History of Rome* and Thirlwall's *History of Greece*.[25] It should not be assumed that the *Eclectic* regarded with equal favour all the work which the liberal Anglicans produced. It objected to Whately's resting his arguments for sabbath observance on the authority of the church, believing this to be a Popish doctrine, and it demanded sabbatarian legislation to which Whately was opposed. It did not believe that Milman's *History of the Jews* was altogether innocent of the charge of generating scepticism, though it refused to attribute to him any wilful design to promote rationalism. But when these strictures are weighed in the balance, it is clear that there was a marked sympathy between liberal Anglicanism and orthodox dissent which compared favourably with the silent distrust which they exhibited towards Brougham, or the outright hostility felt towards Sydney Smith, the doyen of older Whig clerics, many of whose works the *Eclectic* deplored as 'anti-scriptural and irreligious'.[26]

The Whigs' liberal Anglicanism also appealed to the Anglican Evangelicals who stood at the opposite end of the liberal coalition from that of Nonconformity. In this respect the liberal Anglican Whigs were able to bridge the gap between, on the one hand, Independents and Congregationalists, and, on the other, liberal Evangelical Church-of-England men, in a way in which it had been impossible for the Foxites to anticipate. There was, indeed, a marked correspondence between moderate Evangelical and liberal Anglican thought. James Stephen, for example, the Evangelical anti-slavery leader, was no unlikely admirer of Thomas Arnold, of whom he wrote: 'I like him hugely. I have seldom met a man more to my taste.' Although such Evangelicals as Stephen grounded their faith on 'experience' or 'persuasion' rather than 'any series of dogmatical propositions', this did not mean that reason played no part in their understanding of religious conviction. Stephen certainly rejected the validity of an emotionally over-indulgent

[25] *Eclectic Review*, 3rd ser., v (1831), 115, 133; ibid., x (1835), 43; ibid., xv (1836), 321; *Eclectic Review*, 4th ser., v (1839), 68, 102.
[26] *Eclectic Review*, 3rd ser., iii (1830), 486, 508; ibid., iv (1830), 52, 55; *Eclectic Review*, 4th ser., vi (1839), 233.

contemplation of one's sinfulness as a necessary prelude to the realization of faith. Writing to Henry Venn, who was preparing a life of his grandfather, John Venn, Stephen commented: 'I believe a multitude of people make religion consist chiefly in saying the worst things possible of themselves . . . I shd. regret that your grandfather gave his countenance to so pitiable a folly.' When Henry Taylor, a colleague at the Colonial Office, entertained religious doubts, Stephen recommended Locke's *Reasonableness of Christianity*, of which Stephen had 'a very high opinion', to allay his fears. Taylor remarked upon Stephen's 'firmness of faith' with 'philosophical habits of thought'. It should therefore come as no surprise that Stephen explicitly approved of Hampden's method of biblical interpretation. He agreed with the Regius Professor that propositions in the Scriptures were not the first premises of mathematical axioms, but matters of fact. Consequently interpretations of these facts were not refutable deductions, but varying opinions. From this Stephen drew the tolerant conclusion 'that there must be a very large mutual indulgence even in cases of avowed difference of opinion'.[27] His Evangelical toleration, without any diminution of faith (according to Lord Granville he was 'fervently religious'), was akin to that of liberal Anglicanism.[28]

But even these widespread sympathies could not guarantee the stability of the coalition. There were limits to the liberal Anglicans' toleration of dissenting demands which became more extreme as the decade proceeded. Discontented with the ineffectiveness of parliament, self-conscious of their growing strength, distrustful of a temporizing London leadership, orthodox provincial Dissent came of age in the late 1830s: anti-Establishmentarian, in favour of suffrage reform and supporting free trade. The new generation of Nonconformist leaders, which included Edward Miall of Leicester and John Bright of Rochdale, was ready to campaign for the redress of their grievances in the provincial towns, using local societies (such as the Leicester Voluntary Church Association of 1839) and local newspapers (such as the *Leeds Mercury*), and prefer-

---

[27] C. E. Stephen, *The Right Hon. Sir James Stephen* (private circulation only, London, 1906), 64, 182; CUL Addit. MSS 7888 (Stephen Papers), box II fo. 134: Stephen to Venn, 22 Mar. 1834; ibid., box II letterbook I, 127: fragment of a letter not sent, Stephen to S. Wilberforce, 5 Aug. 1838; Bod. MSS Eng. Misc. f. 56: Taylor Diary, 26 June, 21 July 1837.   [28] Taylor *Autobiography*, ii. 301.

ring local agitation to national negotiation. What was notice-
able, for example, in the campaign to abolish church-rates
was the transference of political activity from parliament to
direct action in the country, particularly in contesting the
levying and payment of church-rates, as undertaken most
notoriously by William Baines of Leicester and John
Thorogood of Chelmsford—the consequence being their
imprisonment. In these militant activities English Dissenters
received the support of the Irish Catholic leader, O'Connell.
In January 1840 he attended and spoke at a dinner of the
Manchester Anti-Corn-Law Association, while in the following
February he supported the Radical Duncombe's motion on
the Thorogood church-rate case. The following January
O'Connell addressed a public demonstration against church-
rates held at Leicester.[29] From the autumn of 1838 the Irish
leader had been moving towards a break with Whiggery,
soliciting the aid of the violently anti-Whig Archbishop of
Tuam, MacHale, in the formation of the Precursor Society,
which was instituted to agitate for, among other things, the
extinction of compulsory support for the Anglican Church and
the extension of the franchise; in April 1840 he founded the
Repeal Association in the expectation that the Tories would
form the next government.[30]

Such developments within Catholic and Protestant Dissent
were anathema to the liberal Anglicans. They challenged the
very basis of liberal Anglicanism itself, and in so doing revealed
the limits to Whig concessions. In November 1837 Russell had
committed himself to opposing any further extensions of the
franchise, while he had always been a strong advocate of the
Established Church. Likewise the Whigs had always been
defenders of constitutional and legal proprieties. The consequence was that by the end of the 1830s, as the leadership of
Nonconformity slipped out of the hands of the moderate
orthodox Dissenters such as Josiah Condor, the editor of the
Eclectic Review, Joshua Wilson, a founder of the Congregational
Union, and Henry Waymouth, the chairman of the Dissenting
Deputies, the disruption of the liberal coalition became an

[29] M. R. O'Connell (ed.), *The Correspondence of Daniel O'Connell* (Dublin, 1972–1980),
vi. 291, 304, 394; ibid., vii 7.
[30] Fitzpatrick, *Corresp. of Daniel O'Connell*, ii. 147, 149, 229.

ever-increasing threat. These moderate Dissenters had been
prepared to suppress their principled commitment to voluntaryism in exchange for Whig concessions on matters of practical reform; their provincial successors, less willing to
compromise, insisted on turning grievances into issues of
principle which the Whigs felt unable to concede. Once supporters of the abolition of church-rates, by the end of the decade
the Whig government refused to countenance this measure,
Russell declaring in 1840, on a church-rate abolition motion,
'that the established Church was founded on just, and wise,
and sound principles'.[31] Reflecting on Russell's speech, the
Eclectic remarked that the Whig leader appeared 'concerned
to disencumber himself of the confidence of the Dissenting
body', even if he refrained 'from plainly telling them to be
gone'.[32] This was indeed one of the central problems for the
government in the late 1830s. Unable to appease—on religious
issues at least—an increasingly radicalized Protestant Dissent
and O'Connellite Catholicism, it seemed as though the liberal
coalition which liberal Anglican and 'young' Whigs had
formed so successfully in the mid-1830s would collapse by the
end of the decade. The inherent instability of the various
groups which had collected around the Whigs on the issue of
ecclesiastical reform once more threatened to disrupt the
liberal alliance.

It is the purpose of the remainder of this chapter to illustrate
further the vicissitudes of the liberal coalition, and hence the
extent to which the liberal Anglicans succeeded in holding the
party together, with reference to one specific issue—anti-
slavery. The movement for the abolition of slavery in the
British West Indies was a coalition of denominational and
philanthropic interests which reflected the whole range of the
liberal alliance in general. Its parliamentary leader was
Thomas Fowell Buxton, an Evangelical brewer and, until his
defeat in 1837, MP for Weymouth. Other MPs who participated in anti-slavery bodies such as the London Anti-Slavery
Society or the Central Negro Emancipation Society included
the Independent Edward Baines, the Quaker Joseph Pease,
the Catholic O'Connell, and the liberal Anglican Thomas

[31] *Hansard.* 3rd ser., lii (1840), 94.
[32] *Eclectic Review*, 4th ser., vii (1840), 346.

Spring Rice. The political range was as great as the denominational. Radicals, such as William Ewart and C. P. Villiers,
joined forces with more conservative MPs such as the
Yorkshire baronet Sir George Strickland and William Evans
(who retired from the representation of Leicester on the ground
that he was not sufficiently radical for his constituents).
Although the anti-slavery movement did embrace such Tories
as Sandon and Sir Eardley Wilmot, it was predominantly
liberal in outlook. Of 29 MPs known to be active members of
anti-slavery organizations, 20 were liberal and 8 conservative
(the political affiliation of one is unknown); of the conservatives, 6 were members of one body only, Buxton's African
Civilization Society, which had deliberately sought out bi-
partisan support. Of the 134 candidates returned in the 1832
election pledged to the abolition of slavery whose political
affiliation is identifiable, all but 8 were liberals.[33] The anti-
slavery cause was not confined to Westminster alone, but also
received the support of Nonconformity in the country.
Drescher has estimated that more than one British male in
five over the age of fifteen years probably signed the anti-
slavery petitions of 1833, while three-fifths of the 5,020 petitions
of that year were produced by Dissent.[34] Such popularity in
the country did not lack the support of Nonconformity's institutions. In July 1832 the Protestant Dissenting Deputies urged
that the 'Friends of Humanity and of the Christian Religion'
should only support abolitionist candidates in the forthcoming
elections.[35] Other denominational organizations also
supported the cause: the Wesleyan Conference declared that
slavery was 'contrary to the immutable principles of Christianity', while the Quaker Meeting for Sufferings was primarily
responsible for funding the London Anti-Slavery Society and
the Agency Committee.[36] By these means the parliamentary

[33] Names of the MPs are taken from I. Gross, 'Commons and Empire 1833–41',
D.Phil. thesis, (Oxford 1975), apps 6, 7, 8 & 9; Rhodes House MSS Brit. Emp.s.444
(Buxton Papers), xxx sect. 1, fos. 164–6: MPs subscribing to the African Civilization
Society after the first meeting, 23 July, 1839; Anstey, 'Religion and British Slave
Emancipation', 50.

[34] Ibid., 51; S. Drescher, 'Public Opinion and the Destruction of British Colonial
Slavery', J. Walvin (ed.), *Slavery and British Society 1776–1846* (London, 1982), 26.

[35] Guildhall Lib. MSS 3083 (Minutes of the Dissenting Deputies), viii. 105: 26 July
1832.

[36] Rhodes House MSS Brit. Emp.s.18 (BFASS), C9 fo. 41: Newton to Tredgold,
7 Aug. 1840; H. Temperley, *British Anti-Slavery 1833–70* (London), 1972, 15–6.

campaign was linked to provincial liberalism; it was, indeed, the special task of the Agency Committee 'to appeal to the people' and so secure the aid of 'provincial respectability'.[37] The anti-slavery coalition thus extended from Whigs in the metropolis to orthodox Dissenters in northern and midland industrial towns.

Such a diverse coalition not surprisingly entertained many divergent views. The 1830s witnessed a series of conflicts between London and the provinces, Anglican and Nonconformist, Radical and Liberal, over the means most suitable to effect an improvement in the condition of the negro slave. The first, and perhaps the most famous, of these was that between the London Anti-Slavery Society and its Agency Committee. The latter desired to mount a populist campaign in the country, while the former preferred to rest its hopes on negotiations at Westminster. The consequence was that the Agency Committee eventually constituted itself an independent organization.[38] In the course of the 1830s two personalities dominated this conflict between populism and quietism. On the one hand Joseph Sturge, the Birmingham Quaker and leader of the British and Foreign Anti-Slavery Society, saw himself as the representative of provincial Radical Dissent, fighting a righteous cause independent of party. Unwilling to indulge in political compromises, he preferred to trust in popular support for success. Buxton, on the other hand, the friend of leading Whig politicians and heir to the political mantle of the Clapham Sect, relied primarily on negotiation and conciliation to further his cause. To this end, in a period of unstable government, he was prepared to cultivate friendships with members of both the Whig and Tory parties. As these two leaders mooted new schemes, while old ones became outmoded, the formation and folding of anti-slavery societies—a notable feature of the period—became an institutional sign of the movement's fragmentation. In 1834 the Agency Committee reorganized itself as the British and Foreign Society for the Universal Abolition of Negro Slavery and the Slave Trade, but by 1835 it had ceased to exist. In November 1837 the Central Emancipation Committee was formed to replace it and 1839 saw the

[37] G. Stephen, *Anti-Slavery Recollections*, ed. H. Temperley, (London, 1971), 127, 160.
[38] Temperley, *British Anti-Slavery*, 13.

establishment of Sturge's British and Foreign Anti-Slavery Society. The original London Anti-Slavery Society suspended its operations in March 1839, its successor being the Society for the Extinction of the Slave Trade and for the Civilization of Africa which Buxton founded in June 1839. If in the later 1830s these various approaches produced conflict and disunity in the slavery movement, at the beginning of the decade such divisions were subordinated to the demand for the immediate abolition of slavery: the Whig party and its liberal allies then offered the only hope of achieving slave emancipation.

In the 1820s the Tory government, adhering to Canning's Resolution of May 1823, committed itself to the policy of amelioration. The object was a gradual improvement of the condition of the slaves until they were deemed capable of enjoying civil privileges. But by the mid-1820s there was growing disillusionment with the efficacy of this policy. Missionaries such as John Smith and W. J. Shrewsbury were badly treated by the West Indian planters, while an illicit slave trade continued to flourish in Mauritius. Meanwhile in parliament prominent Whigs identified themselves with the abolitionist cause. Thomas Spring Rice was present at the first meeting of the London Anti-Slavery Society and became one of its Vice-Presidents; Buxton retrospectively referred to him as 'My old friend and coadjutor on Mauritius and Slavery matters.' In 1826 Morpeth declared himself to be in favour of abolition, and Milton attended meetings of the Anti-Slavery Society to which Althorp also subscribed. Mulgrave's father (Foreign Secretary in Pitt's Cabinet) had been an abolitionist, an attitude which his son inherited: the Whigs were to send him to Jamaica as Governor-General to oversee the implementation of the Act of 1833. In the 1830 election Russell pledged himself to the emancipationist cause. Of the 198 MPs who spoke or voted on the abolitionist side in the 1820s, 150 were members of the Whig opposition, while only 24 acted with the government. When the Anti-Slavery Society at its General Meeting of May 1830 changed its policy from tacitly agreeing with amelioration to demanding immediate abolition, it looked to the Whig party for support.[39]

[39] I am greatly indebted to P. F. Dixon, 'The Politics of Emancipation', (D.Phil. thesis), *passim* for the account given in this and the following para. See also Rhodes

The Whig leadership, however, had never committed the party as a whole to support abolition. Grey took little interest in the anti-slavery question and personally detested Wilberforce. A Whig government in November 1830 did not necessarily herald the advent of abolition, and, indeed, in the early years of its existence the Whigs continued the policy of amelioration. It was not until November 1832 that the government agreed in principle to immediate abolition as a consequence of what was in effect the collapse of the gradualist approach. Christmas 1831 saw a slave rebellion in Jamaica followed by an attack on Baptist missionaries. This provoked both West Indian planters and anti-slavers to demand an inquiry into the government's policy. But even after the government had amended its policy, its commitment to the emancipationist cause was half-hearted. In December 1832 Howick, then Under-Secretary at the Colonial Office, drew up a plan for immediate emancipation based on papers written by two government officials, Henry Taylor and James Stephen. The Cabinet, however, declined to adopt this scheme, and the government did not mention the slave issue in the King's Speech at the opening of the 1833 Session. This forced Buxton to give notice that he would bring on a motion for the abolition of slavery on 19 March. The reluctance of the government to take action also caused Howick to resign, and he retired to the back-benches to agitate for abolition.[40] The changes in the Cabinet following the reorganization of the Irish government in April 1833 did not augur well for the emancipationist cause. They brought Stanley to the Colonial Office with, as his new Under-Secretary, John Shaw Lefevre, a man who was so afraid of his superior that he never opened his 'lips in the shape of counsel or remonstrance'.[41] It was still uncertain how the government would act.

Stanley prepared his scheme for emancipation isolated from those in his office who were acquainted with the West India

House MSS Brit. Emp.s.444 (Buxton Papers), xiii. fo. 209: Buxton to Philip, 16 Sept. 1834; ibid., xiii. fo. 64: newspaper cutting for May 1834, reporting an Address from the Bible, Missionary, and Anti-Slavery Societies of Whitby to Lord Mulgrave.

[40] Bod. MSS Eng. Lett.d.7 (Taylor Papers), fos. 204–5: Taylor to his father, 7 Jan. 1833; Kriegel, *Holland House Diaries*, 207; C. Buxton, *Sir Thomas Fowell Buxton*, 313; Grey Papers, box 24 file 3: Howick to Grey, 3 Apr. 1838.

[41] Grey Papers, C3/1B: Howick Jour., 1 Mar. 1834.

question, and without consulting such bodies as the Anti-Slavery Society which had a direct interest in the preparation of the legislation. Henry Taylor complained: 'Stanley leaps into his seat, gets the gout, gets the grippe, goes down into his county to be re-elected & gives his spare time to the invention of a scheme for settling the W. India question without holding a word of communication with Howick, Stephen or myself.' The resulting plan, published in *The Times* of 11 May, was, he thought, 'more crude, ignorant & shallow than even the course which he had adopted had given reason to expect'.[42] The uproar which followed publication induced Stanley to consult Stephen, but even so the plan presented to parliament on 14 May excited disfavour. Its two most controversial proposals were first that slaves were to be apprentices to their former owners (for eleven years in the case of praedial and six years in the case of non–praedial slaves) before enjoying complete liberty; second, that the planters were to receive a loan of £15 million as compensation. Opposition from anti-slavery bodies resulted in the reduction of the apprenticeship to six and four years respectively, but in order to be fair to the planters the loan was turned into a £20 million gift. Not surprisingly this angered the Agency Committee which opposed compensation in any case as 'an indirect participation in the crime' of slave-holding. It also displeased the Anti-Slavery Society and its leader Buxton. Although these were prepared to acquiesce on the ground of its necessity, they were unhappy at the unconditional nature of the gift. Buxton thus moved an amendment, albeit unsuccessfully, to the effect that one half of the sum should not be paid until the apprenticeship had ceased. Holland recorded that in the course of the debate on the Bill, Howick accused the government of being 'little better than slavedrivers, pirates, freebooters and what not'.[43]

Given these circumstances, despite the passing of the Abolition of Slavery Bill on 28 August 1833, it was not surprising that relations between Grey's government and the anti-slavery movement deteriorated. James Stephen, the leading

---

[42] Bod. MSS Eng. Lett.d.7 (Taylor Papers), fos. 206 ff.: Taylor to Miss Fenwick, 12 May 1833.

[43] G. Stephen, *Anti-Slavery Recollections*, C. Buxton, *Sir T. F. Buxton*, 324, 343; Kriegel, *Holland House Diaries*, 234.

abolitionist in the Colonial Office, became increasingly discontented under Stanley's stewardship. In September, he accused the Secretary of State of treating him with 'indifference'; unable to influence the course of policy, he complained 'I sit down daily to my business with feelings approaching disgust . . . nor do I feel as I once did, the invigorating hope that the exertion I make is speeding on its way a great and useful design'. Consequently he pressed to be removed from his office, frustrated at being Hay's (the Permanent Under-Secretary) and Stanley's subordinate.[44] Moreover many thought Stanley's implementation of the Abolition Act to be lax. The Whig measure had left the actual responsibility for passing the regulations relating to the conditions and terms of the apprenticeship to the local legislatures, subject to the approval of the Colonial Office. In the case of Jamaica these ran counter to the intentions of the British Act, transforming the apprenticeship, so the abolitionists argued, into an alternative form of slavery. At the time Stephen complained that the Jamaica Act was drawn up in a hurry, 'principally for the purpose of securing immediately the proportion of the [£]20 millions to which that island will be entitled'. As counsel to the Colonial Office he unsuccessfully attempted to persuade Stanley to resist some of its clauses. James Spedding, who became a clerk in the Colonial Office in 1835, noted later that Stanley had treated the Jamaica Assembly in too flattering and courteous a manner. 'To this original mistake', he suggested, 'most of the imperfections . . . in the working of the new system may be distinctly traced.'[45]

The truth was that only a section of the Whig party, the liberal Anglican Whigs such as Rice, Howick, Russell, and Mulgrave, actively favoured the abolitionist cause. Even Brougham, who in the 1830 election had been returned as MP for Yorkshire partly on the strength of his abolitionist sympathies, proved to be lukewarm when in government.

[44] Bod. MSS Eng. Lett.d.7 (Taylor Papers), fo. 213: Stephen to Taylor, 11 Sept. 1833; CUL Addit. MSS 7888 (Stephen Papers), box II fo. 1: Howick to Stephen, 18 Apr. 1834.

[45] Grey Papers, C3/1B: Howick Jour., 1 Mar. 1834; P. Knaplund, *James Stephen and the British Colonial System 1813–1847* (Madison, 1953), 108–10; [J. Spedding], 'The Negro Apprenticeship System', *Edinburgh Review*, lxvi (1838), 489–90; Rhodes House MSS Brit. Emp.s.444 (Buxton Papers), xvii. fo. 86: Buxton to Pease, 19 Mar. 1838.

Holland, perhaps the only old Whig exception to this rule, noted that the Chancellor 'uniformly abstained' from cabinet discussions on the subject, 'either quitting the room or confining his remarks to some personal reflection on those publick men who took part in debates'.[46] It was not until after the change in the Whig leadership which took place in 1834–5 that the Whigs regained the confidence of the anti–slavery movement. In the course of these manœuvres, two temporizing Colonial Secretaries, Ripon and Stanley, left the government, to be replaced by Spring Rice, who declared that 'during the last 16 or 17 years my political life has connected me with those men who in and out of parliament had advocated the cause of Abolition'.[47] He appointed Stephen to be his Assistant Under-Secretary, which had the effect of securing 'a great pacification' in the Colonial Office.[48] Harmony was also restored with Buxton, whose daughter commented that 'it is comfortable for my father to have Mr. Rice in the Colonial Office & not a little he seems to me to tyrannise over him in his daily visitations there'. For his part Rice described his relationship with Buxton as one of 'intimate and confidential friendship'.[49] Under Melbourne's premiership, Mulgrave and Howick entered the Cabinet, both committed abolitionists, and when Grant replaced Rice as Colonial Secretary in 1835 a Clapham Sect Evangelical held in 'great affection' by James Stephen took over the Colonial Office.[50]

The liberal Anglicans' alliance with Buxton as leader of the anti-slavery movement extended beyond the single issue of emancipation. Buxton was a national spokesman for the liberal Evangelicals in which capacity he furthered the Whig cause. He brought the anti-slavery movement within the field of liberal Anglican politics. Although he claimed to be independent of party ('I vote as I like', he once declared), his brother-in-law advised him: 'Do not let thy independence of all party

---

[46] Kriegel, *Holland House Diaries*, 208.

[47] NLI MSS 551 (Monteagle Papers): copy Rice to Foster, 19 June 1835.

[48] Bod. MSS Eng. Lett.d.7 (Taylor Papers), fo. 202: Taylor to Southey, 9 Sept. 1834.

[49] Rhodes House MSS Brit. Emp.s.444 (Buxton Papers), xiii. fo. 91: P. Buxton to S. Buxton, 22 July 1834; ibid., xiii fo. 321: Rice to Buxton, 11 Feb. 1835.

[50] CUL Addit. MSS 7888 (Stephen Papers), box II vol. 1, 23: copy Stephen to Taylor, 7 Aug. 1830.

be the means of leading thee away from *sound whiggism.*' His son was certainly happy to classify him as 'a thorough Whig'.[51] In the 1835 election he made clear his adherence to a form of moderate Whiggery akin to that of Spring Rice. At the same time as he admitted: 'I am no radical, I am no destructive', he was disinclined to support Wellington's and Peel's government, saying as regards the former: 'we have tried him and know him well . . . I distrust his government'. A pious churchman, he was won over to Russell's cause of appropriating the surplus funds of the Irish Church for the purpose of national education, as he informed Lord Sheffield: 'I am happy to tell you that his proposal provides for the Protestant Church as it is . . . & gives the surplus to Education . . . Had he given it to the Irish Landlords or to the Catholic Clergy I must have voted against it.'[52] Like the liberal Anglicans with whom he associated, Buxton firmly believed in the possibility of teaching common truths of Christianity to all regardless of sect, so much so that he wished to make teaching from the Scripture Extracts compulsory in Irish national schools. Even the Whigs had considered this impractical. In June 1836 he composed an admonitory letter to Morpeth, the Chief Secretary for Ireland, on the matter. As well as endorsing Whig toleration of Catholics he supported liberal endeavours to conciliate protestant Dissent. If he did support Andrew Johnstone's amendment to the Whig church-rate measure of 1837 (which proposed to appropriate the surplus funds of the church not to the relief of this grievance, but to the further supply of religious instruction), it was only after considerable doubt. His daughter remarked that 'The thing has already given him 4 bad nights & I am thoroughly vexed at it & do wish he would keep clear of these questions.'[53]

Buxton also acted as a linchpin between liberal Anglicans and Evangelical Dissent. The Protestant Dissenting Deputies, for example, asked him to present to the Commons their petition praying for the abolition of slavery; in 1835 he took

[51] C. Buxton, *Sir T. F. Buxton*, 83, 93, 396.

[52] Rhodes House MSS Brit. Emp.s.444 (Buxton Papers), xiii. fo. 292: report of Buxton's election speech at Weymouth, Jan. 1835; ibid., xiii. fo. 404: copy Buxton to Suffield, 25 Mar. 1835

[53] Rhodes House MSS Brit. Emp.s.444 (Buxton Papers), xv. fos. 51 ff.: draft Buxton to Morpeth, June 1836; ibid., xv. fo. 216: P. Johnston to her brother, 11 Mar. 1837.

the chair at the annual meeting of the Baptist Mission.[54] In part his association with Dissent was an accident of birth: his mother was a Quaker, his father Anglican. But it was also a relationship which he deliberately fostered when in 1805 he married into the Quaker Gurney family.[55] There were, indeed, many connections between the liberal Evangelicalism of Buxton and the moderate Dissent which his brother-in-law and fellow leader of the anti-slavery movement, Joseph John Gurney, represented. For Gurney was the leading English exponent of Evangelical Quakerism, by which he meant the religion of the New Testament 'without addition, without diminution, & without compromise'.[56] Gurney's particular insistence on the importance of biblical study, although he never altogether abandoned the doctrine of the indwelling light, brought him into the inner circles of liberal Evangelical Anglicans. In his home town of Norwich he was active in the Lancasterian school and the Auxiliary Bible Society; he became friends with Simeon, Daniel Wilson, and Adam Sedgwick.[57] He was also an active liberal. In 1818 he had spoken on behalf of his cousin, Richard Hanbury Gurney, on his election to the Commons as a Whig, and in 1833 he himself seriously considered standing for parliament (another Quaker cousin, Joseph Pease, had become MP for Durham in 1832).[58] He approved particularly of Buxton's stance on Irish appropriation, commending his brother-in-law's speech: 'Thy course was clear ... no other could be taken on real Christian grounds. I much like thy amendment. It was just the thing wanted.'[59]

---

[54] Guildhall Lib. MSS 3083 (Minutes of the Dissenting Deputies), viii. 90: 24 May 1832; *Baptist Magazine*, xxvii (1835), 303.

[55] C. Buxton, *Sir T. F. Buxton*, 3.

[56] Gurney Papers, MSS 111 fo. 750: Gurney to his children, 21 June 1840.

[57] Ibid., MSS 111 fo. 24: A. Gurney to Gurney, 13 Feb. 1838]; ibid., MSS 111 fo. 836: D. Wilson to Gurney, 3 Aug. 1841; D. Swift, *Joseph John Gurney* (Connecticut, 1962), 50–51, 53, 124.

[58] Ibid., 92, 101.

[59] Rhodes House MSS Brit. Emp.s.444 (Buxton Papers), xiii. fo. 428: Gurney to Buxton, 5 Apr. 1835. On Buxton's suggestion, Russell in Apr. 1835 amended his Irish Church resolution (which brought down the Tory government) to the effect that the surplus revenues of the Irish Church should be appropriated for the purpose of 'moral and religious' and not merely 'general' education. See *Hansard*, 3rd ser. xxvii (1835), 770.

Both the Anglican Buxton and the Dissenter Gurney understood their politics to be the product of their religious speculations. Gurney urged Buxton to occupy 'a Wilberforce station'
on public matters of importance, a position which would
answer the question: 'What is the mind of Christianity on the
subject?'[60] For both, the cornerstone of their Christianity was
faith in the saving power of Christ. In his journal for 1812
Gurney wrote: 'I do humbly desire to be enabled to look to
Christ as a precious Saviour who has shed his blood for my
justification and given his spirit for my sanctification.' Buxton
likewise noted in his common-place book that 'a Christian
faith . . . is beyond doubt the great point to be obtained'. For
such evangelicals, good works, although they were not a path
to salvation, were a sign of possessing this faith. Buxton
contended that 'supposing . . . that faith be imparted, the next
step is to make my practice correspond with my faith'.
Commenting on the example of St Paul, the Evangelical noted
that his constant practice, having laid the foundation of faith,
was 'to demand that upon it we should build an edifice of
good works' and so to intimate 'that good works naturally
follow from sound faith'.[61] These good works were not simply
philanthropic undertakings, but duties in the sight of God.
Buxton remarked with regard to his role in the anti-slavery
movement: 'It has pleased God to place some duties upon me
with regard to the poor slaves and these duties I must not
abandon . . . Grant O God that I may be enabled by thy
Holy Spirit to discharge my solemn duties to them'.[62] The
inspiration for the performance of these divine obligations was
other-wordly, even if the parliamentary forum in which they
were performed was mundane.

Unfortunately for the Whigs not only did such men as
Buxton, Gurney and Stephen constitute only one section of
the anti-slavery movement, but their's was a section which
diminished in importance as the decade wore on. Clapham
Sect Evangelicals in any case had only ever been a minority
of Evangelicals in parliament. Of the 45 MPs whom Bradley

---

[60] Ibid.
[61] Swift, *Joseph John Gurney*, 47; Rhodes House MSS Brit. Emp.s.444 (Buxton
Papers), iv. fo. 307: 1 Feb. 1835.
[62] C. Buxton, *Sir T. F. Buxton*, 281.

listed as having Evangelical inclinations in 1830, only 19 were categorized as inclined towards the Saints; of these, even when the Canningites are included, only 14 had liberal affiliations.[63] By the 1830s the Recordite wing of the Evangelical movement, distrusting rationalism, insistent on scriptural purity, increasingly antagonistic towards Popery and intolerant of Catholics, was dominant. As a comparison between Buxton and his son-in-law (Andrew Johnston, the Whig MP for St Andrew's district and elder of the Church of Scotland) indicates, the Evangelical wing of the anti-slavery movement was not immune to this trend. When in 1835 Buxton was prepared to support the Irish appropriation clause, Johnston abstained on Russell's resolution. He objected to teaching the Bible in the adulterated form of the Irish Education Board's scripture extracts, and looked instead to the government to fund the despatch of missionaries to Ireland who would preach the Gospel in Gaelic.[64] Likewise in 1837 Johnston's sense of evangelizing mission predominated over his liberal sympathies. Then, with the belated help of his father-in-law, he proposed that the surplus fund to be created by a rearrangement of church lands be applied not to the relief of Dissenters' grievances, but to church extension. Buxton, by way of contrast, found Johnston's speech on that occasion 'too high churchy'.[65]

This was only one instance of how Buxton and like-minded Evangelicals such as James Stephen were increasingly isolated from mainstream Evangelicalism, which in the 1830s became less tolerant religiously and more conservative politically. Edward Bickersteth, for example, one of the founders of the Evangelical Alliance, who by 1833 had become a pre-millenialist (and so sceptical of the liberal Evangelical aim of bringing about a converted and righteous earth by human agency), resigned his membership of Buxton's Anti-Slavery Society on account of its association with Brougham and

[63] I. C. Bradley, 'The Politics of Godliness: Evangelicals in Parliament 1784–1832', D.Phil. thesis (Oxford, 1974), 276–87.

[64] Rhodes House MSS Brit. Emp.s.444 (Buxton Papers), xiii. fo. 418: P. Johnston to her brothers, 28 Mar. 1835; *Hansard*, 3rd ser., xxvii (1835), 795.

[65] Rhodes House MSS Brit. Emp.s.444 (Buxton Papers), xv. fo. 216: P. Johnston to her brother, 11 Mar. 1837; ibid., xv. fo. 297: R. Buxton to C. Buxton, 23 May 1837; ibid., xv. fo. 300: Buxton to Mrs Johnston, 22 May 1837.

O'Connell. 'The course of public events', he explained, 'has more deeply than ever impressed upon my mind the importance of attention to the plain Christian principle, "Be not unequally yoked with unbelievers." '[66] Likewise the *Record*, the organ of these more extreme Evangelicals, in 1833 denounced the anti-slavery movement as, in Drescher's words, 'an ungodly alliance between Dissenters and contaminated radicals'.[67] In October 1834 the *Eclectic Review* noticed the increasing incidence of Evangelical attacks on Dissent.[68] In such circumstances, liberal Evangelicals such as James Stephen were suspected of heterodoxy. In 1849 Stephen, by then Regius Professor of Modern History at Cambridge, published his *Essays in Ecclesiastical Biography* which resulted in his being accused of heresy: Bonner Hopkins, another Cambridge don, suggested he was unsound on the doctrine of the incarnation and had rejected the damnatory clauses of the Athanasian Creed.[69] Stephen defended himself in a letter to the editor of the Evangelical *Christian Observer*, declaring that he had avowed 'the same religious opinions distinctly and even emphatically' over the previous 35 years as he had in the published work. It was the orthodoxy, not Stephen, which had changed. In 1906 his biographer described his religious outlook as 'latitudinarian', but Stephen himself in 1852 claimed to adhere 'to the theological views of my old Clapham friends'.[70] By the end of the nineteenth century they had ceased to be recognizably orthodox.

The consequence of the increasing prevalence of Recordite views was that the Anglican wing of the anti-slavery movement tended towards Toryism. In the 1830s the Tory party were willing to exploit Evangelical discontent in a bid to extend political support. In 1835 the new Conservative government

---

[66] Rhodes House MSS Brit. Emp.s.18 (B.F.A.S.S.), C/2 fo. 26: Bickersteth to Stokes, 20 May 1835; W. J. Ervine, 'Doctrine and Diplomacy: Some Aspects of the Life and Thought of the Anglican Evangelical Clergy 1797–1837', Ph.D. thesis (Cambridge 1981), esp. Chs 6 & 7.

[67] Drescher, 'Public Opinion and the Destruction of British Colonial Slavery', 37.

[68] *Eclectic Review*. 3rd ser., xii (1834), 301.

[69] W. Hopkins, *Some Points of Christian Doctrine considered* (Cambridge & London, 1849).

[70] CUL Addit. Mss 7888 (Stephen Papers), box II fo. 131/448: copy Stephen to the editor of the *Christian Observer*, 15 May 1852; C. E. Stephen, *Sir James Stephen*, 204, 292.

was certainly aware that Buxton's views were worth cultivating. Lord Aberdeen, Peel's Foreign Secretary, summoned the anti-slavery leader to Downing Street, and Buxton found 'him in his professions as much to my mind as any of his predecessors'.[71] By 1840 the association between anti-slavery and the Tory party was even closer, so much so that Hobhouse declined to assist at a meeting of the African Civilisation Society at Exeter Hall. He reported that 'The principal speakers were conservative. Inglis, Sandon &c., &c., & the whole meeting was evidently got up to impress the Prince [Albert] with the unpopularity of our party.'[72] In 1841 it was a Tory anti-slavery motion, proposed by Sandon as an amendment to the government's budget proposals, which precipitated the dissolution of the Whig administration. Buxton himself was forced to take note of this increasingly illiberal trend. Thus on the sub–committees of his African Civilisation Society he included two Tory MPs, T. D. Acland and William Gladstone. In a similar fashion, at a meeting of the society in 1840 Buxton had to request O'Connell not to speak in order not to offend the Tories; when he refused, the organ was set to work to drown his words.[73] While superficially maintaining non-partisanship, the African Civilisation Society drifted towards the Tory party.

At the same time the Nonconformist wing of the movement was becoming radicalized. Both moderates such as Gurney and the more extreme members of the movement such as Sturge abhorred slavery because it was sinful. For example, Stephen affirmed: 'I hold the practice of slavery . . . to be a practice which God has forbidden,—& from which therefore man should desist, be the expense or risk what it may.'[74] But the more extreme members alone understood this to imply disapproval of using this-wordly tools of negotiation to achieve a Christian end. Compromise smacked of expediency and so of the abandonment of Christian principle and of a trust in

[71] Rhodes House MSS Brit. Emp.s.444 (Buxton Papers), xiii. fo. 404: Buxton to Suffield, 25 Mar. 1835.

[72] BL Addit. MSS 56562 (Broughton Papers): Hobhouse Diary, 1 June 1840.

[73] Rhodes House MSS Brit. Emp.s.444 (Buxton Papers), xxx. sect. 1, fo. 324: list of subcommittees of African Civilization Society; ibid., xix fo. 299a: Buxton to Anna & Charles, 10 June 1840; Gurney Papers, MSS 111 fo. 115: A. Gurney to Gurney, 2 June 1840.

[74] Bod. MSS Eng. Lett.c.3 (Taylor Papers), fo. 84 Stephen to Taylor, 23 June 1827.

Providence. Sturge declared: 'When the Christian is convinced that the principle upon which he acts is correct, I believe it does not become him to examine too closely his probability of success but rather to act in the assurance that if he faithfully does his part, as much success will attend his efforts as is consistent with the will of that Divine leader under whose banner he is enlisted.'[75] In the course of 1835 such extremists as Peter Clare, the Quaker leader of the Manchester abolitionists, Sturge, and George Stephen, brother of James Stephen, began to believe that the Anti-Slavery Society under Buxton's leadership was furthering the interest of the Whigs at the expense of those of the slaves. They regretted Buxton's withdrawal of his motion on 19 June 1835, calling for a committee of inquiry into the conduct of the planters; they objected even more strongly to Buxton's suggestion that Mauritius should receive its share of the £20 million compensation in exchange for the abolition of the apprenticeship. Stephen wrote to *The Times* and published an anonymous article in the *Christian Advocate* attacking this proposal; on the day of the article's publication (30 November), Sturge resigned from the committee of the Anti-Slavery Society. He justified his action with the words: 'I can no longer satisfactorily co-operate with those who appear to me to act upon the principle that the end sanctifies the means'.[76]

Such actions were not simply signs of discontent within the anti-slavery movement. They were also indications of the emergence of provincial radical Dissent. The moderate Quaker John Gurney was at heart something of a metropolitan Whig. He lived in a country house Earlham Hall, and worked in the Norwich bank established on a fortune made two generations previously. He was a close friend of the local Whig bishop, Henry Bathurst, and as a child witnessed the visits of William Frederick, later Duke of Gloucester, to the family home. From 1803 to 1805 he had studied at Oxford under a former Anglican clergyman, John Rogers, who had renounced holy orders to

[75] H. Richard, *Memoirs of Joseph Sturge* (London, 1864), 90.

[76] Rhodes House MSS Brit. Emp.s.444 (Buxton Papers), xiv. fo. 147a: Clare to Buxton, 3 Sept. 1833; ibid., xiv. fo. 176: copy Buxton to Z. Macaulay, 4 Dec. 1835; ibid., xiv. fos. 187 a-c: Sturge to Buxton, 30 Nov. 1835; ibid., xiv. fo. 221: Sturge to Buxton, 17 Dec. 1835.

become a Friend.[77] By contrast Sturge left school when fourteen years old and made his own fortune as a corn factor, transferring his business from Worcester to Birmingham in 1822. There he joined the radical Birmingham Political Union and took an active part in opposing the levy of church-rates in the city. In 1835 he helped to found the Birmingham Voluntary Church Society. Later he was to be one of the earliest members of the Anti-Corn-Law League while his Chartist sympathies led him to found the Complete Suffrage Union in 1842.[78] These activities offended the liberal Anglican values of the Whigs since they put popular agitation above constitutional procedure, dogmatic voluntaryism above the maintenance of a liberal establishment, radical reform above constitutional conservatism. Sturge was to the anti-slavery movement what Miall was to become to the voluntaryist cause.

After 1833 the liberal Whigs were thus faced with a dilemma in their dealings with the anti-slavery movement. Their favourite collaborators, men such as Buxton, Gurney, and James Stephen, who had emerged as prominent leaders in the course of the 1820s and who held out the prospect of support for liberal Anglican doctrines, were being outflanked by other sections of the anti-slavery coalition. On the one hand, in accordance with religious fashion, Anglican Evangelicals were becoming increasingly Tory in their general political affiliation, unwilling to lend support to such pet liberal Anglican schemes as Irish appropriation, national education, and the relief of Dissenters' grievances. On the other hand, the Nonconformist wing of the movement, demanding immediate action when the Whigs offered only amelioration, was associated with policies which were equally anathema to whiggery. In these attitudes they were joined by O'Connell, who by 1838 had emerged as the friend and follower of Sturge.[79] At first the Whigs refused to make their choice and continued to support Buxton, even when he could not control the movement in the country, and so depended on, and was constrained by, Tory support. Eventually the Whigs were to adopt a bold strategy, circumventing the issue altogether, further splitting the anti-slavery movement, and regrouping the liberal coalition around

[77] Swift, *Joseph John Gurney*, passim.   [78] Richard, *Joseph Sturge*, passim.
[79] See, e.g., O'Connell, *Corresp. of Daniel O'Connell*, vi. 151–2.

a new legislative initiative. The first anti-slavery agitation which confronted the Whigs after emancipation was the demand for the abolition of the apprenticeship, a matter which arose in 1837 following Sturge's return from his tour of the West Indies.

The institution of the apprenticeship in 1833 gave the planters ample opportunity to subvert the intentions of the Abolition Act, since it had conferred on them the power to establish the conditions of its operation. The Marquis of Sligo, a former Governor-General of Jamaica, remarked: 'To me it appears impossible to deny that much abuse of the intentions of the Abolition Act has taken place—and that every species of evasion within the letter of the law—certainly far beyond its spirit—has prevailed'.[80] The abolitionists complained that the consequence was that the apprentices were not treated, as Stanley had promised, as the equivalent of 'workmen in England', but continued to be slaves in all but name. The Jamaica Assembly, for example, had refused to arrange the 40.5 hours of compulsory labour so as to include Friday afternoons as well as Saturdays as free time, thus preventing apprentices from properly cultivating their own lands. Although the British government employed stipendiary magistrates, supposedly independent of the planters, to oversee the operation of the Act, the means of penal enforcement remained under the Assembly's control. The consequence was that the flogging of females in the workhouses and the use of the treadmill continued. At the same time the planters attempted to limit the authority of the independent agencies. They transferred jurisdiction over produce-stealing cases from the stipendiary to the general body of magistrates and reduced the size of the police force, which was under the control of the executive, in order to increase reliance for the enforcement of law and order on the militia, which—to a considerable extent—was composed of overseers and book keepers from the estates.[81] Parliamentary means of drawing attention to these abuses were largely unsuccessful. Buxton recalled that witnesses

[80] [P. Howe], *Jamaica under the Apprenticeship System: By a Proprietor* (London, 1838), p. i.
[81] *Hansard*, 3rd ser., xlii (1838), 46–7; W. L. Mathieson, *British Slave Emancipation 1838–1849* (London, 1932), 14; [Howe], *Jamaica under the Apprenticeship System*, 76–81.

summoned by the Select Committee of 1836 refused to repeat in public the evidence they have given in private. 'The consequence', he noted, 'was that I failed in making out a case for immediate Emancipation.'[82] —

A second Select Committee, which reported in June 1837, was equally discouraging to those who favoured the immediate abolition of the apprenticeship.[83] The defeat of Buxton in the 1837 election further weakened the parliamentary wing of the movement, leaving it both leaderless and confused. In November William Evans, the MP for North Derbyshire, was asked to move the renewal of the Apprenticeship Committee, but was reluctant to do so on the ground that it would have made him leader of the anti-slavery movement, a post for which he felt himself unworthy.[84] In this vacuum, as the parliamentary movement foundered, Sturge, acting as leader of the Birmingham Anti-Slavery Society, seized the initiative. At the end of October a meeting of Midland anti-slavery bodies took place in Birmingham; by the beginning of November the Birmingham society, under the names of John Riland, Joseph Sturge and William Morgan, issued a circular for a meeting of anti-slavery delegates to be held on 14 November at Exeter Hall, its purpose to represent the opinions of those in favour of 'Immediate Emancipation'.[85] Sturge intended this to be a provincial and Radical gathering—a rejection of the dilatory leadership of the London committee. Consequently no person living within a ten-mile radius of London received an invitation and the first day's proceedings saw a bitter attack on Buxton and his policies.[86] The latter recalled that George Thompson 'anathematized me in a thundering Philippic', while Sturge 'picked out every point, every occasion, in which I had acted against his views'. William Forster, the future Liberal Cabinet minister who was present at the meeting, referred to 'hot-headed people' who 'took to abusing Uncle B[uxton]'.

[82] Rhodes House MSS Brit. Emp.s.444 (Buxton Papers), xv. fo. 146: Buxton to Dyer, 20 Dec. 1836.

[83] Temperley, *British Anti-Slavery*, 38.

[84] Rhodes House MSS Brit. Emp.s.444 (Buxton Papers) xv. fo. 167a: Evans to Buxton, 18 Nov. 1837.

[85] Ibid., xvi. fo. 159v: circular of the Birmingham Anti-Slavery Society; ibid., xvi. fo. 159x: minute of the Midland Anti-Slavery Societies, 25 Oct. 1837.

[86] Ibid., xvii. fo. 31: 'The Schism in the Anti-Slavery Party', *Christian Advocate*, 15 Jan. 1838.

Although the meeting, by way of apology, eventually passed resolutions lauding Buxton, the attempt at reconciliation did not hide the fact of schism. Following what was intended to be a conciliatory meeting with Sturge, Buxton noted: 'We shall act therefore as independent bodies, yet in concert, they urging the Abolition of the Apprenticeship & I endeavouring to turn their excited vigour to my own purposes.'[87]

Buxton deliberately stayed aloof from this Radical cause. As early as November 1835 he expressed his apprehension that the chief danger to abolition came not so much from the existence of apprenticeship as from the possibility that the planters might pass a vagrancy law, which would be 'Slavery in reality and for a permanence'. He knew that his sanguine appreciation of the state of apprenticeship was not shared by all his colleagues in the anti-slavery movement, noting that in parliament neither Charles Lushington, nor Edward Baines, nor Thomas Thornley, all liberals with a tendency towards Radical Reform, agreed with him. Before Joseph Sturge and John Scoble set out on their journey to the West Indies he warned them to be wary of their prejudices against apprenticeship. 'I have thought . . . that both of you took rather too gloomy a view of the state of things in our colonies', he wrote; the mass of the negroes 'are much better off than during the time of slavery.'[88] Consequently, when Sturge called the Exeter Hall meeting on his return to England, Buxton resolved not to attend, declaring to Josiah Forster that 'It would be against conscience for me to approve the plan of demanding the extinction of the Apprenticeship'. He thought instead that the energies of the agitators should be more productively channelled into demanding the emancipation in the following year of the non–praedial slaves, improving the education of the negroes, and ensuring that vagrancy laws were not passed.[89] The Anti-Slavery Society supported Buxton in this stance. When its committee met on 16 November to discuss the Exeter Hall resolutions, it resolved to continue 'for the present to act

[87] Gurney Papers, MSS 1 fo. 164: Forster to Gurney, 29 Nov. 1837; Rhodes House MSS Brit. Emp.s.444 (Buxton Papers), xvii. fo. 3k: Buxton to Gurney, 16 Dec. 1837.

[88] Ibid., xiv. fo. 143: Buxton to Z. Macaulay, 13 Nov. 1835; ibid., xv. fo. 91: Buxton to Z. Macaulay, 6 Sept. 1836; ibid., xv. fo. 109j: Buxton to Sturge, 9 Oct. 1836.

[89] Ibid., xvi. fos. 159e–l: printed copy Buxton to Forster, 3 Nov. 1837; ibid., xvi. fo. 164: Buxton to Forster, 10 Nov. 1837.

independently'. It also issued a statement which, while it attempted to mitigate the differences between the two bodies, acknowledged that since the prayer to abolish the apprenticeship 'may not be conceded', it 'did not feel exonerated from the duty of demanding that the Imperial Act in its spirit and letter should be carried into full execution'.[90]

As a consequence of the Exeter Hall meeting, the Central Emancipation Committee was formed. This operated as the Agency Committee had earlier in the decade, acting as a co-ordinating committee for the numerous auxiliary societies which had sprung up in the provinces. The attempt to arouse popular enthusiasm proved successful. 'Sturge', reported Buxton, 'has set our good old friends over the kingdom mad, mad, mad with just indignation at the abuses of the Apprenticeship and just as mad in the measures they propose to take.'[91] In these agitations the anti-slavers were joined by militant Dissent. The *Baptist Magazine*, reviewing Sturge's and Harvey's *The West Indies in 1837*, declared 'that the time is come, when it is the duty of the British public to call for immediate abolition of the apprenticeship'. The *Eclectic Review* was no less committed to this view. In its January issue, it commented that the facts of the apprenticeship were 'the facts of slavery'. It attacked Buxton's policy of dissent as displaying 'a timidity and neglect of sound principle at which we are surprised', and demanded an Agency-Committee-style agitation. O'Connell was also in favour of more vigorous agitation, and addressed meetings of the Anti-Slavery Society to this effect.[92] The popular cause first reached parliament when Brougham proposed in the Lords on 20 February 1838 the total abolition of the apprenticeship. On 29 March Sir George Strickland rose in the Commons to propose the resolution 'That this House is of opinion that apprenticeship in the British colonies as established in the year 1833 should cease and determine on the 1st of August in the present year.'[93]

---

[90] Rhodes House MSS Brit. Emp.s.20 (Anti-Slavery Society Minutes), E2/5 p. 53: 16 No. 1837; ibid., Brit. Emp.s.444 (Buxton Papers), xvi. fo. 214: Buxton to Stokes, 13 Dec. 1837.

[91] Rhodes House MSS Brit. Emp.s.444 (Buxton Papers), xvii. fo. 3g: Buxton to Gurney, 16 Dec. 1837.

[92] *Baptist Magazine*, xxx (1838), 15; *Eclectic Review* 4th ser., iii (1838), 69, 77; O'Connell, *Corresp. of Daniel O'Connell*, vi. 151.   [93] *Hansard*, 3rd ser., xlii (1838), 41.

The Whig government continued to pursue the policy established by Buxton, rejecting provincial Radicalism in favour of liberal moderation. Indeed in February 1838 Sir George Grey, the Evangelical Under-Secretary for the Colonies, invited Buxton to re-enter parliament—an invitation which he refused while commenting: 'it makes me sad that Lord Glenelg's character [the Colonial Secretary] is so much misunderstood by some people',[94] The government's defence was that by the Act of 1833 a compact had been made with the West Indian proprietors in which it was acknowledged that the period of apprenticeship formed part of the compensation for abolition. Since the West Indians had not significantly breached that compact, parliament in its turn was not entitled to do so.[95] At the same time the government agreed with Buxton that there had been infractions of the spirit of the Act, and so proposed to legislate accordingly a decision which, incidentally, had been taken long before the popular agitation reached Westminster, even if it was not announced until Brougham proposed his motion.[96] Sir George Grey declared that the government's Abolition Act Amendment Bill was designed 'to meet every existing evil, to compel . . . a compliance with the human and judicious system of management in the regulation of the hours of labour and the grant of allowances, and to supply those defects in the existing laws which the Colonial Legislatures . . . [have] failed to supply'.[97] Moreover, at least one member of the Cabinet, Howick, was prepared to agree to the abolition of the apprenticeship if the West Indian proprietors were prepared to concur. On 26 March Bernal, the West Indian representative, proposed to a meeting of West Indian proprietors a number of resolutions which Howick had drafted, recommending to the colonial legislatures the immediate abolition of the apprenticeship. These they unanimously rejected. Consequently the Cabinet, albeit with some trepidation, adhered to their decision of 24 March to oppose Strickland's motion.[98]

[94] Rhodes House MSS Brit. Emp.s.444 (Buxton Papers), xvii. fo. 50: Buxton to Sir George Grey, 23 Feb. 1838.
[95] *Hansard*, 3rd ser., xlii (1838), 68 ff.
[96] Grey Papers C3/3: Howick Jour., 17 Feb. 1838.
[97] *Hansard*, 3rd ser., lxii (1838), 95.
[98] BL Addit. MSS 56559 (Broughton Papers): Hobhouse Diary, 24 Mar. 1838.

The trepidation was justified. Although the government had a majority of 54, if the Tories voting on either side are subtracted, the government was in a minority of 10, and its opponents included O'Connell and 32 Irish MPs.[99] In a division on a similar motion proposed by Sir Eardley Wilmot on 22 May, which took place in a thin House when 24 friends of the government were absent, the government was in a minority of three.[100] The Whigs' difficulties were increased by the fact that in March Buxton had renounced his previous stance and instead sided with the followers of Sturge. He explained in a letter (which was never sent) to the anti-slavery delegates who met at Fendell's Hotel on 22 March: 'The Public has responded to your call with a more generous and more enthusiastic unanimity than I had dared to expect. The will of the nation has been powerfully declared in favour of the Abolition of the Apprenticeship.' Buxton not only saw Glenelg and Rice on 26 March to explain his volte-face, but also made preparations to attend a meeting of the anti-slavery delegates. In effect this was an attempt at reconciliation with the wing of the movement he had spurned in 1837.[101] Consequently moderate anti-slavers such as Lushington supported Strickland's motion, while the government found itself in the company of Tories such as Sandon and Gladstone.[102] This was worrying for the Whigs. It meant that the anti-slavery movement was increasingly dominated by provincial militants with whom the Whigs had little desire to associate, militants who demanded not only abolition, but voluntaryism and Radical reform as well. Sir George Grey moved and carried a motion on 28 May declaring that the House would not adopt any proceedings to give effect to Wilmot's motion. The Radical wing of the anti-slavery movement had found the limits to liberal Anglican toleration of their agitation.[103] None the less it did not mean that the liberal Whigs had abandoned the negro. They still hoped that a united Whig-liberal coalition existed on the anti-slavery

[99] Ibid., 31 Mar. 1838; O'Connell, *Corresp. of Daniel O'Connell*, vi. 153.

[100] BL Addit. MSS. 56559 (Broughton Papers): Hobhouse Diary, 22 May 1838; *Hansard*, 3rd ser., xliii (1838), 123.

[101] Rhodes House MSS Brit. Emp.s.444 (Buxton Papers), xvii. fo. 92: Buxton to Anti-Slavery Delegates, 22 Mar. 1838; ibid., xvii. fo. 114: E. N. Buxton to Mrs Johnston, 28 Mar. 1838.

[102] *Hansard*, 3rd ser., xlii (1838), 257–60.   [103] Ibid., xliii (1838), 376.

issue, and with this expectation they maintained a close association with Buxton.

Since his parliamentary defeat in 1837, Buxton had turned his attention away from the particular plight of the negroes in the West Indies to the continued prevalence of the slave trade off the coast of Africa. As he wrote in August 1837, 'The subject which now chiefly occupies my mind is the Slave Trade—I am well convinced that the Government is altogether wrong in its mode of going to work.'[104] He argued that it was insufficient to attack the trade in slaves as a form of piracy; rather what was needed was to stop the trade at its source, namely the African who sold his child. He regarded it as a fact that the African had 'acquired a taste for the productions of the civilized world'. The solution therefore was to exploit this taste by instituting a more profitable trade in which Africans could acquire western artefacts by exchanging them not for people, but for agricultural produce. Buxton suggested that trading posts for this purpose should be established on the Niger together with agricultural settlements: the idea was to allow commerce to encourage Christianity.[105] In the spring of 1838 the government, under attack from the anti-slavery movement, was particularly vulnerable to such suggestions. Forster believed that Buxton had great influence at the Colonial Office because he had not been a party to the 'Movement' for the abolition of the apprenticeship. Andrew Johnston's wife noted that the government was lamenting Buxton's absence from parliament because it meant that there was 'no one to transact business with'. Thus when Buxton first mooted his plan to Rice in early April, the minister offered to place it before the Cabinet. In April and May Buxton saw Palmerston, Howick, and Glenelg; by the middle of August he had distributed a printed version of his plan to all Cabinet members.[106]

[104] Rhodes House MSS Brit. Emp.s.444 (Buxton Papers), xvi. fo. 123: Buxton to Jeremie, 25 Aug. 1837.
[105] T. F. Buxton, *Letter on the Slave Trade to the Lord Viscount Melbourne and the other Members of His Majesty's Cabinet Council* (London, 1838).
[106] Rhodes House MSS Brit. Emp.s.444 (Buxton Papers), xvii. fo. 105: J. Forster to W. Forster, 26 Mar. 1838; ibid., fo. 124: Mrs Johnston to C. Buxton, 6 Apr. 1838; ibid., fo. 130: Buxton to Miss Gurney & Miss Buxton, 9 Apr. 1838; ibid., fo. 141a: Buxton to A. Gurney, 4 May 1838; ibid., fo. 152: Buxton to Miss Gurney, 19 May 1838; ibid., fo. 188: Buxton to Mr and Mrs Johnston, 14 Aug. 1838.

Members of the Cabinet were privately somewhat sceptical of Buxton's scheme, Melbourne thinking that the obstacles and objections to it were numerous, an opinion in which Russell concurred.[107] Minto, in charge of the Admiralty, produced a memorandum challenging Buxton's assumption that the profits which were derived from the slave trade were such that no 'honest combination of all nations' could abolish the commerce by a system of treaties. Minto, indeed, thought treaties and protocols would be more effective than the introduction of legitimate commerce for, as he noted, 'the whole habits and pursuits of natives cannot be changed in a day'.[108] Palmerston, for his part, believed Buxton's scheme to be 'a wild and crude idea'.[109] Nevertheless the Cabinet agreed on 23 November to do something about Buxton's proposal. The latter reported to Gurney that the ministers 'all admit that the facts are placed beyond dispute. They tell me that they want no further evidence of the extent and horrors of the trade; and they admit in very strong terms that they are converts to the views which I have developed'.[110] By December the Cabinet had agreed to five points of a nine-point plan of 'practical suggestions' drawn up by Buxton, were favourable to a further two and only refused to commit themselves on one. Those agreed to included the purchase of Fernando Po from the Spanish government, to be used as a trading post; the sending out of persons to make treaties with native chiefs for the suppression of the slave trade and for the purchase of territory suitable for the cultivation of tropical goods; and the encouragement of British subjects to trade with these settlements. By the end of the year Andrew Johnston thought Buxton was acting 'as a sort of non-commissioned though high member of the Cabinet'.[111]

[107] BL Microfilm 859/6 (Melbourne Papers): Melbourne to Russell, 3 Sept. 1838; Broadlands MSS MEL-RU (Melbourne Papers), fo. 55: Russell to Melbourne, 6 Sept. 1838.

[108] Memo n.d. [by Minto], enc. Minto's presentation copy of T. F. Buxton's *Letter on the Slave Trade* deposited in Bod.

[109] J. Gallagher, 'Fowell Buxton and the New Africa Policy 1838–1842', *Cambridge Historical Journal*, x (1950), 40.

[110] BL Addit. MSS 56560 (Broughton Papers): Hobhouse Diary, 23 Nov. 1838; C. Buxton, *Sir T. F. Buxton*, 454.

[111] Rhodes House MSS Brit. Emp.s.444 (Buxton Papers), xvii. fo. 282: 'Practical Suggestions on Africa connected with the Slave Trade', 5 Dec. 1838; ibid., fos. 299a–c:

The expedition up the Niger, which Buxton had requested, eventually set sail in May 1841. Its outcome was disastrous. Of the 145 white men who set out on the expedition, 130 suffered from fever and 40 died. The model farm lasted barely a year.[112] These events heralded the collapse of Buxton's scheme. In January 1843 the African Civilization Society, which Buxton had founded in 1839 to further his cause with the public, was wound up.[113] In part this outcome was the consequence of Whig negligence. Two changes of Colonial Secretary and the temporary resignation of the government in 1839 caused considerable delays. Government retrenchment resulted first in the government's refusal to buy steamers for the expedition, and subsequently in its agreement to purchase only three instead of the four requested by Buxton.[114] But the African disaster was also the consequence of incompetence on the part of the expedition's organizers. According to the scheme which Buxton presented to Normanby in August 1839, the steamers were to leave England not later than November, and to enter the Niger very early in January. In the event the expedition set sail in May and entered the Niger in August, at the height of the rainy season when the risk of malaria was at its greatest. Moreover the expedition entered the river through the Nun mouth, although Buxton had been warned that it was one 'of the most deadly spots in all the coast of Africa & equal if not even worse than Sierra Leone'.[115] The Whig Cabinet had been justified (if not altogether for the right reasons) in its initial scepticism of Buxton's plan.

The Whigs had supported Buxton in any case because they thought that his views would set the tone of the anti-slavery movement for the coming year. Melbourne believed Buxton's book, his *Letter on the Slave Trade*, written in 1838 and presented

Buxton to Mrs Buxton, 22 Dec. 1838; ibid., fo. 302: A. Johnston to Miss Gurney & Miss Buxton, 28 Dec. 1838.

[112] Gallagher, 'Buxton and the New Africa Policy', 56–7.

[113] Rhodes House MSS Brit. Emp.s.444 (Buxton Papers), xx a. fo. 331: [?] to Miss Gurney, 25 Jan. 1843.

[114] Ibid., xviii fo. 377: Buxton to Mrs Buxton, 10 Sept. 1839; ibid., fo. 379: A. Johnston to Mrs Johnston, 11 Sept. 1839.

[115] Ibid., fo. 352: Buxton to Normanby, 24 Aug. 1839; ibid., xxvii. fo. 173: draft memo by A. Johnston, May 1839; ibid., xxx. fo. 25: J. McQueen to Buxton, 29 Apr. 1839; ibid., xxxi. fo. 243: note of a conversation with Capt. Beecroft, 21 May 1838; Gallagher, 'Buxton and the New Africa Policy', 55.

to ministers, 'gave notice of the course which will be taken and the questions which will be pressed by the Saints and Dissenters in the next Session.'[116] In this he was mistaken. Buxton was unable to reunite the anti-slavery movement around his campaign to colonize Africa. Lushington reported a meeting in Manchester to support the African Civilization Society as a 'failure'. 'I must not leave you in the dark', he continued. 'All those classes who were our former friends are gone or lukewarm.' Buxton himself expressed his disappointment that Dissenters in Dorsetshire had not been in favour of his scheme.[117] After 1838 he was able to garner the support of the Saints, but the more popular aid of the Dissenters eluded him. The leading Nonconformist periodical, the *Eclectic Review*, criticized the African Civilization Society on the ground that 'the truly religious population of Britian', which included 'the great bulk of the anti-slavery friends', did not believe—as Buxton appeared to—that Christianity would follow civilization in Africa. In view of the continued prevalence of slavery and, in his view, the government's encouragement of it, O'Connell believed Buxton's society to be 'a humbug'. Even more importantly, Sturge, the leader of the Nonconformist and militant wing of the movement, true to his Quaker principles, attacked Buxton's proposed remedy on pacifist grounds: Buxton had advocated the increased use of armed cruisers and the expedition itself was to carry weapons. Writing to Gurney, Sturge explained: 'I cannot see how we can mix ourselves up with a society whose founder & whose committee have given . . . direct encouragement to an armed force.'[118]

The consequence was that there were two rival anti-slavery movements in the late 1830s, each vying for the same constituency: that led by Buxton and that led by Sturge who in 1839 founded the British and Foreign Anti-Slavery Society to further the abolition of the slave trade 'by [such] moral and religious means only as will not directly or indirectly sanction the

[116] Broadlands MSS GC/ME (Palmerston Papers), fo. 229: Melbourne to Palmerston, 3 Sept. 1838; BL Microfilm 859/5 (Melbourne Papers): Palmerston to Melbourne, 4 Sept. 1838.

[117] Rhodes House MSS Brit. Emp.s.444 (Buxton Papers), xix. fos. 455k–l: Lushington to Buxton, 29 Oct. 1840; ibid., xx. fo. 10: Buxton to Bingham, 3 Nov. 1840.

[118] *Eclectic Review*, 4th ser., viii (1840), 465; O'Connell *Corresp. of Daniel O'Connell*, vi. 382–3; Gurney Papers, MSS i. fo. 411: Sturge to Gurney, 16 Oct. 1840.

employment of an armed force for its persecution or suppression'.[119] Although Buxton nominally sat on the committee of the BFASS, he never attended its meetings.[120] The BFASS indeed actively campaigned against Buxton's own society. In Bury St Edmund's, when a local noble family attempted to form an auxiliary society in connection with the African Civilization Society, a member of the BFASS started publishing letters in the local newspaper to show 'the impracticability of that society'. Likewise, when a similar society was mooted in Bristol, John Scoble commented that 'This must be prevented if possible.' It was Samuel Gurney's belief that the agents of the BFASS spoke against the African Civilization Society in the course of their travels.[121] Thus, in supporting Buxton it was impossible for the Whigs to recapture their alliance with the anti-slavery movement as a whole. One section of it was becoming increasingly wedded to Sturgeite Radicalism, while the other was becoming increasingly wary of offending the Tories by appearing to be too demonstrably Whig. This lesson the government was to learn in 1839 when the West India question resurfaced: the liberal coalition fragmented and the Whigs found themselves abandoned.

Despite the refusal of the Whigs in April and May 1838 to abolish the apprenticeship unilaterally, the local assemblies in the course of that summer proceeded to do so on their own account. By July, apprenticeship had ceased in all the West India colonies. This created more problems than it solved since it meant that the slaves achieved their freedom in a society which had not yet adapted to these new conditions, a society in which the control of law and order primarily rested with planters who were antagonistic to the newly liberated negroes. The government's Abolition Amendment Act, which had dealt with such issues as the use of the treadmill and the flogging of women, applied only to the apprentices. As soon as the apprenticeship ceased, 'there was no security' against

---

[119] Rhodes House MSS Brit. Emp.s.20 (Anti-Slavery Society Minutes), E2/6 i. 1: 27 Feb. 1839.

[120] Rhodes House MSS Brit. Emp.s.444 (Buxton Papers), xix. fo. 302: Buxton to Stephen, 25 June 1840.

[121] Rhodes House MSS Brit. Emp.s.18 (B.F.A.S.S.), C6 fo. 151: Fennell to Tredgold, 9 Dec., 1840; ibid., C10 fo. 27: Scoble to Tredgold, 15 Nov. 1840; ibid., C110 fo. 22: Gurney to Sturge, 24 Oct. 1840.

The Anti-Slavery Movement 289

the negro being committed to prison under the vagrancy law, and against 'his being treated there as he had been formerly treated when a slave without any power on behalf of the executive government to interfere on his behalf'.[122] The government consequently introduced a West India Prison Bill in the House of Lords, which empowered the local governments to take over the control of the prisons. By October 1838 this Act had reached Jamaica. The Assembly there not only refused to pass it, but also declined to conduct any business with the exception of passing certain Bills necessary to maintain the public credit. The Governor-General, Sir Lionel Smith, prorogued the Assembly which, on its recall, refused once more to conduct public business. The Governor responded by dissolving the Assembly, but the new Assembly, which met on 18 December, confirmed the resolutions of its predecessor, in consequence of which it was also prorogued. Smith, the Governor-General, sent a despatch to London stating that 'no House of Assembly can now be found that will acknowledge the authority of the Queen, Lords and Commons to enact laws for Jamaica or that will be likely to pass just and prudent laws for the large portion of the negro population lately brought to freedom.'[123]

By the middle of January 1839 the Colonial Office had taken action, and Henry Taylor had drawn up a minute for submission to the Cabinet.[124] Taylor proposed that the assemblies in all the chartered West India colonies should be abolished and replaced by legislatures on the model of those in the Crown Colonies, in which the power of the Crown was paramount.[125] By the time the measure reached Cabinet on 28 January, it had been reduced to a proposal for the suspension of the Jamaica Assembly for a limited period. Howick, the most prominent anti-slaver in the Cabinet, described Glenelg's presentation as 'a most wretched statement' of 'a most paltry measure'. In his turn he drew up an alternative, more comprehensive plan, advocating the suspension for two years of the assemblies in all the chartered colonies, and the granting of power to the Governor and Councils to pass first, such

[122] Temperley, *British Anti Slavery*, 41; *Hansard*, 3rd ser., xlvi (1839), 1255.
[123] Mathieson, *British Slave Emancipation*, 21; *Hansard*, 3rd ser., xlvi (1839). 1244–7.
[124] Taylor, *Autobiography*, i. 249–50.
[125] Ibid., i. 260.

temporary laws as might be necessary, and second, with the aid of Commissioners from London, such permanent laws as would meet with the approval of parliament and the Queen-in-Council. The Cabinet would only agree to a proposition restricted to Jamaica, whereupon Howick threatened to resign. He explained to Melbourne: 'I am so deeply convinced that the final success of the great experiment of the abolition of slavery . . . will be greatly endangered that . . . I have to request that you will lay before the Queen my humble resignation.' He finally agreed to stay in office in order to prevent Russell from joining him in resignation. As a concession, in part, to Howick's and Russell's concern for the fate of the negro (as well, it should be added, for the safety of Canada, then in revolt), Glenelg left the Colonial Office and Normanby took his place, bringing with him as his Under-Secretary the Evangelical Henry Labouchere.[126] The new ministers eventually agreed on a compromise. On 9 April Labouchere moved for leave to bring in a Bill for the suspension of the Jamaican constitution for five years, its legislative functions to be exercised by the Governor and Council alone, and, pacifying Howick, to add to the Council three councillors to be sent from London. The goverment once more acted in the name of the anti-slavery movement.[127]

The government's measure was controversial since it offended the liberal and Radical doctrine that the rights of representative assemblies should be respected. Peel shrewdly noted on the announcement of the Bill that it contradicted the principle of Durham's Report with respect to Canada, that executive officers should be made responsible to popular assemblies.[128] The Jamaica Bill was thus a direct challenge to the militant anti-slavers of the previous year (who had pressed for the abolition of the apprenticeship) to decide between their Radicalism and their anti-slavery, between opposing and supporting the Whig government. These became the predominant issues in the course of the subsequent debate, especially after 26 April when Peel declared his opposition and the

---

[126] Grey Papers C3/4: Howick Jour., 28, 30 Jan., 4, 9 Feb. 1839; ibid., box 150 file 5, fo. 5: paper by Howick, 30 Jan. 1839; BL Microfilm 859/4 (Melbourne Papers): Howick to Melbourne, 31 Jan. 1839, Russell to Howick, 31 Jan. 1839; BL Addit. MSS 56560 (Broughton Papers): Hobhouse Diary, 30 Jan. 1839.

[127] *Hansard*, 3rd ser., xlvi (1839), 1260.   [128] Ibid., 1282.

prospect of a Whig defeat became likely.[129] Hume declared the government's proposal to be 'totally unnecessary', and accused the Whigs of 'adopting Tory maxims, suspending constitution after constitution and rendering everything insecure'. Conversely, his Radical colleague and Durham's chief secretary in Canada, Charles Buller, was a decided supporter of the Bill, not because the Assembly had refused to implement the Prisons Act ('Nothing is clearer than the duty of the supreme legislative authority to respect the independent exercise of that authority'), but because he recognized the need to fit the political institutions of Jamaica to the altered state of society produced by emancipation.[130] In the division of 6 May, however, the government majority was reduced to five, ten Radicals voting against the Whigs. On 7 May the Cabinet met and agreed to resign, Palmerston noting that the decision 'was brought about more by internal than external causes, jealousies, discontents'.[131] In 1839 the Whig government fell, in part on the anti-slavery issue, influenced by the desire to place the Tories, or so it was believed, in the 'Most unpopular of all possible situations'. In his resignation speech, Melbourne declared that his loss of office was on account of being unable to carry into full effect the Emancipation Act.[132]

Regrettably, the Whigs' plight did not so much rally the anti-slavery movement to the government as indicate the movement's apathy to the continuance of the liberal administration. As early as 12 April Lushington wrote to Buxton asking him what should be done to support the government. Buxton replied that he was in the middle of preparing his book on the slave trade, and so reluctant to come up to town to do anything. In any case, he argued, any activity they undertook would be ineffectual unless the Sturgeites agreed to agitate public opinion.[133] On 18 April Sturge's BFASS came into

[129] Ibid., xlvii (1839), 575; BL Addit. MSS 56560 (Broughton Papers): Hobhouse Diary, 26 Apr, 1839.

[130] *Hansard*, 3rd ser., xlvii (1839), 825–7, 841, 844.

[131] Ibid., 972; Grey Papers C3/4: Howick Jor., 6 May 1839; BL Addit. MSS 56560 (Broughton Papers): Hobhouse Diary, 6, 7 May 1839.

[132] BL Microfilm 859/2 (Melbourne Papers): Ebrington to Melbourne, 2 May 1839; Rhodes House MSS Brit. Emp.s.444 (Buxton Papers), xviii. fo. 92e: Lushington to Buxton, 8 May 1839.

[133] Ibid., fos. 48a–d: Lushington to Buxton, 12 Apr. 1839; ibid., fo. 50: Buxton to Lushington, 13 Apr. 1839.

existence at Exeter Hall, but the society's minutes for that
month contain no mention of the government's plan to suspend
the Jamaican constitution. Johnston complained with respect
to Sturge that 'the little man who affects to head the Anti-
Slavery party at the present time is not inclined to patronize
the Government because they will not "go the whole Hog"
with his radicalism'. The Whigs complained 'with too much
justice' of being deserted by the anti-slavery movement.[134]
When Lushington again asked Buxton what the anti-slavers
ought to do to aid the Whigs, the former leader replied:
'Nothing occurs to me'; two days later he added: 'You will
wonder at my apathy.'[135] Buxton was indeed wary of being
linked too closely to the Whigs on what was understood to be
a party issue, knowing that his scheme to abolish the slave
trade relied equally on the support of Tories such as Gladstone
and Sandon.[136] The most Buxton had been prepared to do was
to summon a meeting of the London Anti-Slavery Society on
26 April in order to pass a resolution approving the suspension
of the Jamaican constitution and to order the printing of a
pamphlet, for circulation among MPs, defending the action.
It was a hollow gesture. The previous March the society had
agreed to suspend its operations.[137] The movement which had
gathered around the Whigs in 1830 was too fragmented to be
recreated in 1839.

By 1841 the Whigs had learnt this lesson. The government
was then prepared to lose the support of a substantial section
of the anti-slavery movement. As part of the 1841 budget, as
well as proposing the reduction of duties on corn to a fixed
and moderate level, the Chancellor of the Exchequer wished
to increase revenue by substantially lowering duties on the
importation of foreign sugar from 63s. per hundredweight to
36s., as compared with the existing duty, which he proposed
to continue, of 24s. on colonial sugar. Baring hoped thereby

[134] Ibid., fo. 73: A. Johnston to Plumptre, 30 Apr. 1839; ibid., fo. 92b: Lushington
to Buxton, 7 May [1839].
[135] Ibid., fo. 93: Buxton to Lushington, 8 May 1839; ibid., fo. 94: Buxton to
Lushington, 10 May 1839.
[136] Ibid., fo. 92n: Lushington to Buxton, 9 May [1839].
[137] Rhodes House MSS Brit. Emp.s.20 (Anti-Slavery Society Minutes), E2/5, 112:
12 Mar. 1839; ibid., 114: 26 Apr. 1839; [J. Beldam], *Reasons for Temporarily Suspending
the Constitution of Jamaica* (London, 1839).

to raise an additional revenue of £660,000.[138] The BFASS objected to the measure as offering encouragement to slavery. At its meetings of 26 March and 5 May it prepared a memorial and resolutions protesting against the measure which it presented to Lord Melbourne and had printed in the newspapers.[139] Its argument was that in encouraging the consumption of sugar, the reduction of duties would also encourage the slave-holding countries of Cuba and Brazil to increase their production of slave-grown sugar, and so increase the incidence of slavery. Buxton, in a rare moment of agreement with Sturge, also attacked the government's plan as offering an inducement to slave owners. Writing to the Duchess of Sutherland, he asked: 'Shall England which has hitherto been the only hope of Africa . . . by a single act do more for the promotion of the Slave Trade than it has ever done by its suppression . . . ?'[140] When the issue reached parliament in the guise of an amendment tabled by the Tory Sandon, the anti-slavery movement marshalled its political forces. Dr. Lushington declared that the Whig measure would 'lower them in the faces of Europe'; Wilmot described the introduction to England of slave-grown sugar as 'a detestable object'; and Sandon himself declared that the government's proposal would defeat 'the great experiment' of emancipation.[141]

The Whigs treated the issue as one of expediency rather than principle. Whereas the most committed anti-slavers such as G. W. Alexander believed that the cause was in compliance with apostolic commands, and hence could admit of no doubt with regard to its beneficial effects, the Whigs treated emancipation purely as an experiment, the benefits of which had to be proven. As Joseph Beldam remarked, its success needed to be judged against 'the moral arithmetic of life.'[142] The Whig government's justification for its action was twofold. First, the government argued that free labour should be able to compete

[138] *Hansard*, 3rd ser., lvii (1841), 1306; ibid., lviii (1841), 474.

[139] Rhodes House MSS Brit. Emp.s.20 (Anti-Slavery Society Minutes), E2/6, 362: 26 March 1841; ibid., 383–4: 5 May 1841.

[140] Rhodes House MSS Brit. Emp.s.444 (Buxton Papers), xx. fos. 155–6: Buxton to Duchess of Sutherland, 10 Feb. 1841.

[141] *Hansard*, 3rd ser., lviii (1841), 53, 80, 446.

[142] G. W. Alexander, *Some Observations on an Article in the Edinburgh Review on the Grounds and Objects of the Budget* (London, 1841), 8; [J. Beldam], *A Review of the Late Proposed Measure for the Reduction of the Duties in Sugar* (London, 1841), 21.

successfully with slave-labour. There was consequently no reason to suppose that in the long-run slave-grown sugar would drive out free-grown sugar. Moreover, if it were the case that free-grown sugar was more profitable, this would act as an inducement to other countries to abolish slavery. Second, the government argued that the plight of the West Indians had to be weighed against the condition of the British manufacturing population. Russell maintained that 'Having done all that we could in the generosity of our nature for the people in that country [the West Indies] . . . I do not think that we should be justified in giving our attention exclusively to their interests . . . whilst the people of this country were suffering from want of the common comforts and necessaries of life.' He proceeded to contrast what he called 'the extreme comfort' of the people of Jamaica with the poverty of the labouring populations of Bolton and Manchester, concluding that the introduction of cheap sugar, one 'of the most essential articles of the most moderate and temperate diet', would be of greater benefit than the continued protection of the freed West Indians—a protection which in any case would restrict their industry and enterprise.[143]

The Whig decision to flout the anti-slavery movement was based on the knowledge not only that the movement had distanced itself from Whiggery, but also that it had become too fragmented to be considered a strong liberal cause. The reunion of Buxton and Sturge on the issue of sugar hid the fact that many members of the anti-slavery movement in the country, at a time of manufacturing depression, preferred the prospect of industrial progress, brought about by free trade, to the continued existence of self-denying ordinances. Auxiliary societies from Bradford, Manchester, Derby, Preston, and elsewhere signified their opposition to the resolutions of the London Committee of the BFASS: 18 notices of dissent were recorded in the letter books of the Anti-Slavery Society.[144] Likewise many Nonconformists were prepared to place their adherence to free trade above their commitment to emancipation. The Unitarian MP for Manchester, Mark Philips,

---

[143] *Hansard*, 3rd ser., lviii (1841), 31–2, 262–9.
[144] See, Rhodes House MSS Brit. Emp.s.18 (BFASS) C/4–10, *passim*: letterbooks of the BFASS.

declared his support for the government's measure as did Greg, his colleague in the city's representation.[145] Such support was most clearly demonstrated in the attendance in August 1841 of 645 ministers at a conference held in Manchester to oppose the Corn Laws. These were primarily Dissenters affiliated to liberal politics: only two Anglicans attended, and the Tory leadership of the Wesleyans refused to send an official deputation.[146] The Whigs also drew support for their measure from Radicals such as Charles Buller, Charles Villiers, William Ewart, and O'Connell himself. Indeed all ten of the Radicals who had voted against the government on the suspension of the Jamaican constitution supported the ministry on Sandon's amendment.[147]

In proposing the reduction of the foreign sugar duties in conjunction with a fiscal policy of increasing revenue by stimulating trade, the Whigs gathered to their fold almost all the sections of the liberal alliance which had been drifting apart on the anti-slavery issue. Even some prominent moderate anti-slavers such as Sir George Strickland and William Evans, who might have been expected to follow Buxton's lead, joined the government in the lobbies on what was in effect an issue of no confidence. If 1839 indicated the disintegration of the liberal alliance on the issue of anti-slavery, 1841 demonstrated how it was possible to repair the damage by the invocation of another rallying cry, comparable to that of the original emancipationist fervour of 1830. Nevertheless the course of the anti-slavery movement in the 1830s revealed just how difficult it was for the liberal Anglicans to maintain the coalition on which their success depended. Even more important, it demonstrated a disquieting divergence of ends among the variance sections of the alliance. While liberal Anglicans such as Russell or Howick might have had much in common with Evangelicals such as Buxton or Dissenters such as Gurney, they differed widely in their political views from other nominally liberal Evangelicals such as Johnston or nominally liberal Dissenters such as Sturge, who were more representative of the trends in each of their respective sections of the

[145] *Hansard*, 3rd ser., lviii (1841), 127, 532.
[146] *Report of the Conference of Ministers of All Denominations on the Corn Laws* (Manchester, 1841), iii, 90, 145.   [147] *Hansard*, 3rd ser., lviii (1841), 97, 585, 609, 668–9.

coalition. There were limits within the liberal movement to the political support the liberal Anglicans could expect to receive. The question the Whigs had to face in the 1840s was whether such disagreements outweighed the advantage of alliance; whether the moderate free-trade cause could bind the Evangelicals, liberal Anglicans, Dissenters, Irish, and Radicals together as Reform, the emancipation of the slaves, Irish Church Reform, education, and the relief of Dissenters' grievances had done in the previous decade.

As the 1841 election was to demonstrate, in the short-term the so-called 'free trade' budget of 1841 enabled the Whigs to sustain their liberal Anglican coalition. Although Betty Kemp has called the elections a 'Whig disaster',[148] this is to judge them in isolation from the catastrophic defeat towards which the Whigs appeared to be heading in the winter of 1840–1. In six by-elections held between November 1840 and May 1841, the Whigs failed to retain their seats, losing three in February. These losses represented almost half the total number of gains which the Tories made between the election of 1837 and the dissolution of 1841.[149] In parliament the government was also weak, so much so that at the end of April 1841 it was forced to withdraw the Irish Registration Bill. Melbourne concluded: 'I feel we shall be greatly beat at a General Election.'[150] The task which the Whigs faced was less that of securing electoral victory—an impossible aspiration—than that of ensuring that defeat was honourable and that the party entered opposition united. In this regard fighting the election on a moderate free trade issue proved a good stratagem. As Poulett Thomson, now Lord Sydenham, noted, the advantage of the 1841 budget was that 'it does not meddle with religious prejudices, it does not relate to Ireland. It does not touch on any theoretical questions on which parties have so long been divided. It is a new flag to fight under'.[151] At the same time it did not associate the party with the extremist Anti-Corn-Law Leaguers whom such prominent, free-trading Whigs as Fitzwilliam opposed. Hugh Fortescue, expressing his pleasure at this circumstance,

[148] B. Kemp, 'The General Election of 1841', *History*, xxxvii (1952), 150.
[149] H. S. Smith, *The Register of Parliamentary Contested Elections* (2nd edn., London 1842), *passim*.
[150] Sanders, *Lord Melbourne's Papers*, 418.
[151] PRO 30/22 4A (Russell Papers), fo. 334: Sydenham to Russell, 15 May 1841.

admitted to being 'enchanted at the prospect of fighting an election on the issue.[152] Howick, the former Whig Cabinet minister who had recently attacked the government on the Irish registration question, acknowledged that 'something of this kind was wanted to unite the liberal party'.[153] The only members of the liberal coalition seriously disaffected by the government's proposals were the county members. Robert Gordon, a long-standing proponent of the Corn Laws, resigned from the government on the introduction of the budget, while Lord Worsley and Thomas Hodges, representing Lincolnshire and Kent respectively, declared in parliament their opposition to the measure.

But in electoral terms such opposition was not significant. As Joseph Parkes, the Whig election agent, noted, the Whigs had only 43 or 44 county MPs in England and Wales (out of a total of 159) after the 1837 election. The Whig county representation had declined steadily since 1832, regardless of the Corn Law and free-trade questions. Parkes claimed further that the government had long well known 'that nearly half of this class of the liberal Representation was lost' at the next dissolution, 'be it when or by whom made'.[154] Parkes was accurate in his prediction. According to Melbourne, the upshot in the counties represented a considerable success for the party. Writing to his private secretary, William Cowper, he declared that 'The Counties are not worse than I expected. Indeed better, for I thought we should lose them all.'[155] The budget proposals were not universally unpopular in the country as Palmerston reported from Taunton. The measure, he wrote, 'is popular in this town & I am told will not hurt us with the farmers in the rural district'.[156] Nevertheless the real contest was fought in the towns. Parkes expected that the free-trade question would lose the Whigs votes in the agricultural boroughs and gain them in the larger commercial

---

[152] DCRO MSS 1262M/LI (Fortescue Papers), fo. 197: Fortescue to Ebrington, 1 May 1841.

[153] NLS MSS 15052 (Ellice Papers), fo. 65: Howick to Ellice, 14 July 1841.

[154] PRO 30/22 4 A (Russell Papers), fo. 279: Parkes to Russell, 7 May 1841.

[155] Broadlands MSS MEL/CO (Melbourne Papers), fo. 38: Melbourne to Cowper, 14 July 1841.

[156] BL Microfilm 859/6 (Melbourne Papers): Palmerston to Melbourne, 17 June 1841.

districts, with the overall result that Whig numbers would be about 300.[157] In this estimate he was about ten seats too optimistic, but the failure, he noted, was not so much due to English and Welsh as to Irish seats.[158] In England the Whigs made an overall gain of five seats from the Tories in boroughs with electorates greater than 1,000: of the 58 borough seats with electorates over 2,000, the Whigs won 43.[159] Although such victories were not sufficient to off-set the losses (which, since they included the seats of Morpeth and Howick, two prominent Whig leaders, were notable), they did mean that the government's overall defeat was by no means discreditable. Ellice, the chief manager of the 1841 election fund, believed that had the Whigs dissolved on any other issue, the Conservative majority would have been double what it was (150, not 75). The free-trade cry had rejuvenated the Whig party which had been tottering in government. 'Here we are landed out of all our difficulties', wrote Ellice, 'with a . . . party more willing to go into opposition than they would have been to embark on another attempt [to form a government]. In what better situation could people have prayed us to be placed?'[160] The 1841 election proved that the liberal Anglican coalition had sufficient strength in it to survive the rigours of the late 1830s and still emerge as a formidable opposition to the challenges Peel was to make to Whig policies in the course of the 1840s. If there were strains in the liberal coalition, it was by no means a spent and redundant force.

*

In 1846, after only five years in opposition, and following the split in the Conservative party caused by Peel's abolition of the Corn Laws, the Whigs once more took office. Lord John Russell, the leading liberal Anglican Whig, assumed his rightful position of leader of the Whig party and Prime Minister. Howick, now Earl Grey, became Secretary for War and Colonies, Hobhouse returned to the Board of Control, and

---

[157] PRO 30/22 4 A (Russell Papers), fo. 279: Parkes to Russell, 7 May 1841.
[158] BL Microfilm 859/15 (Melbourne Papers): Parkes to Melbourne, 15 July 1841.
[159] Blake, *Conservative Party from Peel to Churchill*, 44, 46.
[160] NLS MSS 15044 (Ellice Papers), fo. 68: Ellice to Parkes, 16 July, 1841.

Morpeth held the office of First Commissioner of Woods and Forest, later moving to the Duchy of Lancaster. In these positions they added more causes to the Whig political agenda. In 1849 Russell took up the cry of moderate parliamentary reform with the intention of granting the vote to all independent citizens. At the Colonial Office Grey instituted the policy of introducing responsible self-government in settlers' colonies. Morpeth set up the General Board of Health in 1848. These were all signs that Whiggery had not as yet become a fossilized, exclusively aristocratic, and landed connection. In retrospect such initiatives may appear to be the final flowerings of a decaying political party, but to hold such a view is to over-indulge in the vice of hindsight. If Russell's government was the last purely Whig administration, the Whigs as a political group were to form an important part of subsequent Liberal administrations until at least 1886.[161] Even more important, such Whigs helped to set the political agenda of Victorian England. The question of parliamentary reform despite Palmerton's lack of enthusiasm, periodically agitated administrations until the passing of the Second Reform Act in 1867. Colonial expansion was a perennial preoccupation of politicians as the empire grew in India and the Far East in the 1850s and 1860s, and in Africa in the 1880s. Despite the abolition of the General Board of Health in 1854, issues of social reform did not altogether slip from political view, with the consequence that Liberal administration abolished flogging in the army in 1868, passed an elementary Education Act in 1870, and granted trade unions legal status in 1871. Most significantly, the nineteenth-century Liberal party established a form of non-sectarian Christian polity following the repeal of the Test and Corporation Acts and Catholic Emancipation. It permitted Nonconformists the right to sit on municipal corporations, to enter the ancient universities, not to pay church-rates and to be subject only to a civil registration at birth, marriage, and death. This practical religious toleration, one of the main

---

[161] Harold Macmillan has suggested an even later date for the end to Whig influence, remarking that 'the last of the great Whig figures to make a striking impact was Lord [5 Marquis of] Lansdowne' who held office in Asquith's wartime coalition government. See H. Macmillan, *The Past Masters* (London, 1978), 192. Macmillan, in his turn, has been described as being 'at heart, a Whig'. See G. Hutchinson, *The Last Edwardian At No. 10* (London, 1979), 9.

planks of nineteenth-century liberalism, was also the chief cause of the liberal Anglican Whigs. This essay has explored the intellectual and political origins of their stance. In so doing it has contributed to an understanding not only of the history of English liberalism, but also of the foundations of Victorian politics. Whether in practice non-sectarian politics has ever truly existed in the manner these liberals desired, and in the name of which they proposed legislation, is for the reader to judge.

Bibliography

PRIMARY SOURCES

I. *Unpublished Manuscript Sources*

Balliol College, Oxford:
  Jenkyns Papers (on loan to Prior's Kitchen, Durham University)
Baring Brothers:
  Northbrook (F. T. Baring) Papers
B[erkshire] C[ounty] R[ecord] O[ffice] (Reading):
  3rd Earl Radnor Papers
Bod[leian] Library, Oxford:
  4th Earl of Clarendon Papers
  Correspondence of Bishop Copleston
  Graham Papers (Microfilm)
  Lovelace–Byron Papers
  Oxford University Archives
  Bishop Shuttleworth Papers
  Taylor Papers
  Wynter Papers
Borthwick Institute, York:
  1st Viscount Halifax Papers (Charles Wood)
B[ritish] L[ibrary], London:
  1st Baron Broughton (Hobhouse) Papers
  Bishop Butler Papers
  Halifax (Charles Wood) Papers
  Holland House Papers
  Melbourne Papers (Microfilm)
  Russell Papers
  3rd Earl Spencer Papers
  Sturge Papers
  Wellesley Papers
British Library of Political and Economic Science, London School of Economics, London:
  C. P. Villiers Papers
Brock, M. G., Warden of Nuffield College, Oxford, transcripts in the possession of:
  Ellice Papers
  Grey Papers

Knowsley Papers
Lambton Papers
C[ambridge] U[niversity] L[ibrary]:
  Cam[bridge] Univ[ersity] Papers
  Hey Papers
  Sedgwick Papers
  Stephen Papers
  University Archives
Castle Howard, York:
  Carlisle (Morpeth) Papers
Christ Church College, Oxford:
  College Archives
  T. V. Short's Commonplace Book
Congregational Library, London:
  Hadfield Correspondence
  Wilson Papers
D[evon] C[ounty] R[ecord] O[ffice], Exeter:
  Copleston Papers
  Fortescue (Ebrington) Papers
Dr Williams's Library, London:
  General Body of Protestant Dissenting Ministers
  Minute Books
  Protestant Society Minute Books
Durham County Record Office:
  Pease Papers
Durham University:
  2nd Earl Grey Papers
  3rd Earl Grey (Howick) Papers
  Temple Chevallier Papers
  Thorp Papers
Guildhall Library, London:
  Protestant Dissenting Deputies Minute Books
  United Committee Minute Books
Hertford County Record Office:
  Melbourne Papers
Historical Manuscripts Commission, London:
  Broadlands Papers (Palmerston Papers, Melbourne Papers)
John Rylands Library, Manchester:
  Kay-Shuttleworth Papers
  Monteagle (Spring Rice) Papers
Lambeth Palace Library, London:
  Blomfield Papers
  Howley Papers

Longley Papers
Whately Papers
Longford Castle, Salisbury:
  3rd Earl Radnor Papers
Mulgrave Castle, Whitby:
  Normanby (Mulgrave) Papers
N[ational] L[ibrary] of I[reland]:
  Monteagle (Spring Rice) Papers
N[ational] L[ibrary] of S[cotland]:
  Ellice Papers
  Minto Papers
  Rutherford Papers
Nottingham University Library:
  Ossington (J. E. Denison) Papers
Oriel College, Oxford:
  Hampden Papers
  Hawkins Papers
P[ublic] R[ecord] O[ffice], Kew:
  Russell Papers
Pusey House, Oxford:
  3rd Earl Radnor Papers
Queen's College, Oxford:
  Derby (Stanley) Papers, in the custody of the Provost, the Rt. Hon. The Lord Blake
Rhodes House Library, Oxford:
  Buxton Papers
  B[ritish] [And] F[oreign] A[nti-] S[lavery] S[ociety] Papers
Scottish Record Office:
  Dalhousie (Fox Maule) Papers
Society of Friends, London:
  Allen Papers
  Gurney Papers
S[taffordshire] C[ounty] R[ecord] O[ffice]:
  Hatherton (E. J. Littleton) Papers
  Leveson-Gower Papers
  Lichfield Papers
T[rinity] C[ollege], C[ambridge]:
  Blakesley Papers
  Houghton Papers
  Peacock Papers
  Thirlwall Papers
  Whewell Papers
  Wordsworth Papers

University College, London:
  Brougham Papers
  Parkes Papers
  Russell Papers (Ogden MSS)
  W[est] S[ussex] C[ounty] R[ecord] O[ffice], Chichester:
  Bessborough (Duncannon) Papers
  Goodwood (Richmond) Papers

The Earl of Shelburne refused permission to consult the papers of the 3rd Marquis of Lansdowne.

II. *Official Publications*

Hansard's Parliamentary Debates, 2nd and 3rd series.
The Parliamentary History of England
Parliamentary Papers 1836, vi, xxxvi.
Parliamentary Papers 1837, viii.
Parliamentary Papers 1837–8, xxxvi.
Parliamentary Papers 1839, xli.
Parliamentary Papers 1840, xl.
Parliamentary Papers 1852–3, xciv.
Parliamentary Papers 1854, xv.

III. *Newspapers and Periodicals*

Baptist Magazine
British Critic
Cambridge Chronicle
Eclectic Review
Edinburgh Review
Fraser's Magazine
Gentleman's Magazine
Monthly Repository
Morning Chronicle
Quarterly Journal of Education
Quarterly Review
The Times

IV. *Printed Primary Works*

Articles, books, diaries, letters, nineteenth-century biographies, pamphlets, sermons, and tracts.

Ainslie, G., *An Historical Account of the Oaths and Subscriptions required in the University of Cambridge on Matriculation and of all Persons who proceed to the Degree of Master of Arts* (Cambridge, 1833).
Alexander, G. W., *Some Observations on the Concluding Portion of an*

Article in the Edinburgh Review on the Grounds and Objects on the Budget in a Letter to the Editor of the Morning Chronicle (London, 1841).

Allen, J., *A Charge delivered to the Clergy of the Diocese of Bristol at the Primary Visitation of that Diocese in October 1835* (London, 1835).

—— *A Charge delivered to the Clergy of the Diocese of Ely at the Second Quadrennial Visitation of that Part of the Diocese comprising the Isle of Ely and the County of Cambridge and at the Primary Visitation of the Other Part of the Diocese, held on June, July, and August 1841* (London, 1841).

—— *A Charge delivered to the Clergy of the Isle of Ely and the County of Cambridge at the Primary Visitation of that Part of the Diocese of Ely in September 1837* (London, 1837).

Allen, W., *Life: With Selections from his Correspondence* (London, 1846).

Arnold, T. (ed.), Thucydides, *Peloponesian War* (8th edn., Oxford, 1874).

—— *Fragments on Church and State* (London, 1845).

—— *Sermons: Chiefly on the Interpretation of Scripture* (London, 1845).

—— *Fragment on the Church* (London, 1844)

—— *Introductory Lectures on Modern History* (Oxford, 1842).

—— 'The Oxford Malignants and Dr Hampden', *Edinburgh Review*, lxiii (1836), 225–39.

—— *Principles of Church Reform* (4th edn., London, 1833).

—— *Thirteen Letters on our Social Condition* (n.p., 1832).

—— *Sermons* (London, 1829–34).

Aspinall, A. (ed.), *Three Early Nineteenth-Century Diaries* (London, 1952)

Aspland, R. B., *Memoir of the Life, Works, and Correspondence of Revd Robert Aspland of Hackney* (London, 1850).

Austin, S., *On National Education* (London, 1839).

Baines, E., *The Life of Edward Baines* (2nd edn., London, 1859).

Baring, T. G. (ed.), *Journals and Correspondence of Francis Thornhill Baring, Lord Northbrook* (2 vols., London, 1905).

Bateman, J., *The Life of the Right Revd Daniel Wilson, DD.* (2 vols., London, 1860)

Beldam, J., *A Review of the Late Proposed Measure for the Reduction of the Duties in Sugar* (London, 1841).

—— *Reasons for Temporarily Suspending the Constitution of Jamaica* (London, 1839).

Blagbourne, J., *The Revenues of the National Universities considered, with a View to their being opened to Dissenters: Being a Reply amongst Others to the Arguments of Dr Turton, Dean of Peterborough* (London, 1835).

Blakesley, J. W., *Conciones Academicae: Ten Sermons preached before the University of Cambridge* (London, 1843).

—— *Thoughts on the Recommendations of the Ecclesiastical Commission, particularly in Reference to their Probable Influence on the State of the Universities* (London, 1837).

Bloomfield, B. C. (ed.), *The Autobiography of Sir James Kay-Shuttleworth* (London, 1964).

Blomfield, A., *A Memoir of C. J. Blomfield* (2nd edn., London, 1864).

Boone, J. S., *Sermons* (London, 1853).

[Brewster, D.], 'Lord Brougham's Discourse on Natural Theology', *Edinburgh Review*, lxiv (1837), 263–302.

Brougham, H., *Life and Times* (London, 1871).

—— 'A Discourse of Natural Theology', *Collected Works* (11 vols., London and Glasgow, 1855–61), vi.

—— *A Letter on National Education to the Duke of Bedford, KG*, (Edinburgh, 1839).

—— 'The Education Bill', *Edinburgh Review*, lxvi (1838), 439–49.

—— 'Remarks on an Article in the *Edinburgh Review*, No. 135, on the Times of George the Third and George the Fourth', *Edinburgh Review*, lxviii (1838), 191–262.

—— 'National Education', *Edinburgh Review*, lxv (1837), 245–64.

—— *Speech on the Education of the People May 21 1835* (London, 1835).

—— 'Library of Useful Knowledge', *Edinburgh Review*, li (1830), 526–8.

—— *Objects, Advantages, and Pleasures of Science* (London, 1830).

—— 'Diffusion of Knowledge', *Edinburgh Review*, xlvii (1828), 118–34.

—— 'London University and King's College', *Edinburgh Review*, xlviii (1828), 235–58.

—— 'SDUK', *Edinburgh Review*, xlvi (1827), 225–44.

—— 'New University in London', *Edinburgh Review*, xlii (1825), 346–67.

—— *Practical Observations upon the Education of the Poor* (16th edn., London, 1825).

—— 'Scientific Education of the People', *Edinburgh Review*, xli (1824), 96–122.

—— 'Establishments at Hofwyl', *Edinburgh Review*, xxxii (1819), 487–507.

—— 'Mr Fellenberg's Establishments at Hofwyl', *Edinburgh Review*, xxxi (1818), 150–65.

Burgon, J. W., *Lives of Twelve Good Men* (London, 1889).

Burnet, J., *The Lecture delivered in the Town Hall, Birmingham, at a Public Meeting of the Birmingham Voluntary Church Society on Thursday Evening, February 23, 1836* (Birmingham, 1836).

Bury, J. P. T. (ed.), *Romilly's Cambridge Diary 1832–1842* (Cambridge, 1967).

Butler, J., *The Analogy of Religion, Natural and Revealed, to the Constitution and Course of Nature* (London, 1834).

—— *Works*, ed. W. E. Gladstone (3 vols., Oxford, 1896).

Butler, S., *A Charge delivered to the Clergy of the Archdeaconry of Derby and at the Visitations at Derby and Chesterfield, June 26 and 27, 1834* (London, 1834).

—— *A Charge delivered to the Clergy of the Archdeaconry of Derby at the Visitations at Derby and Chesterfield June 25 and 26, 1835* (London, 1835).

—— *Thoughts on Church Dignities* (London, 1839).

—— *Thoughts on the Present System of Academic Education in the University of Cambridge. By Eubulus* (London, 1822)

Butler, S., *The Life and Letters of Dr Samuel Butler* (London, 1896)

Buxton, C., *Memoirs of Sir Thomas Fowell Buxton, Bart.* (London, 1866).

Buxton, T. F., *Letter on the Slave Trade to the Lord Viscount Melbourne and Other Members of Her Majesty's Cabinet Council* (London, 1838).

Cameron, C. R., *Does Dr Hampden's Inaugural Lecture imply any Change in his Theological Principles?* (Oxford, 1836).

Central, Society of Education, *First Publication* (London, 1837).

—— *Second Publication* (London, 1838).

—— *Third Publication* (London, 1839).

Chalmers, T., *Lectures on the Establishment and Extension of National Churches* (Glasgow, 1838).

Church, R. W., *The Oxford Movement: Twelve Years 1833–1845* (London, 1922).

Church Rate, *A Full Report of the Great Meeting in the Town-Hall on Friday, December 5, 1834* (Birmingham, 1834).

Church-Rate Abolition Society, *Plain Hints to Rate Players respecting the Proposition of Church Rates* (London, 1838).

Churton, E., *A Letter to an Edinburgh Reviewer on the Case of the Oxford Malignants and Dr Hampden* (London, 1836).

Clark, J. W. and Hughes, T. M., *Life and Letters of the Revd Adam Sedgwick* (Cambridge, 1890).

Colquhoun, J. C., *The System of National Education in Ireland: Its Principle and Practice* (Cheltenham, 1838).

Coleridge, S. T., *On the Constitution of Church and State* (London, 1839).

Combe, G., 'State of Massachusetts', *Edinburgh Review*, lxxiii (1841), 486–502.

Conder, E. R., *Memoir of Josiah Conder* (London, 1857).

Conybeare, W. J., 'Church Parties', *Edinburgh Review*, xcviii (1853), 273–342.

Copleston, E., *Remains; With an Introduction by R. Whately* (London, 1854).
—— *An Enquiry into the Doctrines of Necessity and Predestination* (London, 1821).
Copleston, W. J., *Memoir of Edward Copleston, DD, Bishop of Llandaff* (London, 1851).
Cousin, V., *On the State of Education in Holland*, trans. L. Horner (London, 1838).
Creighton, M., *Memoir of Sir George Grey* (London, 1901).

Dalby, W., *The Real Question at Issue between the Opponents and the Supporters of a Bill now before the House of Commons* (London, 1834).
Dale, R. W., *The Old Evangelicalism and the New* (London, 1889).
—— *The Life and Letters of John Angell James* (London, 1861).
Davenport-Hill, R. and F., *A Memoir of Matthew Davenport Hill* (London, 1878).
Davison, J., *Discourses on Prophecy* (London, 1824).
Davys, G., 'Danger of Delay in Religion', *Original Family Sermons* (London, 1833).
—— *A Sermon preached in the Cathedral Church of St Paul on Thursday, June 27, 1833 at the Festival of the Sons of the Clergy* (London, 1833).
Denison, E., *A Charge delivered to the Clergy of the Diocese of Salisbury at the Primary Visitation of Edward, Lord Bishop of Salisbury in August and September 1839* (Salisbury, 1839).
—— *The Church the Teacher of her Children: A Sermon preached at St Margaret's Westminster on Sunday, May 12th, 1839* (Oxford, 1839).
—— *Speech of the Lord Bishop of Salisbury on behalf of the Diocesan Board of Education at a Meeting held in Salisbury on Wednesday, October 9, 1839, the Rt. Hon. The Earl of Shaftesbury in the Chair* (Salisbury, 1839).
—— *A Review of the State of the Question respecting the Admission of Dissenters to the Universities* (London, 1835).
Dickinson, C., *Pastoral Epistle from His Holiness the Pope to Some Members of the University of Oxford* (London, 1836).
—— *Observations on Church Reform* (Dublin, 1833).
Douglas, Mrs Stair, *The Life and Selections from the Correspondence of William Whewell, DD* (London, 1881).
Dunn, H., *Sketches* (London, 1848).
—— *A Reply to the Misrepresentations of the Revd Francis Close* (2nd edn., London, 1839).
—— *National Education, the Question of Questions; Being an Apology for the Bible in Schools for the Nation With remarks on Centralization and the Voluntary Societies and Brief Notes on Lord Brougham's Bill* (2nd edn., London, 1838).

Duppa, B. F., 'Industrial Schools for the Peasantry', *Central Society of Education. First Publication* (London, 1837).

—— 'Lord Brougham's Bill for Promoting Education in England and Wales', *Central Society of Education. Second Publication* (London, 1838).

[Eden, C. P.], *Self-Protection: The Case of the Articles. By Clericus.* (Oxford, 1835).

Eden, R., *A Plan of Church Reform with a Letter to the King* (6th edn., London, 1832).

[Anon.], *1835 and 1772: The Present Attack on Subscription compared with the Last in a Letter to 'A Resident Member of Convocation' occasioned by some Remarks in his 'Letter to the Earl of Radnor'. By a Resident Member of Convocation* (Oxford, 1835).

[Anon.], *Elucidations of Dr Hampden's Theological Statements* (Oxford and London, 1836).

Evangelical Voluntary Church Association, *Advocacy of the Voluntary Principle on Religious Grounds Only* (London, n.d.).

—— *The Church: An Appeal in Behalf of its Freedom* (London, 1841).

Evans, R. W., *A Statement respecting the Lectures at Present given on the Subject of the New Testament in Trinity College Cambridge* (Cambridge, 1834).

Fitzpatrick, W. J. (ed.), *Correspondence of Daniel O'Connell* (2 vols., London, 1888).

—— *Memoir of Richard Whately* (London, 1864).

Foster, J., *The Established Church: Letters on the Voluntary Principle by a Quiet Looker-On. Published in the Morning Chronicle of the 2nd and 3rd October 1834* (London, 1834).

Fox, H. R. V. (Lord Holland), *Further Memoirs of the Whig Party*, ed. Lord Stavordale, (London, 1905).

—— *Memoirs of the Whig Party during My Time*, ed. 4th Lord Holland (London, 1852–4).

Fulford, R. and Strachey, L. (eds.), *The Greville Memoirs* (8 vols., London, 1938).

Gladstone, W. E., *The State in Its Relations with the Church* (4th edn., Farnborough, 1969).

[Gleig, G. R.], 'Lord Brougham on Natural Theology', *Fraser's Magazine*, xii (1835), 375–93.

Gooch, G. P. (ed.), *Later Correspondence of Lord John Russell 1840–1878* (London, 1925).

Gower, R., *My Reminiscences* (London, 1895).

—— ed., *Stafford House Letters* (London, 1891).

Grey, Lt. Gen. Hon. C., *Some Account of the Life and Opinions of Charles, Second Earl Grey* (London, 1861).

Grey, H. G., *The Colonial Policy of Lord John Russell's Administration* (London, 1853).

Grinfield, E. W., *Reflections after a Visit to the University of Oxford on the Occasion of the Late Proceedings against the Regius Professor of Divinity in a Letter to the Rector of Lincoln College* (Oxford and London, 1836).

Hall, F. R., *A Letter to R. M. Beverley Esq.*, (Cambridge, 1834).

[Hamilton, W.], 'Admission of Dissenters to the Universities', *Edinburgh Review*, lx (1834), 202–30.

—— 'The Universities and the Dissenters', *Edinburgh Review*, lx (1835), 422–45.

Hampden, H. (ed.), *Some Memorials of R. D. Hampden, Bishop of Hereford* (London, 1871).

Hampden, R. D., *Introduction to the Second Edition of the Bampton Lectures of the Year 1832* (London, 1837).

—— 'The Scholastic Philosophy considered in its Relation to Christian Theology', *The Bampton Lectures for 1833* (2nd edn., London, 1837).

—— *Observations on Religious Dissent with Particular Reference to the Use of Religious Tests in the University of Oxford* (2nd edn., Oxford, 1834).

—— *An Essay on the Philosophical Evidence of Christianity* (London, 1827).

Hare, J. C. (ed.), *John Sterling Essays and Tales* (London, 1848).

—— *The Better Prospects of the Church: A Charge to the Clergy of the Archdeaconry of Lewes delivered at the Visitation in 1840* (2nd edn., London, 1840).

—— *Sermons preach in Herstmonceux Church* (London and Cambridge, 1841).

—— *The Victory of Faith and Other Sermons* (Cambridge, 1840).

—— *Portions of the Psalms* (London, 1839).

—— *A Vindication of Niebuhr's History of Rome from the Charges of the Quarterly Review* (Cambridge, 1829).

Haviland, J., *A Letter to the Members of the Senate on the Subject of the Subscriptions required of Medical Graduates in the University of Cambridge* (Cambridge, 1833).

Hawkins, E., *A Dissertation upon the Use and Importance of Unauthoritative Tradition* (London, 1889).

—— *The Duty of Private Judgement* (London, 1838).

[——] *A Letter to the Earl of Radnor upon the Oaths, Dispensations, and Subscriptions to the XXXIX Articles at the University of Oxford* (Oxford, 1835).

Henslow, J. S., *Address to the Reformers of the Town of Cambridge* (Cambridge, 1835).

Herbert, W., *Works* (3 vols., London, 1842).

Hey, J., *Lectures in Divinity* (4 vols., Cambridge, 1796).
Hildyard, J., *Five Sermons* (London, 1841)).
Hill, M. D., *Answer to a Letter from the Secretary of a Society for Political Instruction* (London, 1836).
Hill, M. D. and Hill, R., *Public Education* (2nd edn., London, 1825).
Hinds, S., *An Inquiry into the Proofs, Nature, and Extent of Inspiration, and into the Authority of Scripture* (Oxford, 1831).
—— *The History of the Rise and Early Progress of Christianity* (London, 1828).
Hobhouse, J. C., *Recollections of a Long Life*, ed. Lady Dorchester (London, 1909–11).
—— *A Supplicatory Letter to Lord Viscount Castlereagh* (London, 1819).
—— *A Trifling Mistake in Thomas Lord Erskine's Recent Preface shortly noticed and respectfully corrected in a Letter to His Lordship by the Author of the 'Defence of the People'* (London, 1819).
Holroyd, M. (ed.), *Memorials of the Life of George Elwes Corrie* (Cambridge, 1890).
Holyoake, G. J., *Life of Joseph Rayner Stephens* (London, n.d.).
Hopkins, W. B., *Some Points of Christian Doctrine considered with Reference to Certain Theories put forth by the Right Hon. Sir J. Stephen, KCB, LLD* (Cambridge and London, 1849).
Howard, G. W. F. (Lord Morpeth), *The Vice-Regal Speeches and Addresses, Lectures, and Poems of the late Earl of Carlisle, KG*, ed. J. J. Gaskin (Dublin, London, and Edinburgh, 1865).
—— *Lectures and Addresses in Aid of Popular Education* (London, 1852).
—— *Report of Speech at the Dinner of Freeholders at Saddleworth* (Manchester, 1830).
—— *The Last of the Greeks: Or the Fall of Constantinople. A Tragedy* (London, 1828).
[Howe, P.] (2nd Marquis of Sligo), *Jamaica under the Apprenticeship System. By a Proprietor* (London, 1838).
Hull, W. W., *Remarks intended ot show how far Dr Hampden may have been Misunderstood and Misrepresented during the Present Controversy at Oxford* (2nd edn., London, Oxford and Cambridge, 1836)
Hume, D., *Natural History of Religion*, ed. A. T. W. Colver (Oxford, 1976).
—— *Enquiries Concerning the Human Understanding*, ed. L. A. Selby-Bigge (2nd edn., Oxford, 1957).
—— *Dialogues concerning Natural Religion* (London, 1779).
—— *The History of Great Britain* (Edinburgh, 1754).
—— *Philosophical Essays concerning Human Understanding* (London, 1748).
Kay-Shuttleworth, J., *Four Periods of Public Education* (London, 1862).

Keble, J., *National Apostasy* (Oxford, 1833).
King, W., *A Discourse on Predestination: With Notes by Revd Richard Whately* (Oxford, 1821).
Kriegel, A. D. (ed.), *The Holland House Diaries 1831–1840* (London, 1977).
Lancaster, T. W., *Strictures on a Late Publication of Dr Hampden* (Oxford, 1836).
Lascelles, C. (ed.), *Extracts from the Journals kept by George Howard, Earl of Carlisle* (Printed for private circulation only, London, 1871).
Lee, S., *Some Remarks on the Dean of Peterborough's Tract entitled 'Thoughts on the Admission of Persons without regard to their Religious Opinions to Certain Degrees in the Universities of England* (Cambridge, 1834).
Le Marchant, D., *Memoir of John Charles, Viscount Althorp, Third Earl Spencer* (London, 1876).
[Anon.], *A Letter to His Grace the Archbishop of Canterbury explanatory of the Proceedings at Oxford on the Appointment of the Present Regius Professor of Divinity. By a Member of the University of Oxford* (3rd edn., London, 1836).
Locke, J. *An Essay concerning Human Understanding*, ed. P. H. Nidditch (Oxford, 1979).
Longley, C. T., *A Charge delivered to the Diocese of Ripon at the Triennial Visitation in July and August 1841* (London, 1841).
—— *A Charge delivered to the Diocese of Ripon at the Primary Visitation of the New Diocese in July and August 1838* (London, 1838).
Lonsdale, H., *The Worthies of Cumberland* (6 vols., London, 1872).
Macaulay, T. B., *History of England from the Accession of James the Second* (London, 1899).
—— *Critical and Historical Essays* (London, 1894).
—— 'Church and State', *Edinburgh Review*, lxix (1839), 231–80.
—— *A Speech delivered in the House of Commons in the Debate of Wednesday, March 2 1831 on Lord John Russell's Motion for Leave to bring in a Bill to amend the Representation of the People in England and Wales* (London, 1831).
McGregor, J., *The Common Sense View of the Sugar Question addressed to all Classes and Parties: By MBT* (2nd edn., London, 1841).
Maltby, E., *A Charge delivered to the Clergy of the Diocese of Durham* (n.p., 1837).
—— *A Charge delivered to the Clergy of the Archdeaconry of Lewes at the Primary Visitation of Edward, Lord Bishop of Chichester in May 1834* (London, 1834).
[Marriott, C.], *Meaning of Subscription* (Oxford, 1835).
Maurice, F. D., *The Kingdom of Christ*, ed. A. R. Vidler (London, 1958).

—— *Subscription No Bondage: By Rusticus* (Oxford, 1835).

Maxwell, H. (ed.), *Life and Letters of the Fourth Earl of Clarendon* (2 vols., London, 1913).

—— *The Creevey Papers* (2 vols., London, 1903).

Miall, A., *Life of Edward Miall* (London, 1884).

Miller, J., *Conspectus of the Hampden Case at Oxford in a Letter to a Friend* (London, 1836).

Milman, H. H., *Address delivered at the Opening of the City of Westminster Literary, Scientific, and Mechanics' Institute* (2nd edn., London, 1837).

—— 'The Church and the Voluntary System', *Quarterly Review*, liii (1835), 174–215.

Moore, T., *Memoirs, Journal, and Correspondence*, ed. Lord John Russell (8 vols., London, 1853–56).

Morgan, T., *A Lecture on the Views and Designs of the Birmingham Voluntary Church Society delivered in Cannon-Street Meeting House, April 14th, 1836. Published under the Direction of the Committee* (Birmingham, 1836).

Mozley, T., *Reminiscences, Chiefly of Oriel College and the Oxford Movement* (London, 1882).

Musgrave, T., *A Charge delivered to the Clergy of the Diocese of York, June 1849 at the Primary Visitation of Thomas Archbishop of York* (3rd edn., London, 1849).

Newman, J. H., *Apologia Pro Vita Sua* (London, 1966).

Noel, Byron, A. I., *What de Fellenberg has done for Education* (London, 1839).

[Anon.], *A Non-Resident M. A.'s Self-Vindication for attending to support the Vote of Censure on Dr Hampden's Writings* (Oxford, 1836).

[Anon.], *Notices of the Viceroyalty of the Late Earl of Bessborough* (Dublin, 1847).

Otter, W., *A Charge delivered to the Clergy of the Diocese of Chichester in June 1838 at His Primary Visitation* (London, 1838).

Paley, W., *A View of the Evidence of Christianity in Three Parts with Annotations by Richard Whately DD* (London, 1859).

—— *The Principles of Moral and Political Philosophy* (19th edn., London, 1811).

[Anon.], *The Pamphlets in Defence of the Oxford Use of Subscription to the XXXIX Articles at Matriculation published in Collected Form* (Oxford and London, 1835).

Parker, C. S., *Life and Letters of Sir James Graham* (2 vols., London, 1907).

—— *Sir Robert Peel* (2nd edn., London, 1899).

Pattison, M., *Memoirs* (London, 1885).

Peacock, G., *Observations on the Statutes of the University of Cambridge* (London, 1841).

Perry, C., *Clerical Education* (London, 1841).

Phipps, C. H. (The Earl of Mulgrave), *Speech in the House of Lords on Friday, 12th of February 1841 on moving the Second Reading of the Drainage of Buildings Bill* (London, 1841).

—— *Speech in the House of Lords on Monday, 27th November 1837 on the Motion of the Earl of Roden for Certain Papers referring to the State of Ireland* (2nd edn., London, 1837).

—— *The English At Home* (London, 1830).

—— *The English in France* (London, 1828).

Pillans, J., 'National Education', *Edinburgh Review*, lviii (1833), 1–30.

Pinney, T. (ed.), *The Letters of Thomas Babington Macaulay* (Cambridge, 1976), iii.

Pius, Father, *Life of Father Ignatius of St Paul* (Dublin, 1866).

Political Economy Club, *Minutes, Members, Attendances, and Questions 1821–1882* (London, 1882), iv.

—— *Names of Members 1821–1860, Rules of the Club, and List of Questions Discussed 1833–1860* (London, 1860).

Powell, B., *A Supplement to Tradition Unveiled* (London and Oxford, 1840).

—— *State Education considered with Reference to Prevalent Misconceptions on Religious Grounds* (London and Oxford, 1840).

—— *Tradition Unveiled: Or, an Exposition of the Pretensions and Tendency of Authoritative Teaching in the Church* (London, 1839).

—— *Remarks on a Letter from the Revd H. A. Woodgate to Viscount Melbourne Relative to the Appointment of Dr Hampden* (Oxford and London, 1836).

—— *Rational Religion Examined: Or, Remarks on the Pretensions of Unitarianism; Especially as compared with those Systems which professedly discard Reason* (London, 1826).

Pryme, G., *Autobiographic Recollections* (Cambridge, 1870).

[Pusey, E. B.], *Dr Hampden's Past and Present Statements compared* (Oxford, 1836).

—— *Dr Hampden's Theological Statements and the Thirty-Nine Articles compared by a Resident Member of Convocation* (Oxford, 1836).

—— *Questions respectfully addressed to Members of Convocation on the Subjoined Declaration which is proposed as a Substitute for the Subscription to the Thirty-Nine Articles at Matriculation* (Oxford, 1835).

—— *Remarks on the Prospective and Past Benefits of Cathedral Institutions in the Promotion of Sound Religious Knowledge and of Clerical Education* (2nd edn., London, 1833).

Religious Freedom Society, *Report presented at the First Annual Meeting* (London, 1840).

—— *Report of the Conference of Ministers of All Denominations on the Corn*

Laws held in Manchester August 17, 18, 19, 20, 1841 (Manchester, 1841).
Rice, T. Spring, 'Distress of the Manufacturing Districts—Cause and Remedies', *Edinburgh Review*, lxxvii (1843), 190–227.
—— 'The Late Session', *Edinburgh Review*, lxxv (1842), 241–274.
—— 'Ministerial Plan of Education', *Edinburgh Review* lxx (1839), 149–80.
—— *Speech on the Repeal of the Union* (London, 1834)
—— 'Financial Measures of the Government', *Edinburgh Review*, lviii (1833), 144–51.
—— 'Ireland', *Edinburgh Review*, lvii (1833), 248–72.
—— 'Mr Sadler's School of Italian Economists', *Edinburgh Review*, l (1830), 344–63.
—— 'The Education of the Irish Poor', *Edinburgh Review*, xliii (1825), 197–224.
Richard, H., *Memoirs of Joseph Sturge* (London, 1864).
Rigg, J. H., *Modern Anglican Theology* (London, 1857).
Roberston, W., *Life and Times of the Rt. Hon. John Bright* (London, 1883).
Russell, G. W. E., *A Short History of the Evangelical Movement* (London, 1915).
—— *The Household of Faith* (London, 1902).
Russell, J., *Recollections and Suggestions 1813–1873* (Boston, 1875).
—— *Essays on the Rise and Progress of the Christian Religion in the West of Europe* (London, 1873).
—— *Selections from the Speeches of Earl Russell 1817–1841 and from Despatches 1859–1865 with Introductions* (2 vols., London, 1870).
—— *The Life and Times of Charles James Fox* (3 vols., London, 1859–66).
—— *The Causes of the French Revolution* (London, 1832).
—— *The Establishment of the Turks in Europe* (London, 1828).
—— *Memoirs of the Affairs of Europe from the Peace of Utrecht* (London, 1824, 1829).
—— *Don Carlos* (London, 1822).
—— *The Nun of Arrouca* (London, 1822).
—— *An Essay on the History of English Government and Constitution from the Reign of Henry VIII to the Present Time* (1st edn., London, 1821).
—— *Ibid.* (2nd edn., London, 1823).
—— *Essays and Sketches of Life and Character by a Gentleman who has left his Lodgings*, ed. J. Skillet (London, 1820).
—— *The Life of William Lord Russell* (2nd edn., London, 1820).
Russell, J. F. S., *My Life and Adventures* (London, 1923).
Russell, R. (ed.), *The Early Correspondence of Lord John Russell 1805–40)* (2 vols., London, 1913).

Sanders, L. C. (ed.), *Lord Melbourne's Papers* (London, 1889).

Sandwith, H., *A Reply to Lord John Russell's Animadversions on Wesleyan Methodism* (London, 1830).

Schleiermacher, F., *A Critical Essay on the Gospel of St Luke* (London, 1825).

Scrope, G. P., *Memoirs of the Life of the Rt. Hon. Charles, Lord Sydenham GCB* (London, 1843).

Sedgwick, A., *A Discourse on the Studies of the University* (Cambridge, 1834).

—— *Four Letters to R. M. Beverley* (n.p., 1834).

Selwyn, W., *Extracts from the College Examinations in Divinity for the Last Four Years: With a Letter to the Lecturers and Examiners in the Several Colleges* (Cambridge, 1834).

Sewell, W., *A Second Letter to a Dissenter on the Opposition of the University of Oxford to the Charter of the London College* (Oxford and London, 1834).

—— *Thoughts on Subscription in a Letter to a Member of Convocation* (Oxford and London, 1834).

—— *Thoughts on the Admission of Dissenters to the University of Oxford and on the Establishment of a State Religion: In a Letter to a Dissenter* (Oxford and London, 1834).

Short, T. V., *Parochialia* (London, 1842).

—— 'The Song of Simeon', *Original Family Sermons* (London, 1834), iv.

—— *A Letter addressed to the Very Revd The Dean of Christ Church on the State of the Public Examinations in the University of Oxford* (Oxford, 1822, reprinted with appendix, 1829).

Shuttleworth, P. N., *The Last Three Sermons preached at Oxford in 1839 and 1840* (London, Oxford, and Cambridge, 1875).

Simpson, J., *A Second Letter to the Most Noble the Marquis of Lansdowne* (n.p., 1839).

Slaney, R. A., *Speech in the House of Commons on Thursday, November 30, 1837 On the State of Education of the Poorer Classes in Large Towns* (London, 1837).

[Anon.], *Specimens of the Theological Teaching of Certain Members of the Corpus Committee at Oxford 'Professing themselves to be wise'* (London, 1836).

Smith, N. C., *Selected Letters of Sydney Smith* (Oxford, 1981).

Smith, S., 'Letters to Archdeacon Singleton', *Collected Works* (London, 1854).

[Spedding, J.], 'The Jamaica Question', *Edinburgh Review*, lxix (1839), 527–56.

—— 'The Negro Apprenticeship System', *Edinburgh Review*, lxvi (1838), 477–522.

Spencer, J. C., *Letters of Lord Althorp* (privately printed, n.d.)

Stanley, A. P. (ed.), *Memoirs of Edward and Catherine Stanley* (London, 1879).

—— 'Archdeacon Hare', *Quarterly Review*, xcvii (1855), 1–28.

—— *Life and Correspondence of Thomas Arnold, DD* (6th edn., London, n.d.)

Stanley, E., *A Charge delivered to the Clergy of the Diocese of Norwich at the Primary Visitation in July 1838* (Norwich, 1838).

—— *A Sermon preached at His Installation on Thursday August 17 1837* (2nd edn., Norwich, 1837).

[Anon.], *State of Parties in Oxford from the Public Prints* (Oxford, 1836).

Stephen, C. E., *The Right Hon. Sir James Stephen* (Printed for private circulation only, London, 1906).

Stephen, G., *Anti-Slavery Recollections*, ed. H. Temperley (London, 1971).

Stovell, C., *Hints on the Regulation of Christian Churches adapted to the Present State of Affairs: To which are added Remarks on the Voluntary System in Relation to Its Spiritual Importance* (London, 1835).

Sumner, G. H., *Life of C. R. Sumner, Bishop of Winchester* (London, 1876).

[Symons, B. P.], *A Letter to a Non-Resident Friend upon Subscription to the Thirty-Nine Articles at Matriculation: By a Senior Member of Convocation* (Oxford, 1835).

Taylor, H., *Correspondence*, ed. E. Dowden (London, 1885).

—— *Autobiography* (2 vols., London, 1885).

Thirlwall, C., *Letters Literary and Theological* (London, 1881).

—— *A Charge to the Clergy of the Diocese of St David's by Connop, Lord Bishop of St David's delivered at his Primary Visitation, October 28, 1842* (London, 1842).

—— *A Letter to Thomas Turton, DD* (Cambridge, 1834).

—— *A Second Letter to the Revd Thomas Turton DD* (Cambridge, 1834).

Thom, J. H. (ed.), *Life of the Revd Blanco White* (London, 1845).

Thomas, V., *The Reasonableness of the Academic Ordinance of 1581 requiring Subscription at Matriculation* (Oxford, 1835).

Thomson, A., *The Claims of the Dissenters on the Government of the Country: A Letter addressed to the Rt. Hon. Lord Viscount Melbourne* (Edinburgh, 1836).

Thorp, C., *A Short Sketch of the Life of the Ven. Charles Thorp. Archdeacon of Durham* (Newcastle, 1862).

—— *A Charge to the Clergy of the Archdeaconry of Durham and of the*

Officiality of the Dean and Chapter delivered at Berwick on Tweed, July 24 and at Durham August 2, 1838 (Durham, 1838).

Thorpe, W., *A Review of the Revd J. E. Bennett's Letter to Lord John Russell* (London, 1850).

Torrens, W. M., *Memoirs of Rt. Hon. William, 2nd Viscount Melbourne* (2 vols., London, 1878. New edn. 1890).

Tuckwell, W., *Pre-Tractarian Oxford* (London, 1909).

Turton, T., *Thoughts on the Admission of Persons without Regard to their Religious Opinions to Certain Degrees in the Universities of England* (Cambridge and London, 1834).

Waddington, G., *Three Lectures on National Education* (London, 1845).

Walpole, S., *Life of Lord John Russell* (2 vols., London, 1889).

Wardlaw, R., *National Church Establishments Examined: A Course of Lectures delivered in London during April and May 1839* (London, 1839).

Watson, R., *Anecdotes* (London, 1817).

Whately, E. J., *Life and Correspondence of Richard Whately DD* (London, 1875).

Whately, R., *Dr Paley's Works: A Lecture* (London, 1859).

—— *The Kingdom of Christ* (London, 1841).

—— *Charges and Other Tracts* (London, 1836).

—— *A Speech in the House of Lords on a Bill for the Removal of Certain Disablilities from Her Majesty's Subjects of the Jewish Persuasion* (London, 1833).

—— *The Duty of Christians to diffuse Religious Instruction* (London, 1832).

—— *Scriptural Education in Ireland* (London, 1832).

—— *Introductory Lectures on Political Economy* (London, 1831).

—— *The Duty of those who disapprove of the Education of the Poor* (London, 1830).

—— *The Errors of Romanism traced to their Origins in Human Nature* (London, 1830).

—— *Thoughts on the Sabbath* (London, 1830).

—— *Elements of Rhetoric* (Oxford, 1828).

—— *Essays on Some of the Difficulties of the Writings of St Paul* (London, 1828).

—— *Elements of Logic* (London, 1827; revised edn. 1844).

—— *Letters on the Church by an Episcopalian* (London, 1826).

—— *Essays on some of the Peculiarities of the Christian Religion* (Oxford, 1825).

—— 'The Use and Abuse of Party Feeling', *The Bampton Lectures for 1822* (Oxford, 1822).

—— *The Christian's Duty with Respect to the Established Government and the Laws considered in Two Sermons preached before the University of Oxford* (Oxford, 1821).

—— *Historic Doubts Relative to Napoleon Buonaparte* (London, 1819).

Whewell, W., *On the Principles of English University Education* (London, 1838).

—— *Additional Remarks on Some Parts of Mr Thirlwall's Two Letters on the Admission of Dissenters to Academical Degrees* (Cambridge, 1834).

—— *Remarks on Some Parts of Mr Thirlwall's Letter on the Admission of Dissenters to Academical Degrees* (Cambridge, 1834).

Whishaw, J. *The Pope of Holland House*, ed. Lady Seymour (London, 1906).

[Wilberforce, H.], *The Foundation of the Faith Assailed in Oxford: A Letter to His Grace the Archbishop of Canterbury. By a Clerical Member of Convocation* (London, 1835).

Woodgate, H. A., *A Letter to Viscount Melbourne on the Recent Appointment to the Office of Regius Professor of Divinity in the University of Oxford* (London, 1836).

Wordsworth, C., *On the Admission of Dissenters to reside and graduate in the University of Cambridge: A Letter to the Rt. Hon. Viscount Althorp MP* (Cambridge, 1834).

—— *A Second Letter to the Rt. Hon. Viscount Althorp MP* (Cambridge, 1834).

Wyse, T., 'Prussian Education', *Central Society of Education. Third Publication* (London, 1839).

—— 'Education in the United Kingdom', *Central Society of Education. First Publication* (London, 1837).

—— *Education Reform* (London, 1836).

Wyse, W. M., *Notes on Education Reform in Ireland during the First Half of the Nineteenth Century compiled from Speeches, Letters, &c contained in the Unpublished Memoirs of the Hon. Sir Thomas Wyse, KCB* (Waterford, 1901).

Yates, R., *The Church in Danger* (London, 1815).

SECONDARY SOURCES

I. *Printed secondary works*

Aarsleff, H., *The Study of Language in England 1780–1860* (Princeton, 1967).

Akenson, D. H., *The Irish Education Experiment* (London, 1970).

Alexander, J. L., 'Lord John Russell and the Origin of the Committee of Council on Education', *Historical Journal*, xx (1977), 395–415.

Allen, P., *The Cambridge Apostles* (Cambridge, 1978).

Annan, N. G., 'The Intellectual Aristocracy', J. H. Plumb (ed.), *Studies in Social History: A Tribute to G. M. Trevelyan* (London, 1955).

Ansty, R., 'Religion and British Slave Emancipation' in D. Eltis and J. Walvin (eds.), *The Abolition of the Atlantic Slave Trade*, (Madison, Wisc., 1981).

—— *The Atlantic Slave Trade and British Abolition 1760–1810* (London, 1975).

Auchmuty, J. J., *Sir Thomas Wyse 1791–1862* (London, 1939).

—— *Irish Education: A Historical Survey* (Dublin and London, 1937).

Baker, W. J., *Beyond Port and Prejudice* (Orono, Maine, 1981).

—— 'Julius Charles Hare: A Victorian Interpreter of Luther', *South Atlantic Quarterly*, lxx (1971), 88–101.

Ball, N., *Her Majesty's Inspectorate 1839–1849* (London, 1963).

Ball, W. W. Rouse, *Notes on the History of Trinity College, Cambridge* (London, 1899).

Balleine, G., *A History of the Evangelical Party* (London, 1911).

Bamford, T. W., *Thomas Arnold* (London, 1960).

Barker, E., 'Elie Halévy', *English Historical Review*, liii (1938), 79–87.

Barry, P. C. 'The Holy See and the Irish National Schools', *Irish Ecclesiastical Record*, xcii (1959), 90–105.

Batterberry, R., 'The Synod of Ulster and the National Board', *Irish Ecclesiastical Record*, lvi (1940), 548–61.

Beales, D. E. D., 'Peel, Russell, and Reform', *Historical Journal*, xvii (1974), 873–82.

Bell, A., *Sydney Smith* (Oxford, 1980).

Bellot, H. H., *University College, London 1826–1926* (London, 1929).

Best, G. F. A., *Temporal Pillars* (Cambridge, 1964).

—— 'The Whigs and the Church Establishment in the Age of Holland and Grey', *History*, xlv (1960), 103–18.

—— 'The Evangelicals and the Established Church in the Early Nineteenth Century', *Journal of Theological Studies*, x (1959), 63–78.

—— 'The Protestant Constitution and Its Supporters, 1800–1829', *Transactions of the Royal Historical Society*, 5th series, viii (1959), 105–27.

—— 'The Religious Difficulties of National Education in England 1800–1870', *Cambridge Historical Journal*, xii (1956), 155–73.

Binfield, C., *So Down to Prayers: Studies in English Nonconformity 1780–1920* (London, 1977).

Binns, H. B., *A Century of Education* (London, 1908).

Binns, L. E., *The Evangelical Movement in the English Church* (London, 1928).

Blake, R., *The Conservative Party from Peel to Churchill* (London, 1972).

Bourne, K., *Palmerston: The Early Years 1784–1841* (London, 1982).

Brent, R., 'The Whigs and Protestant Dissent in the Decade of Reform: The Case of the Church Rates, 1833–1841', *English Historical Review* (forthcoming).

Brilioth, Y., *The Anglican Revival* (London, 1933).

Brock, M. G., *The Great Reform Act* (London, 1973).

Broderick, J. F., 'The Holy See and the Irish Movement for the Repeal of the Union with England 1829–1847', *Analecta Gregoriana*, lv (Rome, 1951).

Brose, O., *Church and Parliament* (Stanford and London, 1959).

Brown, F. K., *Fathers of the Victorians* (Cambridge, 1961).

Brown, L., *The Board of Trade and Free Trade Movement 1830–1842* (Oxford, 1958).

Brown, S. J., *Thomas Chalmers* (Oxford, 1982).

Buckley, J. K., *Joseph Parkes of Birmingham* (London, 1926).

Burgess, H. J., *Enterprise in Education* (London, 1958).

Burn, W. L., *Emancipation and Apprenticeship in the British West Indies* (London, 1937).

Burroughs, P., 'Lord Howick and Colonial Church Establishments', *Journal of Ecclesiastical History*, xxv (1974), 381–405.

Burrow, J. W., *A Liberal Descent* (Cambridge, 1981).

—— 'The Uses of Philology in Victorian England', R. Robson (ed.), *Ideas and Institutions of Victorian Britain* (London, 1967).

Butler, P., *Gladstone: Church, State, and Tractarianism* (Oxford, 1982).

Butterfield, H., *Historical Development of the Principle of Toleration in British Life* (London, 1956).

—— *The Englishman and His History* (Cambridge, 1944).

—— *The Whig Interpretation of History* (London, 1931).

Cameron, R. H., 'The Melbourne Administration, the Liberals, and the Crisis of 1841', *Durham University Journal*, xxxviii (1976), 83–102.

Cannadine, D., *Lords and Landlords: The Aristocracy and the Towns 1774–1967* (Leicester, 1980).

—— 'Aristocratic Indebtedness in the Nineteenth Century: The Case Re-opened', *Economic History Review*, 2nd series, xxx (1977), 624–50.

Cannon, S. F., *Science in Culture: The Early Victorian Period* (New York, 1979).

—— 'Scientists and Broad Churchmen: An Early Victorian Network', *Journal of British Studies*, iv (1964), 65–88.

Carey, F. P., *Archbishop Murray of Dublin* (Dublin, 1951).

Chadwick, W. O., *The Victorian Church* (London, 1966), part 1.

Chase, M., *Elie Halévy* (New York, 1980).

Clark, G. S. R. Kitson, *The Making of Victorian England* (London, 1962).

Clive, J., *Macaulay* (New York, 1975).

—— *Scottish Reviewers* (London, 1957).

Close, D., 'The Formation of a Two-Party Alignment in the House of Commons between 1832 and 1841', *Historical Journal*, lxxxiv (1969), 257–77.

Collini, S., Winch, D., and Burrow, J., *That Noble Science of Politics* (Cambridge, 1983).

Condon, M. C., 'The Irish Church and the Reform Ministries', *Journal of British Studies*, iv (1964), 120–142.

Cookson, J. E., *Lord Liverpool's Administration: The Crucial Years 1815–1822* (Edinburgh and London, 1975).

Costello, N., *John MacHale* (Dublin and London, 1939).

Coupland, R., *The British Anti-Slavery Movement* (London, 1933).

Cowherd, R., *The Politics of English Dissent* (London, 1959).

Cowling, M. J., *Religion and Public Doctrine in Modern England* (Cambridge, 1980).

Cullen, M. J., 'The Making of the Civil Registration Act of 1836', *Journal of Ecclesiastical History*, xxv (1974), 39–59.

Davie, G. E., *The Scottish Enlightenment* (London, 1981).

—— *The Social Significance of the Scottish Philosophy of Common Sense* (Dundee, 1973).

—— *The Democratic Intellect* (Edinburgh, 1961).

Davis, R. W., *Dissent in Politics 1780–1830: The Political Life of William Smith MP* (London, 1971).

—— 'The Strategy of Dissent in the Repeal Campaign 1820–1828', *Journal of Modern History*, xxxviii (1966), 374–93.

Dinwiddy, J., 'Charles James Fox and The People', *History*, lv (1970), 342–59.

—— 'Charles James Fox as Historian', *Historical Journal*, xii (1969), 23–34.

Distad, N. M., *Guessing At Truth* (Sheperdstown, 1979).

—— 'The Philological Museum 1831–1833', *Victorian Periodicals Newsletter*, v (1972), 27–30.

Ditchfield, G., 'Parliament, the Quakers, and the Tithe Question 1750–1835', *Parliamentary History*, iv (1985), 87–114.

Dobson, J. L., 'Bruce Castle School at Tottenham and the Hills' Part in the Work of the SDUK', *Durham Research Review*, iii (1961), 74–84.

—— 'The Hill Family and Educational Change in the Nineteenth Century', *Durham Research Review*, iii (1960), 1–11.

Drescher, S., 'Public Opinion and the Destruction of British Colonial Slavery', J. Walvin (ed.), *Slavery and British Society 1776–1846* (London, 1982).

Edwards, M. S., 'The Resignation of Joseph Rayner Stephens', *Proceedings of the Wesley Historical Society*, xxxvi (1967), 16–21.
Ellis, D. and Walvin, J. (eds.), *The Abolition of the Atlantic Slave Trade* (Madison, Wisc., 1981).
Engel, A. J., *From Clergyman to Don* (Oxford, 1983).
Evans, E. J., *The Contentious Tithe* (London, 1976).
—— 'Some Reasons for the Growth of English Rural Anti-Clericalism c. 1750–c. 1830', *Past and Present*, lxvi (1975), 84–109.

Finlayson, G. B. A. M., *The Seventh Earl of Shaftesbury* (London, 1981).
Forbes, D., *The Liberal Anglican Idea of History* (Cambridge, 1950).
Frappell, L. O., 'Coleridge and the "Coleridgeans" on Luther', *Journal of Religious History*, vii (1973), 307–23.
Fraser, D., 'The Fruits of Reform: Leeds Politics in the Eighteen-Thirties', *Northern History*, vii (1972), 89–111.
Fraser, P., 'Party Voting in the House of Commons 1812–1827', *English Historical Review* lxxxi (1983), 763–784.

Fulford, R., *Samuel Whitbread* (London, 1967).
Furley, O., 'The Humanitarian Impact', C. J. Bartlett ed., *British Pre-eminent* (London, 1969).

Gallagher, J., 'Fowell Buxton and the New Africa Policy 1838–1842', *Cambridge Historical Journal*, x (1950), 36–58.
Garland, M. M., *Cambridge Before Darwin* (Cambridge, 1980).
Gash, N., *Aristocracy and People* (London, 1979).
—— *Politics in the Age of Peel* (London, 1953).
—— *Reaction and Reconstruction in English Politics 1832–1852* (Oxford, 1965).
—— *Sir Robert Peel: The Life of Sir Robert Peel after 1830* (London, 1972.
Goldstron, J. M., 'Richard Whately and Political Economy in School Books 1833–1880', *Irish Historical Studies*, xv (1966), 131–46.
Gowland, D. A., *Methodist Secessions* (Manchester, 1979).
Gross, I., 'Parliament and the Abolition of Negro Apprenticeship 1835–1838', *English Historical Review*, xcvi (1981), 560–76.
Guggisberg, K., *Philipp Emanuel v. Fellenberg* (2 vols., Bern, 1953).

Halévy, E., *A History of the English People in the Nineteenth Century* (London, 1949–52).
Hamburger, J., *Macaulay and the Whig Tradition* (Chicago, 1976).
Harrison, B., *Peaceable Kingdom* (Oxford, 1982).
Harvey, A. D., 'The "Talents" Ministry', *Historical Journal*, xv (1972), 619–48.
Heesom, A., *The Founding of the University of Durham* (Durham Cathedral Lecture, Durham, 1982).

Hempton, D., *Methodism and Politics in British Society 1750–1850* (London, 1984).

Henriques, U., *Religious Toleration in England 1787–1833* (London, 1961).

Hilton, B., 'The Role of Providence in Evangelical Social Thought', D. Beales and G. Best (eds.), *History, Society and the Churches: Essays in Honour of Owen Chadwick* (Cambridge, 1985).

—— *Corn, Cash, Commerce: The Economic Policies of the Tory Governments 1815–1830* (Oxford, 1977).

Hobsbawm, E. J and Rudé, G., *Captain Swing* (London, 1969).

Hone, A., *For the Cause of Truth* (Oxford, 1982).

Hoppen, K., *Elections, Politics, and Society in Ireland 1832–1885* (Oxford, 1984).

Huch, R. K., *The Radical Lord Radnor: The Public Life of Viscount Folkestone, Third Earl of Radnor 1779–1869* (Minnesota, 1977).

Hurt, J., *Education in Evolution* (London, 1971).

Hutchinson, G., *The Last Edwardian at No. 10* (London, 1979).

Ilchester, The Earl of, *Chronicles of Holland House 1820–1900* (London, 1937).

Isichei, I., *Victorian Quakers* (Oxford, 1970).

Jay, E., *The Religion of the Heart: Anglican Evangelicalism and the Nineteenth-Century Novel* (Oxford, 1979).

Johnson, D. W. J., 'Sir James Graham and the "Derby Dilly"', *University of Birmingham Historical Journal*, iv (1953–4), 66–80.

Johnson, R., 'Educational Policy and Social Control', *Past and Present*, xlix (1970), 96–119.

Jones, G. Stedman, *Languages of Class* (Cambridge, 1983).

Kebbel, T. E., *The Life of the Earl of Derby* (London, 1893).

Kemp, B., 'The General Election of 1841', *History*, xxxvii (1952), 146–57.

Kerr, D. A., *Peel, Priests, and Politics* (Oxford, 1982).

Knaplund, P., *James Stephen and the British Colonial System 1813–1847* (Madison, Wisc., 1953).

Kriegel, A. D., 'Liberty and Whiggery in Early Nineteenth-Century England', *Journal of Modern History*, lii (1980), 253–78.

—— 'The Irish Policy of Lord Grey's Government', *Historical Journal*, lxxxvi (1971), 22–45.

—— 'The Politics of the Whigs in Opposition 1834–35', *Journal of British Studies*, vii (1968), 65–91.

Larkin, E., 'The Quarrel among the Roman Catholic Hierarchy over the National System of Education in Ireland 1838–41', R. B. Browne (ed.), *The Celtic Cross* (West Lafayette, Ind., 1964).

Levy, S. Leon, *Nassau W. Senior 1790–1864* (Newton Abbot, 1970).

Lloyd-Jones, H., Pearl, V., Worden, B. (eds.), *History and Imagination* (London, 1981).

MacCarthy, D. and Russell, A. (eds.), *Lady John Russell: A Memoir: With Selections from Her Diary and Correspondence* (3rd edn., London, 1926).

Machin, G. I. T., *Politics and the Churches in Great Britain 1832–1868* (Oxford, 1977).

—— 'The Disruption and British Politics', *Scottish Historical Review*, li (1972), 20–51.

—— *The Catholic Question in English Politics 1820–1830* (Oxford, 1964).

Macintyre, A. D., *The Liberator: Daniel O'Connell and the Irish Party 1830–1867* (London, 1965).

McKerrow, R. E., 'Richard Whately on the Nature of Human Knowledge in Relation to the Ideas of His Contemporaries', *Journal of the History of Ideas*, xlii (1981), 439–55.

—— 'Whately's Earliest "Rhetoric"', *Philosophy and Rhetoric*, xi (1978), 43–58.

McLachlan, H., *The Unitarian Movement in the Religious Life of England* (London, 1934).

Macmillan, H., *The Past Masters* (London, 1978).

MacSuibhne, P., *Paul Cullen and His Contemporaries* (5 vols., Naas, Eire, 1961–77).

Mallock, W. H., and Ramsden, G. (eds.), *Letters, Remains, and Memoirs of Edward Adolphus Seymour, Twelfth Duke of Somerset KG* (London, 1893).

Mandler, P., 'Cain and Abel: Two Aristocrats and the Early Victorian Factory Acts', *Historical Journal*, xxvii (1984), 83–109.

Manning, B. L., *The Protestant Dissenting Deputies* (Cambridge, 1952).

Manning, H. T., 'Who ran the British Empire 1830–1850?' *Journal of British Studies*, v (1965), 88–121.

Marsh, P. (ed.), *The Conscience of the Victorian State* (Syracuse, N.Y., 1979).

Mathieson, W. L., *British Slave Emancipation 1838–1849* (London, 1932).

—— *English Church Reform 1815–1840* (London, 1923).

Matthew, H. C. G., 'Edward Bouverie Pusey', *Journal of Theological Studies*, new series, xxxii (1981), 101–124.

—— (ed.), *The Gladstone Diaries* (10 vols., Oxford, 1968–to date), v, vii.

Mayne, E. C., *The Life of Lady Byron* (London, 1929).

Mineka, F. E., *The Dissidence of Dissent: The Monthly Repository 1806–1838* (Chapel Hill, NC, 1944).

Mitchell, A., *The Whigs in Opposition 1815–1830* (Oxford, 1967).

Mitchell, L., *Holland House* (London, 1980).

Morrell, J. and Thackray, A., *Gentlemen of Science* (Oxford, 1981).

Murphy, J., *Church, State, and Schools in Britain 1800–1970* (London, 1971).

—— *The Religious Problem in English Education* (Liverpool, 1959).

Murray, D. J., *The West Indies and the Development of Colonial Government 1801–1834* (Oxford, 1965).

Newbould, I. D. C., 'Whiggery and the Dilemma of Reform: Liberals, Radicals, and the Melbourne Administration 1835–9', *Bulletin of the Institute of Historical Research*, liii (1980), 229–241.

Newsome, D., 'Fathers and Sons', *Historical Journal*, vi (1963), 295–310.

Norman, E. R., *Church and Society in England 1770–1970* (Oxford, 1976).

Oakes, C. G., *Sir Samuel Romilly 1757–1818* (London, 1935).

O'Connell, M. R. (ed.), *The Correspondence of Daniel O'Connell* (8 vols., Dublin, 1972–80).

Olphin, H. K., *George Tierney* (London, 1934).

O'Raifertaigh, T., 'Mixed Education and the Synod of Ulster 1831–1840', *Irish Historical Studies*, ix (1955), 281–99.

O'Reilly, B., *Life of John MacHale* (2 vols., New York and Cincinnati, 1890).

Owen, R. A. D., *Christian Bunsen and Liberal English Theology* (Montpelier, Vt., 1924).

Parkin, R., *The Central Society of Education* (Leeds, 1975).

Parry, J. P., 'Religion and the Collapse of Gladstone's First Government', *Historical Journal*, xxv (1982), 71–101.

Patterson, A. T., *Radical Leicester* (Leicester, 1954).

Payne, E. A., *The Baptist Union: A Short History* (London, 1959).

Paz, D. G., *The Politics of Working-Class Education in Britain 1830–1850* (Manchester, 1980).

Peel, A., *These Hundred Years* (London, 1931).

Penny, N., 'The Whig Cult of Fox in Early Nineteenth-Century Sculpture', *Past and Present*, lxx (1976), 94–105.

Pfleiderer, O., *The Development of Theology in Germany since Kant and Its Progress in Britain since 1825* (London, 1893).

Phillips, D, Z., *Religion without Explanation* (Oxford, 1976).

Ponsonby, J., *The Ponsonby Family* (London, 1929).

Prest, J., *Lord John Russell* (London, 1972).

Preyer, R. O., 'Julius Hare and Coleridgean Criticism', *Journal of Aesthetics*, xv (1957), 449–60.

Proby, W. H. B., *Annals of the 'Low Church' Party in England down to the Death of Archbishop Tait* (London, 1888).

[Anon.], 'The Protestant Society for the Protection of Religious

Liberty', *Congregational History Society Transactions*, vi (1915), 364–76.

Quinlan, M. J., *Victorian Prelude: A History of English Manners 1700–1830* (New York, 1941).

Rashid, S., 'Richard Whately and Christian Political Economy at Oxford and Dublin', *Journal of the History of Ideas*, xxxviii (1977), 147–55.

Reynolds, J., *The Evangelicals at Oxford 1735–1871* (Appleford, Oxon., 1975).

Rice, C. D., 'Humanity sold for Sugar'. The British Abolitionist Response to Free Trade in Slave-Grown Sugar', *Historical Journal*, xiii (1970), 402–18.

Rich, R. W., *The Training of Teachers in England and Wales during the Nineteenth Century* (Bath, 1972).

Roberts, M., *The Whig Party 1807–1812* (London, 1939).

Rogers, P., *Father Theobald Matthew* (Dublin, 1943).

Rubinstein, W. D., *Men of Property* (London, 1981).

Salter, F. R., *Dissenters and Public Affairs in Mid-Victorian England* (London, 1967).

—— 'Political Nonconformity in the Eighteen-Thirties', *Transactions of the Royal Historical Society*, 5th series, iii (1953), 125–43.

Sanders, C. R., *Coleridge and the Broad Church Movement* (Durham, NC, 1942).

Saunders, L. J., *Scottish Democracy 1815–1840* (Edinburgh, 1950).

Shannon, R., *Gladstone* (London, 1982), i.

Short, K. R. M.,'London's General Body of Protestant Ministers: Its Disruption in 1836', *Journal of Ecclesiastical History*, xxiv (1973), 377–93.

—— 'The English Regium Donum', *English Historical Review*, lxxxiv (1969), 59–78.

—— 'Baptists and the Corn Laws', *Baptist Quarterly*, xxi (1965–6), 309–20.

Silber, K., *Pestalozzi: The Man and His Work* (London, 1960).

Silver, H., *The Concept of Popular Education* (London, 1965).

Skeats, H. S. and Miall, C. S., *History of the Free Churches in England 1688–1891* (London, 1891).

Smith, H., *The SDUK 1836–1846: A Social and Bibliographical Evaluation* (Halifax NS, 1974).

Smith, E. A., *Whig Principles and Party Politics: Earl Fitzwilliam and the Whig Party 1748–1833* (Manchester, 1975).

Smith, F., *The Life and Work of Sir James Kay-Shuttleworth* (Bath, 1974).

Smith, N. C. (ed.), *Selected Letters of Sydney Smith* (Oxford, 1981).

Soloway, R., *Prelates and People 1782–1852* (London, 1969).

Southgate, D., *The Passing of the Whigs* (London, 1962).
Speller, J. L., 'Alexander Nicholl and the Study of German Biblical Criticism', *Journal of Ecclesiastical History*, xxx (1979), 451–59.
Spring, D., 'Aristocracy, Social Structure, and Religion in the Early Victorian Period', *Victorian Studies*, vii (1963), 263–80.
Stewart, W. A. C., and McCann, W. D., *The Educational Innovators* (2 vols., London, 1967–8).
Stirling, A. M. W., *Coke of Norfolk and His Friends* (London, 1908).
Swanston, H. F. G., *Ideas of Order* (Assen, Netherland, 1976).
Swift, D., *Joseph John Gurney* (Connecticut, 1962).
Temperley, H., *British Anti-Slavery 1833–1870* (London, 1972).
Thirlwall, J. C. Jr., *Connop Thirlwall* (London, 1936).
Thomas, W. E., 'Lord Holland', *History and Imagination*, eds. H. Lloyd Jones, V. Pearl. B. Worden (London, 1981).
—— 'The Philosophic Radicals', P. Hollis (ed.), *Pressure from Without* (London, 1974).
Thompson, F. M. L., 'Whigs and Liberals in the West Riding 1830–1840' *English Historical Review*, lxxxiv (1959), 214–39.
—— *English Landed Society in the Nineteenth Century* (London, 1963).
Trevelyan, G. M., *Lord Grey of the Reform Bill* (London, 1929).
Turner, F. M., *The Greek Heritage in Victorian Britain* (New Haven, Conn., 1981).
Underwood, A. C., *A History of the English Baptists* (London, 1947).
Vincent, J. R., *The Formation of the British Liberal Party* (London, 1972).
—— *Pollbooks: How Victorians Voted* (Cambridge, 1967).
'The Electoral Sociology of Rochdale', *Economic History Review*, xvi (1963–4), 76–90.
Walsh, J. D., 'Origins of the Evangelical Revival', G. V. Bennett and J. D. Walsh (eds.), *Essays in Modern English Church History in Memory of Norman Sykes* (London, 1966).
—— 'The Magdalene Evangelicals', *Church Quarterly Review*, clix (1958), 499–511.
Ward, J. T., *Sir James Graham* (London, 1967).
Ward, W. R., 'Church and Society in the First Half of the Nineteenth Century', R. Davies, A. R. George, G. Rupp (eds.), *A History of the Methodist Church in Great Britain* (London, 1978), ii.
—— *Religion and Society in England 1790–1850* (London, 1972).
—— 'The Tithe Question in England in the Early Nineteenth Century', *Journal of Ecclesiastical History*, xvi (1969), 67–81.
—— *Victorian Oxford* (London, 1965).
Wasson, E. A., 'The Coalitions of 1827 and the Crisis of Whig Leadership', *Historical Journal*, xx (1977), 587–606.
Welch, P. J., 'Contemporary Views on the Proposals for the Aliena-

tion of Capitular Property in England 1832–40', *Journal of Ecclesiastical History*, v (1954), 184–95.

White, J. F., *The Cambridge Movement* (Cambridge, 1979).

Whiting, C. E., *The University of Durham* (London, 1932).

Willis, R. W., '"An Handful of Violent People": The Nature of the Foxite Opposition 1794–1801', *Albion*, viii (1976), 236–54.

Winstanley, D. A., *Early Victorian Cambridge* (Cambridge, 1940).

Woolley, S. F., 'The Personnel of the Parliament of 1833', *English Historical Review*, liii (1938), 240–62.

Young, G. M., 'Portrait of an Age', G. M. Young (ed.), *Early Victorian England* (Oxford, 1951).

Zegger, R. E., *John Cam Hobhouse* (Columbia, 1973).

II. *Unpublished theses*

Bradley, I. C., 'The Politics of Godliness: Evangelicals in Parliament 1784–1832', D. Phil. thesis (Oxford, 1974).

Brent, R., 'The Emergence of Liberal Anglicanism: The Whigs and the Church 1830–1841', D. Phil. thesis (Oxford, 1985).

Clarke, J. C., 'From Business to Politics: The Ellice Family 1760–1860, D.Phil. thesis. (Oxford, 1972).

Close, D. H., 'The General Elections of 1835 and 1837 in England and Wales', D.Phil. thesis (Oxford, 1967).

Corsi, P., 'Baden Powell', D.Phil. thesis (Oxford, 1980).

Custance, R. H., 'The Politics of Lord Melbourne to 1841', D.Phil. thesis (Oxford, 1977).

Dixon, P. F., 'The Politics of Emancipation: The Movement for the Abolition of Slavery in British West Indies 1807–1833', D.Phil. thesis (Oxford, 1971).

Ervine, W. J., 'Doctrine and Diplomacy: Some Aspects of the Life and Thought of the Anglican Evangelical Clergy 1797–1837', Ph.D. thesis (Cambridge, 1981).

Gross, I., 'Commons and Empire 1833–1841' D.Phil. thesis (Oxford, 1975).

Mandler, P., 'Peers, Paupers, Proletarians' (unpublished dissertation, 1982).

Newbould, I. D. C., 'The Politics of the Cabinets of Grey and Melbourne and Ministerial Relations with the House of Commons 1830–41', Ph.D. thesis (Manchester, 1971).

Nockles, P., 'Continuity and Change in Anglican High Churchmanship in Britain 1792–1850', D.Phil. thesis (Oxford, 1982).

Orchard, S. C., 'English Evangelical Eschatology 1790–1850', Ph.D thesis (Cambridge, 1969).

Sellers, I., 'Social and Political Ideas of Representative Unitarians 1795–1850', B.Litt. thesis (Oxford, 1956).
Short, K. R. M., 'A Study in Political Nonconformity: The Baptists 1827–1845 with Particular Reference to Slavery', D.Phil. thesis (Oxford, 1972).
Stange, D. C., 'British Unitarianism and the Crisis of American Slavery 1833–1865', D.Phil. thesis (Oxford, 1981).
Toon, P., 'Evangelical Reactions to Tractarianism', D.Phil. thesis (Oxford, 1977).
Walsh, J. D., 'The Yorkshire Evangelicals in the Eighteenth Century', Ph.D. thesis (Cambridge, 1956).
Wasson, E. A., 'The Young Whigs: Lords Althorp, Milton, and Tavistock and the Whig Party 1809–1830', Ph.D. thesis (Cambridge, 1976).
Wilmer, H., 'Evangelicalism 1785–1835' (Hulsean Prize Essay, Cambridge University, 1962).

III. *Reference Works*

Allibone, S. A., *A Critical Dictionary of English Literature and British and American Authors to the latter half of the Nineteenth Century* (Philadelphia, 1870–91).
[Anon.], *Church of England Biographies*, 2nd series, ii (London, n.d.).
Dod, C. R., *Electoral Facts from 1832 to 1853 Impartially Stated*, ed., *H. J. Hanham* (Brighton, 1972).
Foster, J., *Alumni Oxonienses 1715–1886* (Oxford, 1888).
Gibbs, V. (ed.), *The Complete Peerage: By G.E.C.* (London, 1910).
Houghton, W. (ed.), *The Wellesley Index to Victorian Periodicals 1824–1900* (Toronto and London, 1966–79).
Montague-Smith, P. (ed.), *Debrett's Peerage and Baronetage* (London, 1979).
Pine, L. G., (ed.), *Burke's Genealogical and Heraldic History of the Peerage, Baronetage, and Knightage* (102nd edn., London, 1959).
Smith, H. S., *The Register of Parliamentary Contested Election* (2nd edn., London, 1842).
Stephen, L., and Lee, S. (eds.), *Dictionary of National Biography* (London, 1908–9).
Stenton, M. and Lees, S. (eds.), *Who's Who of British Members of Parliament* (3 vols., Brighton, 1976), i.
Venn, J. A., *Alumni Cantabrigienses* (Cambridge, 1940), part ii.

Index

relations with Whigs 22–4, 39–40, 76,
190, 255–8, 260–2
and university reform 184–5, 191–2,
200, 206–7, 209
voluntaryists 15, 199, 277, 283
*see also different denominations and
individual grievances*
Normanby, 1st Marquis of: *see*
Mulgrave, 2nd Earl
Northampton, 2nd Marquis of 224

O'Connell, D. 39, 80, 83, 252, 262, 274
and 1841 budget 295
and anti-slavery 262, 275, 277, 281,
283, 287
and English Dissenters 261
Grey on 27, 81
and Irish appropriation 98–9
political emergence of 32
relations with Whigs 93–6, 99–100,
254, 257
Rice on 51
role in 1834 disruption 79
role in 1835 govt. 67–8, 102
on Whig judicial appointments 99–
100
Otter, W., Bp. of Chichester 119, 203
Owen, W. 219

Paley, Revd W. 62, 115, 136, 150–3, 169,
199, 204, 207
Palmer, R. 106
Palmerston, 3rd Viscount 20, 25–6, 50,
76, 107, 110–11, 126, 242, 284–5,
291, 297, 299
politics in 1835: 95
religion 117–18
Parkes, J. 255, 297–8
Parliamentary Reform 4, 32, 34, 38, 47,
296
Parnell, H. 20, 74, 130
Parr, S. 41
Peacock, G. 138, 140–2, 144, 146
on oaths 206
university reform 190–1, 199, 209–10,
213
Pease, J. 252, 262, 271
Peel, R., 2nd Bt. 6, 135, 212, 275, 298
and 1839 crisis 249, 290–1
and elementary education 218, 250
and English tithes 6
and first govt. 80
and Irish Church 87–8
Perry, C. 188, 213

Pestalozzi, J. H. 234, 236–8
Philhellenism 55
Philips, M. 252, 294–5
Phillpotts, H., Bp. of Exeter 7, 193
Pitt, W. 127, 265
and church reform 3–4
and political economy 22
Whig view of 49
Plumptre, Revd H. W. 122
Powell, Revd B. 139, 141, 145, 147–9,
168, 176, 247–8
Powell, W. 130
Presbyterians (Irish) 223–4
Primitive Methodism 12–13
Protestant Dissenting Deputies 255, 257,
261
and anti-slavery 263, 270
and education 248, 251
and J. Russell 258
Pryme, G. 133, 135, 192
Pusey, E. B. 148, 170, 173, 183, 201, 210,
212, 215, 217
Pusey, P. 215

Quakers 271
and anti-slavery 263, 276, 287
and English tithes 9

Radicals 17, 34, 40, 43, 296
and anti-slavery 46–7, 263, 279–80,
283, 290–1
and education 248–9
and English tithes 11
excluded from power 27, 102, 282
on Fox 31
and free trade 295
Grey's view of 81
and Irish Church 67
politics in 1820s: 38–9, 49, 55
role in 1835: 92–3, 96, 97–8
Radnor, 3rd Earl of (Viscount
Folkestone) 28, 34, 107, 113, 123,
125–7, 130–2, 140–2, 201–2, 206
Reid, T. 110
Reformation 60–1, 121, 176–7, 214
Regium Donum 256
Repeal movement 23, 51, 67, 99, 261
Rice, S. Spring 140, 146
Rice, T. Spring, 1st Baron Monteagle
16, 43, 51, 58, 102, 133–4, 137–9,
270
and anti-slavery 262–3, 265, 268–9,
283–4
Cabinet Minister 78